STERNDALE'S MAMMALIA OF INDIA

STERNDALE'S MAMMALIA OF INDIA

A New and Abridged Edition, thoroughly revised and with an Appendix on the Reptilia

BY

FRANK FINN, B.A., F.Z.S.
LATE DEPUTY SUPERINTENDENT
INDIAN MUSEUM, CALCUTTA

GYAN

Published by

GYAN

Gyan Publishing House
5, Ansari Road
Daryaganj, New Delhi-110002
Phone: 011-47034999, 9811692060
E-mail: books@gyanbooks.com

Distribution Network
gyanbooks.com
India, USA, Canada, UK, Australia, France

ISBN : 978-81-212-2931-9 (PB)
First Published, 1929

2nd Impression 2021

Printed at: Gyan Press, Delhi.

Sterndale's Mammalia of India
Author: Frank Finn

STERNDALE'S
MAMMALIA OF INDIA

A New and Abridged Edition, thoroughly revised and with an Appendix on the Reptilia

BY

FRANK FINN, B.A., F.Z.S.

LATE DEPUTY SUPERINTENDENT INDIAN MUSEUM, CALCUTTA

CALCUTTA AND SIMLA

THACKER, SPINK & CO.

BOMBAY: THACKER & CO. LIMITED

MADRAS: HIGGINBOTHAMS

1929

Reduced from original Picture
by
R. A. STERNDALE, F.R.G.S., F.Z.S., etc.

Slow Loris in upright posture.

(*See page* 22.)

CONTENTS

		PAGE
MAMMALIA, *Introduction*		1
,,	order *Primates*	3
,,	,, *Chiroptera*	25
,,	,, *Dermoptera*	41
,,	,, *Insectivora*	43
,,	,, *Carnivora*	53
,,	,, *Cetacea*	123
,,	,, *Sirenia*	133
,,	,, *Rodentia*	134
,,	,, *Ungulata*	173
,,	,, *Edentata*	260
REPTILIA		264
AMPHIBIA		335
INDEX		341

PREFACE

In preparing the present revised and abridged edition of Sterndale's well-known work, the editor has quoted the author's original observations verbatim as far as possible, and has relied on condensation and on the omission of unnecessary matter, and of such as is only likely to be of interest to specialists, for reduction of the volume to the compass of a practical manual for beginners. Thus in most groups only such species as are likely to attract attention are dealt with, though in some all are described.

Sterndale's arrangement has been adhered to as far as possible, and the scientific names are for the most part those used by him and by Blanford in his standard work, the "Mammalia" volume in the *Fauna of British India* series. To this, particularly in the matter of vernacular names and of distribution, the editor has been especially indebted; and he has also to express his thanks to Messrs. Longmans, Green & Co. for permission to use certain illustrations from Tennent's *Natural History of Ceylon*.

In addition to granting permission this old firm of publishers were kind enough to supply electrotypes from the original woodcuts, a small enough technical point, but of great value as far as the appearance of the book is concerned.

The section on Reptiles, which are dealt with on similar lines to the Mammals, is the work of the editor alone, and here also he has to acknowledge especial obligations to the *Fauna* series, while his thanks are due to Colonel R. Knowles, I.M.S., for allowing the reproduction of illustrations from his Chart of the Poisonous Snakes of India, and again to Messrs. Longmans for others from the above-mentioned work.

The work of revision was started by me in 1927. It has been in many ways a labour of love, and I venture to express a hope that it may effectually supply a need that undoubtedly exists at the present time.

I would like to express my thanks for the assistance in publishing this book, so fully rendered by the late Mr. W. T. Spink, who, to my great grief, passed away while the work was in progress.

FRANK FINN.

MAMMALIA OF INDIA

INTRODUCTION

THE Mammals are distinguished from all other animals by nourishing their young with milk, and, as a general rule, by their hairy covering, though this is often, as in ourselves, much reduced. There are generally, however, a few hairs to be met with on the nakedest of mammals, even the fish-like whale tribe, which can in any case be

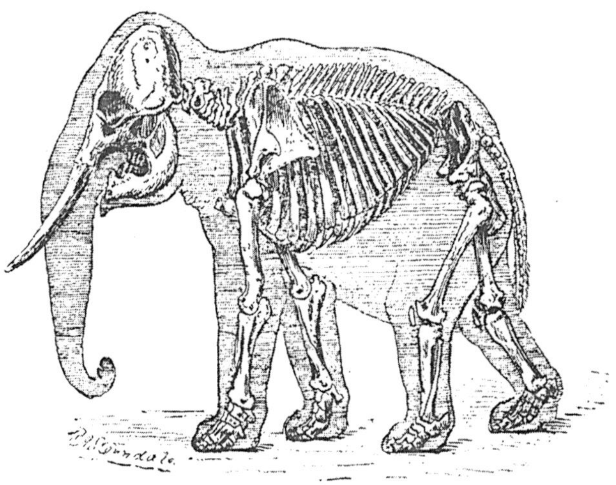

Elephant, showing the relations of the mammalian skeleton to the external form.

distinguished from true fish by the absence of gill-slits and the horizontal instead of vertical tail-fin.

The class of Mammals is divided into three sub-classes, two of which, the *Monotremata* or Egg-laying Mammals, and the *Marsupialia* or

Pouched Mammals, are not represented in India, and so do not concern us here.

The third sub-class, *Eutheria* or ordinary mammals, is divided into several Orders, the members of which are easily distinguishable, *as far as Indian species are concerned*, as follows:—

The *Primates* or Monkeys and Lemurs, by having all the limbs provided with an opposable first toe, in fact, in the form of hands.

The *Chiroptera* or Bats, by the extreme elongation of the finger-bones to support a web which forms wings.

The *Cetacea* or Whales and Dolphins, by their fish-like body, covered even on the muzzle with close bare tight skin.

The *Sirenia* or Dugongs, by the combination of fish-like form with a thick-lipped hairy muzzle.

The *Ungulata* or Hoofed Animals, by the blunt hoofs which terminate their toes.

The remaining orders all have paws, not hands, wings, fins, or hoofs. Of these:

A typical Insectivore, the Bulau.

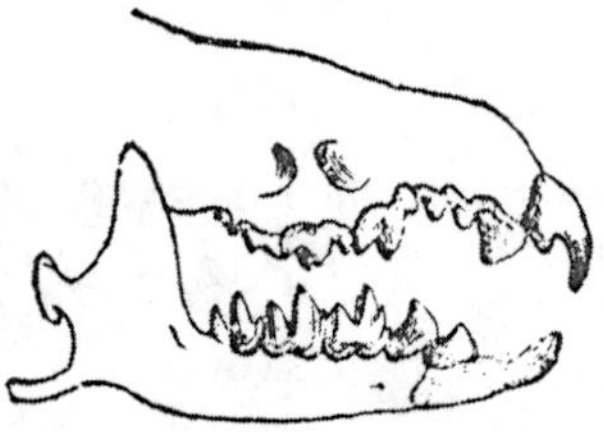

Fore-part of the skull of an Insectivore (Shrew, magnified) to show dentition.

The *Insectivora* or Shrew tribe, which are all smaller than a Rabbit, are distinguished by their long projecting snout, the end of which is far in front of the mouth.

The *Carnivora* or Flesh-eaters, by their large canine teeth in conjunction with absence of any of the above described peculiarities.

The *Rodentia* or Gnawers, by having two large chisel-tipped front teeth in the front of each jaw, and a long gap between these and the grinders.

The *Edentata* by having no teeth at all, and scaly bodies.

There remains one queer beast which is generally chummed up with the *Insectivora*, but is so different that it is better placed in an order by itself, the *Dermaptera*; this is the Cobego (*Galeopithecus*), which differs from all other beasts in having all four paws webbed (though it is not aquatic) in combination with a flounce or parachute-skin uniting the limbs and the tail.

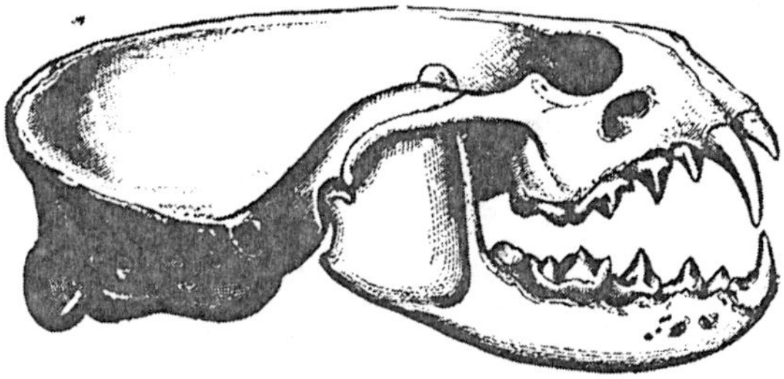

Skull of Carnivore (Otter) to show dentition.

ORDER PRIMATES

Formerly called Quadrumana, this order is divided into two sub-orders, the *Anthropoidea* or Apes and Monkeys, and the *Lemuroidea* or Lemurs. The former are easily distinguished by their broad, more or less human faces, the Lemurs having narrow foxy muzzles.

Of the Monkey section, representatives of two families are found in India, the *Simiidæ* or true Apes, which are all tailless, and the *Cerco-*

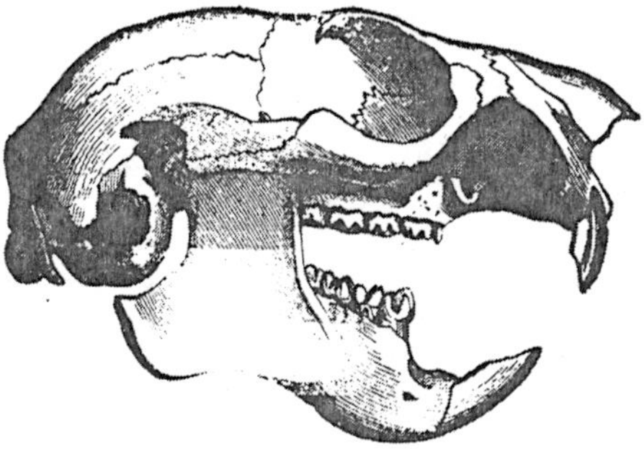

Skull of Rodent (Flying Squirrel) to show dentition.

pithecidæ or Old-World tailed Monkeys. None of the great anthropoid apes occur in our Eastern territory, the only representatives of the ape family there being the Gibbons, which, with the long arms of the Orangs and the receding forehead of the Chimpanzee, possess the callosities (bare seat-patches) of the true monkeys, but differ from them in having neither tail nor cheek-pouches. They are true bipeds on the ground, applying the sole of the foot flatly, with the big toe widely separated. They seldom, however, leave the trees or bamboos, where they travel by swinging themselves along with their arms. Unlike our other monkeys, they have long canines in both sexes.

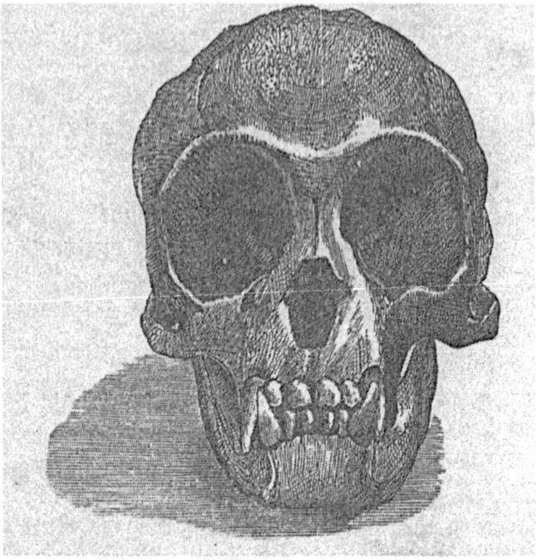

Skull of Gibbon, showing Primate dentitions.

THE HOOLOCK

OTHER NAMES.—Scientific: *Hylobates hooluck.* Native: *Hooluck, Hookoo.*

HABITAT.—Garo and Khasia Hills, Valley of Assam, and Arakan.

DESCRIPTION.—Males deep black, marked with white across the forehead. Females vary from brownish-black to whitish-brown. About two feet in length of body. Sterndale says:

"I think of all the monkey family this Gibbon makes one of the most interesting pets. It is mild and most docile, and capable of great attachment. Even the adult male has been caught, and within the short space of a month so completely tamed that he would follow and come to a call. One I had for a time, some years ago, was a most engaging little creature. Nothing contented him so much as being allowed to sit by my side with his arm linked through mine, and he would resist any attempt I made to go away. He was extremely clean in his habits, which cannot be said of all the monkey tribe. Soon after he came to me I gave him a piece of blanket to sleep on in his box, but the next morning I found he had rolled it up and made a sort of pillow for his head, so a second piece was given him. He was destined for the Queen's Gardens at Delhi, but unfortunately on his way up he got a chill, and contracted a disease akin to consumption. During his illness he was most carefully tended by my brother, who had

White-handed Gibbon. Hoolock.

a little bed made for him, and the doctor came daily to see the little patient, who gratefully accepted his attentions; but, to their disappointment, he died. The only objection to these monkeys as pets is the power they have of howling, or rather whooping, a piercing and somewhat hysterical 'Whoop-poo! whoop-poo! whoop-poo!' for several minutes, till fairly exhausted. They are very fond of swinging by their long arms, and walk something like a tipsy sailor. A friend, resident on the borders of Assam, tells me that the full-grown adult pines and dies in confinement. I think it probable that it may miss a certain amount of insect diet, and would recommend those who cannot let their pets run loose in a garden to give them raw eggs and a little minced meat, and a spider or two occasionally."

In its wild state this Gibbon feeds on leaves, insects, eggs and small birds. They drink by dipping up water with their hands, sliding down on overhanging boughs to do this.

WHITE-HANDED GIBBON

OTHER NAMES.—Scientific: *Hylobates lar.*

HABITAT.—Arakan, Lower Pegu, Tenasserim, and the Malayan Peninsula.

DESCRIPTION.—Has invariably white hands and feet, and generally a white ring encircling the face. It is, however, found in every variety of (body) colour, from black to brownish, and variegated with light-coloured patches, and occasionally of a fulvous white. About the size of the Hoolock. First and middle fingers sometimes joined.

The White-handed Gibbon, according to Tickell, does not go in such large troops as the Hooluck, and has a quite different note. He saw a party escape from a Karen garden, which they had been plundering, carrying the spoil in their feet—showing how much they depend on the hands for locomotion. The young are born in the beginning of the cold weather, and cling to the mother for more than half a year. Of the tailed monkeys, the Langurs or Leaf-Monkeys (*Presbytes, Semnopithecus*) are characterised by their slender bodies and long limbs and tails, and the absence or rudimentary nature of the cheek-pouches; finally, they are to be distinguished by the peculiar structure of the stomach, which is singularly complicated, almost as much so as in the case of Ruminants, consisting of three divisions: first, a simple pouch, second, a wide sacculated portion; third, a narrow elongated canal, sacculated at first, and of simple structure towards the termination. As a matter of fact, these monkeys resemble Ruminants in their diet, feeding more on leaves than on anything else.

"The species of this genus of monkey," says Sterndale, abound throughout the Peninsula. All Indian sportsmen are familiar with their habits, and have often been assisted by them in tracking the tiger. Their loud whoops and immense bounds from tree to tree when excited, or the flashing of their white teeth as they gibber at their lurking foe, have often told the shikari of the whereabouts of the object of his search. The *Langurs* take enormous leaps, twenty-five feet in width, with thirty or forty in a drop and never miss a branch."

Jerdon's statement that they can run with great rapidity on all-fours is qualified by McMaster, who easily ran down a large male on horseback by getting him out on a plain. Strychnine, which kills

Common Langur or Entellus.

the common Bandar or *Rhesus*, has no effect on *Langurs*, at any rate on the common species, as much as five grains having been given in an hour without effect, and two days later even ten !

The Langurs all have the tail longer than the body, and side-whiskers meeting under the chin in a short beard ; they also have eyebrows of bristly black hair, often very long.

COMMON LANGUR, HANUMAN OR ENTELLUS

OTHER NAMES.—Scientific : *Presbytes* or *Semnopithecus entellus*. Native : *Langur*, *Hanuman*, Hindi ; *Wanur*, *Makur*, Mahratti ; *Musya*, Canarese.

HABITAT.—Bengal and Central India.

DESCRIPTION.—Pale dirty straw-colour, or ashy grey, darker on the shoulders and rump, paler on the head and lower parts; hands, feet, and face black. Male's head and body 30 in. long, tail 43 in.

"The *Entellus* monkey," says Sterndale, "is in some parts of India deemed sacred, and is permitted by the Hindus to plunder their grain-shops with impunity. . . . In the forest the *Langur* lives on grain, fruit, the pods of leguminous trees, and young buds or leaves. The female has usually only one young one, though sometimes twins. The very young babies have not black but light-coloured faces, which darken afterwards. I have always found them most difficult to rear, requiring almost as much attention as a human baby. Their diet and hours of feeding must be as systematically arranged; and if cow's milk be given it must be freely diluted with water—two-thirds to one-third milk when very young, and afterwards decreased to one-half. They are extremely susceptible to cold. In confinement they are quiet and gentle whilst young, but the old males are generally sullen and treacherous. Jerdon says, on the authority of the *Bengal Sporting Magazine* (August 1836) that the males live apart from the females, who have only one or two males with each colony, and that they have fights at certain seasons, when the vanquished males receive charge of all the young ones of their own sex, with whom they retire to some neighbouring jungle. Blyth notices that in one locality he found only males of all ages, and in another chiefly females. I have found these monkeys mostly on the banks of streams in the forests of the Central Provinces; in fact, the presence of them anywhere in arid jungles is a sign that water is somewhere in the vicinity. They are timid creatures, and I have never seen the slightest disposition about them to show fight, whereas I was once most deliberately charged by the old males of a party of *Rhesus* monkeys. I was at the time on field service during the Mutiny, and seeing several nursing mothers in the party, tried to run them down in the open and secure a baby; but they were too quick for me, and on being attacked by the old males, I had to pistol the leader."

Blanford doubts the above story of the fights, but quotes an account of a "faction fight" between two troops containing both sexes.

HIMALAYAN LANGUR

OTHER NAMES.—Scientific: *Semnopithecus* or *Presbytes schistaceus*. Native: *Langur*, Hindi; *Kamba Suhú*, Lepcha; *Kubup*, Bhotia.

HABITAT.—Himalayas from Nepal to beyond Simla.

DESCRIPTION.—Like the Bengal Langur, of which some have

considered it only a race, but it runs larger, with longer coat and more massive jaws and teeth; the colour is also more distinct, slate-grey or dark brown; feet pale, head and underparts creamy.

It ranges up to at least 11,000 ft., and has often been seen sporting about in snow-laden trees.

MADRAS LANGUR

OTHER NAMES.—Scientific: *Semnopithecus* or *Presbytes priamus.* Native: *Gandangi*, Telegu; *Musya*, Canarese; *Kunde Wanderu*, Cingalese.

HABITAT.—Coromandel Coast and Ceylon.

DESCRIPTION.—Differs from the Bengal Langur in having a reddish wash over the head and back, and the hands and feet whitish above, not black. Head crested.

Tennant writes of it in Ceylon: "At Jaffna and other parts of the island where the population is comparatively numerous, these monkeys become so familiarised with the presence of man as to exhibit the utmost daring and indifference. A flock of them will take possession of a palmyra palm, and so effectually can they crouch and conceal themselves amongst the leaves that, on the slightest alarm, the whole party becomes invisible in an instant. The presence of a dog, however, excites such irrepressible curiosity that, in order to watch his movements, they never fail to betray themselves. They may be frequently seen congregated on the roof of a native hut. . . . The child of a European clergyman stationed near Jaffna having been left on the ground by the nurse, was so teased and bitten by them as to cause its death."

The three light-coloured Langurs are all very much alike; in all the hair radiates on the crown, and the Hanuman or Common Langur has not always the hair on the hands and feet black, as the editor has seen in three specimens. An ancient Himalayan Langur in the British Museum is more like the plains variety.

MALABAR LANGUR

OTHER NAMES.—Scientific: *Semnopithecus hypoleucus, Semnopithecus* or *Presbytes Johni.* Native: *Vella Manthi*, Malayalim.

HABITAT.—The Malabar Coast from N. Lat. 14° to Cape Comorin.

DESCRIPTION.—Above dusky brown, slightly paling on the sides; head fulvous, darkest on the crown, limbs and tail almost black; beneath yellowish white. Hair of crown radiating as in the Entellus group, and colour, at any rate on the sides, sometimes not much darker; size rather smaller than Hanuman. Young specimens are sooty-brown all over. This monkey abounds in forests, and does not frequent villages, though it will visit gardens and fields, where, however, it shuns observation.

Mr. R. J. Pocock, in an able paper in the *Journal* of the Bombay Natural History Society (vol. xxxii. 1928), treats these three last Langurs as sub-species of the Entellus.

NILGIRI LANGUR OR WANDEROO

OTHER NAMES.—Scientific: *Semnopithecus Johni*, *Semnopithecus* or *Presbytes jubatus*. Native: *Turuni*, *Kodan*, *Pershk*, Toda; *Korangu*, Baduga and Kurumba; *Karing Korangu*, Malayalim.

HABITAT.—The Nilgiri Hills, the Animalais, the Palnis, the Wynaad, and all the higher parts of the ranges of the Ghats as low as Travancore.

This, the true *Semnopithecus Johni*, which has been sometimes confused with the last, is a very striking and distinct species, with the head hair long but not radiating, the body dark glossy black throughout, the head tawny; old specimens have a grey rump-patch, and females a cream one inside each thigh. Young ones are all black. The head and body are about 2 ft. long, the tail longer.

This very handsome monkey does not as a rule descend lower than 2,500 ft.; having been persecuted for its fine fur, and by some castes for food, it is shy, and when the woods it haunts are beaten, executes a noisy retreat.

Mr. Pocock regards this as a sub-species of the Ceylon Wanderoo presently to be noticed.

CAPPED LANGUR

OTHER NAMES.—Scientific: *Semnopithecus* or *Presbytes pileatus*.

HABITAT.—Assam, Chittagong, Tipperah, N. Arakan and Upper Burma in part.

DESCRIPTION.—Cap black, long cheek-whiskers white, body-fur slate-colour above, cream to auburn—the latter in old males—below. Face black, fingers black or yellow. Infant specimens have flesh-coloured faces and close pale golden fur. Size rather smaller than the Hanuman.

Sterndale says: "Dr. Anderson says that a young one he had was of mild disposition, which, however, is not the character of the adult animal, which is uncertain, and the males when irritated are fierce, and determined in attack. No rule, however, is without its exception, for one adult male, possessed by Blyth, is reported as having been an exceedingly gentle animal."

A pair that lived for years at the London Zoo before the war were most charming and nice-mannered animals. The female would even bring her infant young—of which she had three at different times—up to the bars when visitors were present, showing no jealous ferocity, as monkeys so commonly do when carrying small young. Two of them duly changed their infant golden fur for the colours of the adult, which in this particular pair only differed in the male's tints being a little purer; but the first-born, though also golden at birth, assumed a dark brown coat against which the white whiskers showed up very distinctly. This was evidently a hybrid; for originally a male Hanuman had shared the Capped pair's quarters, and the fact that it was much darker than he and browner than its female parent, and on the whole resembled the Ceylonese Purple-faced Langur presently to be noticed, is paralleled by several cases in which hybrid birds have resembled species not concerned in their origin.

BANDED OR WHITE-THIGHED LANGUR

OTHER NAMES.—Scientific: *Semnopithecus femoralis.*

HABITAT.—Tenasserim, Malay Peninsula, and Siam.

DESCRIPTION.—A crest, with a whorl on each side of it on the forehead. Colour blackish-brown, extremities black; inside of thighs white, and sometimes other white markings below. Face black with white lips. Infant specimens are white with a sooty band from poll down spine on to tail.

BARBE'S LANGUR

OTHER NAMES.—Scientific: *Semnopithecus* or *Presbytes Barbei.*

HABITAT.—Tipperah, Upper Burma, Kakhyen Hills, Tenasserim.

DESCRIPTION.—Black with dark-blue face. Lips often light.

"More information," says Sterndale, "is required about this monkey, which was named by Blyth after its donor to the Asiatic Society, the Rev. J. Barbe. Dr. Andersen noticed it in the valley of the Tapeng in the centre of the Kakhyen Hills, in troops of thirty to fifty, in high forest trees overhanging the mountain streams. Being seldom disturbed, they permitted a near approach." A couple in the Calcutta Zoo in the 'nineties were very handsome animals, with the quiet manners usual in Langurs.

PHAYRE'S OR SILVERY LANGUR

OTHER NAMES.—Scientific: *Semnopithecus* or *Presbytes Phayrei, Semnopithecus cristatus.* Native: *Myouk-myek-kweng hpyu,* Burmese; *Myouk-hgnyo,* Arakan and Tavoy; *Geng,* Talain; *Dáthwa* and *Shawá me,* Karen.

HABITAT.—Arakan, Bassein, North Tenasserim.

DESCRIPTION.—Dusky grey-brown above and on cheeks, back

shining or silvery; white below, orbits, eyelids, and lips white, rest of face livid-black. Infant specimens are straw-coloured, as is so often the case with Langurs, recalling the golden hair of our children which so often becomes darker. Size rather smaller than Hanuman.

This monkey inhabits forests on the banks of streams, and is shy, wary, and seldom seen. The old males will sometimes stay and bark, rather like a Hanuman, from a safe perch. The young whine and sometimes mew very like a cat, according to Blyth.

DUSKY LANGUR

OTHER NAMES.—Scientific: *Semnopithecus* or *Presbytes obscurus*. Native: *Lotong*, *Lotong-itam*, Malay.

HABITAT.—Malayan Peninsula, Tenasserim, Siam.

DESCRIPTION.—Greyish or brownish-black, with a whitish tuft on the nape, face black, with the mouth and eyelids whitish. Young golden tan, this colour remaining longest on the end half of the tail, as the animal turns dark grey. Length 21 in., with the tail 32 in.

The species is commonest in the Malay Peninsula. Like the last two, it appears to be a local race of the Javan Langur *pyrrhus*.

RUTLEDGE'S LANGUR

OTHER NAMES.—Scientific: *Semnopithecus rutledgii*.

HABITAT.—Unknown.

DESCRIPTION.—Head with a very well-defined erect median compressed crest. General colour black, grey-tipped, lower surface paler and greyer, hands and feet black, tail black above, yellow below, grey at tip, whiskers long, backwardly and upwardly divided, and broadly tipped with yellowish-grey, beard greyish; face bluish-black Seventeen inches long, tail 2 ft. and half an inch.

As this animal may prove to occur in Indian limits, the above description abstracted from Anderson's *Zoological Results of the Expedition to Yun-nan* (1878), is inserted here, though Blanford ignores it.

PURPLE-FACED LANGUR OR WANDEROO

OTHER NAMES.—Scientific: *Semnopithecus* or *Presbytes cephalopterus* or *thersites*. Native: *Kallu Wanderu* and *Elli Wanderu*, Cingalese. *Wanderu* is simply the general Cingalese name for monkey.

HABITAT.—Low country of Ceylon.

DESCRIPTION.—Dark brown or black, hindquarters silver-grey, tail dark grey, long pointed side-whiskers and throat white, framing the purple face. Body 20 in. long, tail 24 in.

Malabar Langur. Madras Langur.

Wanderoo. Toque Monkey.

This monkey has been much and long confused with the Lion-tailed Macaque, shortly to be noticed, which also is a dark animal with conspicuous light whiskers, though really very different in many ways. There has also been some confusion due to variation in colour, a brown variety having been named as *thersites*.

Tennant says of it that " It is an active and intelligent creature, little larger than the common bonneted macaque, and far from being so mischievous as others of the monkeys of the island. In captivity it is remarkable for the gravity of its demeanour and for an air of melancholy in its expression and movement, which are completely in character with its snowy beard and venerable aspect. In disposition it is gentle and confiding, sensible in the highest degree of kindness, and eager for endearing attention, uttering a low plaintive cry when its sympathies are excited. It is particularly cleanly in its habits when domesticated, and spends much of its time in trimming its fur and carefully divesting its hair of particles of dust. Those which I kept at my house, near Colombo, were chiefly fed upon plantains and bananas, but for nothing did they evince a greater partiality than the rose-coloured flowers of the red hibiscus (*H. rosa-sinensis*). These they devoured with unequivocal gusto; they likewise relished the leaves of many other trees, and even the bark of a few of the more succulent ones."

In a wild state the Wanderoo lives in small troops of ten or fifteen individuals, and does not range to heights above 1,300 feet.

BEAR LANGUR OR GREAT WANDEROO

OTHER NAMES.—Scientific: *Semnopithecus* or *Presbytes ursinus*. Native: *Maha Wanderu*, Cingalese.

HABITAT.—Mountains of Ceylon.

DESCRIPTION.—Bears much the same relation to the common Wanderoo of the plains as the Himalayan Langur does to the low-country Hanuman or Entellus, being a larger and longer-coated animal; the hair on the flanks reaches 5 in. in length. The general colour is dark brown or greyish-black, redder in the young, with the whiskers white.

The hairy coat in these mountain races of monkeys is no doubt related to the cooler temperature, which also probably indirectly accounts for their larger size by delaying maturity, for it is well-known to animal breeders and may be observed in tropical human races that early breeding is most deleterious to size. Mr. Pocock treats this animal as a race of the common Wanderoo.

The celebrated Ceylon White Monkeys, formerly considered as a species (*senex* or *albinus*) are varieties of either the lowland or of the upland Wanderoo.

The Macaques (*Macacus*) or Bandars are a less specialised group, more compactly built than the last and with ordinary stomachs. They are also less herbivorous in their diet, eating frogs, lizards, crabs, and insects, as well as vegetables and fruit. Their callosities (seat-pads) and cheek-pouches are large. Their tails vary much in length, and the shorter-tailed species used to be placed in a separate genus *Inuus*, not at all reasonably, the tail being, as we know from some of our domestic animals, the sheep, dog, and cat, excessively liable to variation, and hence unimportant in classification. The males exceed the females in size and strength most noticeably in this group.

LION-TAILED MONKEY

Other Names.—Scientific: *Inuus* or *Macacus silenus*. Native: *Nil bandar*, Bengali; *Shia bandar*, Hindi; *Nella manthi*, Malabari; *Singalika*, Canarese; *Kondamachu*, Telugu; *Kurankarangu*, Tamil.

Habitat.—Western Ghats, especially in Cochin and Travancore.

Lion-tailed Monkey.

Description.—Tail tufted at end, not more than three-quarters the length of head and body; head surrounded with a full ruff of very long whiskers, more developed than in any Langur. These are grey, the rest of the coat and the bare face black. Infants have no whiskers, and the face is flesh-coloured. Head and body about 20 in. long, tail 10 to 15 in.

In its dark face and wide frill, and to some extent in its dignity of bearing, this Bandar resembles the aristocratic Langurs more than its very vulgar-looking genus-fellows, all the rest of which are pale-faced and beardless, while even their whiskers are very short or wanting. It is therefore not surprising that it has been confused with the Wanderoo Langurs.

It is somewhat sulky and savage, and is difficult to get near in a wild state. Jerdon says that he met with it only in dense unfrequented forest, and sometimes at a considerable elevation. It occurs in troops of from twelve to twenty. It has long been well known in captivity, unlike the delicate Langurs, so that it is no wonder that it has usurped the name of one of these.

RHESUS MONKEY OR COMMON BANDAR

OTHER NAMES.—Scientific: *Inuus* or *Macacus rhesus*. Native: *Bandar*, Hindi; *Markat*, Bengali; *Wandar*, *Puriz*, *Púnj*, Kashmir; *Gye*, Ho Kol.

HABITAT.—From the base of the Himalayas, south to the Godavari; it ranges some thousands of feet uphill in places.

Common Bandar or Rhesus.

DESCRIPTION.—Short, close side whiskers, no beard, hair on head lying straight back, tail not more than half length of head and body, hindquarters naked round the seat-pads. Coat brown, becoming redder or yellower behind. Face and other bare parts flesh-coloured or red, the latter especially in old females, not so much in males. Male with head and body up to 22 in. long, female much less.

A bright pale auburn or golden variety, with very light and European-looking hands and face, appears not to be rare; the finest male the editor ever saw, nearly twenty years old, was of this type, also two young ones, which struck him as more active than normal animals. The eyes of these blonds were hazel, as in others. Old females become very fat and pursy like some humans.

Sterndale only says: "This monkey is too well-known to need description. It is the common acting monkey of the *bandar-wallas*, the delight of all Anglo-Indian children, who go into raptures over the romance of *Munsar-ram* and *Chameli*, their quarrels, parting, and reconciliation, so admirably acted by these miniature comedians."

It is, so far as the editor knows, the commonest monkey in captivity generally; at any rate, it was always plentiful in the Calcutta animal market in his time (the 'nineties), and has been with English dealers (who know it as *Rhesus*) ever since. It has sometimes bred in captivity. At the end of the war a number of immature specimens were placed in the large aviary, previously and now used for parrots, in the London Zoo. This contains a little pond, and the monkeys took to the water with surprising readiness, not only swimming, but diving from the surface and plunging in from a height. The latter, however, they did feet first, and swam with the dog-stroke. The biped Gibbon is unable to swim, like untaught man, and throws up its arms in the same way.

HIMALAYAN MONKEY

OTHER NAMES.—Scientific: *Inuus* or *Macacus pelops*, *Macacus assamensis*.

HABITAT.—Himalayas to Upper Burma; said to reappear in the Sunderbunds.

DESCRIPTION.—Like the other mountain monkeys already noticed among the Langurs, this differs from its lowland relative in being larger and with more fur; in particular it has a beard, and the hind-quarters clothed up to the seat-pads. It also is of a uniform shade of brown, not reddish or greyish anywhere; but its face is sometimes darker.

This monkey is stouter in build and less active than the ordinary Rhesus, but if the same form really recurs in the low flat sweltering Sunderbunds, it does not look as if it were a true species at all; in fact, it seems to the editor probable that in all these cases of hill-and-plains pairs of allied forms the two cannot be called fully distinct species, but only local races.

PIG-TAILED MONKEY

OTHER NAMES.—Scientific: *Inuus* or *Macacus nemestrinus*. Native: *Myouk-padi*, Burmese; *Ta-o-ti*, at Tavoy; *Bruh*, Malay.

HABITAT.—Tenasserim to Borneo.

DESCRIPTION.—A long-legged, long-muzzled, short-tailed, rather baboon-like monkey, with a short close coat of brown of various shades, generally light; a conspicuous black crown patch, and a stripe of the same colour often running down the back. Tail thin and poorly furred, not much longer than the head. Size very variable; sometimes bigger than any Rhesus.

This monkey is noted for its docility, and in Bencoolen is trained to be useful as well as amusing. According to Sir Stamford Raffles, it is taught to climb the cocoa-nut palms for the fruit for its master, and to select only those that are ripe.

In captivity it is particularly lively, and has a curious habit of standing erect and holding its thighs with its hands. Another trick is carrying the tail curved like an S when excited. As Blanford says, it must be only the females and young that are trained as fruit-pickers, the old males being savage and dangerous. The gestation period is nearly eight months, and young have been born in captivity.

Pig-tailed Monkey.

BURMESE PIG-TAILED MONKEY

Other Names.—Scientific: *Inuus* or *Macacus leoninus*. Native: *Myouk-mai*, Burmese; *Myouk-la-haing*, Arakanese.

Habitat.—Upper Burma and Arakan.

Description.—More thick-set than the common Pig-tail, with a shorter and broader head bearing a distinct horseshoe-shaped crest on the forehead, of very stiff hairs where the convexity projects towards the brows. Hair very long on the neck and shoulders, up to 3 in. Short, full whiskers and beard. General colour brown, paler below, the sides of the head and the stern grey, lower back black, extending over the upper surface of the tail; crest also black. Females are greyer, with no black on the upper parts except on the tail, and much smaller than the male, which is nearly 2 ft. long from muzzle to stern.

Very little is known about the habits of this monkey—the fact that old males are fierce and young and females docile, applies to very many monkeys, and indeed other mammals and birds.

STUMP-TAILED MONKEY

OTHER NAMES.—Scientific: *Inuus* or *Macacus arctoides.*

HABITAT.—Kakhyen Hills, Cochin China, probably hills south of Assam, and Tipperah.

DESCRIPTION.—Tail a mere stump, almost or quite naked, not more than 2 in. to a body of about 2 ft. Hair on fore-quarters up to 4½ in. long. Colour dark brown, with bare face and stern bright red.

Practically nothing is known about this monkey, which is believed to inhabit hilly country. Blanford quotes an account of two specimens Davison met with apparently allied to it, but both, though adult, and one was a male, were very small, standing only 15 in. high when erect. They had tails less than an inch long and turned on one side, flesh-coloured face and hands, and cream-coloured fur tinged with rusty above; they smelt very bad and had shrill voices. The editor once got for the Zoo in Calcutta a monkey which closely corresponded in nearly all these points, though he took it to be young; it was clingingly affectionate in manner. Both Davison and Bingham also saw in the Tenasserim mountains large tailless monkeys, which were not Gibbons, more or less red in colour, so there is evidently some remarkable new monkey in that region, which, as Blanford suggests, may be related to the stump-tailed species.

BONNET MONKEY

OTHER NAMES.—Scientific: *Macacus radiatus* or *sinicus.* Native: *Bandar*, Hindi; *Makadu*, *Wanar*, *Kerda*, Mahratta; *Manga*, *Kadaga*, Canarese; *Kurangu*, Tamil; *Koti*, Telegu; *Koranga*, *Vella manthi*, Malayalam; *Mucha*, Kúrg; *Kodan*, Toda.

HABITAT.—Southern India, extending up to near Bombay and the Godavari.

DESCRIPTION.—A long-tailed monkey with no whiskers (except straggling hairs) or beard, and a cap of radiating hair on the crown. Brown in colour, paler below, with flesh-coloured face and a very low-caste look. Not quite so large as the Rhesus or Bandar, but with a tail about as long as the head and body. The male is much bigger about the head than the female.

It takes the place, in the south, of the Common Bandar of Northern India, both in general familiarity in the wilds and in being the monkey commonly kept to show off tricks; it is also freely exported to Europe, and so nearly as familiar in menageries as the Common Bandar.

Group of Macaques.
Rhesus, Bonnet, Crab-eating and Toque.

TOQUE MONKEY

OTHER NAMES.—Scientific: *Macacus pileatus* or *sinicus*, *Macaca sinica*. Native: *Mishi Bandar*, Hindi; *Rilawa*, Cingalese.

HABITAT.—Ceylon, generally distributed over the island.

DESCRIPTION.—Very like the Bonnet Monkey, but a smaller, slimmer, and altogether better-looking animal. Its coat is longer, rougher, and yellower, especially on the head, where it radiates as in the Bonnet, but stands up more into a kind of top-knot. The face is flesh-coloured and free from whiskers or beard, but the ears dark, not pale like the face as in the Bonnet, of which Blanford is inclined to consider it only a local variety, though the two look more different than do some of the Langurs commonly reckoned as distinct. A specimen of the Bonnet from Travancore he cites as presenting some of the points of the Toque may have been an escaped specimen of this or a hybrid with one, for no wild animals are carried about so much or so liable to escape and thrive as the commoner and hardier monkeys.

This is the best-known monkey in its native island. "In Ceylon," says Sterndale, "it takes the place of our Rhesus monkey with the conjurers. . . . It also, like the last [the Bonnet] smokes tobacco; and one that belonged to the captain of a tug steamer, in which I once went down from Calcutta to the Sandheads, not only smoked, but chewed tobacco." It is known in Ceylon as the Red monkey, from the auburn tinge of its coat; the dark lips are also noticeable.

CRAB-EATING MONKEY

OTHER NAMES.—Scientific: *Macacus cynomolgus.* Native: *Kra*, Malay; *Myouk-ta-nga*, Burmese; *Ta-o-tan*, Tavoy and Arakan; *Kamui-awut*, Talain; *Da-ouk*, *Sha-ok-li*, Karen.

HABITAT.—Burma to Siam and Malay Islands, also Nicobars, where it was probably introduced.

DESCRIPTION.—A most variable monkey, but recognisable by combining a whiskered face with a tail about as long as the head and

Common or Crab-eating Macaque Monkey.

body. The coat is dark- to golden-brown, the face either flesh-coloured or dark, and the shade of the coat and face do not necessarily correspond. Many have white eyelids. The size of body is about that of the common Bandar.

The Crab-eating monkey, as its name implies, feeds a good deal on crabs, for it especially frequents the edges of estuaries and tidal creeks. It is not surprising that it swims and dives well—a wounded male, escaping from a boat, has been known to dive for a distance of 50 yds.

It is very freely exported, and is probably the next commonest monkey to the Rhesus in the animal trade. Young specimens were often offered in the Calcutta animal market as "pocket monkeys."

The Lemuroid section of the Primates has two representatives only in our limits, both belonging to the typical family *Lemuridæ*, tailless or nearly so, and smaller than any of our monkeys, from which their great eyes and especially their foxy muzzles also distinguish them. They also have the fore-finger and great toe very short, and ending in a claw instead of a nail like the others.

SLOW LORIS

OTHER NAMES.—Scientific: *Nycticebus tardigradus*. Native: *Sharmindi billi*, Hindi; *Lajjar bánar*, Bengali; *Myouk-moung-ma*, Burmese; *Myouk hlioung*, Tavoy; *Kasyng*, Talain; *Tacheng*, Karen; *Kukang*, Malay.

HABITAT.—Eastern Bengal to Borneo.

DESCRIPTION.—A thick-set little animal about the size of a half-grown cat, with short ears and stump tail almost hidden in the close thick fur, which varies in colour, being grey in the larger specimens from the north, reddish-grey in the smaller southern race; a brown ring round the eyes, and a more or less well-developed brown streak on the crown and back.

It is nocturnal and omnivorous, eating any soft vegetable food or small animal it can get hold of. Tickell says: "This animal is tolerably common in the Tenasserim provinces and Arakan, but, being strictly nocturnal in its habits, is seldom seen. It inhabits the densest forests, and never by choice leaves the trees. Its movements are slow, but it climbs readily, and grasps with great tenacity. If placed on the ground, it can proceed, if frightened, in a wavering kind of trot, the limbs placed at right angles. It sleeps rolled up in a ball, its head and hands buried between its thighs [whence, no doubt, its Hindi name of "bashful cat"], and wakes up at the dusk of evening to commence its nocturnal rambles. The female bears but one young at a time." The illustration showing it erect is from a sketch by Colonel Tickell, who saw a captive specimen stalk a cockroach and rise to throw itself on it—needless to say, without success, though the same trick would doubtless answer with a sleeping lizard or bird in the woods.

SLENDER LORIS

OTHER NAMES.—Scientific: *Loris gracilis*, *Loris tardigradus*, *malabaricus*, *lydekkerianus*. Native: *Tevángu*, Tamil; *Devánga-pilli*, Telegu; *Nala manushya*, *Adavi manushya*, Canarese; *Una happolava*, Cingalese.

HABITAT.—Southern India and Ceylon, not ascending the hills to any height.

DESCRIPTION.—A quite tailless, very thin and lanky little creature of the size of a rat, with huge eyes set in a dark patch, and fair-sized ears. Fur very short and soft, greyish or, in the young, reddish-brown. Several species have been described, but as the animal has been known to naturalists for over a century and these distinctions have

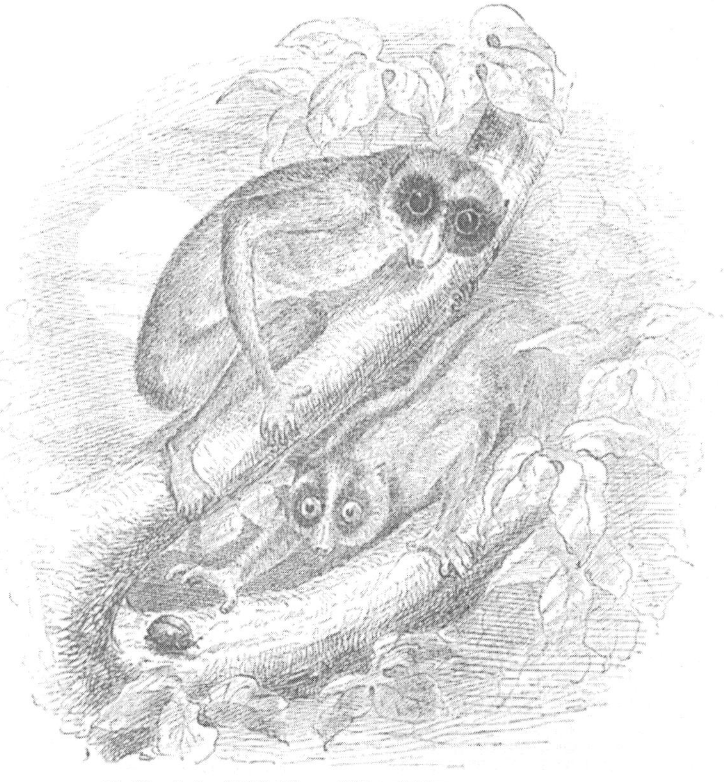

Slender Loris (above). Slow Loris (below, reduced).

been only recently made, they can hardly be of much importance. It was first described from Ceylon.

Sterndale says: "This, like the last, is nocturnal in its habits, and from the extreme slowness of its movements is called in Ceylon 'sloth.' Its diet is varied—fruits, flower and leaf buds, insects, eggs and young birds. Sir Emerson Tennent says the Sinhalese assert that it has been known to strangle pea-fowl at night and feast on the brain, but this I doubt. Smaller birds it might overcome. Jerdon states that in confinement it will eat boiled rice, plantains, honey or syrup and raw meat. These little creatures double themselves up when they sleep, bending their head down between their legs. Although so sluggish generally, Jerdon says they can move with considerable agility when they choose." The eyes of this Loris are regarded as a medicine or charm by natives, and procured by a method too disgustingly cruel to write about, so the sale alive of these little creatures should be looked into and regulated.

The native story about pea-fowl-garrotting certainly sounds wildly improbable; but, although an old bird would very likely injure the little ghoul in its struggles and certainly drag him to the ground—where he would least like to be—it must be remembered that pea-chicks are hatched with wing-feathers showing, and perch when small; thus even the tiny Loris could account for one in the manner indicated if he could abstract it from its mother's side, so that the story probably, like so many other wild-seeming native tales, has an element of truth in it after all. A female specimen of this Loris kept captive in Ceylon made a sort of nest in a coir broom in which to bring forth her young.

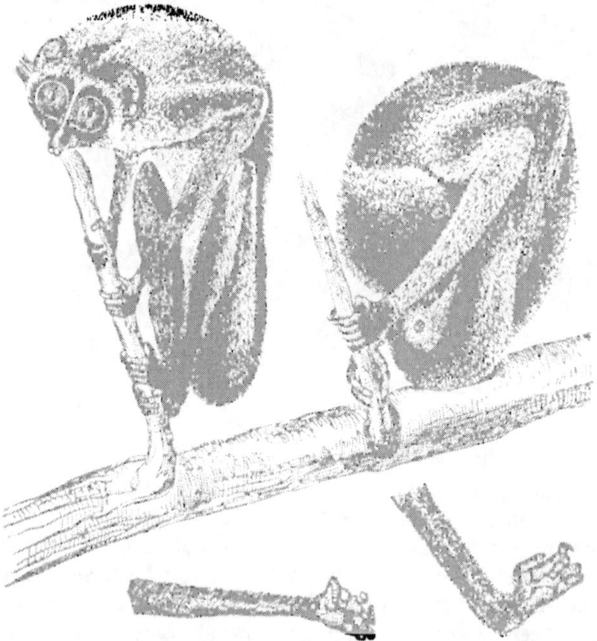

Slender Loris, awake and asleep. Details of hand and foot below.

ORDER CHIROPTERA

The Bats, although now regarded as related to the Insectivora, were once included among the Carnivora, and earlier still among the Primates, and it seems as well to keep them next as Sterndale did, though not including them among the carnivora; for in some respects they do resemble the Primates, notably in having two teats on the breast, bearing only one or two young after a long gestation, which they carry about with them, and being long-lived. Moreover, as we

Bat (Large Painted or Hodgson's) showing relation of the wing-membrane to the fore-limb, and of the leg-web to the tail.

shall see, some of the Insectivora themselves are now thought to come very near the Primates.

The Bats' skeleton does indeed remind one much of a monkey's, with the fingers, except the thumb, very much drawn out. The arms themselves greatly exceed the legs in development, but not much more than in the Gibbons; the breastbone is furnished with a keel, but this is very slight compared with a bird's breast-keel, implying much smaller breast-muscles to move the wings, although bats fly on the average far better than birds. This is probably because the wing-membrane, carried down as it is from little finger to ankle, embraces far more air than a bird's wing, so that the stroke of the wing is much more effective. It will be seen in examining bird-skeletons that many broad-winged and strong-flying species have smaller breast-bones with smaller keels than some which are by no means their equals on the wing.

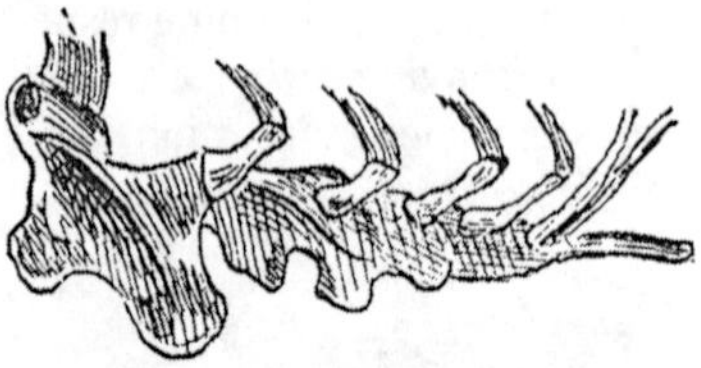

Breast-bone of Flying-Fox, showing the keel for attachment of wing-muscles.

In bats the leg bends upward and forward very freely, and the foot rotates like our hand; they crawl about upside down on boughs, etc., and on the ground creep on all-fours on their stomachs, but are not unable to rise if healthy and uninjured, any more than swifts, which also creep, though on two limbs only, and are credited with the same disability.

In crawling the knee points upwards and outwards. In repose bats hang upside down as a rule, often wrapping themselves in their wings like a cloak. The feet and the thumb with its powerful claw are often used in feeding, and the latter in fighting.

The Bats, like the Primates, are divided into two sub-orders, and, like them, are in one division fox-faced and in the other short-faced. The Fox-bats form the sub-order *Megachiroptera* (large bats) and live mostly on fruit; the short-faced bats are the *Microchiroptera* (small bats), and in the case of all Indian species live on animal food, generally insects. The dimensions, however, overlap considerably, the smallest Fruit-bats being much smaller than many of the other section. The Fox-bats have the second finger generally provided with a small claw, absent in the others, and the tail is short or wanting, and the rudder or inter-femoral membrane which it supports in most bats, cut away almost to vanishing-point. They also have the bony orbit nearly complete, approaching the Primates in this respect. As Sterndale says, "Bats are all nocturnal, with small eyes (except in the case of the frugivorous bats), large ears, and in some cases membranous appendages to the nostrils, which may possibly be for the purpose of guiding themselves in the dark, for it is proved by experiment that bats are not

Head of Fruit-bat (Short-nosed) showing junction of inner margin of ears, characteristic of Fruit-bats.

dependent on eyesight for guidance, and one naturalist has remarked that, in a certain species of bat which has no facial membrane, this delicacy of perception was absent. I have noticed this in one species, *Cynopterus marginatus* [small Fox-bat], one of which flew into my room not long ago, and repeatedly dashed itself against a glass door in its efforts to escape. I had all the other doors closed." The editor has seen the same with two Pipistrelles in England, but as they had been aroused from the hibernation usual to insectivorous bats in cold winter climates, he put it down to the evident weakness of their flight which they could not control—though it certainly seemed as if they also sought the light.

The Fruit-bats are all contained in the single family *Pteropodidæ*.

FLYING-FOX

OTHER NAMES.—Scientific: *Pteropus edwardsii*, *medius*, *vampyrus*. Native: *Badul*, Bengali and Mahratti; *Badur*, *Chamgidar*, Hindi; *Warbagul*, Mahratti; *Toggal bawuli*, Canarese; *Sikat yelle*, Wadari; *Sikurayi*, Telegu; *Barvalu*, Malayalam; *Loco-vaola*, *Wawal*, Cingalese; *Leng-tshwai*, *Leng-nek*, Burmese.

Flying-Foxes, showing positions in repose and feeding.

HABITAT.—All through India, Ceylon, and Burma, but not permanently above the base of the Himalayas.

DESCRIPTION.—A very large tailless fox-headed bat with black wings about 4 ft. in expanse, and a body length of 7 to 10 in., fur black and tan, the lighter colour in front.

Sterndale says: "These bats roost on trees in vast numbers. I have generally found them to prefer tamarinds of large size. . . . I was aware that they went long distances in search of food, but I was not aware of the power they had for sustained flight till the year 1869, when, on my way to England on furlough, I discovered a large flying-fox winging his way towards our vessel, which was at the time more than 200 miles from land. Exhausted, it clung to the fore yard-arm; and a present of a rupee induced a Lascar to go aloft and seize it, which he did after several attempts. The voracity with which it attacked some plantains showed that it had been for some time deprived of food, probably having been blown off shore by high winds. Hanging head downwards from its cage, it stuffed the fruit into its cheeks, monkey-fashion, and then seemed to chew it at leisure. When I left the steamer at Suez, it remained in the captain's possession, and seemed to be tame and reconciled to its imprisonment, tempered by a surfeit of plantains.

"In flying over water they frequently dip down to touch the surface. Jerdon was in doubt whether they did this to drink or not, but McMaster feels sure that they do this in order to drink, and that the habit is not peculiar to the *Pteropodidæ*, as he has noticed other bats doing the same. Colonel Sykes states that he 'can personally testify that their flesh is delicate and without disagreeable flavour'; and another colonel of my acquaintance once regaled his friends on some flying-fox cutlets, which were pronounced 'not bad.' Dr. Day accuses these bats of intemperate habits—drinking the toddy from the earthen pots on the cocoa-nut trees, and flying home intoxicated. The wild almond is a favourite fruit.

"Mr. Rainey, who has been a careful observer of animals for years, states that in Bengal these bats prefer clumps of bamboos for a resting-place, and feed much on the fruit of the betel-nut palm when ripe. Another naturalist, Mr. G. Vidal, writes that in Southern India the *P. medius* feeds chiefly on the green drupe or nut of the Alexandrian laurel (*Calophyllum inophyllum*), the kernels of which contain a strong-smelling green oil on which the bats fatten amazingly; and then they in turn yield, when boiled down, an oil which is recommended as an excellent stimulative application for the hair. I noticed in Seonee a curious superstition to the effect that a bone of this bat tied on to the ankle by a cord of black cowhair is a sovereign remedy, according to the natives, for rheumatism in the leg. Tickell states that these bats produce one at a time in March or April, and they continue a fixture on the parent till the end of May or beginning of June."

This seems a short time for the young animal to become independent, but bats are born of a relative large size and in a very perfect condition. In addition to the foods mentioned above, flying-foxes eat neem, jamoon, and beer fruit, figs of various kinds, and flowers; in Ceylon Mr. W. W. A. Phillipps notices that they will fly from a distance of 30 or 40 miles to feed on *Eucalyptus* flowers, and that they are often on the wing by day.

They are well-known pests to cultivated fruit, but refuse the orange family; and Shortt in 1863 described in the *Proceedings* of the London Zoological Society how he watched them fishing, hovering over water swarming with small fish on the rise, seizing them with their feet, and flying to trees on the bank to eat them. Several were shot in the act, and this very circumstantial account disposes of the idea that the very different action of swooping down and touching water with the muzzle in order to drink has been mistaken for fishing. Moreover there is an American Fishing Bat (*Noctilio leporinus*) which catches its prey with its feet. Much has been written about the riotous and quarrelsome behaviour of flying-foxes at the home trees, but their proceedings when seeking food need further study. They do well in captivity and sometimes breed; one has been known to live for twenty years in England.

KALONG OR MALAY FLYING-FOX

OTHER NAMES.—Scientific: *Pteropus edulis.* Native: *Kluang,* Malay.

HABITAT.—Malay Peninsula and Islands; has been obtained at Mergui and its archipelago.

DESCRIPTION.—Like the Indian Flying-Fox but larger, with narrower ears, only half as wide as long, and broader furry space on the back between the wings. The wings are 5 ft. across, and the fore-arm bone (which, being the largest in the skeleton, is much used in measuring bats) often well over 8 in. long, while in the common species it is less than 7 in. The fur is sometimes all black.

The Kalong is the largest bat known, and resembles the common Flying-Fox in habits. It is also good eating; Wallace compares it to hare; but in preparing fruit-bats for the table, Mr. Phillipps says, care must be taken that the fur, in which resides the rank odour of these bats, does not come in contact with the flesh and taint it.

NICOBAR OR ISLAND FLYING-FOX

OTHER NAMES.—Scientific: *Pteropus nicobaricus.*

HABITAT.—Andamans and Nicobars.

DESCRIPTION.—Like the common Indian species, but with the ears blunter and quite half an inch shorter, and the fur darker, often all black in females and young.

FULVOUS FRUIT-BAT

OTHER NAMES. — Scientific: *Xantharpyia amplexicaudata, Pteropus leschenaultii.*

HABITAT.—From the Persian Gulf to Timor, including most of India, Ceylon, and Burma, but local.

DESCRIPTION.—General form much like that of the Flying-fox, but ears rounded and a small tail present; size less than half that of the common species; forearm not 4 in., and expanse under 2 ft. Fur short and downy, light brown; skin of wings dark brown.

A voracious fruit-eater and strong flyer, travelling at least sixteen miles out from home in search of food. Near Moulmein it has been known to feed on shell-fish exposed by the tide. It often haunts caves.

SMALL OR SHORT-NOSED FOX-BAT

OTHER NAMES.—Scientific: *Cynopterus marginatus.* Native: *Cham-gadili*, Bengali; *Chota badur*, Hindi; *Lenzwe, Lenwet*, Burmese.

HABITAT.—The same as the large Indian Fox-bat, but extending east through the Malay Islands to the Philippines; the commonest species in our area next to the Flying-fox.

DESCRIPTION.—Brown, either yellowish or greyish, in tint; wings dusky brown, ears edged with white. Size rather less than last species, like which it has a small tail. Fore-arm 3 in., expanse 18 in.

This little Fox-bat has the light easy flight of an insectivorous bat, not the slow heavy stroke of the big Flying-fox. It also hangs upon clusters on trees, especially plantains and Palmyra palms, but males are often found solitary. It is very voracious, especially favouring plantains, guavas, and mangoes, and will eat more than its own weight in three hours, the food passing through its body almost unchanged. Although so different in size and flight, in voice it much resembles the large Flying-fox, which chatters and cackles, not squeaking like an ordinary bat. Two insular species need no notice.

PIGMY FRUIT-BAT OR SMALL LONG-TONGUED FRUIT-BAT

OTHER NAMES.—Scientific: *Carponycterus minima*, *Macroglossus minimus*.

HABITAT.—Warm Sikkim valleys east through Burma and Malaysia to Australia.

DESCRIPTION.—The smallest of all Fox-bats, about the size of an ordinary insectivorous bat, from which its long narrow muzzle will distinguish it. The body is not much more than 2 in. long, the forearm less than 1½ in.—not half the size of the common small Fruit-bat. The tongue is long and brush-like, adapted for licking out the contents of fruit. This little bat roosts in trees, but is sometimes found in sheds, etc. Its fur is brown in colour and long.

DOBSON'S LONG-TONGUED FRUIT-BAT

OTHER NAMES.—Scientific: *Eonycteris spelæa*.

HABITAT.—Farm Caves, Moulmein; Cambodia and Java.

DESCRIPTION.—Another brush-tongued species, with thin short dark brown fur, and a little smaller than the common small Fox-bat. Like the last species, it has a short tail, but it differs from all our other Fruit-bats in having no claw on the index finger, all the wing-fingers being clawless as in ordinary bats. It appears to live in caves.

The Insectivorous Bats or *Microchiroptera* are an exceedingly numerous group, over a hundred species being found in our Eastern Empire; and, in accordance with the plan of this revision, no attempt will be made to give descriptions of all these, but certain species will be selected, which, by reason of their abundance or of some striking peculiarity in appearance or habits, are likely to attract attention. As Sterndale, who attempted to describe all the Indian species then known, says, "Much is to be discovered concerning them. Very little is known of the habits of these small nocturnal animals. . . . We see them flit about rapidly in the dusky evening, and capture one here and there, but, after a brief description, in most cases very uninteresting to all save those who are 'bat fanciers,' what can be said about them?" More is probably to be gained by most people in studying the ways of those which *are* easy to identify than by trying to learn the lot; and

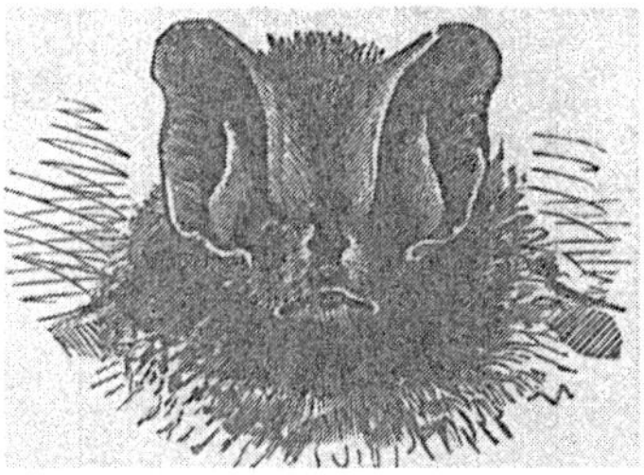

Head of Insectivorous Bat (*Barbastelle*). Showing short face and tragus or inner earlet.

fortunately the notable species above mentioned and now to be dealt with include representatives of all the families of the sub-order found in our limits.

These are distinguished as follows: The Vampires * (*Nycteridæ* or *Vampyridæ*) by having a "nose-leaf" or horizontal skinny crest on the nose, and a tragus or "earlet" a sort of supplementary inner ear-lobe. The Horse-shoe Bats (*Rhinolophidæ*) by having a nose-leaf, but no tragus, the ear being simply single-lobed as in Fruit-bats. The Free-tailed Bats (*Emballonuridæ*) by having the tail projecting either in the middle of the leg-web or from its hinder margin. Finally, the most Typical Insectivorous Bats (*Vespertilionidæ*) by having a tragus but no nose-leaf, and the tail, as in the Horse-shoe Bats, included in the web that unites it to the legs right up to the tip.

We have two easily-distinguished species of Vampires.

INDIAN VAMPIRE

OTHER NAMES.—Scientific: *Megaderma lyra, spectrum, Lyroderma lyra.*

HABITAT.—India and Ceylon, and perhaps Burma.

DESCRIPTION.—A rather large bat (forearm about 2½ in.) with very large ears united for some distance from the base and containing a bifid tragus, a long lyre-shaped nose-leaf, and no tail, though the leg-web, which usually includes it, is present. Eyes larger than in most insectivorous bats; fur grey, wing-membranes dark brown.

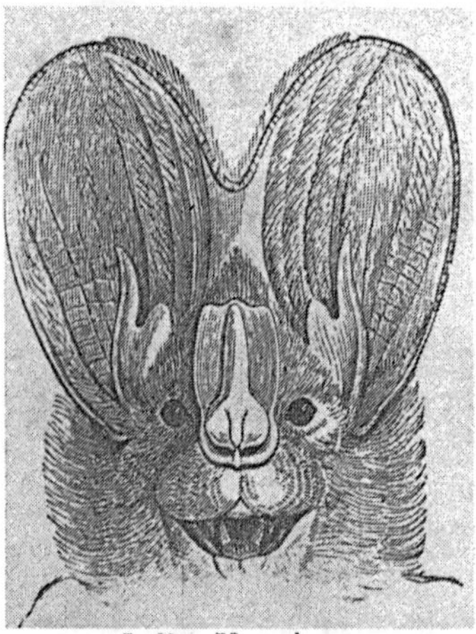

Indian Vampire.

This bat, often called "False Vampire" to distinguish it from the American Vampires, inhabits buildings and caves during the day, and often comes into verandahs and rooms at night to seek prey or devour it. It flies low, and when chased in a room shows less endurance than most bats. Though it eats insects, it preys as much or more on small vertebrates, taking smaller bats, birds, lizards, frogs, and even fish. It even devours some of the bones of its prey.

* Not to be confused with the true vampires of America (*Phyllostomatidæ*), the only family of this sub-order not represented in the East.

MALAY VAMPIRE

OTHER NAMES.—Scientific: *Megaderma spasma.*

HABITAT.—Tenasserim to the Malay Islands, and Ceylon; possibly Travancore.

DESCRIPTION.—Very like the last, but smaller, with the ears not joined so far up, the outer limb of the tragus longer, and the nose-leaf very different, having a heart-shaped pattern.

This bat needs further study, as its feeding-habits may be different from the Indian Vampire's, though this is unlikely.

Of the Horse-shoe Bats (*Rhinolophidæ*) we can only make a selection here.

Malay Vampire.

Large Horse-shoe Bat.

GREAT EASTERN HORSE-SHOE BAT OR LARGE LEAF-BAT

OTHER NAMES.—Scientific: *Rhinolophus luctus, perniger.*

HABITAT.—A mountain bat, inhabiting moderate heights in the Himalayas, and ranging into Southern India, Ceylon, and the Malay region to the Philippines.

DESCRIPTION.—A large black long-furred bat with the forearm nearly 3 in. long. Ears large, longer than head, and pointed, with a large rounded lobe on the outer margin (not to be mistaken for a tragus, which is, as above stated, absent in Horse-shoe bats); nose-leaf large and complicated, the upper part like a graduated spire; eyes very small.

This bat roosts both in forests and in caves and buildings, and hangs up in pairs, only one pair being found in a particular haunt, unless there is plenty of space. It flies rather low and heavily, and feeds on beetles, etc.

Dark-brown Leaf-bat.

DARK-BROWN LEAF-BAT

OTHER NAMES.—Scientific: *Rhinolophus tragatus, ferrum-equinum.*

HABITAT.—Moderate heights in the Himalayas.

DESCRIPTION.—Much smaller than the last, with the forearm less than 2½ in.; ears not quite so long as head and scarcely lobed in front; nose-leaf like a barbed spear-head above. Fur reddish brown above, pale grey below.

The form *ferrum-equinum* of this bat is the greater Horse-shoe Bat of English naturalists; this form has only occurred in Gilgit, and only differs from the Indian *tragatus* (which in spite of this name has no tragus) in having three grooves on the lower lip instead of one, so that Dobson was probably right in uniting them, so many European animals extending to the Himalayas.

It associates in numbers in caves, etc., and comes out early.

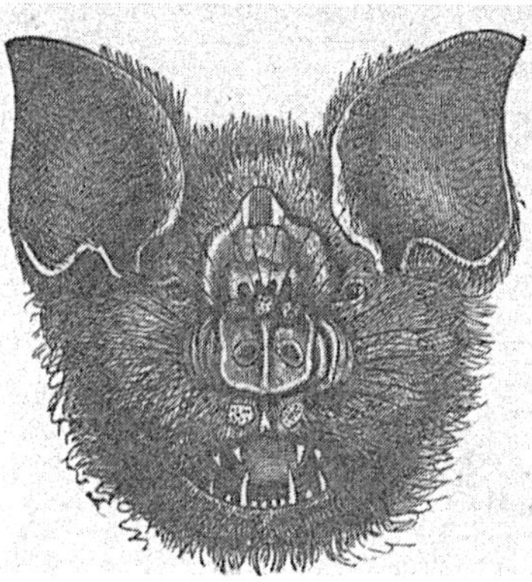

Great Himalayan Leaf-nosed Bat (male).

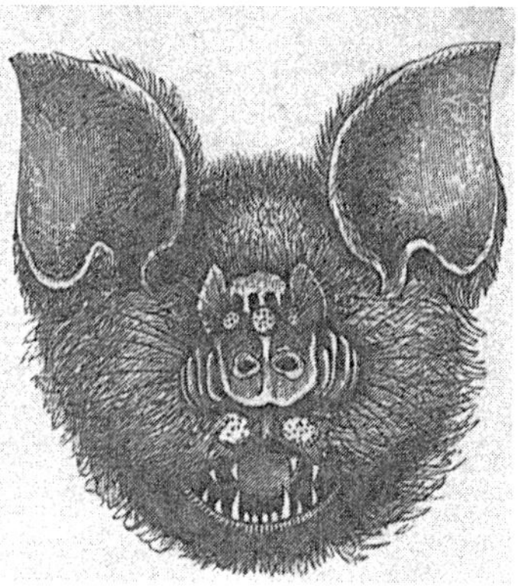

Great Himalayan Leaf-nosed Bat (female).

GREAT HIMALAYAN LEAF-NOSED BAT

OTHER NAMES.—Scientific: *Hipposideros armiger, Phyllorhina armigera.*

HABITAT.—Himalayas and Khasi Hills, China, Penang.

DESCRIPTION.—The largest Indian insectivorous bat, larger than the small flying-fox, with a forearm of nearly 4 in. in males. Ears moderate with concave outer and convex inner margin. Nose-leaf complicated. Lower part of nose-leaf shield-shaped, with four supplementary lobes on each side; upper part much more developed in males than in females. Fur of some shade of brown.

Hutton observed this species roosting in a loft, and noticed that when thus hanging up it had the tail and leg-web turned up over the back. It came out before dark, to hunt beetles and the noisy cicadas, whose notes betrayed them.

The Free-tailed Bats (*Emballonuridæ*) are not numerous in species in India, but some species are common or remarkable.

MOUSE-TAILED BAT

OTHER NAMES.—Scientific: *Rhinopoma microphyllum, Hardwickii.*

HABITAT.—North-Eastern Africa and South-Eastern Asia, including India; east to the Malay Peninsula, but not the Himalayas or Ceylon.

DESCRIPTION.—A rather small drab bat, with a forearm often not much over 2 in., but easily distinguished from all others by having a long tail only included at the base in the very short leg-web, so that it looks like a mouse's. Ears large, broad, pointed, joined at the base, with a small tragus; eyes rather larger than usual in insectivorous bats, snout rather long and pig-like.

This is generally called the long-tailed bat, but some species have the tail as long or longer, the peculiarity of the present one being the freedom of the tail from the leg-web; the tail is flexible, but does not seem to be prehensile, so its use is doubtful; as in some Egyptian specimens the tail is wanting, it would seem that there is a tendency here to degeneration, first the web having been nearly lost, while the tail is following suit, and the species may end up in having neither tail nor much leg-web, as has happened in most of the fruit-bats.

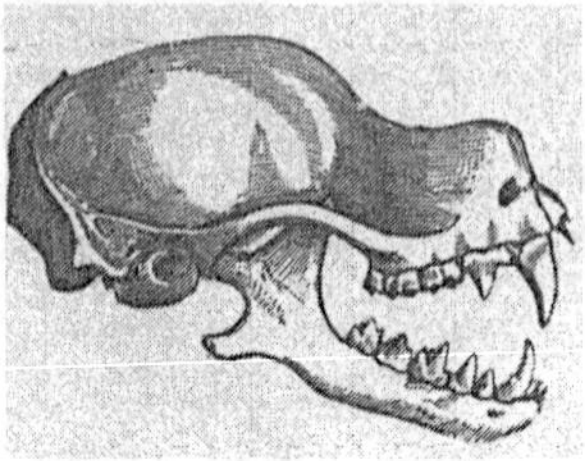
Skull of Mouse-tailed Bat.

The species is a haunter of caves and buildings, and in the cold weather is found to have a huge mass of fat at the hinder and under part of the body, on which it presumably lives during hibernation.

LONG-ARMED SHEATH-TAILED BAT

OTHER NAMES.—Scientific: *Taphozous longimanus.*

HABITAT.—Southern India, Ceylon and Burma, east to Tenasserim; Southern Central Provinces.

DESCRIPTION.—A rather small bat with the short tail projecting through the middle of the leg-web instead of being enclosed in it to the end as usual. Muzzle rather pointed, ears moderate, with a short broad-ended tragus; a pocket or pouch on the chin in males, only represented in females by a groove. Fur black or brown, buff in the young. Forearm about 2½ in.

The name "long-armed" is not particularly appropriate to this bat; in fact, the scientific name does not mean this, but "long-handed," and the wings, which are elongated-webbed hands, are long and narrow in these free-tailed bats. It frequents buildings, and so is common about large towns.

POUCHED SHEATH-TAILED BAT

OTHER NAMES.—Scientific: *Taphozous saccolæmus, Saccolæmus saccolæmus.*

HABITAT.—Indian Peninsula and Ceylon, and east through Burma to Java.

DESCRIPTION.—Similar in form to the last but rather larger, and with a chin-pouch in the female as well as the male, though much larger in the latter sex. Fur very variable, dark to light brown, sometimes spotted with white, or white below.

Also a common haunter of caves and buildings.

WRINKLED-LIPPED BAT

OTHER NAMES.—Scientific: *Nyctinomus plicatus.*

HABITAT.—India east to Malaysia, but not the Himalayas or Ceylon.

DESCRIPTION.—A rather small bat with broad round ears joined at the base and very short tragus, especially noticeable by its deep hound-like lips marked with vertical wrinkles. Wings long and narrow, legs very short, tail fairly long, quite half of it projecting from the leg-web. Forearm nearly 2 in. long. Fur black to brown, paler below.

This peculiar-looking and easily recognisable bat is a high and powerful flyer, and haunts caves and buildings in large numbers, the Phagat caves in the Moulmein district harbouring "countless myriads" of them. Many of the small bats, by the way, do not trouble about hanging up by their hind legs in the orthodox way of bats, but cram themselves into any crevice anyhow.

The remaining bats of the family *Vespertilionidæ* are just the ordinary bats, far the most numerous in species and the most widely-distributed. They have no eccentricities in faces or tails, but some have other remarkable points.

LONG-EARED BAT

OTHER NAMES.—Scientific: *Plecotus auritus.*

DISTRIBUTION.—Europe and temperate Asia, including the higher Himalayas.

DESCRIPTION.—A very small bat with the longest ears of any animal known, well over an inch long, while the forearm is not much over an inch and a half; the tragus alone would make a respectable ear for any bat of the size, and sticks out like an ear when the bat is hanging up in repose, the ears themselves being tucked under the wings. The fur is light-brown above, paler below.

Long-eared Bat.

This is a well-known bat at home, hiding in hollow trees and old buildings, and flying late and dodgily, but not very fast; but when an attempt is made to capture it in a room it shows much endurance.

NOCTULE BAT

OTHER NAMES.—Scientific: *Vesperugo noctula.*

HABITAT.—Europe, Africa, and Asia; it has been found in India in Nepal and Sikkim, and again in Ceylon and Singapore; it even inhabits Sumatra and Java.

DESCRIPTION.—A typical ordinary small insectivorous bat, though at home it seems large compared to the commoner little Flittermouse or Pipistrelle. Its ears are of moderate size with a small round tragus, and its fur chestnut; the forearm is about 2 in. long.

The Noctule haunts hollow trees, and flies high and early, living much on beetles.

Noctule Bat.

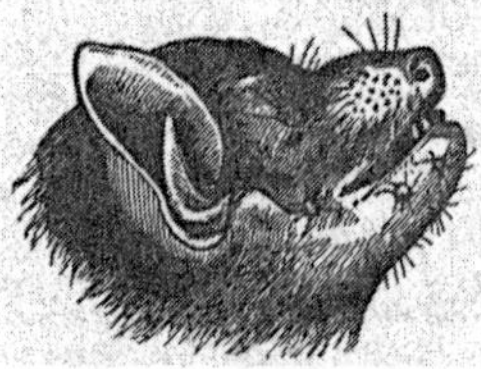

Common Yellow Bat.

COMMON YELLOW BAT

OTHER NAMES.—Scientific: *Nycticejus* or *Scotophilus temminckii.*

HABITAT.—Southern Asia east to the Philippines; not ascending the Himalayas very high.

DESCRIPTION.—Like the Noctule, an ordinary small bat, with a forearm about 2 in. long, but the tragus is long and narrow. The fur varies from greyish to yellowish-brown above and white to yellow below, some specimens being quite bright.

This is almost the commonest bat in India, and as it haunts buildings and comes out early, is particularly noticeable; it feeds a great deal on white ants, and has a rather slow and steady flight. Some specimens are much larger than others.

HARLEQUIN BAT

OTHER NAMES.—Scientific: *Nycticejus* or *Scotophilus ornatus.*

HABITAT.—Eastern Himalayas in warm valleys, and east to Yunnan.

DESCRIPTION.—Similar in size and form to the last, but with longer ears. Colour rich yellow-brown, with white stripes down the back and breast, and a white crown-patch and collar; legs and fingers sometimes reddish.

This bat deserves notice here only for its remarkable colour, for it is a local species.

HAIRY-WINGED BAT

OTHER NAMES.—Scientific: *Harpyiocephalus harpyia.*

HABITAT.—Himalayas and Khasi Hills.

DESCRIPTION.—Rather larger than the common yellow bat, with separately projecting nostrils and very strong teeth; fur soft and full, spreading out on to the wing-membrane at the sides and covering the legs and leg-web. Colour rusty drab, grizzled with white, as far as the shoulders; hind quarters and leg-web deep bay; underparts grey.

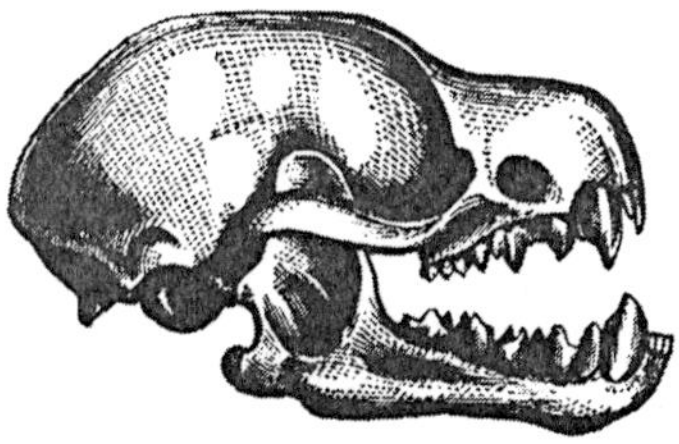

Skull of Hairy-winged Bat.

This peculiar bat, noticeable for its exceptional furriness, feeds on particularly hard-shelled beetles, this accounting for its hyæna-like teeth.

PAINTED BAT

OTHER NAMES.—Scientific: *Kerivoula picta.* Native: *Kehel vulha,* Cingalese.

HABITAT.—India, Ceylon and Burma, but not very common.

DESCRIPTION.—A very small bat, with the forearm barely 1½ in. long, but noticeable for its brilliant colouring, the wings, ears and tail-web being orange, with broad deep wedges of black between the fingers, and the fur orange According to Mr. Phillipps, Ceylon specimens, especially males, often have the light parts of the wing scarlet instead of orange.

This bat is so remarkable, looking more like a large butterfly or moth on the wing than a bat, that it often attracts attention in spite of its comparative rarity. It often resorts to plantains to repose during the day, and is said to be then not conspicuous.

HODGSON'S OR LARGE PAINTED BAT

OTHER NAMES.—Scientific: *Vespertilio formosus.*

HABITAT.—Northern India and China.

Description.—Very like the Painted Bat, but with the fur less richly coloured, though the wings and other bare parts are similar; the size is considerably larger, the forearm being nearly 2 in. long, and the tail is decidedly shorter than the head and body, whereas in the last species it is a little longer.

Like the more familiar Painted Bat, its coloration appears to be protective in repose, but as neither of these bats are abundant, the protection does not seem to be of much service to them.

INDIAN PIPISTRELLE

Other Names.—Scientific: *Vesperugo* or *Vespertilio abramus* or *coromandelicus*.

Habitat.—Central Europe through Asia even down to Northern Australia, including the Indian region generally, even up to 7,000 ft. in the Himalayas.

Description.—The smallest common Indian bat, with a forearm less than 1½ in. long and dark brown fur, often yellowish on the head.

This little creature is the most familiar of all Indian bats, corresponding to its near ally at home, the common Pipistrelle or Flittermouse, and similarly frequenting houses and often coming into rooms, where it flies round so fast that one can only just see that it *is* a bat and not a large moth. Sterndale says it is found in hollow bamboos.

COMMON EUROPEAN BAT

Other Names.—Scientific: *Myotis* or *Vespertilio murinus*.

Habitat.—Europe and the Himalayas.

Common European Bat.

Description.—About as big as the common yellow bat, but with a much longer and more pointed nose, as long as a small fruit-bat's, and larger eyes and ears; fur brown above, whitish below.

Although it has only once been found in England, this is the common bat of Europe, and is worth mention here, because Hutton found that in confinement it would kill and partly eat smaller bats, so that its habits require further investigation, as it may turn out to be partially carnivorous like the Vampire. It haunts caves and buildings, and flies low and slowly late in the evening.

ORDER DERMOPTERA

The two closely-allied species of curious animals which compose this order stand quite by themselves, though the genus (*Galeopithecus*) has been referred at different times to the Bats, the Lemurs and the Insectivora. They are about the size of a small cat, with strong, curved, compressed, rather cat-like claws--which, however, are not retractile —long limbs, the forearm being especially long, and a very perfect parachute-membrane. Altogether they look like an abortive attempt at a bat, and in some ways are bat-like in their habits, but their teeth are unlike those of any other animal, the incisors being more or less notched, especially the two central lower pairs, which are like miniature combs.

COBEGO OR COLUGO

Other Names.—Scientific: *Galeopithecus volans*. Native: *Myouk-hloung-pyan*, Burmese; *Kubong*, Malay.

Habitat.—Mergui, east to Borneo, and Siam.

Description.—Fur olive-brown, mottled with irregular whitish spots and blotches; the pile is short, but exquisitely soft; head and brain very small; tail long and prehensile. The membrane is continued from each side of the neck to the fore-feet, thence to the hind feet, again to the tip of the tail. All the feet have five webbed toes.

This animal is nocturnal in its habits, and very sluggish in its motions by day, at which time it usually hangs from a branch suspended by its four paws, its mottled back assimilating closely to the rugged bark of the tree; it is especially herbivorous, possessing a very voluminous stomach and long intestines. Wallace, in addition, says of it, that its brain is very small, and it possesses such tenacity of life that it is very difficult to kill; he adds that it is said to have only one at a birth, and one he shot had a very small blind naked little creature clinging closely to its breast, which was quite bare and much wrinkled. There are four teats placed here. Raffles, however, gives two as the number produced at each birth. Dr. Cantor says that in confinement plantains constitute the favourite food, but deprived of liberty it soon dies. In its wild state it "lives entirely on young fruits and leaves; those of the cocoa-nut and *Bombax pentandrum* are its favourite food, and it commits great injury to the plantations of these" (*Horsfield*). Regarding its powers of flight, Wallace says: "I saw one of these animals run up a tree in a rather open space, and then glide obliquely through the air to another tree on which it alighted near its base, and immediately began to ascend. I paced the distance from one tree to the other, and found it to be 70 yards, and the amount of descent not more than 35 or 40 ft., or less than one in five. This, I think, proves that the animal must have some power of guiding itself through the air, otherwise in so long a distance it would have little chance of alighting exactly upon the trunk." Both Blanford and

Cobego.

Sterndale call the animal "Flying Lemur," but this misleading name ought to be dropped. A recent observer has seen it give a flap when changing direction, so that it comes very near true flight. The voice is said to be a harsh, disagreeable croaking sound, and the gait on the ground a succession of short awkward flapping jumps.

The only other species inhabits the Philippines.

ORDER INSECTIVORA

These are mostly small animals of, with few exceptions, nocturnal habits. Their chief characteristic lies in their pointed dentition; the skull is elongated, the bones of the face and jaw especially, and those of the latter are comparatively weak. The limbs are short, five-toed, and plantigrade, and the animals are all possessed of clavicles like the preceding orders; the teats are placed on the abdomen and are more than two. The long pig-like nose is, as stated in the diagnosis of the Order (p. 2), the readiest means of distinguishing an Insectivore from other small mammals; the teeth vary much in detail, and their peculiarities are best noted under the separate families, of which there are four in India. All are easily distinguishable, as follows:—

The Moles (*Talpidæ*) are little sausage-shaped animals with very short limbs and tail and no noticeable eyes or ears.

The Shrews (*Soricidæ*) are like long-nosed, small-eyed mice or rats.

The Hedgehog family (*Erinaceidæ*) are much larger, generally about the size of guinea-pigs, and prickly and short-tailed. Two shrew-like animals are, however, referred to it, the characters of which will be given when they come to be dealt with.

The Tupaias * (*Tupaiidæ*) are like long-nosed squirrels.

There are more of these little animals recorded from India than there are of the Primates, but as they are, even more than the smaller kinds of bats, animals for the specialist, it is not necessary here to allude to more than about half of them.

Of the moles (*Talpidæ*) we have two species, easily recognisable by their sausage-shaped body, clad in very soft fur, very short tail, and very large, broad, long-nailed fore-paws which seem to spring straight from the trunk. The eyes are covered by skin, and there are no external ears. Moles are burrowing animals, living on earth-worms and underground grubs. In India they are confined to the hills.

SHORT-TAILED MOLE

OTHER NAMES.—Scientific: *Talpa micrura*. Native: *Pariam*, Lepcha; *Biyukantyem*, Bhutanese.

HABITAT.—South-western Himalayas and hills south of Assam.

DESCRIPTION.—About 5 in. long, tail only about an eighth of an inch and buried in the fur. Colour, steely black (brown in many dried skins), snout and feet flesh-colour.

* A true squirrel with a long muzzle, and extraordinarily like a Tupaia, exists, but is not found in India. Its teeth are, of course, unlike the Tupaia's.

This mole appears not to form mole-hills like the common mole of Europe.

WHITE-TAILED MOLE

OTHER NAMES.—Scientific: *Talpa leucura.*

HABITAT.—Khasi and Naga Hills, up to 10,000 ft.; valley of the Sittoung River.

DESCRIPTION.—Smaller than the last, with a shorter muzzle but longer tail, which is about a quarter of an inch long and covered with rather long white hair. Body-fur brown in preserved specimens, but may be black.

The European Mole (*Talpa europæa*, *T. macrura* of Hodgson) may perhaps occur, but Blanford doubts if Hodgson's specimen was obtained in India, as no one else has found it there, and thinks there may have been some confusion of specimens. It may be distinguished from our Indian moles by having the eyes open, and especially by the tail being over an inch long.

Sterndale thinks he got moles of some sort in the Satpura Range, but says he had not then devoted much attention to the smaller mammals, and may have mistaken some kind of shrew for them.

The Rev. H. Baker thought he found moles in Malabar; they had mole-like velvety fur, but this was black above and white below, unusual for moles; yet the feet were mole-like, and it is possible that more moles remain to be discovered in India.

The Shrews (*Soricidæ*) are far the most numerous and widely spread family of Insectivores; they have two large, pointed, rather hooked incisors in the front of the upper jaw, and two more, also large but very slightly curved, opposing them in the lower. The other incisors are small, as are the canines, which are only found in the upper jaw, and all these are in contact at their bases. (See illustration on p. 2.)

COMMON MUSK-SHREW OR MUSK-RAT

OTHER NAMES.—Scientific: *Chachundar*, Hindi; *Sondeli*, Canarese; *Kondeli*, Malayalam; *Kune-miyo*, Cingalese; *Anachiwa-gagar*, Kashmiri; *Kywek-tsút*, Burmese; *Chundi*, Kol.

HABITAT.—Towns and other human habitations in India, Ceylon, and Burma; it has spread to some ports on the Indian Ocean outside India.

DESCRIPTION.—Distinguished from an ordinary rat by its long snout, very small eyes, comparatively short tail, small ears and bluish-grey fur. The snout, ears, feet, and tail are flesh-coloured, and the scanty fur on the extremities white. Head and body length about 6 in., tail about 4 in. Sometimes a reddish-brown-backed specimen is found, and young ones are dark grey.

One of the most familiar of Indian mammals, and a useful insect destroyer. It is nocturnal, hiding during the day in drains, etc. Sterndale says, apropos of the story, now generally discredited, of its tainting corked bottles of wine, etc., "We had once been talking at the mess about musk-rats; someone declared a bottle of sherry had been tainted, and nobody defended the poor little beast but myself, and I was considerably laughed at. However, one night soon after, as I was dressing for dinner, I heard a musk-rat squeak in my room. Here was a chance. Shutting the door, I laid a clean pocket-handkerchief on the ground next to the wall, knowing the way in which the animal usually skirts round a room; on he came and ran over the handkerchief, and then, seeing me, he turned and went back again. I then headed him once more and quietly turned him; and thus went on till I had made him run over the handkerchief five times. I then took it up, and there was not the least smell. I then went across to the mess house, and, producing the handkerchief, asked several of my brother officers if they could perceive any peculiar smell about it. No, none of them could. 'Well, all I know is,' said I, 'that I have driven a musk-rat five times over that handkerchief just now.'" As this experiment shows, a musk-rat does not give off its scent, which emanates from the flank-glands found in shrews, unless disturbed; and any liquors found to be tainted must have been so by the tainting of the corks, European-bottled samples being always free. The musk-rat has been known to eat bread, and to tackle a large frog and a scorpion.

Sterndale also says: "When I was at Nagpore in 1864, I made friends with one of these shrews, and it would come out every evening at my whistle and take grasshoppers out of my fingers. It seemed to be very short-sighted, and did not notice the insect till quite close to my hand, when, with a short swift spring, it would pounce upon its prey." This looks as if, in the experiment above quoted, the shrew when it turned was aware of his proximity by scent rather than sight.

He also says: "Whilst marching as a Settlement Officer in the district of Seeonee, I noticed that one of my camels had a sore back, and on inquiring into the cause was told by the natives that a musk-rat (our commonest shrew) had run over him," comparing this with the former English belief that a shrew could cause domestic animals pain and injury by running over them.

Musk-shrews are born blind, and the young are presumably, like those of most insectivores, several in number.

BROWN MUSK-SHREW

OTHER NAMES.—Scientific: *Crocidura murina.*

HABITAT.—Much the same as that of the last, but extending east to Malaysia and China.

DESCRIPTION.—Very similar to the last, but brown, blackish-brown or dark grey; skin of feet, ears and tail dark, with brown hair. The size in these, as in other shrews, varies, especially as young ones are not distinguishable externally from adults, and this species and the last appear to interbreed, some specimens being intermediate.

Indeed, Dobson very reasonably suggested that the common musk-rat is really only a semi-domesticated (*i.e.* self-domesticated) race of this shrew, which generally frequents woods, though occasionally entering houses and outbuildings. It does not smell so strong as the common musk-shrew. The natives in some places at any rate distinguish the two and consider this dark species venomous.

Blanford says this belief is without foundation; but if so, why should it attach to the less familiar variety and not to the common one? It may be that this large " wild " shrew may, without, of course, being really venomous, inflict a deleterious bite at times, and have thus started a bad reputation ages ago (civilisation being so much more ancient in the East), which has spread westwards, and incidentally become transferred there to shrews generally.

INDIAN PIGMY SHREW

OTHER NAMES.—Scientific: *Crocidura perrotteti.*

HABITAT.—Southern India, Bengal, Assam, Tenasserim.

DESCRIPTION.—A very small brown animal less than 2 in. long without the tail, which is less than 1½ in. long.

This is doubtfully distinct from another tiny shrew (*C. hodgsoni*) found in the Himalayas, and from the European Pigmy Shrew *C. etrusca,* one of the smallest known mammals; its minute size is likely to attract notice, and its habits have not been recorded and so deserve study. Anderson showed, however, that one could have five young.

It may here be mentioned that the frequent occurrence of dead but apparently uninjured shrews in England in autumn has been accounted for by the suggestion that they only live one year. It would be worth while to keep a musk-shrew captive and see if it were short-lived; a common rat dies of old age at five, and a mouse at two, and shrews may well be shorter-lived even than this. The editor has, however, seen a musk-shrew slip through the bars of an ordinary canary-cage quite easily, so that a cage covered with fine wire-netting would be needed to confine the subject of any experiment. Chopped raw meat, table-scraps, and any available insects would serve as food.

HIMALAYAN WATER-SHREW

OTHER NAMES.—Scientific: *Chimarrogale himalayica, Crossopus himalayicus.* Native: *Ung lagniyu*, Lepcha; *Chupitsi*, Bhutia.

HABITAT.—Khakyen Hills and South-eastern Himalayas, at moderate elevations.

DESCRIPTION.—Snout furry and well-whiskered, eyes and ears very small, feet broad and fringed with white hairs, tail rather long. Colour of fur dark grey, paler and browner below, tail white underneath. Size rather smaller than the musk-shrew.

This shrew appears to resemble the European water-shrew in habits, and to feed, like it, on small water-animals.

McMaster saw a black water-shrew near Nagpur, which, Blanford suggests, may be an undescribed species.

European Hedgehog.

The hedgehog family (*Erinaceidæ*) comprises five species of hedgehogs in our area, and two curious shrew-like animals, the teeth of which agree more closely with those of the hedgehogs than with shrews' teeth.

Hedgehogs are large for Insectivores, but small as mammals go generally, being about the size of guinea-pigs or less, with very short inconspicuous tails, and a covering of short spines above, and of fur on the underparts. Their eyes are not so small as those of shrews, nor are their noses quite so long, but are still quite piggish enough to distinguish them from baby porcupines, to say nothing of the teeth and other characters into which it is not necessary to enter here, except to say that the tiny tail is quite different from any porcupine's, and that the great chisel incisors of the spiny rodent, and its want of canines, contrast with the pointed and separated incisors of the hedgehogs, which, also, possess canines, though these are short and triangular.

Hedgehogs feed on insects and other small animals, and are nocturnal, hiding in holes during the day. When in fear of an enemy they roll themselves into a ball, presenting spines only at all points. They are not nearly so familiar in India as they are at home, where our single species is one of the commonest wild mammals, and is often kept as a pet. In this species there are several nearly naked young at a birth, whose spines are at first pale and soft.

In adults the spines are ringed with dark brown or black and white, the proportion of the colours varying with different species. In some, too, there is a parting in the spines on the crown, absent in others.

The general native names for hedgehogs are *Kánta chua*, *Kanderna*, or *Sonh*, in Hindi; *Jaho*, *Tar-java*, in Sindhi.

HARDWICKE'S OR COLLARED HEDGEHOG

OTHER NAMES.—Scientific: *Erinaceus collaris, grayi.*

HABITAT.—Northern India, but not in the hills.

DESCRIPTION.—No parting in spines on crown; feet and claws well developed, as in the European hedgehog, but ears much larger; colour on the whole dark, though more than half of the spines from their base is white. Fur on the underparts and legs dark brown, but the chin white, this colour sometimes running back and up the neck, but not forming a real collar.

Length about 7 in., ear longer than tail, which is 1 in., and bluntly pointed.

Sterndale says: "I have found this species in the Punjab, near Lahore. One evening, while walking in the dusk, a small animal, which I took to be a rat, ran suddenly between my legs. Now I confess to an antipathy to rats, and, though I would not willingly hurt any animal, I could not resist an impulsive kick, which sent my supposed rat high in the air. I felt a qualm of conscience immediately afterwards, and ran to pick up my victim, and was sorry to find that

I had perpetrated such an assault on an unoffending little hedgehog, which was however only stunned, and was carried off by me to the Zoological Gardens." He also quotes Hutton, saying that "when touched they have the habit of suddenly jerking up the back with some force, so as to prick the fingers or mouth of the assailant, and at the same time emitting a blowing sound, not unlike the noise produced when blowing upon a flame with a pair of bellows."

LARGE-EARED OR AFGHAN HEDGEHOG

OTHER NAMES.—Scientific: *Erinaceus megalotis.*

HABITAT.—Afghanistan, but extends to Quetta.

DESCRIPTION.—Our largest hedgehog, growing to 1 ft. in length; large-eared also, but not so much so as the last, in spite of the name. The ears are as a matter of fact no longer than the tail, which in this large species is $1\frac{1}{2}$ in. long; they are pointed in form. There is no parting on the forehead among the spines, which are brown at the base, and the feet and claws are well developed, the spines being also long, the longest just over 1 in. The fur is dark brown below, and white on the chin, as in the last species.

According to Hutton, this hedgehog feeds on slugs, snails, worms, insects, and lizards, and hibernates from about the end of October to February.

ANDERSON'S HEDGEHOG

OTHER NAMES.—Scientific: *Erinaceus jerdoni.*

HABITAT.—Sind and Punjab.

DESCRIPTION.—Another dark species with large rather pointed ears and well-developed feet, but with a parting dividing the spines on the crown. Ear longer than tail, spines dark at base; fur below very dark, but shading through whitish brown on the chest to white on the throat. Length $7\frac{1}{2}$ in.

Blanford thought it probable that the Long-spined Hedgehog (*Erinaceus macracanthus*) of Afghanistan and Persian Baluchistan would be found to range into our area.

It is of the same type as the last, with the parting on the crown, dark colour, and large ears and feet, but is larger and has very long spines, and the white of the throat extends down to the breast.

SMALL-FOOTED OR SOUTH-INDIAN HEDGEHOG

OTHER NAMES.—Scientific: *Erinaceus micropus.* Native: *Mollu-yelli*, Tamil.

HABITAT.—Southern India, in the plains and on the eastern slopes towards the base of the Nilgiris. Its northern limits are not known.

DESCRIPTION.—A short-eared, small-footed, pale-coloured hedgehog, only 6 in. long. Spines with a parting on the forehead, ears rounded, and not projecting above them, this being the shortest-eared of our species. The tail is also exceptionally short, half an inch, so that the ears, short as they are, double it. Spines only one dark band, near the tip, otherwise yellow or white; fur on forehead, flanks, throat and chest white; feet, snout, belly, and rump brown. The fur is very thin.

PAINTED HEDGEHOG

OTHER NAMES.—Scientific: *Erinaceus pictus.*

HABITAT.—The North-West from Agra and Goona to Sind.

DESCRIPTION.—A small-footed pale-coloured species with a parting on the crown, like the last, and with the same colouring and pattern, but a shorter and broader head, and longer ears, which appear above the spines, though rounded as in the last species. Size averaging larger than this.

This animal hides in holes or under grass in the day, often in old fox-earths.

Blanford called it Stoliczka's Hedgehog, but this name is not descriptive, and a bad exchange for Sterndale's, although the animal is not more conspicuously variegated than the South-Indian kind.

The Gymnuras, or Hedgehog-Shrews, are, as stated above, very shrew-like, but one is easily distinguished by being far larger than any shrew, and the other by its short tail; their teeth also differ from those of shrews in the fact that the central incisors have not the supplementary cusp at the base, and are smaller and less hook-like, while the other incisors are not in contact with them, and the canine is large enough to be noticeable; the first grinder is also a large conspicuous triangular tooth.

The two species differ so much that the old plan of keeping them in separate genera seems more sensible than "lumping" them.

BULAU OR RAFFLES' GYMNURA

OTHER NAMES.—Scientific: *Gymnura rafflesii.*

HABITAT.—Malay Peninsula to Borneo.

DESCRIPTION.—Like a giant musk-rat in form, with a fur composed of a soft woolly under-coat mixed with long bristles. Colour black and white in varying proportions, the white generally occupying the head and fore-parts except a black eye-patch. Some are all white. Body about 1 ft. long, tail three-quarters length of head and body, scaly, and bristly below. Canines well developed, larger than central incisors.

This curious-looking animal has a smell which is equally curious—and far from pleasant—described by the great collector Davison as resembling Irish stew that had gone bad! It hides under tree-roots by day and feeds on insects. In our area it has only been found in the extreme south of Tenasserim.

SMALLER GYMNURA

OTHER NAMES.—Scientific: *Hylomys suillus*, *Gymnura suilla*.

HABITAT.—Burma to Java.

DESCRIPTION.—Like a rather small musk-rat with a short thin tail barely 1 in. long. Fur reddish-brown above, yellowish-white below. Canines much smaller than first incisors, but bigger than the others; first grinder the largest tooth in the jaw.

This animal, which used to be classed with the next family, is very little known; Blanford could not get a specimen to examine, but one can now be seen mounted in the small mammal gallery at the South Kensington Natural History Museum.

The squirrel-like climbing Insectivores known as Tupaias or Tree-shrews (*Tupaiidæ*) are a very distinct family, differing from our other Insectivores in having large eyes—part of their resemblance to squirrels—and in being, like those animals, of diurnal habits. They are also partly vegetable feeders, and hold their food in their paws while eating.

Their long noses, and the low set of their small rather human-like ears on the head, rather spoil their looks, but they are exceptionally interesting little animals, and the latest authority on them, Mr. Le Gros Clark, in a paper in the "Proceedings of the Zoological Society for 1926," regards them as showing distinct affinities to the Lemurs. We have only three species.

The Malay name *Tupai* simply means "squirrel," but it is better to call them Tupaias than degrade them to the level of shrews with a prefix, and English people are never likely to call a squirrel by any foreign name, so no confusion is likely.

The teeth of Tupaias, like those of shrews, show projection of the lower incisors, which is a lemurine point, as is also the surrounding of the orbit by bone which they show. Both incisors and canines are small, and none of these front teeth are in contact as in shrews,

MADRAS OR ELLIOT'S TUPAIA

OTHER NAMES.—Scientific: *Tupaia ellioti.* Native: *Múnghil anathan*, Tamil; the name means Bamboo-squirrel, so Indians as well as Malays call these animals squirrels.

HABITAT.—Forests of Indian Peninsula.

DESCRIPTION.—About as big as a rat, with coarse but smooth hair and a long bushy tail and long nose. Colour grizzled yellowish-brown, reddish on the back, under-parts nearly white; a pale stripe from below ear to shoulder.

Hardly anything is on record about the habits of this species, which probably much resemble those of the next, except that it does not frequent human abodes.

Malay Tupaia.

MALAY TUPAIA

OTHER NAMES.—Scientific: *Tupaia ferruginea, peguana, chinensis, belangeri.* Native: *Tswai*, Burmese; *Tupai tana*, Malay; *Kalli-tang-zhing*, Lepcha.

HABITAT.—Lower slopes of Himalayas from Nepal east to Assam, the whole of Burma and thence east to Borneo.

Description.—Very like the last, but smaller and with softer fur diversified by coarser and glossier hairs on the back. Colour speckled brown to rusty red, the latter especially in Eastern specimens. Under-parts buff, and the pale shoulder-stripe sometimes indistinct.

This species is a well-known animal in Burma, where it comes about and into houses like the common striped squirrel in India. It lives in pairs or singly, and appears not to be so active as a squirrel, as it is often caught by dogs and cats. It makes a rough nest in trees, and has but one young at a birth, a fact that confirms its primate affinities.

A curious habit is its fondness for bathing, which is a very remarkable habit in a small land mammal. It has a peculiar tremulous whistle, changing to a shrill protracted cry when angry, which is often, as it is pugnacious with its own kind.

NICOBAR TUPAIA

Other Names.—Scientific: *Tupaia nicobarica.*

Habitat.—Nicobar Islands.

Description.—Black and tan in colour, the light hue being on the muzzle, limbs, sides and back of neck; no shoulder-stripe; under-parts pale brown, tail long.

There are no notes about the habits of this species.

Our Tupaias are certainly deserving of more study, especially with regard to their breeding and nursing habits, and this should be easy with the Malay Tupaia in Burma, where it displays such domesticated habits. The editor once got a specimen of this species in Calcutta, and kept it in a small verandah aviary along with a tame dove, feeding it on bread-and-milk, plantains, and cooked meat, as well as butterflies of various kinds, of which it rejected all the "warningly coloured" species, after smelling them. It made no attempt to molest its companion, although the natives of Sikkim say that it there feeds on small birds and mice. Probably it found the dove too large.

ORDER CARNIVORA

The Carnivora, to which order all the most sensational "wild beasts" except a few of the giant Ungulates like the elephant belong, are easily distinguished from most of our other mammals with paws by their large canines and small incisors; those which possess large canines among the Insectivores, such as the moles, being quite different in other ways (see figure below, and skull of otter on p. 3).

The Indian members of the various families represented in the East are also easily recognisable as a rule, as follows :—

The Bears (*Ursidæ*) by their very short tails combined with large size, the smallest being as big as a large dog.

The Hyænas (*Hyænidæ*) by having only four toes on all the feet.

The Cat-Bear or Panda (*Æluridæ*) by its fur-clad soles.

The Cats (*Felidæ*) are so like our domestic cat in structure that this resemblance alone is sufficient to distinguish them.

The Dogs (*Canidæ*) are also distinguishable by their resemblance to our domestic dog (provided the comparison be made with primitive breeds like the Pariah and the Alsatian Wolf-dog).

There remain two families of which the members in each case exhibit great variation in appearance among themselves, and are difficult to distinguish as a whole from each other. These are the Civets and Mongooses (*Viverridæ*) and the Weasels and Badgers

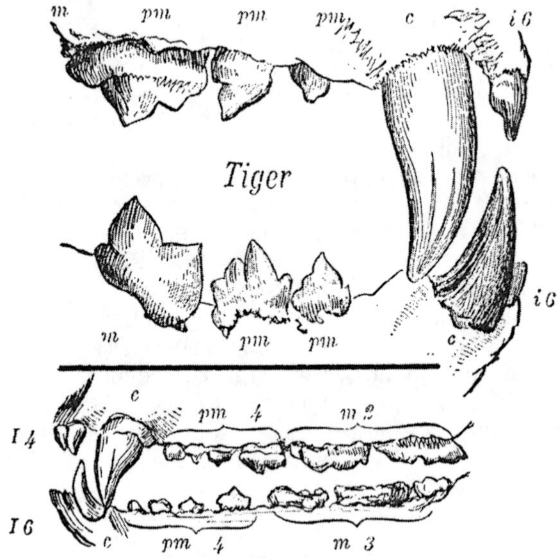

Teeth of Tiger and Black Bear (below).

(*Mustelidæ*), all of which are long-bodied and short-legged compared with other Carnivores. They are, however, closely allied, as is shown by fossil forms, and should perhaps be treated as one family. In any case they are generally distinguishable by the fact that the fur of the *Viverridæ* is generally striped, spotted, or grizzled, and that of the *Mustelidæ* nearly uniform, or dark above and more or less light below.

The grinders in the most truly carnivorous species, as in all the Cats, are sharp-edged and only suited for chopping meat; but many of the order are omnivorous rather than carnivorous, and in these the grinders are broader and more truly deserving of the name, as in the Bears.

None of our carnivores are smaller than a rat, and some are really large animals. They all produce more than one at a birth, and most are solitary and nocturnal in their habits.

The Bear family (*Ursidæ*) are not only large and short-tailed, but plantigrade, placing the whole sole of the foot on the ground in walking. They easily stand and even walk on their hind-legs, and, in spite of their size and heavy build, are good climbers. They like to repose under cover, but do not dig out their own dens, though their large fore-claws are well adapted for digging, and are often so used. Their tracks are very like those made by the human bare foot.

BROWN BEAR

Other Names.—Scientific: *Ursus arctos, isabellinus.* Native: *Lal-bhálu*, *Barf-ka-rinch*, Hindi; *Háput*, Kashmiri; *Drengmo*, Balti; *Drin-mor*, Ladaki; *Brabu*, Kisht-war; *Dúb*, Nepalese; *Tan-khaina*, Tibetan. Sportsmen often call the species Snow Bear or Red Bear.

Habitat.—Most of the Northern Hemisphere in the Old World and Alaska in the New, allowing for local races. In India only at high elevations in the Himalayas, descending to the forest regions in spring and autumn.

Description.—The largest of Indian bears and the most thickly-furred, the length reaching 7 ft. or even more, and the winter fur 8 in. on the back. The summer fur is much shorter. Colour some shade of brown, Himalayan specimens—the so-called Isabelline bear—being paler than European. Cubs, and old animals just after shedding the winter coat, have a white crescent on the chest.

The Brown Bear in the Himalayas feeds more on vegetable than on animal food, though it will sometimes kill even good-sized animals for food, even of its own species, and will eat carrion. Its principal food, however, is grass and other herbs, roots, nuts, and fruit, cultivated as well as wild.

It is also more harmless in character than it is in Europe, and seems never to attack man. It pairs in autumn, and the cubs are born in spring, being, as in other bears, very small in proportion to the parent, only about as big as rats. The cubs of the previous year remain with the mother along with their juniors. They are adult at three years old, and may live (in captivity at any rate) to nearly fifty years of age. In winter they hibernate in caves in the higher part of their range.

Brown Bear.

Their senses are rather dull, with the exception of scent, and this is only moderately good. In attacking, they strike inwards with the fore-paws, like bears generally.

Himalayan Black Bear.

HIMALAYAN BLACK BEAR

OTHER NAMES.—Scientific : *Ursus torquatus*, *tibetanus*, *Helarctos torquatus*. Native : *Bhálu*, *Rínch*, Hindi ; *Mam*, Baluchi ; *Haput*, Kashmiri ; *Sanár*, *Hingbong*, Nepalese ; *Dom*, Bhutia ; *Sona*, Lepcha ; *Mágyen*, Limbo ; *Sutum*, Daphla ; *Situm*, Abor ; *Mapol*, Garo ;

Miephúr, *Musu-bhurma*, Kachári; *Viempi*, Kuki; *Sawom*, Manipuri; *Húghúm*, *Thagua*, *Thega*, *Chúp*, *Sevam*, *Sápá*, Naga; *Wek-won*, Burmese.

HABITAT.—Himalayas from Afghanistan and Baluchistan to the Khirthar Range in Sind, east to Assam and Pegu, Southern China, Hainan, and Formosa. Said to have been shot in Lower Bengal and close to Patli Dun in the North-West Provinces.

DESCRIPTION.—Smaller than the Brown Bear, and generally under 6 ft. in length; fur smooth and shorter than in the brown bear, black with a white chin and white crescent on the chest. The editor has seen one in the London Zoo, which had this mark prolonged with a streak on the abdomen and white toes and claws on the fore-feet; usually the claws are black. This individual walked on its hind-legs more than usual. The hair on the cheeks is unusually full, forming bushy whiskers. An individual without the white crescent is on record.

Except in Baluchistan, the Black Bear is a forest animal; its range is lower in the Himalayas than that of the Brown Bear, from about 10,000 feet to about half that elevation according to season. It is omnivorous like the Brown Bear, but digs and grazes less, and is much more addicted to climbing trees after fruit. It also ravages crops, and attacks village beehives, for it does not fear the neighbourhood of man, and often kills live-stock of all sorts, as well as feeding on carrion, being far more carnivorous than the last species.

Its senses are also keener, and it is a really fierce animal, many casualties, fatal and otherwise, being laid to its account. In fact, it is one of the most dangerous and destructive animals in the East. It swims well, but does not seem to take to the water for pleasure, as the Brown Bear sometimes does in hot weather. It is usually solitary, parties of bears being apparently composed of a female and her grown cubs of more than one season. Young cubs are tameable enough, but are apt to grow troublesome before long.

There is some difference of opinion as to whether this bear hibernates; it certainly has less need to do so than the Brown Bear, living as it does where food is easier to get, and it is probably only semi-torpid in winter, and will come out and search for food if the weather be mild.

MALAY BEAR OR SUN BEAR

OTHER NAMES.—Scientific: *Ursus* or *Helarctos malayanus*. Native: *Bruang*, Malay; *Wek-won*, Burmese.

HABITAT.—Garo Hills east and south to the Malay Peninsula, Sumatra, and Borneo.

DESCRIPTION.—The smallest of our bears, being only about 4 ft. long, and with a very short close coat, so that it looks rather like a very large bob-tailed dog. Colour black, with a grey muzzle and white or yellow crescent on the chest. The claws are large, and white in colour. This bear lives in forest and is the best climber of its tribe, and is decidedly more a vegetable than an animal feeder, though killing prey at times, and even attacking man. It is even fonder of honey than bears generally, and is especially a fruit-eater.

It is better known in captivity than in the wild state, and is a most amusing and active animal, and fairly good-tempered for a bear.

Malay Bear.

Sterndale quotes McMaster as having heard of a bear of this species who delighted in cherry brandy, "and on one occasion, having been indulged with an entire bottle of this insinuating beverage, got so completely intoxicated that it stole a bottle of blacking, and drank off the contents under the impression that they were some more of its favourite liquor. The owner of the bear told me that he saw it suffering from this strange mixture, and evidently with, as may be imagined, a terrible headache." Raffles had one which had more exalted ideas about liquor, and was not satisfied with anything but champagne when invited to his master's table!

Sloth Bear.

SLOTH BEAR

OTHER NAMES.—Scientific: *Ursus labiatus*, *Melursus labiatus*. Native: *Rinch*, *Bhalu*, *Adam-zad*, Hindi; *Bhaluk*, Bengali; *Rikspa*, Sanscrit; *Aswal*, Mahratta; *Yerid*, *Yedjal*, *Asol*, Gond; *Bir Mendi*, Oraon; *Bana*, Kol; *Elugu*, Telugu; *Kaddi* or *Karadi*, Canarese and Tamil; *Pani Karudi*, Malayalam; *Usa*, Cingalese.

HABITAT.—Indian Peninsula and Ceylon, where it is the only bear found.

DESCRIPTION.—Very distinct from all our other bears, and hence reasonably enough placed in a different genus, *Melursus*. Size about that of the Himalayan Black Bear, and colour also black with a white crescent on the chest; muzzle grey as in the Malayan Bear, but general appearance very different from either of these two species, owing to the long rough coat and large loose lips. Claws very large, and white. No middle incisors in the upper jaw, and grinders small.

This is the most familiar of Indian bears, owing to its inhabiting the low country, though it prefers the hilly parts of this. It is doubtful how far it extends to the eastward.

Sterndale says of it: "Our old friend is so well known that he hardly requires description, and the very thought of him brings back many a ludicrous and exciting scene of one's jungle days. There is frequently an element of comicality in most bear-hunts, as well as a considerable spice of danger; for, though some people may pooh-pooh this, I know that a she-bear with cubs is no despicable antagonist. Otherwise the male is more anxious to get away than to provoke an attack.

"This bear does not hibernate at all, but is active all the year round. In the hot weather it lies all day in cool caves, emerging only at night. In March and April, when the *mowha*-tree is in flower, it revels in the luscious petals that fall from the trees, even ascending the branches to shake down the coveted blossoms. . . . The Sloth Bear is also partial to mangoes, sugar-cane, and the pods of the *amaltas* or *cassia* (*Cathartocarpus fistula*) and the fruit of the jack-tree (*Artocarpus integrifolia*).

"It is extremely fond of honey, and never passes an ant-hill without digging up its contents, especially those of white ants. . . . Tickell describes the operation thus: 'On arriving at an ant-hill the bear scrapes away with the fore-feet till he reaches the large combs at the bottom of the galleries. He then with violent puffs dissipates the dust and crumbled particles of the nest, and sucks out the inhabitants of the comb by such forcible inhalations as to be heard at 200 yards distance or more.' Insects of all sorts seem not to come amiss to this animal, which systematically hunts for them, turning over stones in the operation.

"The Sloth Bear has usually two cubs at a birth. They are born blind, and continue so till about the end of the third week. . . . The young ones are not difficult to rear if ordinary care be taken. The great mistake that most people make in feeding the young of wild animals is the giving of pure cows' milk. . . . I had considerable experience in the bringing up of young things of all sorts in the Seeonee district, and only after some time learnt the proper proportions of milk and water, and also that regularity in feeding was necessary—two-thirds water to one of milk for the first month; after that half and half.

"The Sloth Bear carries her young on her back—and she seems to do this for some time, as Mr. Sanderson writes that he shot one which was carrying a cub as large as a sheep-dog. . . .

"The British soldier is rather fond of a bear as a pet; and Captain Baldwin tells an amusing story of one which followed the men on to the parade ground, and quite disorganised the manœuvres by frightening the colonel's horse. In 1858 I was quartered for a time with a naval brigade, and once, when there was an alarm of the enemy, Jack went to the front with all his pets, including Bruin, which brought up the rear, shuffling along in blissful ignorance of the bubble reputation to be found in the cannon's mouth.

"Although as a rule vegetarian, yet this species is not altogether free from the imputation of being a devourer of flesh when it comes in its way. In such cases it possibly has been impelled by hunger, and I doubt whether it ever kills for the sake of eating. I have known even ruminants eat meat, and in their case hunger could not have been urged as an excuse. Mr. Sanderson mentions an instance when a Barking Deer he shot was partially devoured by a bear during the night.

"Very few elephants, however steady with tigers, will stand a bear. Whether it is that bears make such a row when wounded, or whether there be anything in the smell, I know not, but I have heard many sportsmen allude to the fact. A favourite elephant I had would stand anything but a bear and a pig. Few horses will approach a bear, and this is one difficulty in spearing them; and for this reason I think bear dancers should be prohibited in towns. Calcutta used to swarm with them at one time. . . . The bear rising to hug its adversary is a fallacy as far as this species is concerned; it does not squeeze, but uses its claws freely and with great effect."

It is also more inclined to attack man unprovoked than almost any other animal, and casualties inflicted by it are unfortunately very common, the victim being often terribly disfigured even if not killed, as the bear strikes at the head and face. Blanford was inclined to consider bears more dangerous than tigers, and the Seeonee bears must have been a very quiet lot, or Sterndale would surely have mentioned ferocity. The editor only once saw one led about in Calcutta.

Sloth Bear, front view.

The so-called Cat-Bear, better known as Panda, is our sole representative of the Raccoon family (*Procyonidæ*), which are chiefly American animals.

Panda or Cat-Bear.

PANDA OR HIMALAYAN RACCOON

OTHER NAMES.—Scientific: *Aelurus fulgens.* Native: *Wah, Yé, Nigalyaponya,* Nepalese; *Wah-donka, Woker,* Bhutanese; *Saknam,* Lepcha.

HABITAT.—South-Eastern Himalayas to China.

DESCRIPTION.—Like a pigmy bear, but with the long tail and broad short face of a cat; eyes small as in a bear, fur long and thick, soles of feet furry.

Colour rich auburn red above and on the tail, which is ringed with light and dark shades; under-parts and limbs black, face largely or mostly white. Length about 2 ft. in head and body, tail about 18 in. Feet plantigrade, as in the bears, but with partially retractile claws.

The Panda or Cat-Bear—the last a name which should be avoided, as it is zoologically incorrect and leads to confusion with the equally ill-named Bear-Cat or Binturong to be noticed later on—is the least carnivorous of our carnivora, living mostly on vegetable substances, such as roots, grass, fruit, acorns, and especially bamboo-shoots. It is said to rob birds' nests, however, of the eggs and young, and to visit villages to steal milk and ghee, a strange habit for an animal which is neither keen of senses, fierce, nor active, on the ground at any rate, though it is a good climber. It is found in pairs or families, and lives in holes in trees or rocks, sleeping during the middle of the day. A pair have been seen high up in a tree making unearthly noises, apparently a nuptial concert as in cats. A male was also observed when excited, to emit a strong odour of musk. The young, which are born in spring, are two in number, and associate with the parents till another litter is due.

The Panda is easily tamed, and will thrive even in a hot climate like that of Calcutta, though living in the temperate belt of the Himalayas. When angry, it rears up and strikes with the fore-paws like a bear, but mews and spits like a cat.

Giant Panda or Pied Bear.

The only old-world relative of the Panda—the Giant Panda or Pied Bear—is found in Moupin in Eastern Tibet, and is of all animals living in the neighbourhood of our area most likely to attract notice. Being a large animal—bigger than the Malay Bear—and very strikingly clad in white fur with black limbs, eye-patches, and shoulder-stripe, it cannot be mistaken for anything else. It is short-tailed like a bear, and a vegetable-feeder like our Panda.

The Weasel family (*Mustelidæ*) includes among its members the badgers and otters, and thus shows in its members a greater range of habits and appearance than our other carnivorous families. The mustelines, however, are all long-bodied, short-legged animals, and have peculiarly-shaped long skulls; the length is due to the large size of the cranial or hinder portion, the face being short.

The neck is almost as thick as the head, and very powerful; in fact, these animals are remarkably strong for their size, and the most active of all the carnivora; many of them hunt by day, and sometimes in parties. The most typical weasels, which show more or less resemblance to our domestic species, the ferret, are very carnivorous and bloodthirsty, but the badgers incline to omnivorous habits, like the bears, which they rather resemble in appearance and gait, being plantigrade. They are also distinguished from typical weasels by their fore-claws being large, much longer than the hind ones.

Hog-Badger.

HOG-BADGER

Other Names.—Scientific: *Arctonyx collaris.* Native: *Bála-súr*, Hindi; *Chomhúvho*, *Thembakso*, Naga; *Nuloang*, Kuki; *No-ok*, Manipuri; *Quado-Waildu*, Mug; *Khwe-htu-wet-hti*, Arakanese; *Khwe-ta-wek-wek-ta-wek*, Burmese.

Habitat.—Nepal and Sikkim, at low elevations, east to Tenasserim and Yunnan. Sterndale heard of it in Seonee, but did not see it.

F

DESCRIPTION.—A short-tailed animal about the size of a small dog, and a combination of pig and bear in appearance, the snout being long and limbs and gait bear-like—in fact, some say the Hindi name should be *Bhálu-súr* (bear-pig) instead of *Bála-súr* (sand-pig). The coat is coarse, grey, and rough on the body, close and white, with longitudinal black streaks, on the head, black or very dark on the limbs. Length of head and body over 2 ft.; tail about 8 in.

The Hog-Badger is omnivorous and nocturnal, passing the day in crevices of rocks or in burrows which it digs. Its scent is keen, but its sight poor, and it readily stands up like a bear.

ASSAM BADGER

OTHER NAMES.—Scientific: *Arctonyx taxoides.*

HABITAT.—Assam and Arakan.

DESCRIPTION.—Only about half the size of the common Hog-Badger (which is also found in the same countries), with brighter though similar colours and a longer and softer coat; the tail is shorter and the nose less pig-like.

Nothing seems to be known about the habits of this animal, of which but few specimens have been obtained.

Indian Ratel.

INDIAN RATEL OR HONEY-BADGER

OTHER NAMES.—Scientific: *Mellivora indica.* Native: *Biju*, Hindi; *Biju-khawar*, Telegu; *Tava karadi*, Tamil; *Bhagru-bhal*, at Bhagulpore; *Bharsiah*, Nepalese; *Usa ban-na*, Kol.

Habitat.—Most of India, but not ascending the Himalayas, and absent from Lower Bengal, the Malabar coast, and Ceylon.

Description.—A good-sized animal, the largest of our mustelines, very squat in build and easily distinguished among Indian animals by its curious colour, black with the crown, nape, and back grey. The tail is short, and there are no external ears.

The head and body measure more than 2 ft., the tail only about 6 in.

So far as is known the Indian Ratel is purely carnivorous, but as it readily takes vegetable food in captivity it probably is not really so, but more or less omnivorous. It is destructive to poultry, and is said by Indians to dig up dead bodies and devour them. Neither Sterndale nor Blanford credit this, but such an act is only to be expected from a carnivore with particularly strong digging claws.

The Indian Ratel is nocturnal, spending the day in holes, while the better-known African species may be met with by day, often hunting for bees' nests in partnership with the birds well known as Honey-guides. One of these is known in the Himalayas, but there it never meets the Ratel, and does not guide men to honey as the African species do. No doubt, however, the Indian Ratel finds and exploits honey-stores somehow.

In captivity it is very tame and lively, and has a curious habit of turning somersaults; while, although supposed to be chiefly a ground animal, it climbs about the wires of a cage actively.

The common African species only differs in having a white border to the grey upper parts, and this apparently only when adult, so it may not really be a fully distinct form.

The Ferret-badgers (*Helictis*) form a link between the badgers and the weasels, being slenderer in form and shorter-legged than the others. They have been called Wolverenes, but this is misleading, the real Wolverene or Glutton of the sub-arctic forests being a sort of gigantic thick-set weasel, larger than any badger.

BROWN OR INDIAN FERRET-BADGER

Other Names.—Scientific: *Helictis orientalis*. Native: *Oker*, Nepalese; *Nyentek*, Malay.

Habitat.—Nepal, Sikkim, and Java.

Description.—About the size of a small cat, with rather long nose and tail, and small but well-developed ears. Fur a mixture of soft and coarse hair, dark brown above, dirty white below; a white stripe down the back, and the cheeks and a forehead-patch also white. Head and body about 16 in. long, tail about half that length.

This animal is found at moderate elevations in forests, but also visits houses at night, where it is useful in destroying cockroaches and other vermin.

GREY OR BURMESE FERRET-BADGER

Other Names.—Scientific : *Kyoung-u-gyi*, Burmese ; *Kyoung-pyan*, Arakanese.

Habitat.—Manipur and Pegu, perhaps Cachar, Tipperah and Arakan.

Description.—Like the last, but with larger teeth, the coloured parts of the face darker, the general hue brownish grey, and the light face-marks and under-side sometimes yellow. One kept by Tickell ate fruit as well as meat, eggs, etc., and was kept chained to a tree, being fierce enough to defy dogs.

It is possible that the Chinese Ferret-badger (*Helictis moschata*), distinguished by having smaller teeth, not only than the present species, but than the Indian one, may occur in Upper Burma.

Marten.

The Martens (*Mustela*), though definitely belonging to the weasel section of the musteline family, are yet rather different from the most typical weasels ; though very long-bodied, they are also long-tailed, and may be compared in size to slim common cats. Also they are very largely climbers, while typical weasels, although climbing well, hunt on the ground. Like true weasels generally, they hunt much by day, but are less purely carnivorous, eating fruit as well as flesh. They have not the atrocious smell which most of the family produce when excited.

WHITE-CHEEKED MARTEN

OTHER NAMES.—Scientific: *Mustela* or *Martes flavigula.* Native: *Múl sampra*, Nepalese; *Tuturala, Chetrala*, Nepal and Kumaon; *Huniah* or *Aniar*, Bhutanese; *Sakku*, Lepcha; *Anga Prao*, Malay.

HABITAT.—Himalayas at moderate elevations, and eastward in mountainous parts through the Indian region to Sumatra in the east and Travancore in the south.

DESCRIPTION.—Fur rather close, especially in the Malay race, tail nearly as long as head and body, rather bushy. Colour generally strikingly variegated, the crown, nape, and extremities being black, the throat and cheeks white, chest yellow, and the rest of the coat light brown. But there is much variation, some even being brown of various shades all over, or dark brown with the usual white and yellow on the throat and breast.

It has been suggested that this last variety is the summer dress, but specimens the editor has watched in the Calcutta and London Zoos have shown no seasonal change; and he considers it more likely that these brown specimens, which are of a more ordinary and inconspicuous colour, probably are survivals of or reversions to an ancestral form, the usual bright-coloured type being of comparatively recent evolution, like a black-and-tan dog compared with a wolf.

The length of the head and body is about 21 in., the tail measuring about 18 in.

The Indian Marten, as this species is sometimes called, associates in pairs or families, and eats birds and mammals of all sizes up to barking-deer fawns, besides fruit and reptiles. It is a most attractive animal from its beauty and activity; one sent by Captain the Hon. C. Shore to the Zoological Society a century ago had been, he says, "caught when not many days old, and was so tame that it was always kept loose about a well, sporting about the windlasses, posts, etc., and playing tricks with the people who came to draw water."

It keeps up a low chuckle when moving about at large, changing to a harsh cry if excited.

BEECH-MARTEN

OTHER NAMES.—Scientific: *Mustela foina.* Native: *Dalla kapak*, Afghan.

HABITAT.—Europe east to the Himalayas at considerable elevations, but not well known.

DESCRIPTION.—Smaller than the last, and more thickly furred, especially on the feet; tail only about half the length of the head and body Colour of some shade of greyish-brown, darker as a rule on the extremities and lighter on the head; more or less of the throat and breast white.

This is a well-known animal in Europe, where it is often called the Stone-Marten; it does not inhabit Britain, as used to be thought, our species at home being the Pine-Marten (*M. martes* or *abietum*), which is now scarce, and is on the Continent wilder and scarcer than the Beech-Marten. That species, indeed, is rather too familiar, as it is inclined to come about houses after poultry.

The Beech-Marten breeds in spring, going with young for nine weeks, and producing a litter of four or five. It is, as Blanford recalls, the animal which Rolleston showed was kept in domestication by the classical ancients before they adopted the cat, which, ages before, had been tamed in Egypt.

The polecats and weasels (*Putorius*) are the most typical members of the present family, very slim and snaky, with long necks, very short legs, and tails moderately long, and about equal in length to half the head and body or a little less. They are the most active of a very active family, most thoroughly carnivorous, and very bloodthirsty; bold as well, for though their usual prey is small mammals and birds, they will attack and overcome creatures vastly their superiors in size. They live in holes, and often hunt by day, sometimes in packs, when, if interfered with, they may even be dangerous to man. They emit a very detestable-smelling liquid when excited from their anal glands. Males are much larger than females in this group.

HIMALAYAN WEASEL

OTHER NAMES.—Scientific: *Putorius subhemachalanus, Mustela subhemachalana.* Native: *Simiong*, Bhutia; *Sang-king*, Lepcha.

HABITAT.—Nepal and Kashmir Himalayas at moderate or high elevations.

DESCRIPTION.—About 1 ft. in length of head and body; chestnut or bay, chin white; often the chest is also marked with white. This weasel seems inclined to be familiar, as Hodgson caught two in his house at Darjeeling.

YELLOW-BELLIED WEASEL

OTHER NAMES.—Scientific: *Putorius* or *Mustela kathiah.* Native: *Kathia nyal*, Nepalese.

HABITAT.—Himalayas from Mussoorie east to Assam and Khasi hills, not ranging very high.

DESCRIPTION.—Under 1 ft. in length of head and body; bay above and on the tail, which is not bushy; deep yellow below.

All that is known about this very pretty little animal is that it is tamed and kept by the Nepalese as a ratter, and also trained to kill fowls, geese, and even sheep and goats; it fixes on the neck artery, and holds on with the persistence of its family—a good example of their powers of killing.

STRIPED WEASEL

OTHER NAMES.—Scientific: *Putorius strigidorsus*, *Mustela strigidorsa.*

HABITAT.—Sikkim.

DESCRIPTION.—About 1 ft. in length of head and body; bay with a white streak along the back and another along the underparts; throat and a broad streak on the chest yellow.

This is a very rare animal, of which only a few specimens are known.

STOAT

OTHER NAMES.—Scientific: *Putorius* or *Mustela erminea.*

HABITAT.—Northern parts of northern hemisphere, ranging into the Arctic. Has occurred in Kashmir.

DESCRIPTION.—Less than 1 ft. in length of head and body, tail with a rather bushy black tip. General colour chestnut above, white or pale yellow below. In cold climates it changes to white in winter except for the black tail-tip, and is then called Ermine, and furnishes a valuable fur.

It has a large litter, five to eight in number, and even in England holds its own well against persecution.

From their size and comparative length of tail the other Himalayan weasels would probably be called stoats in England if they occurred there, the original weasel being a very tiny short-tailed animal.

WHITE-NOSED WEASEL

OTHER NAMES.—Scientific: *Putorius* or *Mustela canigula.* Native: *Kran*, Kashmiri.

HABITAT.—Tibet and probably the Western Himalayas generally; has been obtained at Chamba and Pangi at 8,000 ft.

DESCRIPTION.—Head and body over 1 ft. long, tail rather bushy. General colour chestnut; muzzle and more or less of underparts to chest, white.

There is nothing much on record about the habits of this species—

in fact, there is not very much known about the Indian mustelines generally, and these mountain weasels in particular.

TIBETAN POLECAT

OTHER NAMES.—Scientific: *Putorius larvatus* or *tibetanus*.

HABITAT.—Tibet north of Sikkim; has occurred in Ladak.

DESCRIPTION.—Not quite so slim as the before-mentioned weasels, and the coat looser and less smooth, with long hair intermixed; tail rather bushy. Colour above buff or cream, shaded with black, which is the colour of the long hairs; under-parts and extremities black, and a black patch crossing the white face at the eyes. Head and body about 15 in. long.

Altogether the animal is very like a light-backed edition of the dark or polecat-coloured variety of the ferret, more usually known as a pink-eyed albino with straw-coloured fur; and it seems to bear much the same relation to the European Polecat as the Himalayan Brown Bear does to the European form of that species.

MOTTLED POLECAT

OTHER NAMES.—Scientific: *Putorius sarmaticus*.

HABITAT.—Poland east to Afghanistan and Baluchistan.

DESCRIPTION.—A sleeker-coated animal than the common pole-cat or ferret, but still not so slim as the most typical weasels; tail decidedly bushy and colour unlike that of any other animal, mottled with brown and cream-colour above, black below and on the limbs, with the head black crossed by two semicircular white bands, one before and one behind the ears, and the tail a mixture of brown and white, ending in black. It is smaller than the typical polecat, the head and body being little over a foot in length.

This pretty animal is rare and local in most countries; the neighbourhood of Kandahar and Quetta appears to be its headquarters, as it is common there.

The otters (*Lutra*) are large aquatic weasels with sleek coats of coarse hair concealing a downy underfur, strong tapering tails about half as long as the head and body, broad muzzles, very small ears, short legs, and fully-webbed feet, with short claws, which, as Blanford remarks, leave tracks on mud and sand which are easily recognisable and betray their haunts. They are partially nocturnal, and lie up by day in holes; they are very sociable and playful, good travellers on land and most graceful swimmers. They are to be found in rivers and large tanks or even on the sea-coast, feeding on fish and other aquatic animals, often with the usual weasel wastefulness of life, as when fish after fish is caught and only one bite taken from each. Our three Indian species are all very much alike at first sight and in habits.

Common Otter.

COMMON OTTER

OTHER NAMES.—Scientific: *Lutra vulgaris* or *nair*. Native: *Ud*, *Ud bilao*, *Pani kutta*, Hindi; *Nirnai*, Canarese; *Niru kuka*, Telegu; *Jalmánjar*, Mahratti; *Nirunai*, Tamil; *Dalwai bek*, Wadári.

HABITAT.—Northern Hemisphere in the Old World generally; both hills and plains in India, Ceylon, and some part of Burma—how much not definitely known.

DESCRIPTION.—A large otter between 2 and 2½ ft. in length of head and body; with the naked skin of the end of the snout invading the hairy part of the muzzle in the middle in a slight point; colour brown, usually grizzled with the white tips of the longer hairs, above, cheeks and all underparts more or less pure white, throat and cheeks especially; but this whiteness is only fully developed in adults, the young being pale brown below, on the belly at any rate.

In Europe this otter, which is there larger and redder and seldom grizzled, brings forth its young in winter, two to five forming the litter, and the gestation period being about two months.

Its cry is a yelp or a whistled alarm-call; parties—probably family parties—often hunt in concert to surround fish. Young otters are easily tamed, and these animals are often kept by Indian fishermen for driving fish into nets as a dog drives sheep into a fold.

Sterndale quotes an affecting story from Jerdon about a tame otter the latter possessed and wished to get rid of owing to its fish-stealing habits; he therefore conveyed it in a closed box, by boat, 7 or 8 miles off, and liberated it, returning home when the animal had gone out of sight. But the same evening the faithful beast returned to him where he was in a shed watching the Mohurrum, about 1½ miles from his house.

SMOOTH INDIAN OTTER

OTHER NAMES.—Scientific: *Lutra ellioti, macrodus.* Native: *Ludra*, Sindhi; *Hpyan*, Burmese; *Phey*, Talain; *Bong*, Karen; *Mamrang*, *Aurang*, *Anjing-ayer*, Malay. Presumably these names, which are given by Blanford, also refer, in the case of Indian languages, to the Common Otter, as the two are much alike.

HABITAT.—India generally, but not ascending the Himalayas to any height; east through Burma to the Malay Peninsula.

DESCRIPTION.—A shorter but more stoutly-built animal than the Common Otter, with shorter fur and larger skull and teeth; the fur shows no grizzling on the back, and the white on the underparts does not extend below the chest, except for the tips of the hair in some specimens.

The line of division between the naked nose and the adjacent hairy part runs almost straight across, and is not angulated as in the Common Otter.

It is not surprising that this species has been much confused with the Common Otter, and it still remains to be discovered in what respect it may differ in habits.

SMALL OR CLAWLESS OTTER

OTHER NAMES.—Scientific: *Lutra leptonyx, cinerea.* Native: *Chusam*, Bhotanese; *Suriam*, Lepcha.

HABITAT.—Foot of the Himalayas, Lower Bengal east to Burma, South China, and Java; hill-ranges of Madras Presidency.

DESCRIPTION.—A small otter, with the head and body 2 ft. long or less, and the head short and rounded. But the most noticeable distinction from our other species is in the feet, in which the two middle toes are noticeably longer than the others, and the claws very small or absent.

The white on the under-parts is limited to the neck and shades into brown on the chest.

The name Clawless Otter is not appropriate to this species, as the claws, though very small, are more often present than absent; the scientific name *cinerea*, supposed to be the correct one, is also misleading, as the animal is brown, not cinereous or ash-coloured. Being so distinct as a species, this small otter no doubt has some habits of its own, but these have not been recorded.

The Cats (*Felidæ*), of which our region can boast of more species than any other, are the most perfectly organised of the Carnivora, and the essential peculiarities of their structure are easily studied in our domestic species. The head is broad and short, with large eyes and long moustaches; the incisors very small, the canines large, and the grinders few and sharp-edged, only suited for chopping up meat, the animals of this family being more exclusively addicted to animal food than any other carnivores.

In this family we first come across reduction of the toes, all the mammals previously dealt with having the full number of five digits to each limb; in the cats the inner toe in the hind foot is absent, and in the fore-foot reduced and so elevated that it does not touch the ground in walking, though its claw is well developed and made use of with the others, the cats using their fore-feet freely, like the bears.

The claws are well curved and very sharp, and when not in use for clutching or climbing are drawn back so that their points are well clear of the ground, thus preserving their sharpness. The tongue is rough, the body very supple, and the clavicles or collar-bones very small and lying in the soft tissues unconnected with the rest of the skeleton—they are the "lucky bones" of the tiger.

The cats are generally nocturnal, unsociable, and good climbers; they are nervous and highly-strung, but courageous, though less so than the weasels. They, also, though quick in brief movements, lack endurance, and spend much time in repose when circumstances allow of this.

At different times the family has been cut up into various genera, and these have again been reunited, though the Cheetah has usually been kept distinct. All, however, are undoubtedly very closely allied, and it seems unnecessary to enter into subdivisions here, but to rank all in one genus, so that this coincides with the family.

LION

OTHER NAMES.—Scientific: *Felis leo*. Native: *Sher-babar*, *Singh*, Hindi; *Untia-bagh*, Guzerati; *Sawach*, in Kattywar; *Shingal*, Bengali; *Suh* (lion) *Siming* (lioness), Kashmiri; *Rastar*, Brahui.

HABITAT.—Africa and Western Asia east to Western India, where a few remain in the Gir forest in Kattywar.

DESCRIPTION.—" Distinguished from other Cats by its uniform

tawny colour, flatter skull, which gives it a more dog-like appearance, the shaggy mane of the male, and by the tufted tail of both sexes. From nose to insertion of tail 6 to 6½ ft.; tail 2½ to 3 ft. . . . Young lions when born are invariably spotted" (Sterndale).

To this it may be added that the tail-tuft is black in both sexes, and the male's mane, when well-developed, often black at the ends; it varies much in growth, and the idea that Indian lions were especially maneless is a mistake. The tail-tuft often conceals a horny claw, with which the beast was supposed by the ancients to lash himself into fury. The lion's skull lies level if placed on a flat surface with the lower jaw attached; the tiger's so placed will tilt.

Lion.

The lion is now so nearly extinct in India, though it appears formerly to have been generally distributed through the North-West and Central Provinces, that it is not necessary to say much about so generally well-known an animal, especially as Sterndale had no personal experience of its habits in India, though he says: "Whilst at Seeonee, within the years 1857 to 1864, I frequently heard the native shikaries speak of having seen a tiger *without stripes* which may have been of the present species."

It may, however, be of interest to quote Bishop Heber, writing a century ago, as to the disposition of the lion as compared with the tiger. In describing an unsuccessful tiger-hunt, in which the quarry was not even sighted, he quotes his companion, Mr. Boulderson, collector of the Kulleanpoor district, a keen shikari, as saying that the tiger's aim was to remain concealed, and to make off as quietly as possible, though fighting boldly when at bay. "He added, that the lion, though not so large and swift an animal as the tiger, was generally stronger and more courageous. Those which have been killed in India, instead of running away when pursued through a jungle, seldom seem to think its cover necessary at all. When they see their enemies approaching, they spring out to meet them, open-mouthed, in the plain, like the boldest of all animals—a mastiff dog. They are thus generally shot with very little trouble, but if they are missed, or only slightly wounded, they are truly formidable enemies. Though not swift, they leap with vast strength and violence; and their large heads, immense paws, and the great weight of their body forwards, often enable them to spring on the head of the largest elephants and fairly pull them down to the ground, riders and all."

Some may consider this account exaggerated, though it must be remembered that when formidable animals come into contact with well-armed men, the boldest individuals will be the first to perish, and Blanford, who knew both lions and tigers in nature, and is most cautious, says: "Lions are perhaps bolder than tigers, and certainly much more noisy, their habit of roaring, especially in the evening and night, having necessarily attracted the attention of all who have been in countries infested by them." Add to this the fact that the lion inhabits more open country, and that there is more *kudos* attached to his slaying, and it is easy to see why he has failed to hold his own as the tiger does, though the two beasts have the same general habits and seek similar prey. The lion breeds more freely in captivity than the tiger; hybrids between them have been produced more than once, and are marked with thin and faint stripes, with the mane but just indicated in the male; one is in the London Zoo at the time of writing (1927).

TIGER

OTHER NAMES.—Scientific: *Felis tigris*. Native: *Bagh*, *Sher*, Hindi; *Sela-nagh*, *Go-nagh*, Bengali; *Wahag*, Mahratti; *Nahar*, Central India; *Tut Sad*, Rajmehal; *Nongya-chor*, Gorukhpore; *Púli*, Telegu and Tamil; *Kuli*, Canarese; *Sathong*, Lepcha; *Túkt*, Bhotanese; *Mayar*, Baluchi; *Shinh*, Sindi; *Padar-suh*, Kashmiri; *Lakhra*, Uraon; *Krodi*, Kondh; *Nari*, Kurg; *Parri*, *Búrsh*, Toda; *Keh-na*, Limbu; *Schi*, Aka; *Matsu*, *Garo*, *Kla*, Khasi; *Sa*, *Ragdi*, *Tekhu*, *Khudi*, Naga; *Húmpi*, Kuki; *Sumyo*, Abor; *Sü*, Khamti; *Sirong*, Singpho; *Kei*, Manipuri; *Misi*, Kachari; *Kya*, Burmese; *Kla*, Talain; *Khi*, *Botha-o*, *Tupuli*, Karen; *Htso*, Shan; *Rimau* or *Harimau*, Malay.

HABITAT.—From the southern shore of the Caspian locally through Central Asia and Southern Siberia to Saghalien Island in one direction, and through India and Burma (but not Ceylon) south-east to Java and Sumatra in the other. Although sometimes found as high as 7,000 ft. in the Himalayas, it usually keeps to their bases.

DESCRIPTION.—Sterndale's is "a large heavy-bodied cat, much developed in the fore-quarters, with short, close hair of a bright rufous ground tint from every shade of pale yellow ochre to burnt sienna, with black stripes arranged irregularly and seldom in two individuals alike, the stripes being also irregular in form, from single streaks to loops and broad bands. In some the brows and cheeks are white, and in all the chin, throat, breast, and belly are pure white. All parts, however, whether white or rufous, are equally pervaded by the black stripes. The males have prolonged hairs extending from the ears round the cheeks, forming a ruff."

To this it may be added that cubs are marked like adults, and that aged animals become lighter in colour. A black specimen is on record, seen dead near Chittagong; a notorious "blue tiger" is at the time of this revision (1927) at large in South China, and many white ones are on record, of which the editor has seen three. His Majesty the King exhibits one, shot in Rewa State, at the South Kensington Natural History Museum, and several are or recently were at large in India, so that the white variety appears to be becoming commoner; it is more or less clearly striped.

The subject of the maximum size of tigers has been debated with more zeal than the importance of the matter justifies; Sterndale very properly says: "Care should be taken in measuring that the head be raised, so that the top of the skull be as much as possible in line with the vertebræ. A stake should then be driven in at the nose and another close in at the root of the tail, and the measurement taken between the two stakes, and not round the curves. The tail, which is an unimportant matter, but which in the present system of measurement is a considerable factor, should be measured and noted separately . . . there may be a heavy tiger with a short tail and a light-bodied one with a long tail."

Summing up observations on the point, it may be said that tigers measure about 6 ft. in head and body, with a tail about 1 yd. long, tigresses being 6 in. to 1 ft. shorter in head and body length. Measured "over all" a tiger 10 ft. long is a big one, but a length of 12 feet is now admitted by Blanford, who also records shooting a tigress only 7 ft. 6 in. in total length. Sterndale records a skull of 15¼ in., but 1 ft. is more what one can usually expect in a tiger, and less in a tigress. As to weight, Mr. Hornaday killed a specimen in the Anamalai forest which, measuring 9 ft. 8½ in. over all, weighed 495 pounds, so that a 500-pound tiger is not improbable.

Sterndale quotes this interesting memorandum of Shillingford's as to growth of tigers:

"Cubs one year old measure ..	Males, 4½ ft. to 5½ ft. Females, 4 ft. to 5 ft.
Cubs two years old measure ..	Males, 5½ ft. to 7 ft. Females, 5 ft. to 6½ ft.
Cubs three years old measure ..	Males, 7 ft. to 8½ ft. Females, 6½ ft. to 7½ ft.

When they reach three years of age they lose their 'milk' canines, which are replaced by the permanent fangs, and at this period the mother leaves them to cater for themselves."

He goes on himself to say: "The cubs are interesting pets if taken from the mother very young. I have reared several, but only kept one for any length of time. I have given a full description of Zalim and his ways in *Seeonee*. He was found by my camp followers with another in a nullah, and brought to me. The other cub died, but Zalim grew up into a very fine tiger, and was sent to England. I never allowed him to taste raw flesh. He had a little cooked meat each day, and as much milk as he liked to drink, and he throve well on this diet. When he was too large to be allowed to roam about unconfined, I had a stout buffalo leather collar made for his neck, and he was chained to a stump near the cookroom door. With grown-up people he was perfectly tame, but I noticed he got restless when children approached, and so made up my mind to part with him before he did any mischief. . . . Strange though it may seem to the English reader that a tiger should have any special character beyond the general one for cruelty and cunning, it is nevertheless a fact that each animal has certain peculiarities of temperament which are well known to the villagers in the neighbourhood. They will tell you that such a one is daring and rash; another is cunning and not to be taken by any artifice; that one is savage and morose; another is mild and harmless. . . . So accustomed do the people get to their unwelcome visitor that we have known the boys of a village turn a tiger out of quarters which were reckoned too close, and pelt him with stones. On one occasion two of the juvenile assailants were killed by the animal they had approached too near. Herdsmen in the same way get callous to the danger of meddling with so dreadful a creature, and frequently rush out to the rescue of their cattle when seized. On a certain occasion one out of a herd of cattle was attacked close to our camp, and rescued single-handed by its owner, who laid his iron-bound staff across the tiger's back. . . . He did not seem to think he had done anything wonderful, and seemed rather surprised that we should suppose that he was going to let his last heifer go the way of all the others.

"It is fortunate for these dwellers in the backwoods that but a small percentage of tigers are man-eaters, perhaps not 5 per cent., otherwise village after village would be depopulated; as it is the yearly tale of lives lost is a heavy one.

"Tigers are also eccentric in their ways, showing differences in disposition under different circumstances. I believe that many a shikari passes at times within a few yards of a tiger without knowing it, the tendency of the animal being to crouch and hide till the strange two-legged beast has passed. The narrowest escape I ever had is an instance. I had hunted a large tiger, well known for the savageness of his disposition, on foot from ravine to ravine on the banks of the Pench, one hot day in June, and, giving him no rest, made sure of getting him about three o'clock in the afternoon. He had been seen to slip into a large nullah, bordered on one side by open country, a small watercourse draining into it from the fields; here was one large *beyr* bush, behind which I wished to place myself, but was persuaded by an old shikari of great local reputation to move farther on. Hardly had we done so when our friend bounded from under the bush and disappeared in a thicket, where we lost him. Ten days after this he was killed by a friend and myself, and he sustained his savage reputation by attacking the elephant without provocation—a thing a tiger seldom does. I had hunted this animal several times, and on one occasion saw him swim the Pench River at one of its broadest reaches. It was the only time I had seen a tiger swim, and it was interesting to watch him powerfully breasting the stream with his head well up. Tigers swim readily, as is well known. . . .

"There has been some controversy about the way in which tigers kill their prey. I am afraid I cannot speak definitely on the subject, although I have several times seen tigers kill oxen and ponies. I do not think they have a uniform way of doing it; so much depends upon circumstances—certain it is that they cannot smash in the head of a buffalo with a stroke, as some writers make out, but yet I have known them make strokes at the head, in a running fight, for instance, between a buffalo and a tiger—in which the former got off—and in the case of human beings. Of two men killed by the same tiger, one had his skull fractured by a blow; the other, who was killed as we were endeavouring to drive the tiger out of the village, was seized by the loins. He died immediately; the man with the fractured skull lingered some hours longer. Another case of a stroke at the head happened once when I had tied out a pony for a tiger that would not look at cows, over which I had sat for several successive nights. A tiger and tigress came out, and the former made a rush at the *tattoo*, who met him with such a kick on the nose that he drew back much astonished; the tigress then dashed at the pony, and I, wishing to save the plucky little animal's life, fired two barrels into her, rolling her over just as she struck at his head. But it was too late; the pony dropped at the blow and died—not from concussion, however, but from loss of blood, for the jugular vein had been cut open as though it had been done with a knife. So much for the head stroke, which is, I may say, exceptional. As a general rule I think the tiger bears down his victim by sheer weight, and then, by some means which I should hesitate to define, although I have seen it, the head is wrenched back, so as to dislocate the vertebræ. . . .

"That tigers are carrion feeders is well known, but that sometimes they prefer high meat to fresh I had only proof of once. A tiger killed a mare and foal, on which he feasted for three days; on the fourth, nothing remaining but a very offensive leg, we tied out a fine young buffalo calf for him within a yard or two of the savoury joint. The tiger came during the night and took away the leg, without touching the calf, and, devouring it, fell asleep; in which condition we, having tracked him up the nullah, found and killed him."

Man and his domestic animals are not, of course, what may be called the natural food of the tiger, which in the wilder districts at any rate, lives mainly on the larger game, especially deer of various kinds, nilghai, and female and young wild pigs; even young elephants may be attacked, while on the other hand, small quarry such as monkeys, porcupines, and pea-fowl sometimes fall victims. A tiger has been known to kill bears, and others have been found to eat frogs and even locusts, and in time of flood to feed on fish and reptiles.

Where the durian grows, its fruit is said to be eaten by tigers, and they eat grass medicinally. "The tigress," says Sterndale, "goes with young about fifteen weeks, and produces from two to five at a birth. . . . The native shikaris say that the tiger kills the young ones if he finds them. The mother is a most affectionate parent as a rule, and sometimes exhibits strange fits of jealousy at interference with her young. I heard an instance of this some years ago from my brother, Mr. H. B. Sterndale, who, as one of the Municipal Commissioners of Delhi, took a great interest in the collection of animals in the Queen's Gardens there. Both tiger and leopard cubs had been born in the gardens, and the mother of the latter showed no uneasiness at her offspring being handled by strangers as they crept through the bars and strayed about; but one day, a tiger cub having done the same, the tigress exhibited great restlessness, and, on the little one's return, in a sudden accession of jealous fury she dashed her paw on it and killed it."

Males and females appear to be nearly equal in numbers among the cubs born, the former, if anything, predominating, but some say that among adults females predominate; if this is true, some cause destroys many males—perhaps combats among themselves. They seldom associate with their females when these are in company with cubs, and are generally far less social than lions, which in Africa are often found not only in families, but in what would be called packs in meaner animals—a dozen or even a score.

Tigers also keep more to cover, as has been stated above, and may be expected to occur in any large area of high grass or forest; they also haunt caves and ravines, and prefer the neighbourhood of water, especially in the hot season, when they like wallowing in it. Certain spots are known to be particularly favoured, and the presence of pea-fowl, of both the Indian and Burmese species, is often an indication of a tiger in the neighbourhood, the birds perhaps keeping near him to spy on his movements.

LEOPARD OR PANTHER

OTHER NAMES.—Scientific: *Felis pardus*, *panthera*. Native: *Tendwa*, *Chita*, *Chita-bagh*, Hindi; *Honiga*, Canarese; *Asnea*, Mahratti; *Chinna puli*, Telegu; *Burkal*, Gond; *Bai-hira*, *Tahr-hay*, hill tribes near Simla. Sterndale gives these names for the large form, which he calls the Pard; for the smaller, which he distinguishes as the Panther, he gives *Chita*, *Gorbacha*, Hindi; *Bibia-bagh*, Mahratti; *Kerkal*, Canarese; *Ghur-hai*, hill tribes. Blanford, who unites the two, gives all these names, and also *Tidua*, *Srighas*, Bundelkund; *Sonora*, Korku; *Jerkos*, Rajmehal; *Chiru-thai*, Tamil; *Kutiya*, Singhalese; *Sik*, Tibetan; *Syiak*, Lepcha; *Kajenda*, Manipuri; *Misi-patrai*, *Kam-kei*, Kuki; *Hurrea kon*, *Morrh*, *Rusa*, *Tekhu Khuia*, *Kekhi*, Nagel; *Kya-lak*, *Kya-thit*, Burmese; *Klapreung*, Talain; *Kiché-phong*, Karen; *Rimau-bintang*, Malay. The natives seem in some cases to discriminate the two forms, or perhaps the sexes.

HABITAT.—Africa eastward through Asia, including the Indian Empire, extending into Ceylon, where it is miscalled Cheetah by some people. It is absent from parts of Sind and the Punjab, and from Siberia and the highlands of Tibet, though ranging higher in the Himalayas than the tiger. It is also found in Sumatra.

DESCRIPTION.—Sterndale describes the two extreme forms as

Leopard.

follows: Pard * or large leopard: "A clean, long-limbed, though compact body; hair close and short; colour pale fulvous yellow, with clearly defined spots in rosettes; the head more tiger-like than in the next species; the skull is longer and more pointed, with a much-developed occipital ridge. Head and body from 4½ to 5½ ft.; tail from 30 to 38 in."

Panther or small leopard (this name being given to the larger by Jerdon): "Much smaller than the last, with comparatively shorter legs and rounder head; the fur is less bright; the ground-work often darker in colour, and the rosettes are more indistinct, which is caused by the longer hairs intermingling and breaking into the edges of the spots; tail long and furry at the end. Head and body 3 to 3½ ft., tail 2½ ft."

He also says: "My old district had both kinds in abundance, and I have had scores of cubs, of both sorts, brought to me—cubs which could be distinguished at a glance as to which kind they belonged to, but I never remember any mixture of the two," and "Grant their relative sizes, one so much bigger than the other, and the difference in colour and marking, has it ever been known that out of a litter of several cubs by a female of the larger kind, one of the smaller has been produced, or *vice versâ?*"

Blanford, on the other hand, says that he often cannot distinguish the two forms by the examination of skins, and points out that the difference may very often be due to age, young leopards having the rounder skull without occipital ridge, and the rougher fur. Practically all naturalists now unite the two, and it may be suggested that we have to do with an exceptionally variable species, which in some districts is in process of being segregated into two, complete segregation being as yet prevented by frequent interbreeding. Also, the great differences produced in the individual animal by captivity in the case of the lion, which tends to become in this state richer in colour, fuller in coat, and shorter and broader in skull, would seem to indicate that the development of the leopard may be influenced by its mode of life—that a big-game-hunter may become a big animal, while one that lives on small mammals and on birds may fail to reach the same standard of size and form.

Black leopards, which are not uncommon, especially in the hills of Southern India and the Malay Peninsula, are definitely known to be casual "sports" occurring in the same litter as the ordinary spotted kind. Blanford cites a figure of a white one in Buchanan Hamilton's

* Sterndale says the true leopard is the animal now called Cheetah, in which no doubt he is right; but the name leopard is so well established that it cannot be set aside.

drawings, and the editor has seen a skin which was normal except for having the spots light brown instead of black.

Sterndale says of the large variety: "This is a powerful animal and very fierce as a rule, though in the case of a noted man-eater I have known it exhibit a curious mixture of ferocity and abject cowardice. . . . The concurrence of evidence as to the habits of this species is that it is chiefly found in hilly jungles preying upon wild animals, wild pigs and monkeys, but not unfrequently, as I know, haunting the outskirts of villages for the sake of stray ponies and cattle. The largest pard I have ever seen was shot by one of my own shikaris in the act of stalking a pony near a village." With regard to the above-noted man-eater he says: "At Seconee we had one which devastated a tract of country extending to about eighteen miles in diameter. . . . He was at last killed by a native shikari who, in the dusk, took him for a pig or some such animal, and made a lucky shot; but the tale of his victims had swelled over two hundred during the three years of his reign of terror." In fact, until in recent years a tiger put up an even more terrible record, this animal appears to have been the worst man-eater ever known.

Of the smaller variety, Sterndale says: "This animal is more common than the pard, and it is more impudent in venturing into inhabited places. This is fortunate, for it is seldom a man-eater, although perhaps children may be occasionally carried off. I have before mentioned one which killed and partially devoured a pony in the heart of a populous town, and many are the instances of dogs being carried off out of the verandahs of Europeans' houses. A friend of mine one night, being awoke by a piteous howl from a dog chained to the centre pole of his tent, saw the head and shoulders of one peering in at the door; it retreated but had the audacity to return in a few minutes. Jerdon and other writers have adduced similar instances. It is this bold and reckless disposition which renders it easier to trap and shoot. The tiger is suspicious to a degree and always apprehensive of a snare, but the panther never seems to trouble his head about the matter, but walks into a trap or resumes his feast on a previously-killed carcase though it may have been moved or handled. There is little difficulty in shooting a panther on a dark night. All that is necessary is to suspend, some little distance off, a common earthen *gharra* or water-pot, with an oil light inside, the mouth covered lightly with a sod, and a small hole knocked in the side in such a way as to allow a ray of light to fall on the carcase. No tiger would come near such an arrangement, but the panther boldly sets to his dinner without suspicion, probably from his familiarity with the lights in villages.

"I may here digress a little on the subject of night shooting. Every one who has tried it knows the extreme difficulty of seeing the sights of the rifle on a dark night. The common native method is to attach a fluff of cotton wool. On a moonlight night a bit of wax, with powdered mica scattered on it, will sometimes answer. I have seen diamond sights suggested, but all are practically useless. My plan was to carry a small phial of phosphorescent oil, about one grain to a drachm of oil dissolved in a bath of warm water. A small dab of this, applied to the fore and hind sights, will produce two luminous spots which will glow for about forty or fifty seconds or a minute."

Leopards are good climbers, and much more active in springing than tigers, which seldom lift their hind feet off the ground; they are also more courageous, and more independent of water, though they will cross it if necessary.

Their prey consists of practically anything they can capture, and they will often hide part of a kill up in a tree. In attacking they prefer the throat-hold. The note is a short, harsh, repeated, grating sound, rather like sawing wood, but is not often heard.

They have two to four at a birth, and are supposed to take three years to mature. In captivity they are not very tameable, the black variety being usually especially savage.

Ounce or Snow-Leopard.

OUNCE OR SNOW-LEOPARD

OTHER NAMES.—Scientific: *Felis uncia.* Native: *Iker*, Tibetan; *Sah*, Bhotia; *Bharal-hai*, Simla hill-men; *Thurmagh*, Kunawar.

HABITAT.—Altai, Tibet, and high elevations in the Himalayas generally.

DESCRIPTION.—Shorter in face than the ordinary leopard, and with much longer fur, especially on the tail, which is long and almost bushy. Colour whitish or creamy-grey, with much larger black rings than in the leopard, extremities with solid black spots as in that animal. Head and body rather over 4 ft., tail 1 yd.

The snow-leopard frequents rocky ground, generally high up, but has been found as low as 6,000 ft. in winter. It kills both wild and tame sheep and goats, and also attacks dogs and ponies; no instance appears to have been recorded of its attacking man, and it is not known whether it feeds on alpine rodents and birds, though it probably does so—but little is known of its habits, and it is very rare in captivity.

Clouded Leopard or Tiger.

CLOUDED LEOPARD OR TIGER

OTHER NAMES.—Scientific: *Felis macrocelis, diardi*. Native: *Tungmar*, Lepcha; *Lamchitta*, Khas of Nepal; *Rimau dahan*, Malay.

HABITAT.—Hill ranges of South-Eastern Asia from Sikkim and Bhutan to Siam, the Malay Peninsula, and the islands of Sumatra and Borneo. In the Himalayas it is believed not to range above 7,000 ft.

DESCRIPTION.—Generally smaller than the average leopard, and much lower in build, the legs being short; skull long, with longer canines than any of the cats. Body and tail long; fur close and sleek, and with a very distinct pattern of large patches, placed close together and edged behind with black; ground colour grey or buff, the patches darker. Head and limbs with black spots, and tail black-ringed. The colour is said to change from grey to tawny with age. Head and body over a yard in length, tail a yard or less. The pattern reminds one of a python, eyes brown, with a vertically oval pupil.

The Clouded Leopard or Tiger (which is, as a matter of fact, equally distinct from both) is the most arboreal of the large cats, and is said even to sleep in trees. It preys on birds and mammals, but is not known to attack man, and is particularly tameable in captivity. Its dark eyes give it a much less fierce expression than that of other cats, but it might not be wise to place too much reliance on the presumed harmlessness of this and the last species, for, as we shall see, smaller cats have been known to be aggressive.*

Marbled Cat.

MARBLED CAT

OTHER NAMES.—Scientific: *Felis marmorata.* Native: *Sikmar*, Bhutanese; *Dosal*, Lepcha.

* Since this was written an instance of aggression towards man has been recorded.

HABITAT.—Very much the same as that of the last—the hilly portions of South-Eastern Asia and the adjacent islands.

DESCRIPTION.—Very similar to the last in its coloration, with large, close-set, black-edged patches on a lighter ground, with the limbs black-spotted. Ground colour brownish-grey, becoming redder or yellower with age. Head short, as in small cats generally, and size cat-like, not to be compared with a leopard's, the body and head being under 2 ft., and the tail about 14 in. Legs short.

The Marbled Cat bears much the same relation to the Clouded Leopard that the small common leopard does to the large one, except that in this case the differentiation is very complete, and no one could call the two anything but very distinct species. It is said to be shy and fierce in disposition, but nothing else is known of it.

FISHING CAT OR LARGE TIGER-CAT

OTHER NAMES.—Scientific: *Felis viverrina.* Native: *Mach-bagral*, Bengali; *Bágh-dásha*, *Banbiral*, *Khupyah-bágh*, *Báráun*, Hindi; *Handundiva*, Cingalese.

HABITAT.—Bengal, west to Sind, and east to Burma and the Malay Peninsula and South China; base of the Himalayas to Nepal; Malabar coast and Ceylon.

DESCRIPTION.—One of the largest of our lesser cats, much bigger than a tame cat, with longer head and shorter tail. Fur coarse and dull, brownish-grey with long black spots of varying size and distinctness. Head and body 2½ ft. long, tail about a third of this.

The Fishing Cat is a waterside animal, and feeds much on fish and shellfish. It presumably kills birds, and must kill wild mammals also, for it takes tame ones—dogs, sheep, and even calves—while it is also a child-eater on occasion, for it will take off native infants even up to four months old. It is, in fact, one of the fiercest of the cats, a match for several dogs, and Blyth had one which killed a tame young leopardess twice its size, breaking through a cage-partition to do this. Yet, though it is often fierce in captivity, Blyth had several quite tame ones.

The cat which Mason, in his book on Burma, calls the leopard-cat and cites as having attacked a Karen and badly torn his arm, must have been this species and not the next—he says it is as big as a small dog.

LEOPARD-CAT

OTHER NAMES.—Scientific: *Felis bengalensis*—there are too many others to quote, so many varieties of this species having been mistakenly named as species. Native: *Ban biral*, Bengali; *Jungli billi*, *Chita billi*, Hindi ; *Wagati*, Mahratti ; *Thit-kyoung*, Arakanese ; *Kyethit*, *Kya-gyúk*, *Thit-kyuk*, Burmese ; *Kla-hla*, Talain and Karen ; *Rimau-ákar*, Malay.

HABITAT.—Himalayas west to Simla, Western Ghats, Coromandel, Jeypore, Lower Bengal east to the Philippines.

DESCRIPTION.—One of the smallest of cats, sometimes smaller than the tame cat, with a rather short tail. Colour extremely variable, but the coat always spotted, the spots varying in size, shape, and colour, sometimes all black or all brown, sometimes partly black and partly brown, but not amounting to patches like the big 2-in. broad markings of the Marbled Cat. Tail spotted, at any rate above. Ground colour either reddish or greyish. Young pale brown with ill-defined markings. Head and body about 2 ft., tail about 1 ft., but the head and body may be only 16 in., and the tail under 10 in.

The Leopard-Cat is a forest animal, and largely arboreal, sheltering in hollow trees or rocks. It feeds on birds and small mammals, and steals poultry from villages. It is very savage, and few specimens get tame in captivity. It is said to breed in May, and have three or four kittens at a time. It will cross with tame cats, and Blyth considered that some of the grey varieties were produced in this way.

RUSTY SPOTTED CAT

OTHER NAMES.—Scientific : *Felis rubiginosa*. Native : *Namali pilli*, Tamil in Madras ; *Verewa puni*, Tamil in Ceylon ; *Kula diya*, Cingalese.

HABITAT.—Southern India in the Carnatic, Ceylon, and (rarely) Central India.

DESCRIPTION.—As a species the smallest of all cats, though some varieties of the last are equally small. Colour reddish-grey with rusty spots, or, in the case of some in Ceylon, rusty with black spots. Tail not spotted, by which this species may be distinguished from small specimens of the Leopard-Cat.

Length of head and body 18 in. or less, tail about half of that measurement.

The Rusty-Spotted Cat generally frequents grass cover, but may also be found in jungle in some places. Jerdon had one which would hunt for squirrels, and when only eight months old seized a small gazelle fawn as soon as it saw it, and was with difficulty taken off the back of its neck. Sterndale says : "Jerdon doubted the existence of this cat in Central India, but in 1859 or 1860 I had two kittens brought to me by a Gond in the Seeonee district, and I kept them for many months. They became perfectly tame, so much so that, although for nine months of the year I was out in camp they never left the tents, although allowed to roam about unconfined. The grace and agility of their motions was most striking. I have seen one of them balance itself on the back of a chair, and when one of the pair died it was ludicrous to see the attempts of a little grey village cat, which I got to be a companion to the survivor, to emulate the gymnastics of its wild comrade. At night the little cats were put into a basket, and went on with the spare tents to my next halting place; and on my arrival next morning I would find them frisking about the tent roof between the two canvasses, or scrambling up the trees under which we were pitched. Whilst I was at work I usually had one on my lap and the other cuddled behind my back on the chair. One day one of them, which had been exploring the hollows of an old tree close by, rushed into my tent and fell down in convulsions at my feet. I did everything in my power for the poor little creature, but in vain—it died in two or three minutes, having evidently been bitten by a snake. The survivor was inconsolable, refused food, and went mewing all over the place and kept rolling at my feet, rubbing itself against them as though to beg for the restoration of its brother. At last I sent into a village and procured a common kitten, which I put into the basket with the other. There was a great deal of spitting and growling at first, but in time they became great friends, but the villager was no match for the forester. It was amusing to see the wild one dart like a squirrel up the walls of the tent on to the roof; the other would try to follow, scramble up a few feet, and then, hanging by its claws, look round piteously before it dropped to the ground."

The Rusty-Spotted Cat sometimes haunts drains near villages, and is said to cross with tame cats.

Golden Cat.

GOLDEN OR BAY CAT

OTHER NAMES.—Scientific: *Felis temmincki, aurata.*

HABITAT.—South-Eastern Asia, from Nepal east to Borneo.

DESCRIPTION.—A fairly large cat, bigger even than the Fishing-Cat, and longer-tailed. Colour chestnut, striped with white on the face; ears black, chin and under-part of tail white; under-parts generally pale and more or less spotted. There is a dark brown variety in which the under-part of the tail is still white, and in the editor's time the Calcutta Zoo exhibited a specimen which was glossy black all over. Head and body over 30 in., tail 19 in.

Sterndale quotes Hodgson to the effect that his first specimen "was caught in a tree by some hunters in the midst of an exceedingly dense forest. Though only just taken it bore confinement very tranquilly, and gave evident signs of a tractable disposition, but manifested high courage, for the approach of a huge Bhotea dog to its cage excited in it symptoms of wrath only, not of fear." Other specimens, however, seem to be less tractable.

DESERT CAT

OTHER NAMES.—Scientific: *Felis ornata.*

HABITAT.—Western India.

DESCRIPTION.—A short-furred, pointed-eared cat of a pale sandy colour well covered with small black spots; tail about half as long as head and body, ringed and tipped with black. Size of tame cat—head and body about 20 in.

This cat is not found in forest, but is confined to sandy districts. It breeds with tame cats. The so-called Waved Cat (*Felis torquata*) is now considered to be a tame cat run wild. It differs from the last in having rounder ears and sometimes a longer tail, sometimes a greyer colour, and the spots forming vertical cross-bands on the sides; it is like a tame striped tabby, in fact.

BLACK-CHESTED CAT

OTHER NAMES.—Scientific: *Felis manul.*

HABITAT.—Siberia, Mongolia, and Tibet, entering Ladak in Indian territory.

DESCRIPTION.—Although one of the small cats, about the size of the tame animal, this is a most distinct species, with remarkably broad head and short rounded ears, large eyes—of which the pupil contracts in a circle as in most large cats, not in a slit as usual in the smaller ones—and long close thick fur, the tail being quite bushy. Colour pale grey or buff, with the chest black or brown, the sides and tail scantily barred with black and the latter black-tipped; it is about half the length of the head and body, which measure about 19 in.

Palles' Cat, as this animal is often called after its first describer, was said by him to live in rocky country and feed on small mammals; no doubt it takes birds as well. Sterndale's name "Black-chested" is preferable, as it expresses one of the peculiarities of this remarkable species.

COMMON JUNGLE-CAT

OTHER NAMES.—Scientific: *Felis chaus*. *Khatas*, *Jungli billi*, Hindi; *Banberal*, Bengali; *Berka*, Bhagalpur hillmen; *Mant-bek*, Canarese; *Kada* or *Bella-bek*, Wadari; *Baul*, *Bhaga*, *Mota lahu manpir*, Mahratti; *Jurka-pilli*, Telegu; *Cherru puli*, Malabarese; *Kyoung-tset-kun*, Arakanese; *Gúrba-i-kuhi*, Persian; *Katu punai*, Tamil.

HABITAT.—Northern Africa and through Western Asia to India, Ceylon, and Burma; it is generally distributed in India, ascending the Himalayas to at least 8,000 ft.

DESCRIPTION.—Rather larger than a tame cat, and higher on the legs, with a shorter tail. Ears often with a rudimentary tuft. General colour light reddish-grey or greyish-brown, with few or no dark markings except the black tail-tip, and a few rings preceding it. Head and body about 2 ft. long, tail less than 1 ft. Black specimens are occasionally found; it is possible that some at any rate of these are the produce of crosses with tame cats. A hybrid at the London Zoo resembled the *Felis chaus* in size and build, but was otherwise a "red tabby" in all colour points.

On the other hand, many Indian tame cats have the dull pale sandy of this wild animal, which interbreeds with them, as is said to be the case, as we have seen, with several other species. It must be borne in mind, however, that our tame European cats come from a common African species (*Felis caffra*, *maniculata*, *caligata*) which is sometimes coloured just like this common Indian wild cat, though sometimes greyer and striped. Also the appearance of a character properly belonging to another species does not necessarily imply crossing; the editor, among several earthy-coloured tame cats which frequented the Indian Museum compound, observed one with a very short lynx-like tail, complete with black tip (so evidently not mutilated, although with a slight kink), but this was most certainly not indicative of a cross with the Himalayan Lynx!

The name Jungle-Cat—unless "jungle" be taken simply as an adjective meaning "wild"—is misleading for this species, which frequents open country and grass cover, crops, etc., as well as woodland; as Blyth says, "it even affects populous neighbourhoods, and is a terrible depredator among the tame ducks and poultry, but I have not known him attack geese." The immunity of these was no doubt owing to their well-known vigilance—they were kept about a tank, though there ducks were not safe—not so much to their size, as the editor saw a specimen which had been captured on the premises of the late W. Rutledge of Entally, Calcutta, after getting into a shed and killing half a dozen Black Swans. Blyth further says: "A pair of them bred under my house, and I have . . . been surprised at the most extraordinary humming sound which they sometimes uttered of an evening. Their other cries were distinguishable from those of the domestic cat."

Sterndale says: "It is said to be untameable, but in 1859, at Sasseram, one of the men of my Levy caught a very young kitten, which was evidently of this species. I wrote at the time to a friend about a young mongoose which I had just got, and added, 'It is great fun to see my last acquisition and a little jungle cat (*Felis chaus*) playing together. They are just like two children in their manner, romping and rolling over each other, till one gets angry, then there is a quarrel and a fight, which, however, is soon made up, the kitten generally making the first advances towards a reconciliation, and then they go on as merrily as ever. The cat is a very playful, good-tempered little thing; the colour is a reddish-yellow with darker red stripes like a tiger, and slightly spotted; the ears and eyes are very large; the orbits of the last bony and prominent.'" From what has been said above this was probably a hybrid with a tame cat.

The Chaus is the common wild cat of India, and is a terrible enemy to game, small furred and feathered, as well as to poultry; it would also seem to seek aquatic food, as one has been found wading in deep mud. If not so formidable as the larger Fishing Cat, it has been known to charge when wounded. According to Hodgson it produces three or four kittens twice a year.

LYNX

OTHER NAMES.—Scientific: *Felis lynx, isabellina.* Native: *Patsalan*, Kashmiri.

HABITAT.—Northern Hemisphere, ranging into our area in Gilgit and Ladak.

DESCRIPTION.—The largest of our minor cats, thickset but high on the legs, with well-tufted ears, a very short tail, and full drooping whiskers on the cheeks. Eye with round pupil. Coat full and thick, between grey and fawn in colour, often marked, at any rate in summer, with small black spots; tips of ears and tail black. Head and body nearly 1 yd. long, but tail barely 8 in. Indian specimens strongly incline to be spotless.

Lynxes climb well, and are very destructive both to game and to domestic animals; they seem to hunt in pairs, and a couple have accounted for six sheep in a night, while they are active enough to catch pigeons. Although bloodthirsty, they are particularly tameable if taken young; one kept in Calcutta was noticed to have a particular hatred of tame cats.

Caracal.

CARACAL OR RED LYNX

OTHER NAMES.—Scientific: *Felis caracal.* Native: *Siagush*, Hindi; *Ech*, Ladaki.

HABITAT.—Africa, east to Western Asia, and India, where it is mostly confined to the North-West and Central portions, but ranges through the Peninsula except the Malabar coast.

DESCRIPTION.—A rather tall, slight cat of good size, but smaller than the Lynx proper, with a longer tail and short close coat without whiskers on the cheeks, but with very long ear-tufts, the ears themselves being long; the tail about reaches the hocks. Colour fawn or chestnut, with the ears conspicuously black, sometimes grizzled with white. Kittens are coloured like the adults; they chirp like young thrushes.

The Caracal is rare in India, and little is known about its habits there; it is supposed to favour open country, preying on small ruminants and birds, which latter it will bring down by bounds of a couple of yards off the ground. It is generally surly in captivity, and a starving specimen once attacked a coolie in India; yet it is trained for hunting in some parts of India, and is said to be swifter in proportion than the Cheetah.

Cheetah or Hunting Leopard.

CHEETAH OR HUNTING LEOPARD

Other Names.—Scientific: *Felis jubata*, *Cynælurus jubatus*. Native: *Chita*, Hindi; *Yuz* of its former professional catchers (said by Blanford to be a Persian word); *Kendua-bagh*, Bengali; *Chita pulo*, Telegu; *Chircha, Sibungi*, Canarese; *Laggar* in some districts.

Habitat.—Africa east through South-Western Asia to India, where it is now nearly extinct. It was never found in Burma nor in Ceylon, the animal sometimes called Cheetah in that island being the Leopard.*

Description.—One of the "great cats" being about the size of the average leopard, but differing so much in detail that it has generally been given a genus to itself. It is slim and long-legged, long-tailed also, but with a very short head. The claws are blunt, except that of the small first toe on the fore-foot, but not non-retractile, as Blyth pointed out in the 'fifties of last century.

The fur is coarse and dull, short except on the neck and belly, where it is lengthened and shaggy, forming a mane and fringe; the tail is rather bushy towards the tip. Pupil round and iris dark

* Cheetah is simply the Anglicised spelling of "Chita," spotted, and does not especially apply to this animal; but it is now established as its English name.

brown. Colour fawn with small solid black spots, running into partial rings at the tail-tip ; a very characteristic black line running down from each eye to the mouth. Head and body about 4½ ft., tail about 2½ ft.

"Chita kittens," says Sterndale, "are very pretty little things, quite grey, without any spots whatever, but they can always be recognised by the black stripe down the nose, and on cutting off a little bit of the soft hair I noticed that the spots were quite distinct in the under fur. I have not seen this fact alluded to by others. . . . I had several of them at Seonee."

The cheetah is an animal of open dry country, preying chiefly on antelopes of various kinds ; it occasionally takes sheep and goats, but has not been known to attack man. Although it stalks its prey to some extent, its final rush is very long, and for about a furlong or two it seems to be the swiftest of runners, even pulling down the blackbuck or gazelle in a quarter of a mile. If its rush fails, however, it does not continue the chase, and it can be ridden down and speared, having no endurance. It trips up its victim with the fore-foot, and then fastens on its throat.

It used to be largely captured by a class of skilful hunters and trained for antelope coursing, but the editor was told this year (1927) on good authority, that the cheetahs now so used by Indian magnates are all imported from Africa.

Colonel J. C. Faunthorpe, also, writing in this year's (1927) *Field* (p. 426), says : "There is no doubt that the cheetah is now very rare indeed. General Sir Afzul Ul Mulk of Hyderabad told me that there are now no cheetahs in the Hyderabad territories—a very large area. A few survive in the Berar districts of the Central Provinces. It was found in the Central Provinces when Sir John Hewitt was Chief Commissioner. Rajkumar Sadul Singh of Bikanir . . . shot three cheetah out of a bunch of five, or more, which he came across a year or two ago, when motoring, in Rewah State. I believe Lord Hardinge, when Viceroy, also shot one in Rewah, in the same locality some years before. One specimen, which from its skin must have been very old, was killed by villagers in the Mirzapur district (which borders on Rewah) about two years ago. With these exceptions I have not been able to hear of its existence in recent years." It is evidently high time that this poor animal was protected, as the lion is in the Gir forest.

In the wild state it is more sociable than most cats, the family remaining together for some time, and when tamed, although captured in nooses when full-grown, becomes quite friendly. Young animals are supposed to be unsuitable for hunting, lacking natural teaching, but as pets they are just as good. Sterndale says: "Dr. Jerdon describes one which he brought up from its earliest infancy; his bungalow was next to the one I inhabited for a time at Kampti, and consequently I saw a good deal of Billy, as the leopard was named. At our first interview I found him in the stables amongst the dogs and horses, and, as I sat down on his charpoy, he jumped up alongside of me, and lay down to be scratched, playing and purring and licking my hands with a very rough tongue. He sometimes used to go out with his master, and was gradually getting into the way of running down antelope, when Dr. Jerdon was ordered off on field service."

Cheetah (below) and Leopard (above), showing difference in form.

The Hyænas (*Hyænidæ*) are a very small family related to the civets; as we have only one species, distinguished from all our carnivores by having only four toes on each foot, its general characters may be given in the description.

Striped Hyæna.

STRIPED HYÆNA

OTHER NAMES.—Scientific: *Hyæna striata.* Native: *Taras, Hondar, Jhirak, Harvagh, Lakhar-baghar, Lakra,* Hindi; *Naukra-bagh,* Bengali; *Rerha,* Gondi; *Kirba, Kat-kirba,* Canarese; *Dúmul* or *Kórnagúndu,* Telegu; *Cherak,* Sindhi; *Aptar,* Baluchi; *Hebar kula,* Ho Kol; *Derko Tud,* Rajmehal; *Dhopre,* Korku; *Kaluthai-karuchi,* Tamil.

HABITAT.—Northern Africa east through South-West Asia to India generally, but not Ceylon or Burma, and rare in Lower Bengal.

DESCRIPTION.—A large animal, dog-like in general form, with blunt non-retractile claws, but with a striped coat and long moustaches like a cat; and differing much from either in having the fore-legs longer than the hind and a mane all down the neck and back; tail bushy and rather short. Coat coarse and rather rough, dull grey striped with black or brown. Tongue rough as in cats; eyes dark. Skull rather short and strongly ridged, with large blunt grinders. Head and body about 3½ ft., tail about 1½ ft.

The Hyæna is a solitary animal, generally found in open country, haunting rocks and low cover, and hiding by day in caves or in its own burrows. It lives largely on carrion, and even devours bones, its jaws and teeth being so powerful that it has been seen to snap a buffalo's rib asunder with a single effort. Blanford says he once shot one which was carrying off the hind leg of a nilgai to its den. Sterndale says that most wild animals are too active for it, but that it "is very destructive to dogs, and constantly carries off pariahs from the outskirts of villages. The natives declare that the hyæna tempts the dogs out by its unearthly cries, and then falls upon them. . . . The hyæna is of a timorous nature, seldom, if ever, showing fight. Two of them nearly ran over me once as I was squatting on a deer run waiting for sambhar, which were being beaten out of a hill. I flung my hat in the face of the leading one, on which both turned tail and fled." It preys on sheep and goats, but as it takes these less often than dogs, which are so much more able to defend themselves, it cannot be so cowardly as is supposed—it is rather, perhaps, lacking in resource in an emergency. Little is known about its breeding; the cubs are easily tamed, and show a docile and faithful disposition.

The Civet family (*Viverridæ*), which also includes the mongooses, is the most numerously represented and varied group of carnivores, and, with the exception, possibly, of the jackal among the dogs, comprises our most abundant carnivorous species. They are all short-legged and long-tailed animals, with five toes on all feet; the typical civets are like cats with dogs' muzzles, and the mongooses like ferrets. The coarse speckled or "pepper-and-salt" type of fur, however, distinguishes mongooses from any of the weasels, which they much resemble in habits, the civets being more like cats in ways as well as in coat. Like cats, also, they have long conspicuous moustaches. In fact, they are often called civet-cats, and the native name *Khatas* is applied to some of them as well as to the cats proper. Their fur, however, is not really so rich as in the cats, and is little esteemed by furriers.

The most typical civets (*Viverra*) are fairly large animals, bigger than a tame cat, and not so short-legged as the rest of the family. They have a pouch under the tail which secretes the civet perfume, a sort of pasty substance, formerly much valued in Europe as a scent and still esteemed in the East. Their claws are partially retractile, and their backs maned; they are omnivorous and terrestrial in habits.

LARGE INDIAN CIVET

OTHER NAMES.—Scientific: *Viverra zibetha.* Native: *Khatas,* Hindi; *Mach-bhondar, Bágdas, Pudo-ganla,* Bengali; *Bhran,* Nepalese in Terai; *Nit-biralu,* in Nepal; *Kung,* Bhotia; *Saphiong,* Lepcha; *Khyoung-myeng,* Burmese; *Tangalong,* Malay.

HABITAT.—South-Eastern Asia from Nepal east and south to Siam and Southern China; it extends some distance up the Himalayas, and south as far as Orissa and perhaps further.

DESCRIPTION.—Something between a fox and a tabby cat in

appearance, and exceeding the former in size. Fur iron-grey, with the mane down the back black, and the tail black with narrow white rings. Feet black, throat and chest boldly banded with black and white; legs barred with black and grey near the body, sides sometimes faintly marked. Head and body about 2 ft. 8 in., tail $1\frac{1}{2}$ ft.

This civet is a solitary nocturnal animal, hiding by day in grass or scrub. It will eat almost any animal it can catch, warm-blooded or cold, and is destructive to poultry; it also eats roots and fruit. Its scent is followed by dogs more readily than any other animal's: It breeds in May and June, and has from three to five young; if hunted it takes to water readily.

MALABAR CIVET

OTHER NAMES.—Scientific: *Viverra civettina.*

HABITAT.—Malabar coast.

DESCRIPTION.—Differs from the last in having the hind-quarters boldly marked with large black spots, and a black band along the top of the tail joining the black interspaces between the white rings.

BURMESE CIVET

OTHER NAMES.—Scientific: *Viverra megaspila.* Native: *Kyoung-myeng,* Burmese; *Músang-jehat,* Malay.

HABITAT.—Burma east to Sumatra.

DESCRIPTION.—Larger and shorter-tailed than the Indian civet, with the sides generally well-spotted, and the dark rings on the tail no broader than the light ones, and connected above by a black line. Head and body about 1 yd. long, tail barely 18 in.

The habits of this and the last have not been recorded as differing from those of the Indian civet; it is worth mentioning that the name applied by the Burmese to these animals means "horse-cat," which is rather remarkable, as the small head and long deep powerful neck of these big civets do suggest a horse. The whole build and size are reminiscent of the very early equine ancestor which had paws, in the distant ages when carnivores and ungulates were not so sharply differentiated as they have become in the course of their evolution.

The next species is much smaller and slimmer, with no mane.

SMALL INDIAN CIVET OR RASSE

OTHER NAMES.—Scientific: *Viverra* or *Viverricula malaccensis.* Native: *Mashk-billi, Katas, Kasturi,* Hindi (the last name properly belonging to the Musk-deer); *Gandhagokul, Gandogaula,* Bengali; *Jowádi manjur,* Mahratti; *Punagin-bek,* Canarese; *Púnagú pilli,*

Telegu; *Saiyar*, *Bag-nyul*, Nepalese; *Wa-young-kyoung-byouk*, Arakanese; *Kyoung-kado*, Burmese; *Uralama*, Cingalese.

Small Indian Civet.

HABITAT.—Most of India, extending east to the Malayan Islands and South China, but not found in the Punjab, Sind, or Western Rajputana. It is found in Ceylon, Socotra, the Comoro Islands, and

Madagascar, but except in the first-named island, is supposed to have been artificially introduced.

DESCRIPTION.—Not larger than a common cat, and shorter on the legs, with a longer tail. Coat grey or brown, more or less striped and spotted lengthways with black; tail ringed with black and white. Head and body under 2 ft., tail nearly 18 in.

The small civet is a mixed feeder like the larger kinds, but differs in being a climber, and is not so destructive, though often coming near houses.

The Linsangs or Tiger-Civets (*Prionodon*) are a sort of exaggeration of the Rasse type, *very* long-bodied and short-legged, with very long tails and feet with perfectly retractile claws. They are fine climbers and have sleek soft fur, handsomely marked, but not at all like a tiger's. They appear to be purely carnivorous, unlike most civets, but little is known about them. They have no scent-pouch.

INDIAN LINSANG

OTHER NAMES.—Scientific: *Prionodon pardicolor*. Native: *Zik-chum*, Bhotia; *Súliyú*, Lepcha.

HABITAT.—Sikkim to Yunan.

DESCRIPTION.—About as large as a ferret, pale buff with large black spots running in rows down the back and sides; tail with black rings. Head and body about 15 in. long, tail about 1 ft.

The Linsang is said to live in hollow trees, and feed on small birds; it breeds twice a year, having two at each litter.

BURMESE LINSANG

OTHER NAMES.—Scientific: *Prionodon maculosus*.

HABITAT.—Tenasserim.

DESCRIPTION.—Much larger than the last, about equalling a cat in size; fur grey with large black spots, forming bands along the sides; patches on the back forming broad short cross-bands rather than rounded spots as in the last species. Head and body about 18 in. long, tail about 16 in.

This Linsang has only been procured twice, east of Moulmein and at Bánkasún.

The Musangs or Palm-civets (*Paradoxurus*) are also climbers with retractile claws, but not so slim as the other small civets, though very long-tailed. Their tails are not ringed and their fur not very fine or well marked. They are common animals, but so nocturnal that they are not often seen. They have a scent-pouch, but not the full civet odour, and some can emit a very powerful stench from other posterior glands, which, like the previous species, they possess. They are particularly omnivorous, taking much vegetable food, and all equal cats in size. The name Palm-civet is not very appropriate, as

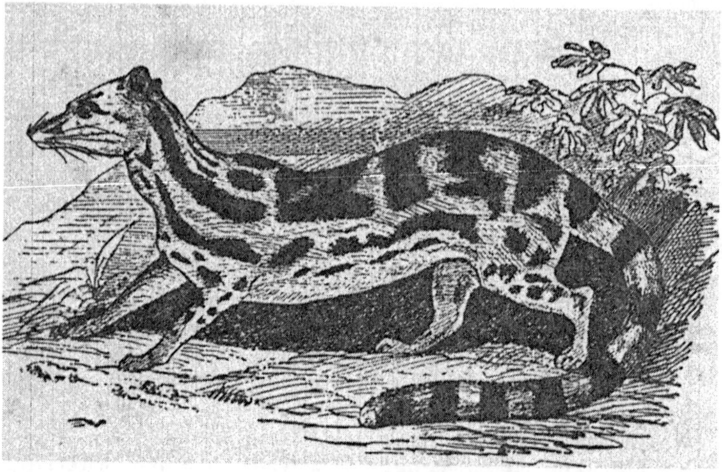

Burmese Linsang.

they do not especially frequent palms; "tree-civet" would be better, but would apply equally well to the three previous species, so it is best to follow Sterndale in using the Malay name Musang, though this appears to be applied to civets generally in Malaysia.

COMMON MUSANG, PALM-CIVET, OR TODDY-CAT

OTHER NAMES.—Scientific: *Paradoxurus musanga, niger, bondar, hermaphroditus*. Native: *Khatas, Menuri, Lakáti, Chingar, Shar-ka-kutta*, Hindi; *Bham, Bhondar*, Bengali; *Ud*, Mahratti; *Kera-hek*, Canarese; *Manu-pilli*, Telegu; *Togot*, Singhbhum; *Kyoung-won-baik, -na-ga*, Burmese; *Khabbo-palaing*, Talain; *Sapo-mi-aing*, Karen; *Musang*, Malay.

HABITAT.—South-Eastern Asia and its adjacent islands, from India and Ceylon to Borneo, but not in the Punjab or Sind.

DESCRIPTION.—About 20 in. in length of head and body, with tail nearly as long; fur coarse, grey and black, varying much in length and colour; in the Indian race it is long and ragged, an indistinct mixture of black and grey, the lighter colour sometimes rather brownish. Muzzle and extremities usually more or less black; young often more or less striped or spotted.

The Burmese race has shorter and closer fur, with the body more or less distinctly striped or spotted on a more or less pure grey ground. In both the tip of the tail may be white. The black mask and the absence of rings on the tail will distinguish this spotted form from the Rasse. The two varieties are ranked by Blanford as distinct species, but he admits this is merely a matter of convenience, so many specimens in Eastern India being intermediate.

Sterndale, who treats them as one, says: "This is a very common animal in India, frequently to be found in the neighbourhood of houses, attracted no doubt by poultry, rats, mice, etc. It abounds in the suburbs of Calcutta, taking up its abode sometimes in outhouses or in secluded parts of the main building. During the years 1865–66 a pair inhabited a wooden staircase in the Lieutenant-Governor's house at Alipore (Belvedere). We used to hear them daily, and once or twice I saw them in the dusk, but failed in all my attempts to trap them. That part of the building has since been altered, so I have no doubt the confiding pair have since betaken themselves to other quarters. In a large banyan tree in my brother's garden at Alipore there is a family at the present time [? 1884, the date of publication of Sterndale's original work], the junior members of which have lately fallen victims to a greyhound, who is often on the look-out for them. As yet the old ones have had the wisdom to keep out of his way.

"They are very easily tamed. I had one for a time at Seeonee which had been shot at and wounded, and I was astonished to find how soon it got accustomed to my surgical operations. Whilst under treatment I fed it on eggs. In confinement it is better to accustom it to live partly on vegetable food, rice and milk, etc., with raw meat occasionally. Its habits are nocturnal. I cannot affirm from my own experience that it is partial to the juice of the palm-tree, for *toddy* (or *tari*) is unknown in the Central Provinces, and I have had no specimens alive since I have been in Bengal, but it has the character of being a toddy-drinker in those parts of India where the toddy-palms grow; and Kellaart confirms the report. It is arboreal in its habits, and climbs with great agility."

The editor has seen it run up a water-pipe in the angle of two walls of the Indian Museum buildings, and trapped two (probably a pair) in the pantry of his quarters there in box-traps—they had been pulling a tin bread-box about and betraying themselves by the noise. He also often found their droppings, full of the seeds of the peepul fig, on the balustrade of the verandah, so that up to the end of the last century, at any rate, the animal was found about Calcutta houses. It is not, however, especially a parasite on man, but is also found in forests, and is probably the most numerous of all Indian carnivores, being so adaptable. It brings forth four to six young. As it eats snakes as well as rats, it deserves protection if provisions, poultry, and garden produce can be preserved from its attacks, which might be done by feeding it on cooked table scraps; an animal with its instinct for self-domestication deserves encouragement, and is no doubt intelligent and worthy of study.

HILL MUSANG OR HIMALAYAN PALM-CIVET

OTHER NAMES.—Scientific: *Paradoxurus grayi.*

HABITAT.—Himalayas from Simla to Nepal, Arakan and the Andamans.

DESCRIPTION.—Larger and longer-tailed than the common plains species, both head and body and tail being about 2 ft., with softer, thicker, and smoother fur, which is plain grey or fawn, but with the face very dark and marked with grizzled whitish streaks.

In fact, the plan of colouring is somewhat like that of the Burmese Ferret-badger, but this is much smaller, with much shorter and bushy tail, and non-retractile claws. This Musang is more addicted to fruit-eating than the common species, and in the Andamans is destructive to pine-apples. The local pigmies eat it, but appear not to use its skin even when they feel the need of clothing.

CEYLONESE OR GOLDEN MUSANG

OTHER NAMES.—Scientific: *Paradoxurus zeylanicus, aureus.* Native: *Kula-wedda*, Cingalese.

HABITAT.—Ceylon.

DESCRIPTION.—A little smaller than the common Indian species, with a decidedly shorter tail. Fur fairly close and soft, chestnut in colour.

Like the last species, this is very partial to fruit.

BROWN MUSANG OR PALM-CIVET

OTHER NAMES.—Scientific: *Paradoxurus jerdoni.* Native: *Kárt-nai*, Malabarese.

HABITAT.—Palni hills and Nilgiris.

DESCRIPTION.—Like the last, smaller and shorter-tailed than the common Musang; fur smoother, dark brown, grizzled on back, and the tail often white-tipped.

Small-toothed Musang.

SMALL-TOOTHED OR WHITE-EARED MUSANG

OTHER NAMES.—Scientific: *Paradoxurus* or *Arctogale leucotis* or *trivirgatus*. Native: *Kyoung-na-ga*, Tenasserim; *Kyoung-na-zwet-phyu*, Arakanese; *Musang-ákar*, Malay.

HABITAT.—Sylhet east to Java.

DESCRIPTION.—This species is sometimes separated as a distinct genus (*Arctogale*) from our other Musangs, on account of its much smaller teeth (except the canines), though in length of head and body and tail (about 2 ft. each) it equals any of them; the first or inner toes on its feet are also further separated from the other digits than in any of the rest. Fur short and soft, brown or grey, with three more or less distinct black bands or rows of spots down the back; extremities black, the face often with a white streak and white tips to the ears.

Little is known about this species except what Sterndale says about a tame one: "I had a specimen of this Paradoxurus given to me early in the cold season of 1881 by Dr. W. Forsyth. I brought it home to England with me, and it is now [? 1884] in the Zoological Society's Gardens in Regent's Park. It was very tame when Dr. Forsyth brought it, but it became more so afterwards, and we made a great pet of it. It used to sleep nearly all day on a bookshelf in my study, and would, if called, lazily look up, yawn, and then come down to be petted, after which it would spring up again into its retreat. At night it was very active, especially in bounding from branch to branch of a tree which I had cut down and placed in the room in which it was locked up every evening. Its wonderful agility on ropes was greatly noticed on board ship. Its favourite food was plantains, and it was also very fond of milk. At night I used to give it a little meat, but not much; but most kinds of fruit it seemed to like.

"Its temper was a little uncertain, and it seemed to dislike natives, who sometimes got bitten; but it never bit any of my family, although one of my little girls used to catch hold of it by the fore-paws and dance it about like a kitten. Its carnivorous nature showed itself one day by its pouncing upon a tame pigeon. The bird was rescued, and is alive still, but it was severely mauled before I could rescue it, having been seized by the neck." This account suggests that the species is mainly a fruit-eater; a thorough carnivore would have settled the unfortunate pigeon at once. Small finches thus seized by an Indian Vampire the editor kept died instantly without a struggle when gripped by the bat, which then bit off and dropped the head.

The very curious beast next to follow is the only member of its genus (*Arctictis*), so its characters can be fully given in the description of the species.

Binturong.

BINTURONG OR BEAR-CAT

OTHER NAMES.—Scientific: *Arctictis binturong*. Native: *Untarong*, Malay; *Myouk-kya*, Burmese; *Young*, Assamese.

HABITAT.—South-East Asia and its adjacent islands, from Assam to Java.

DESCRIPTION.—About the size of a pariah dog, but with short legs and a very long tail; head short and broad, but with a narrow muzzle; eyes and ears small, but the latter with long lynx-like tufts. Fur coarse and ragged, longest on the tail, black in colour, but more or less grizzled, especially on the fore-quarters; young with grey or rusty tippings to the fur. Head and body about 2½ ft., tail nearly as long. Claws partly retractile.

The tail is prehensile, a unique peculiarity among our mammals; the gait is plantigrade, and the movements not very quick.

The animal is omnivorous, devouring fruit and all sorts of animals, even fish and worms—how it gets these last two articles of food it would be interesting to know, as it has not the look of a fisher or digger, but is well adapted for climbing. It lives, as a matter of fact, on trees in forests, coming out at night. It is said to have a loud howl—a curious peculiarity, for the civets as a group are remarkably silent animals.

Though said to be fierce, it is very tameable, but is not common in captivity, and nothing is known about its breeding.

The name Bear-cat applied to it is undesirable, as leading to confusion with the Panda or Cat-bear already described.

The Mongooses or Ichneumons (*Herpestes*) are very distinct from all the other animals of the civet family we have been reviewing. As has been said, they look more like ferrets than cats, and they are also weasel-like in their habits, showing great activity and a very bloodthirsty nature. Unlike weasels, they have not conspicuous moustaches, and when in motion trot instead of galloping. They nearly always have grizzled fur, and this is coarse, and longest at the base of the tail, a peculiarity which distinguishes them not only from weasels, but from all our other animals. Their ears are small, their eyes small and light-coloured, not dark as in typical civets, and their claws strong and not at all retractile. They are as much diurnal as nocturnal, and live on the ground, though able to climb trees on occasion. They are intelligent and easily tamed, and two species are well known in captivity, one of which at any rate has a great reputation as a snake-killer and ratter.

COMMON GREY MONGOOSE

OTHER NAMES.—Scientific: *Herpestes mungo, pallidus, griseus.* Native: *Mangús, Newal, Nyul, Dhor, Rasu,* Hindi; *Mungli,* Canarese; *Yentama,* Telegu; *Koral,* Gondi; *Kiri,* Tamil; *Mugatea,* Cingalese; *Binguidaro, Sarambumbui,* Ho Kol.

HABITAT.—India and Ceylon. Introduced into some of the West Indian and Pacific islands.

DESCRIPTION.—About as big as a ferret, but with a much longer tail. Fur grizzly-grey, rather rough, often rusty on head and feet (where it is short), and sometimes throughout. Eyes reddish-brown, claws dark brown. Head and body about 16 in., tail a little less.

"This animal," says Sterndale, "is familiar to most English residents in the Mofussil; it is, if unmolested, fearless of man, and will, even in its wild state, enter the verandahs and rooms of houses. In one house I know a pair would not only boldly lift the bamboo chicks and walk in, but in time were accompanied by a young family. When domesticated they are capable of showing as much attachment as a dog. One that I had constantly with me for three years died of grief during a temporary separation, having refused food from the time I left. I got it whilst on active service during the Indian Mutiny, when it was a wee thing, smaller than a rat. It travelled with me on horseback in an empty holster, or in a pocket, or up my sleeve; and afterwards, when my duties as a settlement officer took me out into camp, 'Pips' was my constant companion. He knew perfectly well when I was going to shoot a bird for him. He would stand up on his hind legs when he saw me present the gun, and rush for the bird when it fell; he had, however, no notion of retrieving, but would scamper off with his prey to devour it at leisure. He was a most fearless little fellow, and once attacked a big greyhound, who beat a retreat. In a rage his body would swell to nearly twice its size from the erection of the hair, yet I had him under such perfect subjection that I had only to hold up my finger to him when he was about to attack anything, and he would desist. I heard a great noise one day outside my room, and found Master 'Pips' attacking a fine male specimen I had of the great bustard, *Eupodotis edwardsi*, and had just seized it by the throat. I rescued the bird, but it died of its injuries. Through the carelessness of one of my servants he was lost one day in a heavy brushwood jungle some miles from my camp, and I quite gave up all hopes of recovering my pet. Next day, however, in tracking some antelope, we happened to cross the route taken by my servants, when we heard a familiar little yelp, and down from a tree we were under rushed 'Pips.' He went to England with me after that, and was the delight of all the sailors on board, for his accomplishments were varied; he could sit in a chair with a cap on his head, shoulder arms, ready, present, fire!—turn somersaults, jump, and do various other little tricks.

"From watching him I observed many little habits belonging to these animals. He was excessively clean, and after eating would pick his teeth with his claws in a most absurd manner. I do not know whether a mongoose in a wild state will eat carrion, but he would not touch anything tainted, and, though very fond of freshly-cooked game, would turn up his nose at high partridge or grouse. He was very fond of eggs, and, holding them in his fore-paws, would crack a little hole at the small end, out of which he would suck the contents. He was a very good ratter, and also killed many snakes against which I pitted him. His way seemed to be to tease the snake into darting at him, when, with inconceivable rapidity, he would pounce on the reptile's head. He seemed to know instinctively which were the poisonous ones, and acted with corresponding caution. I tried him once with some sea-snakes (*Hydrophis pelamoides*), which are poisonous, but he could get no fight out of them, and crunched their heads off one after the other. I do not believe in the mongoose being proof against snake poison, or in the antidote theory. Their extreme agility prevents their being bitten, and the stiff rigid hair, which is erected at such times, and a thick loose skin, are an additional protection. I think it has been proved that if the poison of a snake is injected into the veins of a mongoose it proves fatal. The female produces from three to four young at a time.

"The cry of the mongoose is a grating mew, varied occasionally by a little querulous yelp, which seems to be given in an interrogative sort of way when searching for anything. When angry it growls most audibly for such a small beast, and this is generally accompanied by a bristling of the hair, especially of the tail."

Sterndale was right in supposing that the mongoose is not proof against snake poison, but it appears to succumb less readily than other small animals. It eats fruit and insects as well as mammals, birds, and reptiles, and makes burrows to live in. It is not only almost the most familiar of our carnivores at large, but is very well known in England as a pet and ratter, and has been introduced into several West Indian and Pacific islands.

RUDDY OR LONG-TAILED MONGOOSE

Other Names.—Scientific: *Herpestes smithi*, *jerdoni*, *monticolus*. Native: *Konda yentana*, Telegu; *Erimakiri-pilai*, Tamil; *Dito*, Cingalese.

Habitat.—Indian Peninsula and Ceylon.

Description.—Fur rather coarse and rough, tail about as long as head and body, with a long black tip. Colour grizzled, either grey or reddish, tail before the tip red. Size variable, but generally considerably larger than common mongoose.

This mongoose is mostly a forest animal.

SMALL INDIAN OR GOLD-SPECKLED MONGOOSE

OTHER NAMES.—Scientific: *Herpestes auropunctatus.* Native: *Mush-i-khourma*, Persian; *Nul*, Kashmiri.

HABITAT.—Mesopotamia east through Northern India to Upper Burma.

DESCRIPTION.—The smallest of our mongooses, and of sleek appearance; it compares with the common species much as a stoat with a polecat. Colour grizzled-brown or grey, the grey specimens being found in the west, as in Sind, which is curious, because it is there that the reddish variety of the common mongoose most often occurs. Head and body about 11 in. long, tail about 8 in.

This animal is as common in captivity as the common mongoose, and no doubt the single specimens of each which were obtained by Cantor in the Malay Peninsula many years ago had been imported; but little is on record about it in the wild state. The editor, though familiar with it in the Calcutta bazaar and in dealers' shops in England, never saw it wild, though he has seen the common species at large in the Calcutta Zoo at Alipore. In captivity in a shop it spits at intruders like a cat, while the common Mongoose remains quiet.

SMALL BURMESE MONGOOSE

OTHER NAMES.—Scientific: *Herpestes birmanicus.*

HABITAT.—Cachar, Manipur, and Pegu, probably Lower Burma generally.

DESCRIPTION.—Much like the last, but dark grizzled brown, and larger, being intermediate in size between it and the common mongoose. Head and body about 14 in. long, tail about 9 in.

NILGIRI BROWN MONGOOSE

OTHER NAMES.—Scientific: *Herpestes fuscus.*

HABITAT.—Hills of Southern India.

DESCRIPTION.—Size generally larger than Common Mongoose, fur not so coarse, dark grizzled brown, tail and feet especially dark. Head and body 18 in., tail nearly as long.

Like the Ruddy Mongoose, this is a woodland form.

CEYLON BROWN MONGOOSE

OTHER NAMES.—Scientific: *Herpestes fulvescens.* Native: *Ram-mugatea*, Cingalese.

HABITAT.—Ceylon.

DESCRIPTION.—Averaging smaller than common mongoose, tail

proportionately shorter; grizzled brown in colour, generally dark. Bare sole of hind-foot not extending to hock as it does in the common mongoose; in this point it agrees with the last species, of which it seems to be simply a small southern race

Stripe-necked Mongoose.

STRIPE-NECKED MONGOOSE

OTHER NAMES.—Scientific: *Herpestes vitticollis*. Native: *Loko-mugatea*, Ceylon.

HABITAT.—Ceylon and the hills of the west coast of India.

DESCRIPTION.—The largest of our mongooses, as big as a cat, and easily distinguished by the black stripe down each side of the neck; the tail has also a long black tip as in the Long-tailed Mongoose, but is much shorter proportionally than in that species. Fur grizzly grey on the head and sometimes elsewhere, but the body, or at any rate the hind part, more often rusty-red without grizzling. Head and body over 20 in. long, but tail not more than 15 in.

The Stripe-necked Mongoose is not uncommon on the Nilgiris, hunting by day, and sometimes at any rate in pairs.

Crab-eating Mongoose.

CRAB-EATING MONGOOSE

OTHER NAMES.—Scientific: *Herpestes urva, Urva cancrivora.* Native: *Arva,* Nepalese.

HABITAT.—Himalayas east to South China, not ranging high up.

DESCRIPTION.—The most distinct of our mongooses, large and rather thick-set and badger-like, with long, coarse, rough iron-grey fur frosted with white tips; but the most striking point is the white stripe along each side of the neck; feet dark or even black. Head and body about 20 in. long, tail about 1 ft.

Although distinctly approaching a badger in appearance, this mongoose is more like an otter in habits, as it feeds on frogs and crabs, and is somewhat aquatic. It has the skunk-like trick of ejecting a foul-smelling fluid from its large anal glands.

The Dogs (*Canidæ*) are, as remarked in the introduction, easily identified by their resemblance to the common pariah dog; otherwise they are not easy to describe, being remarkably well-proportioned animals, with no part of the body strikingly developed, though the bushy tail is noticeable. In their long muzzles they agree with the typical civets, and in having only four toes on the hind-foot,* and the first toe of the fore-foot reduced and elevated, with the cats; but their claws, though strong, are blunt and non-retractile. Their legs are longer than those of nearly all our other carnivora, and they are good and enduring runners. They live on the ground, taking shelter in holes, and are not strictly diurnal or nocturnal. The larger kinds are more or less gregarious, the smaller, or foxes, solitary. They

* Some domestic dogs often have the inner toe on the hind-foot (dew-claw) developed, but it is loosely attached and often double.

are very intelligent, and hold their own with man well on the whole. The common Wolf and Jackal are the most typical.

Wolf.

WOLF

OTHER NAMES.—Scientific: *Canis lupus, pallipes, laniger.* Native: *Bheria,* Northern and Central India; *Bighana, Hondár,* Bundelkhund; *Lándgá,* Gond and Dakhani; *Tola,* Canarese; *Toralu,* Telegu; *Gúrg,* Persian; *Kharma,* Brahui; *Ratnahun,* Kashmir; *Chángú,* Tibetan.

HABITAT.—Northern parts of Northern Hemisphere, including India generally, but not Ceylon or Burma.

DESCRIPTION.—From a large to a medium (pariah)-sized dog in size, with a bushy tail, rather less than half length of head and body. The Indian race is of the smaller size and has a closer, thinner coat than the large wolves of the north, the Tibetan wolves being especially thick and woolly-coated. This variety is found in Ladak; the European wolf in Gilgit, Sind, and Baluchistan.

Colour between grey and buff, more or less clouded with black, Indian specimens being browner than the western type, and the Tibetan form palest, though on the other hand it sometimes produces a black variety. Cubs are sooty-brown with a white patch on the chest. Eyes usually yellow, not brown as in most dogs, but the editor has seen brown eyes in three specimens, two from Arabia and one from Mesopotamia; the small Indian race of wolf seems to spread through Western Asia into Egypt, where it is called a jackal, though Herodotus (who must have known our jackal, which extends through Asia Minor to Greece) called it a small wolf. At any rate, this small warm-climate wolf is the main ancestor of the tame dog, which in some specimens of the Alsatian breed closely resembles it.

Head and body of the Indian race about a yard long, tail nearly half of this; any wolf much over this size belongs to the typical race which has always been *the* wolf, and such specimens may be nearly 4 ft. long in head and body.

As Sterndale says: " Wolves vary greatly in colour. Every one who has seen much of them will bear witness to this. . . . In India one seldom hears of their attacking grown-up men. I remember an instance in which an old woman was a victim; but hundreds of children are carried off annually especially in Central India and the North-West Provinces.

" Stories have been related of wolves sparing and suckling young infants so carried off. . . . The story of the nursing is not improbable, for well-known instances have been recorded of the *feræ*, when deprived of their young, adopting young animals, even of those on whom they usually prey. Cats have been known to suckle young leverets."

Mr. E. C. Stuart Baker has recorded in the Bombay Natural History Society's *Journal* a case of a leopardess carrying off and fostering a child, and the editor quite agrees with Sterndale as to the possibility of wild-animal fosterage of infants, which seem, according to all the accounts, to become hopelessly animal in nature.

Although the wolf kills and eats its descendant the dog, like all other domestic animals it can overpower, fraternisation and interbreeding between the two sometimes occur.

Sterndale says also: " Wolves do, I think, get light-coloured with great age. I remember once having one brought into my camp for the usual reward by a couple of small boys, the elder not more than ten or twelve years of age, I should think. The beast was old and emaciated, and very light-coloured, and, doubtless impelled by hunger, attacked the children, as they were herding cattle, with a view to dining off them; but the elder boy had a small axe, such as is commonly carried by the Gonds, and, manfully standing his ground, split the wolf's skull with a blow—a feat of which he was justly proud."

In India the wolf, though often hunting in couples, appears not to associate in larger packs than six or eight—probably family parties; it is seldom found away from open dry country, and, according to Mr. A. A. Dunbar Brander, writing in *The Field* for 1927, p. 506, has become of late years very rare in many places where it was once common. There is nothing to regret in this, for the wolf is a pest to game as well as domestic stock, to say nothing of its being a continual danger to man, for it helps to spread hydrophobia as well as being a foe to children.

JACKAL

OTHER NAMES.—Scientific: *Canis aureus*. Native: *Srigala*, Sanskrit; *Gidhar*, *Shial*, Hindi; *Kolá*, Mahratti; *Nari*, Canarese; *Nakka*, Telegu; *Nerka*, Gondi; *Shigal*, Persian; *Amu*, Bhotia; *Mye-khwe*, Burmese; *Naria*, Cingalese; *Laraiya*, Bundelkand; *Shal*, *Sháaj* (for male and female), Kashmiri; *Tolágh*, Baluchi; *Karincha*, Ho Kol; *Hiyál*, Assamese; *Meshrong*, Kachari; *Hijai*, *Joksat*, Mikiri; *Hian*, Naga.

HABITAT.—South-Eastern Europe east to Burma, including all India and Ceylon.

DESCRIPTION.—Smaller than an ordinary pariah dog and with shorter ears and tail, the latter bushy, but not more than about a third of the length of the head and body, which measure from 2 ft. to 2 ft. 6 in. in length. Colour tan, with a mixture of black above; tip of tail black. Black, white, and tan varieties have been found.

The wolf is sometimes as dark and red as the jackal, but its much larger size and proportionately longer tail and ears will always distinguish it. Sterndale says: "The jackal is one of our best known animals, both as a prowler and a scavenger, in which capacity he is useful, and as a disturber of our midnight rest by his diabolical yells, in which peculiarity he is to be looked upon as an unmitigated nuisance.

"He is mischievous too occasionally, and will commit havoc amongst poultry and young kids and lambs, but, as a general rule, he is a harmless, timid creature, and when animal food fails he will take readily to vegetables. Indian corn seems to be one of the things chiefly affected by him; the fruit of the wild ber-tree (*Zizyphus jujuba*) is another, as I have personally witnessed. In Ceylon he is said to devour large quantities of ripe coffee-berries; the seeds, which pass through entire, are carefully gathered by the coolies, who get an extra fee for the labour, and are found to be the best for germination, as the animal picks the finest fruit. According to Sykes he devastates the vineyards in the west of India, and is said to be partial to sugar-cane. The jackal is credited with digging corpses out of the shallow graves, and devouring bodies. I once came across the body of a child in a jungle village which had been unearthed by one. At Seeonee we had, at one time, a plague of mad jackals, which did much damage. Sir Emerson Tennant writes of a curious horn or excrescence which grows on the head of the jackal occasionally, which is regarded by the Singhalese as a potent charm, by the instrumentality of which every wish can be realised, and stolen property will return of its own accord! This horn, which is called *Narricomboo,* is said to grow only on the head of the leader of the pack.

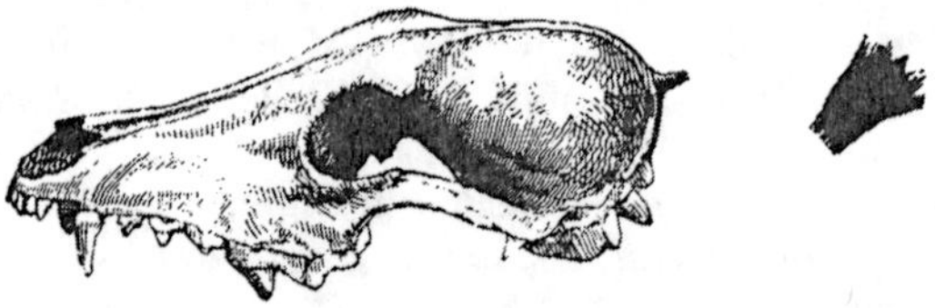

Skull of Jackal, showing bony core of "horn," and detail of latter, showing through the hair.

"The domestic dog is supposed to owe its origin to this species, as well as to the wolf, but all conjecture on this point can be but pure speculation. Certain it is that the pariahs about villages are strikingly like jackals, at least in many cases, and they will freely interbreed." The hybrids are also fertile, at any rate with the dog, but the fact that the wolf sometimes barks like a pariah dog, while the jackal's howl, "Dead Hindoo, where, where—where, where—where, where!" is quite unlike any noise made by any dog, is one argument against any great infusion of jackal blood, to say nothing of the different proportions of tail and ears in the jackal from those of primitive dogs.

The editor has, however, seen an Indian jackal at the Zoo run to and fro for some time with one hind leg tucked up, a common trick in small domestic dogs; it would be interesting to know if this occurs in other canines. The "Pheal" cry of the jackal is apparently an alarm note, occasioned by the proximity of a tiger or leopard, the latter of which is certainly an enemy. The young are brought forth in some hole, and are four in number.

Jackals do not range far up the Himalayas, except near hill stations, and are not so common east of Bengal as in India proper, or found further south of Moulmein. They much affect human habitations, and in the 'nineties; at any rate, were common even in Calcutta; the editor has bolted one from a drain under his front door in the official quarters of the Indian Museum.

The so-called "Wild Dog" which, unlike the wolf and jackal, is not a near relative of the tame dog, has a genus (*Cyon*) of its own.

DHOLE OR WILD DOG

Other Names.—Scientific: *Cyon dukhunensis, rutilans.* Native: *Jungli-kutta*, *Son-kutta*, *Ban-kutta*, *Ram-kutta*, Hindi; *Kolsun*, *Kolasna*, *Kolsa* and *Kolasra*, Mahratti; *Reza-kutá*, *Adavi-kútá*, Telegu; *Shin-nai*, Malabarese; *Eram-naiko*, Gond; *Sakki-sarai*, Hyderabad; *Ramhun*, Kashmiri; *Siddaki*, *Hazi*, *Phari*, Tibetan; *Sá-tum*, Lepcha; *Paoho*, Bhotia; *Bhaosa*, *Bhúnsa*, *Buánsú*, Himalayan tribes; *Taukhwe*, Burmese; *Anjing-utan*, Malay.

Habitat.—Eastern Tibet through the Himalayas south-east through Burma and the Malay Peninsula to Borneo; also Indian Peninsula, but not Ceylon.

Description.—Varies in size and thickness in coat according to district, like the wolf, but is never so large as the bigger wolves, or so small as the jackal. Ears rounded, furry, tail more bushy than in the wolf and jackal; hair between the toes. Not so smartly built as the above two, large-footed, and standing lower at the shoulders than the croup. Teeth fewer than in the typical dogs, the last lower grinders being absent; teats more numerous than ten, which is the typical dog number.

Colour bright rust-red (whence the name Red Dog) with a long purple-black tip to the brush, sometimes containing a more or less pronounced white tuft. Some specimens, however, are duller, even to brownish-grey, but the greater hairiness of the ears, feet, and tail will distinguish these from wolves. Pups are dark sooty-brown.

Head and body about 1 yd. long in the Indian race, tail over 1 ft.; in the Malayan race, which is also much slenderer and thinner-coated, only a little over 2½ ft. The Siberian Dhole, which is larger than the Indian, and pale fawn with very thick fur in winter, is said to be red in summer, and, though there are some small differences in the teeth, may really only bear the same relation to our Dhole as the Siberian Tiger, with its thick pale winter fur, does to the Indian animal.

The wild dog inhabits forest, except in the Upper Indus Valley, where there is none; it is more sociable than the wolf, uniting in packs of from six to twenty in number; the females also sometimes at any rate breed in society, their litters being from two to six in number. Sterndale says: "During my residence in the Seeonee district from 1857 to 1864, I only came across them two or three times. . . . We once heard a very circumstantial account given of a fight, which took place near the station of Seeonee, between a tiger and a pack of these dogs, in which the latter were victors. They followed him about cautiously, avoiding too close a contact, and worried him for three successive days—a statement which should be received with caution. We have, however, heard of them annoying a tiger to such an extent as to make him surrender to them the prey he had killed for himself."

Colonel J. C. Faunthorpe, writing in *The Field* for 1927 (p. 426) says that it is well known that these animals hunt and kill leopards, and expresses his belief in the native story that they kill tigers also. There is no doubt that they are excessively destructive to game, and sometimes to domestic animals, even buffaloes not being safe from them; their method is apparently for some to tear the animal open from behind, while others make a frontal attack. A sambhar stag has been known to have nine inches of his windpipe torn out by a bite, and a Himalayan black bear to be baited till he was shot out of mercy by the witness of the struggle. Although hardly any instance is known of the Indian Dhole attacking man, it fears him little, and the large Siberian race is considered dangerous, so that there is every reason to keep down "red dogs" wherever found. They cannot even claim utility as scavengers, as they hunt for themselves, and soon clear game out of a district. They are very hard to tame, and rarely seen in captivity, but have bred in the London Zoo.

Colonel Faunthorpe suggests that the rapid extermination of the cheetah is due to wild dogs, and, although it has been objected to this that the cheetah inhabits open country and the dhole forest, it must be remembered that the latter can at need hunt in the open, while the cheetah's speed is not lasting, and it is not so good a climber as the leopard.

The Foxes are given a genus to themselves (*Vulpes*) by some naturalists; and certainly our species at any rate stand apart from the previously mentioned canines in their shorter limbs and longer tail—always at least half as long as the head and body and very bushy—as also in their vertical pupil and moustaches well-developed as in cats, which they resemble in being solitary and to some extent in their hunting habits. They are always smaller than the jackal, and feed mostly on birds, small mammals, insects, and fruit.

INDIAN FOX

OTHER NAMES.—Scientific: *Vulpes bengalensis*. Native: *Lomri*, *Lokri*, Hindi; *Kokri*, Mahratti; *Khekar*, *Khikir*, Behar; *Kheksiyal*, Bengali; *Konk*, *Kemp-nari*, *Chandak-nari*, Canarese; *Konka-* or *Gunta-nakka*, *Poti-nara*, Telegu.

HABITAT.—India only, not ascending the hills, or frequenting forest.

DESCRIPTION.—Only about as large as a cat, with large ears and slender nose and limbs, which are more or less rusty, the rest of the fur being grey more or less tinged with reddish; this tinge varies with locality and season, the colour being greyer, as well as the fur longer, in the cold weather. Tip of brush black. Head and body about 20 in., tail about 1 ft.

Sterndale says: "This fox is common, not only in open country, but even in cantonments and suburbs of cities. Hardly a night passes without its familiar little chattering bark in the Dalhousie Square Gardens, or on the Maidan [in Calcutta], being heard; and few passengers running up and down our railway lines, who are on the look-out for birds and animals as the train whirls along, fail to see in the early morning our little grey friend sneaking home with his brush trailing behind him. . . . It also, like the jackal, will eat fruit, such as melons, ber, etc., and herbs. It breeds in the spring, from February to April, and has four cubs. . . . It is much coursed with greyhounds, and gives most amusing sport, doubling constantly till it gets near an earth; but it has little or no smell, so the scent does not lie." When doubling, the fox raises its tail erect; as its scentlessness and its numerous earths put it out of court for ordinary hunting, the jackal is the animal hunted with hounds in India. It is easily tamed, but said to be liable to hydrophobia.

The Indian fox does little harm to poultry, its usual food being rats, lizards, land-crabs, insects, etc., and no doubt small birds. It may not be so common now as Sterndale found it, for the editor never once saw it in seven years in India, though he often noted jackals (always singly) when travelling by rail in the 'nineties.

HOARY FOX

OTHER NAMES.—Scientific: *Vulpes cana*. Native: *Poh*, Baluchi; *Kúrba-shákál*, Persian.

HABITAT.—Baluchistan and South Afghanistan.

DESCRIPTION.—The smallest of our canines, less than the Indian fox, but with a longer tail. Colour grey, including the outside of the ears, which may be dark brown in the Indian fox; forehead and sometimes limbs reddish. Tip of brush black. Head and body 18 in., tail about 14 in. Only two specimens of this fox have been obtained, at Gwadar and at Kandahar.

DESERT FOX

OTHER NAMES.—Scientific: *Vulpes leucopus.* Native: *Lúmri*, *Lokri*, Hindi; *Lombar*, Baluchi; *Rubah*, Persian.

HABITAT.—South-Western Asia from Arabia east to the Punjab and Fatigarh, always in dry districts and desert.

DESCRIPTION.—More like the European than the Indian fox—though not much bigger than the latter—owing to the reddish-brown colour of the face, back, and white-tipped brush. Ears and under-parts dark, flanks pale grey, feet and front of hind-legs white. The upper parts are greyer in summer. The head and body are about 20 in. long, and the tail a little over 1 ft.

The Desert Fox is sometimes found on the same ground as the Indian fox, but is the only fox found in desert; it feeds on gerbilles to a great extent, and is swifter than the Indian Fox. It seems to be little more than a dwarfed desert race of the common European fox.

SMALL TIBETAN GREY FOX

OTHER NAMES.—Scientific: *Vulpes ferrilatus.* Native: *Igur*, Tibetan.

HABITAT.—Tibet, ranging to the Upper Sutlej Valley.

DESCRIPTION.—The most distinct of our foxes, owing to its short brush and ears, which last are only 2 in. long, as against 3 in. in the much smaller Desert Fox. Legs more thickly clad than in our other foxes. Colour buff above, including the ears; sides iron-grey, as is the brush, which is white-tipped; under-parts white. Length of head and body about 2 ft., tail not quite 1 ft.

COMMON FOX OR HILL FOX

OTHER NAMES.—Scientific: *Vulpes alopex, montanus.* Native: *Luh*, *Laash* (male and female), Kashmiri; *Lomri*, Hindi; *Wamu*, Nepalese; *Rubah*, Persian.

HABITAT.—Northern Hemisphere; in India only the Himalayas above 5,000 ft.

DESCRIPTION.—The largest of our foxes, with a particularly fine white-tipped brush, and large black ears. The Indian race is not so red as the English fox, but rather a mixture of buff and iron-grey, but the size will always distinguish it, as the head and body are 2 ft. or more long, and the tail about 18 in.

As in Europe, it is a poultry thief when it gets the chance; but although it has been hunted in India, Jerdon mentioning that in 1865 the 7th Hussars had a pack in Kashmir and killed many, it seldom lives on rideable ground, and so, as above remarked, the jackal takes its place as a beast of chase in the East.

Like most other mammalian orders, the carnivora are divided into sub-orders; those we have been dealing with belong to the sub-order *Fissipedia*, or pawed carnivores, while the other sub-order, *Pinnipedia*, contains the flippered carnivores—seals, sea-lions, and walruses.

None of these are Indian, or ever have been so far as history goes; but there is archæological evidence that one may once have occurred and perhaps resided in our seas. This is the giant seal known as the sea-elephant (*Mirounga proboscidea, angustirostris*) of the southern oceans, which is found in the Pacific even north of the Tropic of Cancer. Indian ancient sculptures portray a monster, known as the *jal-hathi* or water-elephant, as a creature with elephant's fore-quarters and fish's tail, but with the trunk short, no ears, and the teeth of a carnivore. This is not bad as a rough idea of the sea-elephant, in which the male has a short trunk, and, as he reaches about 20 ft. in length, is a worthy rival of the land elephant. A seal's hind flippers look very like a fish-tail, and though the elephant's fore-feet are wrong, the carnivore dentition can hardly be imaginary. Moreover, two sea-fowl of the southern ocean have been met with in Indian seas—a diving petrel by Sundevall a century ago, and by the editor in our time; and the Cape Petrel or "Cape Pigeon" by Captain Legge in Ceylon.

We shall see presently that strange sea-beasts have more than once occurred as single specimens off Indian coasts, just as the walrus does now and then off the British shores.

ORDER CETACEA

The remarkable order *Cetacea*, or whales and porpoises, are a group with no near relations to other mammals, and so fish-like in form that they are commonly called fish. They can always be distinguished from true fish, however, by having the tail-fin horizontal instead of vertical, and by the absence of gill-openings. They differ from the other fish-like order, the *Sirenia* or sea-cows, by having thin lips with few or no bristles, while the blunt, full-lipped muzzle of the *Sirenia* is plentifully studded with short thick hairs. In both orders the hind-limbs are absent, and the fore-limbs fin-like, most so in the Cetacea. Most have a fin on the back.

The nostrils, except in the great sperm-whale, are on the top of the head, forming the so-called blow-hole, from which the animal in large species snorts a jet of spray (no doubt mucus) when it comes up to breathe or blow. It is usually attributed to condensation of the breath, natural in the cold climates in which the beasts are generally met with, but the editor has seen it in Indian waters.

The Cetacea, breathing air as they do, ought to be able to live if they run aground, but they do not survive long in such a case, as their great weight compresses their expansible chests so that they die from slow suffocation, the weak-walled expansible thorax being necessitated by their long stay under water, which requires a deep breath to be taken. They are naked-skinned, animal-feeders, and not prolific, having only one or two young at a birth, and are never under 1 yd. long, while the larger species are unrivalled for size in the animal kingdom. They hardly come into practical zoological politics in India, being mostly marine and rare, so here a selection will be made, and only familiar or very striking species dealt with.

The order falls into two sub-orders, the Whalebone Whales (*Mystacocete*), which have no teeth, but ranges of the horny substance incorrectly called whalebone, used to strain food from the water, and the Toothed Whales (*Denticete*), which have teeth and no whalebone. Three families of the latter occur with us.

The Sperm-Whales (*Physeteridæ*) have teeth only in the lower jaw; the two known species are extremely different, so that they are well placed in different genera.

GREAT SPERM-WHALE OR CACHALOT

OTHER NAMES.—Scientific: *Physeter macrocephalus*.

HABITAT.—Nearly all seas, chiefly the warmer ones; once a common object of pursuit in our area, but only a single specimen has been captured in recent times, stranded at Madras.

DESCRIPTION.—Distinguished from all other cetaceans by the huge square-cut muzzle, with the blow-hole at its tip, so that the "spout" is directed forward. Lower jaw shorter than upper, narrow, with about fifty large teeth. No back-fin, but a hump in its place. Colour black. Male about 20 yds. long, female about half that length; the Madras specimen was about 8 yds.

The Sperm-whale goes in herds, and feeds chiefly on cuttlefish, often of huge size. Old males are solitary, and seem often to be "rogues," attacking ships, which have sometimes been sunk by them. The valuable oil spermaceti is contained in the "case" or upper part of the muzzle, the actual upper jaw being long and beak-like in the skeleton.

PIGMY SPERM-WHALE

Other Names.—Scientific: *Cogia breviceps*, *Euphysetes simus*. Native: *Wonga*, Telegu.

Habitat.—Recorded from North Pacific, Southern Ocean, and Indian seas.

Description.—Like a large dolphin or porpoise, with a well-developed back-fin; head and muzzle of ordinary form and moderate size, bluntly pointed, but differing much from a porpoise's by having the mouth small and some distance back of the snout. About two dozen slender pointed teeth in the lower jaw. Colour black, size up to 10 ft. or more. Blow-hole on top of the head.

A specimen was once obtained at Vizagapatam; nothing is known of the habits. The name "Snub-nosed Cachalot," sometimes applied to this species, is absurd; it is a Cachalot all right, but the nose is not snub, the muzzle being like that of an average fish—or rather a shark in particular, owing to the backward situation of the mouth.

The river dolphins (*Platanistidæ*) are a very small family of cetaceans all of which inhabit fresh water, and never attain a very large size. The characters which distinguish our only species from the more typical dolphins (some of which also inhabit fresh water) will be given in its description.

SUSU OR GANGETIC DOLPHIN

Other Names.—Scientific: *Platanista gangetica*. Native: *Súsú*, *Sús*, Hindi; *Súsúk*, *Sishuk*, Bengali; *Sisúmar*, Sanscrit; *Bhulan*, *Súnsar*, Sindi; *Hiho*, *Seho*, Assamese; *Húh*, Cachar and Sylhet.

Habitat.—Ganges, Indus, and Brahmaputra, following their larger tributaries nearly up to the hills, and descending into their estuaries, but not entering the sea.

Description.—Distinguished from other cetaceans by having the eye, which is small in all of them, so reduced as to be hardly noticeable, and by the square-cut flippers, which are nearly triangular; a low ridge in place of back-fin; head low and rounded, neck distinctly indicated; jaws long and narrow, with about sixty teeth, longer in front than behind, unlike our other cetaceans. Colour slate-colour or black. Length about 7 ft., but said to run up to

12 ft.; the female is considerably larger than the male, which is also thicker-set, with a shorter muzzle, a large female's skull measuring over 7 in. more than a large male's.

The Susu—a name preferable to Gangetic Dolphin, as the animal is very different from typical dolphins, and not confined to the Ganges—is one of the most familiar Indian water-animals. It feeds on prawns and fish, and is solitary; it may be seen in the Hooghly off Calcutta, though seldom noticed except in the cold weather, when it often jumps out of the water. Sterndale says: "Dr. Anderson had one in captivity for ten days, and carefully watched its respira-

Susu or Gangetic Dolphin.

tions. 'The blow-hole opened whenever it reached the surface of the water. The characteristic expiratory sound was produced, and so rapid was the inspiration that the blow-hole seemed to close immediately after the expiratory act.' He states that 'the respirations were tolerably frequent, occurring at intervals of about one-half or three-quarters of a minute, and the whole act did not take more than a few seconds for its fulfilment.' But it is probable that in a free state and in perfect health the animal remains longer under water. It has certainly been longer on several occasions when I have watched for the reappearance of one in the river." The period of gestation is said to be eight or nine months, and usually only one young one at a time is born, between April and July. The young are sometimes caught with their mothers, and are said to cling by the mouth to the base of the parent's flipper.

The flesh of the Susu is eaten by many castes of natives, some of whom compare it to venison and others to turtle. The oil is also useful as an embrocation and illuminant. The creature is quite blind, the eye being imperfectly developed. The teeth undergo great changes, being pointed in youth and becoming very blunt and broad-rooted as the animal becomes aged.

The typical Dolphins (*Delphinidæ*) comprise most of the cetaceans; all our species have teeth of even height in both jaws, pointed flippers, and are of moderate size; the form of the head varies much.

In the Porpoises proper (a name often wrongly given to dolphins generally) there is no projecting beak, and our species has no back-fin.

LITTLE PORPOISE

OTHER NAMES.—Scientific: *Phocæna phocænoides*. Native: *Molagan*, Tamil; *Bhulga*, Mahratti.

HABITAT.—Indian Ocean, but only inshore.

DESCRIPTION.—Our smallest cetacean, measuring about 4 ft.; forehead high and bulging; no projection of the muzzle and no back-fin, but a long triangular patch of warts on the back. Teeth about seventy-two, small, broad lengthways and sharp-edged. Colour black, with light patches about the mouth.

The Little Porpoise feeds on prawns, cuttlefish and true fish, and is generally solitary, though the young is often found with the mother. It haunts shallow water in estuaries and back-waters, and is sluggish, not jumping as dolphins do, but "rolling" like the common porpoise of our home waters.

RIVER PORPOISE

OTHER NAMES.—Scientific: *Orcella brevirostris, fluminalis*. Native: *Lomba-lomba*, Malay.

HABITAT.—Tidal water of rivers running into Bay of Bengal; fresh water of Irrawaddy to a little above Bhamo; Singapore and Borneo.

DESCRIPTION.—High-browed and round-headed, without projection of muzzle, as in the Little Porpoise, but possessing a back-fin and much larger, about 7 ft. long. Colour dark slate in the Indian form, paler in the Burmese, which is also whitish and streaked on the under-parts. Teeth conical, about sixty in number.

Anderson, and Sterndale following him, treat the Indian and Burmese races as distinct; but Mr. Oldfield Thomas unites them—no doubt rightly, as naturalists, specialists in particular, seldom err on the side of "lumping" species. These large river porpoises feed on fish, and are gregarious and playful like sea dolphins. They have a curious habit of rearing up and belching water out of their mouths, and also of standing up in the water, apparently a pairing gesture.

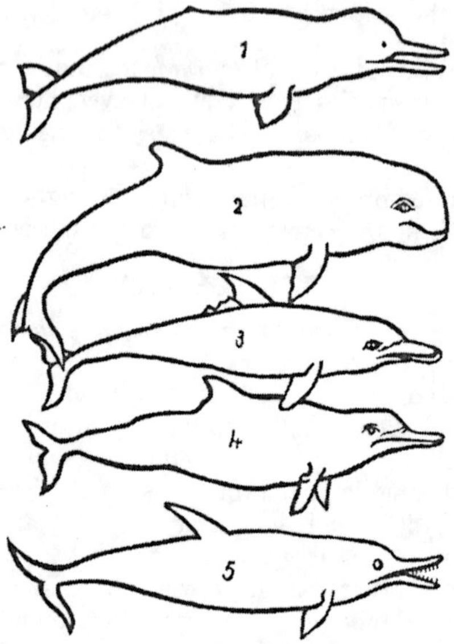

Indian Dolphins in outline. (1) Susu; (2) River Porpoise; (3) Elliot's Dolphin; (4) Speckled Dolphin; (5) Common Dolphin.

The typical Dolphins (*Steno*, *Delphinus*) have low rounded typical foreheads, long, flat, beak-like jaws furnished all along with many narrow pointed teeth, and well-developed back-fins. They are marine, and very swift and lively.

PLUMBEOUS DOLPHIN

OTHER NAMES.—Scientific: *Steno plumbeus*. Native: *Lamaing*, Burmese.

HABITAT.—Indian Ocean.

DESCRIPTION.—About 8 ft. long; lead-colour, with the lower jaw white; jaws very long.

The Plumbeous or Lead-coloured Dolphin is said to be common in Burmese estuaries.

ELLIOT'S DOLPHIN

Other Names.—Scientific: *Steno perniger, gadamu.* Native: *Gadamu*, Telegu.

Habitat.—Indian Ocean east to Australia.

Description.—Length about 7 ft.; colour dark slate above, shading into pale grey below.

SPECKLED DOLPHIN

Other Names.—Scientific: *Steno lentiginosus.* Native: *Bolla-gadimi*, Telegu.

Habitat.—Seas around India.

Description.—About 8 ft. long, pale slate speckled with black and white.

SPOT-BELLIED DOLPHIN

Other Names.—Scientific: *Steno maculiventer.* Native: *Suvva*, Telegu.

Habitat.—Madras coast.

Description.—About 7 ft. long, black above, grey below with dark spots.

COMMON DOLPHIN

Other Names.—Scientific: *Delphinus delphis, pomeegra.* Native: *Pomigra*, Tamil.

Habitat.—Warm and temperate seas generally.

Description.—A very elegant clipper-built dolphin, slim-bodied, with long beak and flippers. About 7 ft. long, dark slate above, white below, more or less buff or grey on the flanks.

The common dolphin is a very swift and playful animal, delighting to accompany ships and sport around them, jumping out of the water and even springing up and turning on its back before the bows. The movements of its tail in swimming are so rapid that the eye cannot follow them—at any rate that has been the editor's experience. Dolphins go in schools, jumping one after the other.

The only other member of the Dolphin family that need be specially noticed here is large enough to be called a whale; it has only once occurred with us, when a shoal was stranded.

INDIAN PILOT WHALE

Other Names.—Scientific: *Globicephalus indicus.*

Habitat.—Only known from the Calcutta Salt Lake.

Description.—About 14 ft. long; head high and rounded, no

beak; a long low back-fin. Teeth about thirty only, confined to the front half of the jaws. Colour slaty-black.

All that is known about this species, which is closely allied to the well-known European Ca'ing Whale or "Blackfish" (*Globicephalus melas*), is that a large shoal was stranded in July, 1852, in the Salt-water Lake, from which Blyth got two specimens.

The well-known Grampus or "Killer-whale" (*Orca gladiator*), found in all seas, and celebrated for its attacks on other cetaceans, is believed to occur in Indian waters. It is the largest of dolphins, 30 ft. long, with a very high conspicuous back-fin, and coloured black above and white below, with white head-patches.

The Whalebone Whales all belong to one family (*Balænidæ*) and all are large, measuring from 20 to 100 ft.

The horny plates of "whalebone" or baleen which form a row on each side of the upper jaw are set edgeways, and their inner sides are frayed out into bristles, so that the roof of the mouth looks as if covered with hair. The two branches of the lower jaw together form a Gothic arch; they are only joined by ligament at the tip, where there is a strong bony union in the toothed whales, this junction in the great Sperm Whale and the Susu extending halfway down the jaw, which is thus narrow for a long way.

The lower jaw with its loose flooring forms a huge spoon, like that of the pelican when feeding; only the bird's lower jaw is only spoon-like at that time, and the whale's is permanently expanded.

These whales feed like ducks on a huge scale, taking in gigantic mouthfuls of water swarming with small animal life, and straining off this water through the baleen plates, while its floating population is stranded on the tongue. Their throats are narrow, and they do not take prey larger than dogfish, and often feed on quite minute creatures. The whale that swallowed Jonah would have been the wide-throated Cachalot—an instance of a man being swallowed by this whale and escaping with his life by being thrown up occurred during the last century.

The Whalebone Whales certainly known from Indian seas all belong to the genus known as Rorquals, Finners, or Finbacks (*Balænoptera*); they are long slim whales with pleated throats, comparatively short baleen plates, and a small fin on the hinder part of the back. When the "Right Whales" (*Balæna*), which have more baleen and blubber, and the Cachalot, were common, Rorquals were little hunted, but now they are the mainstay of the whaling that goes on, steam-whalers and better harpoon-guns having made it possible to attack these swift animals safely, which was rarely done in Sterndale's time.

Rorqual.

Whales seem to have been common in Blyth's time, about the middle of last century. The Rev. H. Baker of Alleppi wrote to him: "Whales are very common on the coast. American ships, and occasionally a Swedish one, call at Cochin for stores during their cruises for them; but no English whalers ever come here that I have heard of." Sterndale says: "I wonder at any whaling vessels coming out of their way after this species, for I have always heard from whalers that the finback is not worth hunting. It is possible that in cruising after sperms they may go a little out of their way to take a finback or two. . . . They are not particularly shy, and will sometimes follow a vessel closely for days. . . . I myself was in a sailing vessel going about five or six knots, when a whale played about for a time, and then rose and spouted just under the bow, covering the forecastle with spray. The captain, who was standing by me, quite expected a shock, and exclaimed, 'Look out! hold on.'" This would be the vertical spout of a whalebone whale—the sperm's forward "blow" would have been flung clear, probably.

GREAT RORQUAL OR BLUE WHALE

OTHER NAMES.—Scientific: *Balænoptera sibbaldi, indica.*

HABITAT.—All seas.

DESCRIPTION.—The largest animal known, from 80 to 100 ft. in length; colour slate, spotted with white on breast, under-parts sometimes yellow, whence the name "sulphur-bottom" sometimes used. Flippers white inside and edged with white below.

Any whale over 80 ft. long would be of this species, and two or three of such have been recorded as stranded; the lower jaw of one from Amherst Island, Arakan, is preserved in the Indian Museum, Calcutta, where in the editor's time it was set up as an arch over the main doorway of the Mammal Gallery, inside. This specimen was said to be 84 ft. long, and the jaw is nearly 21 ft.; a few other bones were preserved.

This monster feeds on particularly small prey, small crustacea, etc. It is supposed to be migratory, but stray specimens may occur in Indian seas in summer, just as migratory birds sometimes occur with us at that time.

PIKE WHALE

OTHER NAMES.—Scientific: *Balænoptera rostrata, edeni.*

HABITAT.—All seas.

DESCRIPTION.—Small for a whalebone whale, about 25 to 33 ft. Black, with the under-parts, inside of flippers, under-side of tail, and a band across outside of flippers, white. There is some doubt, however, as to whether the only example obtained in Indian seas was not a Sei-whale (*Balænoptera borealis*), which runs up to 40 ft. and is less white below, but spotted with white above, and has the fins black on both sides.

This Indian example, stranded in the Sittoung estuary, was 37 ft. long; its skull and some other bones are in the Indian Museum.

These smaller whales feed more on fish than do the giant species.

In dealing with cetaceans it is well to remember Blanford's advice about dolphins, that "skins are difficult to preserve and of no great use in identification; a good sketch to scale and a skeleton are better." No one probably has ever tried to preserve the skin of one of the great whales—it would be literally "too large an order" altogether. As the colours are only or chiefly black, grey, and white, a photograph is a good realistic record.

ORDER SIRENIA

The vegetable-feeding *Sirenia*, or Sea-cows, are really as different from the Cetaceans as are the hoofed mammals from the carnivores, though also fish-like in form with the exception of the horizontal set of the tail-fin. There are very few of them, and only one family (*Manatidæ*), and the characters of ours may be given in the description of the species.

Dugong.

DUGONG

OTHER NAMES.—Scientific: *Halicore dugong*. Native: *Muda ura*, Singhalese; *Duyong*, Malay.

HABITAT.—Warmer parts of Indian Ocean.

DESCRIPTION.—Distinguished from any of our sea mammals by the oval flippers, round, truncated, bristly snout, and nostrils situated between the eyes and end of muzzle. No back-fin. Colour slaty. Teats of female situated under the flippers, while in Cetacea they are in grooves where the groin would be if the animals had hind legs.

Skull very unlike a cetacean's, Roman-nosed like a flamingo's bill, with two tusks in the upper jaw, very deeply rooted, but not projecting in the female, and only slightly in the male; grinders broad and flat-topped, not in the least like cetacean teeth. Length from about 6 ft. to 9 ft. or perhaps even more.

The dugong is purely a coast animal, avoiding both the open sea and fresh water. It feeds on seaweed, and used to be found in herds, but has now been much reduced by wasteful hunting, and badly needs protection, as it is neither active nor intelligent, and is a most useful animal, its flesh being as good as pork and its fat supplying the best of oil. It is said that the nursing female holds her young to the breast with her flipper, and some at any rate of the

Dugong nursing young.

mermaid legends are no doubt traceable to this animal, northerners also getting their ideas of sea-folk from the walrus.

ORDER RODENTIA

With the rodents we come again to mammals with ordinary paws, and our species are at once distinguished from all our other mammals of any shape by the two great incisors in each jaw, followed by a long toothless gap. Shrews, as we have seen, much resemble the commonest type of rodents—rats and mice—even to having two conspicuously large teeth in front of each jaw; but in them these teeth are immediately followed by others, and they are, besides, pointed, whereas those of rodents are chisel-tipped.

These great incisors of the rodents are rootless and ever-growing in adaptation to their hard use in the gnawing so characteristic of these animals, and if one be lost or broken its fellow in the other jaw, having nothing to bite against and wear it down, develops into a tusk-like monstrosity, and often causes death.

The grinders are broad and adapted for chewing vegetable food, which is the mainstay of these gnawers, but many, perhaps most, have a strong omnivorous tendency—too well seen in rats—and take animal food of some kind or other. The mouth is always small, and situated well back of the end of the muzzle, but not nearly so much so as in the insectivores. The moustaches are very well developed.

Rodents are mostly very small, nocturnal, and prolific, but there are numerous exceptions to these rules. They are the most numerous in species of our mammals, and generally abundant individually; only the more conspicuous species will be noticed here.

They are divided into two sub-orders: the *Simplicidentata*, to which the vast majority belong, these having two incisors only in each jaw; and the *Duplicidentata*, including only the Hares and Pikas, in which there are a pair of small incisors in the upper jaw situated behind the large ones and therefore not to be seen unless looked for. As, however, the Hares are all much like their relative the common Rabbit, and the Pikas like soft-furred Guinea-pigs or tailless Rats, it is not necessary minutely to examine their teeth to identify them.

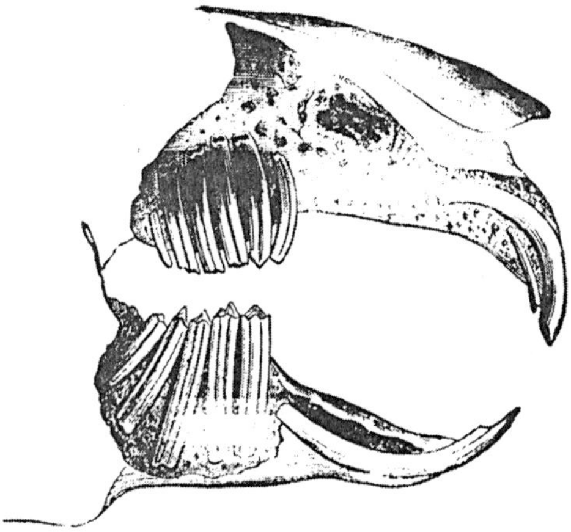

Skull of Rodent (Hare) showing whole of incisors.

Of the *Simplicidentata* we have five families, all likewise very easy to distinguish. They are:

The Squirrels (*Sciuridæ*), animals with bushy tails;

The Jerboas (*Dipodidæ*), kangaroo-like animals with very long hind legs;

The Rats and Mice (*Muridæ*), the general form of which is familiar to every one;

The Mole-Rats (*Spalacidæ*), with thick, heavy, sausage-shaped bodies; and

The Porcupines (*Hystricidæ*), distinguished by their spines.

All of them have a more or less rabbit-like muzzle, the shape of the head not varying as we have seen it does in the Carnivores, Bats, and Primates.

The Squirrels are the most familiar of our rodents, as they are not only common but diurnal as a rule; they are usually slim climbers, but the family also includes the Marmots, which are thick-set burrowers, though also noticeably bushy-tailed in our species. They have five toes on all feet, though the first toe on the forefoot is a mere stump.

The typical squirrels (*Sciurus*) are at once recognisable by their general resemblance to the most familiar of our mammals, the common little striped squirrel; but they are found in three sizes, small species like that above-mentioned, medium-sized ones, and large ones approaching cats in size, which will be treated first. These last are all forest animals, living high up in the trees, and seldom coming to the ground. Squirrels feed mainly on fruit, nuts, and shoots, and build nests in trees.

LARGE INDIAN SQUIRREL

OTHER NAMES.—Scientific: *Sciurus indicus, maximus*. Native: *Kat-berral*, Bengali; *Karat*, *Rasu*, *Ratuphar*, *Jangli gilheri*, Hindi; *Kondeng*, Kol; *Per-warsti*, Gondi; *Bet udata*, Telegu; *Shekra*, Mahratti; *Kes annalu*, Canarese.

HABITAT.—Indian Peninsula east to Manipur.

DESCRIPTION.—A very large squirrel with tufted ears, snub nose, and tail about as long as head and body. Colour maroon-red—almost crimson—or red and black; underparts, face, paws, and a band in front of the ears, buff, and often the forelegs. Tail red and buff, red, black, and buff, or all black. Nose flesh-coloured and eyes light brown, not very dark brown as in most rodents. Head and body about 17 in. long—the reddest variety is the smallest.

The large red squirrel is an inmate of large forests, living and nesting high up, and having a loud cackling cry. Sterndale saw a tame one jump 20 ft. He says: "This squirrel was tolerably common in the forests of Seeonee, and we had one or two in confinement. One belonging to my brother-in-law was so tame as to allow any amount of bullying by his children, who used to pull it about as though it were a puppy or kitten, but I have known others to bite severely and resent any freedom." It is often exported.

LARGE MALAY SQUIRREL OR BLACK HILL SQUIRREL

OTHER NAMES.—Scientific: *Sciurus bicolor, giganteus*. Native: *Shingsham*, Bhotia; *Le-hyuk*, *Satheu*, Lepcha; *Chingkráwah*, Malay; *Leng-thek*, Arakan; *Sheng*, Burmese.

HABITAT.—Himalayas from Nepal east to Burma, Siam, and the Malay countries.

DESCRIPTION.—A little smaller than the last species, but with a longer tail, definitely exceeding the head and body. Ears tufted or plain. Colour black to brown above, including the face, tail, and limbs, buff below; the fur is blackest when newly grown, and sometimes there is in Burmese specimens a pale saddle-mark. Eyes and nose dark.

There is a great deal of variation in colour in this fine squirrel,

Large Indian Squirrel.

some being grizzled or even silvered fawn-colour, but the large size and particularly long tail will always distinguish it. It lives in pairs as a rule, has a loud, harsh, cackling cry, and eats eggs and insects as well as vegetable food.

LARGE GRIZZLED INDIAN SQUIRREL

OTHER NAMES.—Scientific: *Sciurus macrurus.* Native: *Rukiya, Dandolena,* Singalese; *Peria-anathan,* Tamil.

HABITAT.—Southern India and Ceylon.

DESCRIPTION.—The smallest of our three large squirrels, but still a big animal as squirrels go, about 14 in. in length of head and body, with tail about the same. Ears plain or very little tufted. Colour usually grizzly-grey above or on the tail, but sometimes black; sides of head, forearms, a band across the crown, and under-parts pale, buff or dirty white, but toes black. The black-backed variety is confined to high elevations in Ceylon.

The middle-sized squirrels are a very confusing lot of animals, being not only variable but inclined to run into each other, so all that can be done here in their case and in that of the small striped species is to describe certain forms which in view of their peculiar colouring or their commonness are likely to attract notice.

ORANGE-BELLIED HILL SQUIRREL

OTHER NAMES.—Scientific: *Sciurus locria.* Native: *Lokriah*, Nepalese; *Zhamo*, Bhotia; *Kalli*, *Kalli tingdong*, Lepcha.

HABITAT.—Himalayas of Nepal and Sikkim, east through Assam hills to Arakan, at fairly high elevations, up to 8,000 ft.

DESCRIPTION.—About as big as a rat, with tail shorter than head and body, and rather long narrow muzzle. Colour speckled brown above, some shade of orange or rust-red below.

PALLAS'S SQUIRREL

OTHER NAMES.—Scientific: *Sciurus erythraeus.* Native: *Kherwa*, Manipuri.

HABITAT.—Assam south to Chittagong and east to Upper Burma.

DESCRIPTION.—About the same size as the last, but with the tail longer than head and body. Colour very variable, Blanford describing no less than five varieties. Speaking of it as a whole, the upper parts are olive or brown to nearly black, the under-parts bay or chestnut, the end of the tail and the feet more or less red or, in dark forms, black.

ANDERSON'S STRIPE-BELLIED SQUIRREL

OTHER NAMES.—Scientific: *Sciurus quinquestriatus.*

HABITAT.—Kakhyen Hills.

DESCRIPTION.—About 9 in. in length of head and body and of tail, and noticeable for the broad black and white stripes of the under-parts, unique among our squirrels; upper-parts speckled brown.

HOARY-BELLIED HILL SQUIRREL

OTHER NAMES.—Scientific: *Sciurus locroides.*

HABITAT.—Lower levels of the Himalayas from Nepal, extending eastwards and southwards to Arakan, Upper Burma, Eastern Bengal, and Preparis Island.

DESCRIPTION.—Somewhat like the Orange-bellied Hill Squirrel, but with a longer tail and shorter muzzle, and not so richly coloured, speckled brown above, buff, fawn, or greyish below. The black squirrel of Sylhet and Cachar seems to be a melanistic form of this species.

This squirrel is particularly fond of chestnuts, and mostly to be seen when they ripen.

IRRAWADDY SQUIRREL

OTHER NAMES.—Scientific: *Sciurus pygerythrus.*

HABITAT.—Irrawaddy Valley.

DESCRIPTION.—Speckled brown or grey above, more or less rich buff below; tip of tail black. Blanford thinks that Phayre's or the Laterally-banded Squirrel (*S. phayrei*) of Martaban passes into this, as the black bands along the sides which distinguish it vary in distinctness.

GOLDEN-BACKED SQUIRREL

OTHER NAMES.—Scientific: *Sciurus caniceps.*

HABITAT.—Moulmein to Malay Peninsula.

DESCRIPTION.—A very distinct species owing to its broad feet with warts between the pads and to (in some cases) the orange colour of the back. This, however, is seasonal, being only seen in the cold weather, and the southern variety never has it. The general colour is olive above, grey below, and often on the head, southern specimens being darker, and Malayan ones also reddish along the sides.

BLACK-BACKED SQUIRREL

OTHER NAMES.—Scientific: *Sciurus atridorsalis.*

HABITAT.—Lower Pegu and Upper Tenasserim.

DESCRIPTION.—Another form with broad feet and—generally—distinct back-coloration, in this case black; but with no warts between the sole-pads. The striking black back-patch is not known to be seasonal, and the general colouring is very variable, greyish or reddish-brown, with the under-parts bay to buff. Head and body about 8 in., as in the last. This squirrel frequents hedges and thickets, and has a low cackling cry

BAY SQUIRREL

OTHER NAMES.—Scientific: *Sciurus ferrugineus.*

HABITAT.—Burma and Siam.

DESCRIPTION.—Larger than the other medium-sized squirrels, the head and body sometimes reaching 10 in., and the tail considerably exceeding this. Colour chestnut to bay all over, with the exception of the tip of the tail, which may be white.

The rest of our squirrels are all little striped animals, of which there are fewer than of the medium-sized ones; the most noticeable of them will be here characterised. None are as much as 8 in. long in length of head and body.

COMMON STRIPED SQUIRREL OR PALM SQUIRREL

OTHER NAMES.—Scientific: *Sciurus palmarum.* Native: *Gilehri*, Hindi; *Berál*, *Lakhi*, Bengali; *Khadi*, Mahratti; *Alalu*, Canarese; *Vodata*, Telegu; *Urta*, Wadars; *Chitta Anathan*, Tamil; *Lena*, Cingalese; "Tree-rat" of some British soldiers.

HABITAT.—India and Ceylon.

DESCRIPTION.—Brown of some shade, with three cream-coloured stripes all down the back; whitish below, tail grizzled. Head and body about 6 in. long, tail a little longer. The editor has seen two black specimens.

"This beautiful little animal," says Sterndale, "is well known to almost all who have lived in India, and it is one of the most engaging and cheerful of all the frequenters of our Mofussil bungalows, although I have heard the poor little creature abused by some in unmeasured terms as a nuisance on account of its piercing voice. I confess to liking even its shrill chatter, but then I am not easily put out by noises. . . . I can, however, quite imagine the irritation the sharp chirrup-chirrup of this little squirrel would cause to an invalid, for there is something particularly ear-piercing about it; but their prettiness and familiarity make up in great measure for their noisiness. They are certainly a nuisance in a garden, and I rather doubt whether they are of any use, as McMaster says, 'in destroying many insects, especially white ants, and beetles, both in their perfect and larval state,' etc. He adds: 'They are said to destroy the eggs of small birds, but I have never observed this myself.' I should also doubt this, were it not that the European squirrel is accused of the same thing. . . . Our so-called palm squirrel (though it does not affect palms any more than other trees) builds a ragged sort of nest of any fibrous matter, without much attempt at concealment; and I have known it carry off bits of lace and strips of muslin and skeins of wool from a lady's work-box for its house-building purposes. The skins of this species nicely cured make very pretty slippers. They are very easily tamed, and often fall victims to their temerity, in venturing unknown into their owner's pockets, boxes, boots, etc. One I have now is very fond of a mess of parched rise and milk. It sleeps rolled up in a ball, not on its side, but with its head bent down between its legs."

Sterndale, it will be noticed, speaks of this squirrel as frequenting Mofussil bungalows, but in the editor's time at any rate it frequented towns, being common in open spaces in Calcutta, such as the Maidan, and was always present in the grounds of the Indian Museum—there was a nest under the eaves of his quarters. He has also seen it nibbling at the earthen galleries of white ants, and so has no doubt that McMaster was right about its insectivorous propensities.

It is, except in Sind and Baluchistan, where it is scarce, about the most familiar of our mammals, and is especially attached to human habitations and cultivation, not being seen in forest. In the People's Park at Madras it fairly swarmed when the editor visited that place. Captive specimens were always to be seen in the Calcutta markets, but it does not seem common in the home animal trade.

JUNGLE STRIPED SQUIRREL

Other Names.—Scientific: *Sciurus tristriatus*. Native: Same as for the common striped species, and *Anan* in Malabarese.

Habitat.—From Sikkim to South India and Ceylon.

Description.—Like the last, but larger, darker in ground colour and with narrower and shorter pale stripes. Head also broader and muzzle longer.

The Jungle Striped Squirrel is a forest animal, rarely frequenting houses, and only where the common striped species does not occur, besides not showing the same familiarity. Blyth and Jerdon agree in crediting it with a different and much less shrill voice, which is some excuse for keeping it distinct, though Blanford, who does so, suggests that it is the "wild" parent of the common striped squirrel, which may have become a parasite of man like rats and mice.

The case would be even more like that of the Brown and Grey Musk-shrews, but there the house form is larger as well as lighter. He also suggests that Layard's Striped Squirrel (*Sciurus layardi*) of the Ceylon and Travancore hill-forests may also be a variety of the present species; it is larger and darker still, with the central spinal stripe buff, and the side ones darker and less well marked. At any rate all these three are closely related, but Blanford doubts if the next is really near them.

DUSKY STRIPED SQUIRREL

OTHER NAMES.—Scientific: *Sciurus sublineatus.*

HABITAT.—Hill-forests of Ceylon and Southern India.

DESCRIPTION.—Smaller, duller, and less distinctly marked than any of the first striped group, the back-stripes being all short, narrow, and indistinct.

HIMALAYAN STRIPED SQUIRREL

OTHER NAMES.—Scientific: *Sciurus maclellandii.*

HABITAT.—South-East Asia from Sikkim to China and south to Cochin China.

DESCRIPTION.—The smallest and shortest-tailed of the striped squirrels, and the only one with ear-tufts, which are white; colour brown with a black line down the back and two or four pale stripes.

This is not only a high-forest animal, but seldom leaves the trees.

BERDMORE'S SQUIRREL

OTHER NAMES.—Scientific: *Sciurus berdmorei.*

HABITAT.—Martaban to Cochin China, including the Mergui Archipelago.

DESCRIPTION.—The longest-headed of the striped squirrels, and larger than most; brown above, with four cream stripes, white below.

According to Blyth, this species is a true ground-squirrel, not frequenting trees; and it is said to frequent cultivated ground like the common striped squirrel.

The flying-squirrels are distinguished by the broad flounce of furry skin which extends along their flanks, from the wrist, where it is supported by a gristly spur or gaff, to the hind foot; this acts as a parachute to support them in the great leaps they make, and is sometimes more or less supplemented by a leg-web, which is, however, never so well developed as in most bats and in the Cobego. Like that animal, they are nocturnal, but must come out by day at times, as some frequently fall victims to the Golden Eagle. Mr. C. H. Donald has suggested in the *Field* this year (1927) that they stay out after wet nights to dry their fur in the sun. It is possible also that the eagle may hunt later than it is credited with doing—a beast which merely sails from tree to tree ought to be an easy prey even in a bad light.

The first we have to deal with is a very rare and little-known animal, which has a genus to itself.

WOOLLY FLYING-SQUIRREL

OTHER NAMES.—Scientific: *Eupetaurus cinereus.*

HABITAT.—Gilgit and possibly Tibet.

DESCRIPTION.—Apparently the largest of our squirrels, at least equalling the large red species, and with an even longer tail. Fur very dense and long, drab in colour; claws blunt, leg-web very little developed and wrist-spur short.

The habits of this woolly-coated squirrel can only be guessed at; Blanford suggests that it lives in a very cold climate, among rocks rather than trees.

The large Flying-Squirrels of the genus *Pteromys* are well-known animals, well over 1 ft. in length of head and body, with tail considerably exceeding these in length. The wrist-spur is long, generally equalling the forearm in length, and there is a well-developed leg-web extending from heel to heel and enclosing the base of the tail. They are all forest animals.

Large Brown Flying-Squirrel.

LARGE BROWN FLYING-SQUIRREL

OTHER NAMES.—Scientific: *Pteromys oral.* Native: *Ural,* Kol; *Pakya,* Mahratti; *Parachatea,* Malabarese; *Egala dandolena,* Cingalese.

HABITAT.—India east to Tenasserim, Ceylon, and the Mergui Archipelago, but not north of the Ganges.

DESCRIPTION.—The largest of this group of squirrels, about 18 in. in length of head and body, with the tail about 2 ft. Ears tufted. Colour brown, with a mostly black tail, or grey with the tail black-tipped; white on the under-parts, and sometimes chestnut on the upper-part of the flounce.

This fine squirrel does not avoid villages if they are situated in forest; it eats bark and insects as well as fruit and nuts, and has a low, soft, repeated note. It lives in holes and trees, and often sleeps on its back. It is not so active on its feet as ordinary squirrels, but can glide nearly eighty yards through the air.

Flying-Squirrel, showing parachute-skin.

ANDERSON'S OR RED-AND-WHITE FLYING-SQUIRREL

OTHER NAMES.—Scientific: *Pteromys yunnanensis, alborufus.*

HABITAT.—Assam to Yunnan and Eastern Tibet.

DESCRIPTION.—About 18 in. long in head and body; colour bay, more or less mixed with white above, white or yellow below, the hinder back in yellow-bellied specimens also yellow. Tail bay, reddish-grey, or more or less blackish from the tip forwards.

As Mr. W. L. Sclater, according to Blanford, refers specimens of this squirrel from Assam and Burma to the Tibetan *alborufus* race, the two may here be united.

HODGSON'S OR ORANGE-BELLIED FLYING-SQUIRREL

OTHER NAMES.—Scientific: *Pteromys magnificus.* Native: *Suráj-bhagat*, Hindi; *Biyom*, Lepcha.

HABITAT.—Nepal east to Assam Hills, between 6,000 and 9,000 ft.

DESCRIPTION.—Rather smaller than the Large Brown Flying-Squirrel, with shorter and broader head. Colour maroon with a yellow spinal stripe and head-spot, or grizzled chestnut without this. Under-parts light chestnut; tail tipped with black. Blanford thinks the lighter-coloured specimens without back-stripe are in winter coat.

The Red-bellied Flying-Squirrel lives on chestnuts and other hard fruit, young leaves, and shoots, and breeds in hollow trees in the rains, the litter consisting apparently of one only, which when able to shift for itself more or less has the parachute much smaller than in the adult.

LARGE RED FLYING-SQUIRREL

OTHER NAMES.—Scientific: *Pteromys inornatus, albiventer.* Native: *Rusi gugar*, Kashmiri.

HABITAT.—Nepal to Kashmir, ranging up to 10,000 ft

DESCRIPTION.—Shape and (probably) size as in the Large Brown species; colour chestnut, pale or whitish below, cheeks pale grey.

Sterndale says: "This is a common squirrel at Simla. One was killed close to the house in which I was staying in 1880 at the Chota Simla end of the station by a native servant, who threw a stick at it and knocked it off a bough, and I heard of two living ones being hawked about for sale about the same time—which, to my regret, I failed to secure, some one having bought them. They are common also in Kashmir, where they live in holes made in the bark of dead fir-trees. They are said to hybernate during the [cold] season there. A melanoid variety of this species is mentioned by Dr. Anderson as being in the Leyden Museum. It was obtained by Dr Jerdon in

Kashmir, and presented to the Museum by the late Marquis of Tweeddale."

GREY-HEADED FLYING-SQUIRREL

OTHER NAMES.—Scientific: *Pteromys caniceps.* Native: *Biyom-chimbo*, Lepcha.

HABITAT.—Sikkim and Nepal, not above 6,000 ft.

DESCRIPTION.—About the size of the last, but with smaller head and larger ears. Colour reddish-brown, paler and redder below, head grey or brown.

SPOTTED FLYING-SQUIRREL

OTHER NAMES.—Scientific: *Pteromys punctatus.*

HABITAT.—Karennee and Malacca.

DESCRIPTION.—Smaller than the large red species, but still well over 1 ft. in head and body length, and well distinguished by the white spotting on the yellowish-brown head and back; rest of fur pale chestnut, browner on the tail.

The small Flying-Squirrels (*Sciuropterus*) are not only smaller than the last group—the head and body being never more than 1 ft. long and often much less—but have shorter and more or less flat tails; the wrist-spur is shorter, not so long as the forearm, and thus the parachute is narrower, and the leg-web is hardly at all developed, not embracing the tail even at the root. They are pretty little animals, but generally not so brightly coloured as the larger kinds that have just been noticed.

HAIRY-FOOTED FLYING-SQUIRREL

OTHER NAMES.—Scientific: *Sciuropterus pearsoni.*

HABITAT.—Sikkim at moderate elevations, east to Yunnan.

DESCRIPTION.—Feet clothed with long hair, and long tufts to the ears. Colour grizzled brown, parachute black above, chestnut below, belly cream-colour. Head and body of same length as tail, 8 in.

SMALL TRAVANCORE FLYING-SQUIRREL

OTHER NAMES.—Scientific: *Sciuropterus fuscicapillus.*

HABITAT.—Southern India and Ceylon, on the hills.

DESCRIPTION.—Ears small, but with long tufts. Tail decidedly shorter than head and body, which measure 1 ft. Fur reddish-brown above, mixed with blackish, cheeks and under-parts nearly white, tail sometimes tipped white.

SMALL KASHMIR FLYING-SQUIRREL

OTHER NAMES.—Scientific: *Sciuropterus fimbriatus.*

HABITAT.—North-West Himalayas, always fairly high, up to 12,000 ft., and Afghanistan.

DESCRIPTION.—Nearly 1 ft. long in head and body, tail rather more, ears large but not tufted; tail not nearly so flat as usual in these small flying-squirrels. Coat brown above, light in shade but varied with black, more or less pure white below.

As four young have been found in a pregnant female, this species is more prolific than some at any rate of the large ones.

PARTICOLOURED FLYING-SQUIRREL

OTHER NAMES.—Scientific: *Sciuropterus alboniger.*

HABITAT.—Nepal east to Siam and apparently Borneo; in the Himalayas at moderate elevations.

DESCRIPTION.—Tail considerably less than head and body, which are about 10 in.; ears plain. Colour white below and in the young black above, becoming much mixed with greyish or reddish-brown in the adult—a very remarkable change of colour.

HORSFIELD'S FLYING-SQUIRREL

OTHER NAMES.—Scientific: *Sciuropterus sagitta.*

HABITAT.—Pegu, from the Sittoung River east to the Malay countries.

DESCRIPTION.—A small species with short fur and large plain ears. Yellowish-brown above, more or less pure white below. Tail hardly as long as head and body, which are about 6½ in.

PIGMY FLYING-SQUIRREL

OTHER NAMES.—Scientific: *Sciuropterus spadiceus.*

HABITAT.—Arakan to Cochin China.

DESCRIPTION.—The smallest of our flying-squirrels, only about 5 in. without the tail, which is less than the head and body, and comes to a point; ears plain, fur chestnut above, white below, tail and extremities darker.

The flying-squirrels represent the extreme adaptation of squirrels to an arboreal life, but in the opposite direction some non-Indian forms connect the ordinary squirrels with the marmots, of which we have representatives of one genus (*Arctomys*). These bear much the same relation to the squirrels as the badgers to the weasels, being, as remarked above, thick-set burrowing animals. Their ears are very short, and their tails—which vary in length in all our three species—always much shorter than in our squirrels, though still moderately bushy. They are all hill animals with us, and resemble rabbits in their ways, forming warrens, and living on herbs and roots. Their note is a one-syllable cry, not a chatter or cackle.

TIBET MARMOT

OTHER NAMES.—Scientific: *Arctomys himalayanus.* Native: *Brin.* Kashmiri; *Kadia-piu,* Tibetan; *Chibi,* Bhotia; *Lho,* Lepcha; *Pfif,* Niti.

HABITAT.—Rukshu and Ladak, Tibet, Kuenlun range.

DESCRIPTION.—Tail about a quarter of the length of head and body, which measure about 2 ft.; colour fawn mixed above with black, tail-tip and face all dark.

The Tibet marmot lives with us on high elevations, from 13,000 to 18,000 ft. Its note is a chirping bark.

RED OR LONG-TAILED MARMOT

OTHER NAMES.—Scientific: *Arctomys caudatus.* Native: *Drun,* Kashmiri.

HABITAT.—North Kashmir and South Ladak.

DESCRIPTION.—About the size of the last species, but with a much longer tail, about 1 ft. in length. Colour chestnut, the back, tail-tip, and a patch round the eye, black.

The Red Marmot has a long shrill cry, and lives at between 8,000 and 14,000 ft. elevation, in fairly fertile spots.

SMALLER HIMALAYAN MARMOT

OTHER NAMES.—Scientific: *Arctomys hemachalanus.* Native: *Sammiong,* Lepcha; *Jabra, Chipi,* Bhotia.

HABITAT.—Eastern Himalayas.

DESCRIPTION.—The smallest of our species, about two-thirds the size of the others, with a tail of intermediate proportional length, about 6 in. Colour only differing from that of the Tibet marmot in the reddish hue of the sides. At the time Blanford wrote the Mammalia volume on the Fauna of British India this species was only known from captive specimens.

The Rats and Mice (*Muridæ*) are all, as above remarked, recognisable by their resemblance to our too familiar self-domesticated pests, though some differ in detail, especially in form of tail. As in squirrels, the thumb is rudimentary. They are the most omnivorous of the rodents, generally small and active, with very long moustaches, and very numerous both in individuals and in species—over fifty of the latter are recorded from our area, only a few of which are likely to attract the attention of the ordinary observer of animal life. The Wadars or tank-diggers, who eat rats, are great authorities on the family.

The first we have to notice has a genus to itself, and its characters will be given under the sole species.

PEPPER-RAT OR MALABAR SPINY MOUSE

OTHER NAMES.—Scientific: *Platacanthomys lasiurus.*

HABITAT.—Southern Indian hills.

DESCRIPTION.—Small for a rat, but too large to be fairly called a mouse, the head and body being over 4 in., and the tail about the same. Generally appearance very squirrel-like, the tail being bushy, but less so at the root, and the ears longer and narrower than in any squirrel, the moustaches also excessively long, and the back having numerous spines among the fur. Colour chestnut above and on the tail, very pale below, this whitish under-surface sharply defined.

The Pepper-rat, to give it its native name, is common in large old trees in valleys, living in holes which it makes and lines with leaves and moss. It is very destructive to pepper, angely, and jack-fruit, and also indulges in toddy whenever it can get access to a pot. Several may live in one hole, and holes in rocks are used as well as in trees. It was at first classed with the dormice.

The Gerbils or Jerboa-rats (*Gerbillus*) are more like ordinary rats, but have longer hind-legs, so that they are rather like miniature kangaroos, and have a corresponding power of leaping. Their tails are long, and covered with short hair, longer at the tip. They are burrowers, living in dry country.

COMMON INDIAN GERBIL

OTHER NAMES.—Scientific: *Gerbillus indicus.* Native: *Harna-mús*, Hindi; *Jhenku-indur*, Bengali; *Yeri yelka*, Wadars; *Tel yelka*, Yanadis; *Billailei*, Canarese; *Pándhará undir*, Mahratti.

HABITAT.—Baluchistan, India, and Ceylon.

DESCRIPTION.—About the size of the common house-rat—up to 7 in. in head and body, with the tail longer. Hind-foot nearly 2 in. from hock to claws. Fawn above, white below, tail-tuft black.

From its colour and activity in leaping, this pretty rat is called "Antelope-rat" in Hindi. It can clear as much as five yards at a bound, and escape a dog by jumping over its back. It is nocturnal and very prolific, often producing a dozen young at a time, and feeds on grass, roots, and grain, and in 1878–9 was a veritable plague in the Deccan over thousands of square miles—one of the few recorded instances of a rodent plague in India. Sterndale says: "With regard to Kellaart's accusation of its being carnivorous at times, I may say I have noticed such tendencies amongst several other rodents which are supposed to be purely vegetarians. I have also known ruminants take to flesh-eating when opportunity offered." The Gerbil is recommended as a food for trained hawks.

DESERT GERBIL

OTHER NAMES.—Scientific: *Gerbillus hurrianæ.*

HABITAT.—Baluchistan to North-Western India.

DESCRIPTION.—Rather smaller than the last species, with proportionately shorter ears and tail, the last not exceeding the head and body, and the ears being only ¼ in. long, whereas in the last they are more than ½ in. Colour much duller, drab shading into dirty white below, but tip of tail also black.

The Desert Gerbil haunts drier localities than the common species, often actual desert; it is also diurnal, and, though more local, is much commoner than the other species usually is, when the locality is suitable to it.

Of the typical rats and mice the Field-rats or Mole-rats (*Nesocia*) are characterised by a broad blunt muzzle and broad feet; their tails are nearly naked, and scaly as in house-rats. They are mostly outdoor rats, eating grass, roots, and corn, and living in extensive burrows in the ground, the openings marked by heaps of the earth they have thrown out, like mole-hills at home.

SHORT-TAILED FIELD-RAT

OTHER NAMES.—Scientific: *Nesocia hardwickei.*

HABITAT.—Baluchistan to the Punjab.

DESCRIPTION.—About the size of a common house-rat, but with a much shorter tail, which may be as little as half the length of the head and body, which may measure over 8 in. Ears only ½ in. long; fur even, coarse or fine, colour warm light brown, paler below.

The Short-tailed Field-rat is found in fields or waste land; Blanford found two pairs in one earth he dug out.

COMMON FIELD-RAT

OTHER NAMES.—Scientific: *Nesocia bengalensis, providens.* Native: *Kok*, Canarese; *Yenkrai*, Bengali; *Golatta koku*, Yanadis.

HABITAT.—India, Ceylon, and Burma.

Description.—Larger than the last, with longer tail, about three-fourths the length of head and body, which may measure up to 9 in.; ears $\frac{3}{4}$ in. Fur dark brown and coarse, often with many long projecting black hairs, pale below.

This is the common out-door rat of India; it is fierce and solitary, and makes large burrows, sometimes extending over an area of several yards, often on the edges of tanks; it swims well, and is destructive in gardens and fields, eating grain as well as grass and roots, and often making stores of the former. It is bread and meat to the Wadars, who not only eat it, but often get plenty of grain from its burrows, sometimes as much as half a seer in one.

Sterndale says: "In confinement these rats are not engaging pets; they show a considerable amount of surliness and ferocity. I have noticed that on approaching the bars of the cage, one would grind its teeth, put back its ears, and fly at you with a grunt."

This species is one of the rats mainly instrumental in the propagation of plague.

Bandicoot.

BANDICOOT

Other Names.—Scientific: *Nesocia bandicota*, *Mus giganteus*. Native: *Indúr*, Sanscrit; *Ghunse*, Hindi; *Ikria*, Bengali; *Heggin*, Canarese; *Pandikoku*, Telegu; *Ura-miyo*, Cingalese.

HABITAT.—India and Ceylon. (The Australian mammals called bandicoots are not rodents, but small marsupials.)

DESCRIPTION.—Much the largest of our rats, 1 ft. or considerably more in length of head and body, with the tail nearly as much, and attaining a weight of three pounds—nearly half as much as our little Indian fox. Fur dark brown above, drab below, mixed above with long black bristly hairs.

The bandicoot's name in Telegu means pig-rat, owing to its habit of grunting, and no doubt also to its large size. It is best known in South India, and haunts cultivation and human habitations, but Blanford thinks it is also found in forest. It is destructive not only to corn and garden produce, but to fowls; but has far less activity and spirit than our common rat at home, and is not such a difficult proposition for a dog as it looks.

SMALLER BANDICOOT

OTHER NAMES.—Scientific: *Nesocia nemorivaga, elliotanus.*

HABITAT.—Bengal east to the Khasi hills and Formosa.

DESCRIPTION.—Much smaller than the true Bandicoot, but larger than our other rats generally are, the head and body measuring 9 in. or over, and the tail about 8 in. Colour as in the large Bandicoot, but fur less coarse and bristly.

The ordinary and most familiar rats and mice belong to the genus *Mus*, which includes more species than any other genus of mammals, and all have long scaly tails and pointed noses, the latter distinguishing them from the blunt-headed species we have just been discussing. They are the most omnivorous and cunning of all rodents, and hold their own the best.

BROWN RAT OR SEWER-RAT

OTHER NAMES—Scientific: *Mus decumanus.* Native: *Ghar-ka-chuha*, Hindi; (*Chuha* alone is probably applied as generally as our word "rat"); *Demsa-indur*, Bengali; *Manei-ilei*, Canarese; *Gaval-miyo*, Cingalese; *Kymek*, Burmese.

HABITAT.—Supposed to be originally Chinese Mongolia, but this rat is now the most widely distributed mammal over the world except man, by the latter's unwilling assistance. Blanford says it "is certainly not indigenous in India, though now found in all large towns and villages, along the banks of navigable rivers, and on high roads."

DESCRIPTION.—Size very variable, from 7 in. to over 10 in. in head and body, which exceed the tail in length. Ears small, not an inch long, just reaching eye when laid forward. Fur brown above, more or less pure white below, coarse in texture. A black variety occurs in Europe, and among domestic rats, which are descended from this species, white and pied specimens are usual, and a buff form has been bred from a wild English " sport " in recent years.

The longer and more tapering muzzle is the best distinction between this and such of the field-rats as resemble it in size.

This is *the* rat *par excellence* for most people, as it is the best known and most abundant in Europe, but in the tropics it is not so successful as the Black or Roof-Rat. The names " Brown " and " Black " are objectionable for both species, as both may be of either colour in some places.

" Sewer-rat " suits the present species better, as it frequents basements and drains, and when living a wild and independent life is often partly aquatic in its habits, being a good swimmer and diver. It is the most carnivorous of common rats and very cunning and fierce. It is instrumental in spreading plague—this being, as most people know, a rodent disease communicated by fleas—but less so than the Roof-rat.

Sterndale says : " I find there is no bait so enticing to the brown rat as a piece of chicken or meat of any kind. I have heard stories of their attacking children and even grown-up people when asleep, but I cannot vouch for the truth of this beyond what once happened to myself. I was then inhabiting a house which swarmed with these creatures, and one night I awoke with a sharp pain in my right arm. Jumping up I disturbed a rat, who sprang off the bed, and was pursued and killed by me. I found he had given me a nip just below the elbow." This habit of biting people is otherwise well authenticated, and " rat-bite fever," a disease caused by the protozoan parasite *Spirillum morsus-muris*, is communicated in this way.

Sterndale further says : " The brown rat breeds several times in a year, and has from ten to fourteen at a time " (according to Blanford, also as few as four). " It is a difficult matter to stop the burrowing of rats ; the best plan is to fill the holes with Portland cement mixed with bits of bottle-glass broken in small pieces."

The Sewer-rat grows to an especially large size in Calcutta, and is said, according to Blanford, often to be mistaken for the bandicoot, which does not occur there—in fact, even the lesser bandicoot is scarce. The destructiveness of this rat is to some extent compensated for by its hostility to the Black or Roof-Rat, which is worse as a plague distributor, but its influence in this respect is but little felt in India.

COMMON INDIAN RAT OR ROOF-RAT

Other Names.—Scientific: *Mus rattus, alexandrinus;* nearly a score more have been applied to this variable animal. Native: *Chuha*, *Musa*, *Kala-mus*, *Kala-chuha*, Hindi; *Gachua-indur*, Bengali; *Kart yelli*, Tamil; *Ghas-miyo*, *Kala-miyo*, Cingalese.

Habitat.—Nearly the whole world, but, Blanford thinks, "probably indigenous in India and found throughout the country, also in Burma and Ceylon, from the sea-level to an elevation of at least 8,000 ft. Its wide distribution is due to unwilling human transport; it is the commonest rat on ships, and invaded Europe centuries before the Sewer-rat or Brown Rat.

Description.—The typical and original rat; proportions much like those of the mouse on a large scale. Tail usually longer than head and body, which measure 5 to 8 in.; ears large, nearly or quite 1 in. long; when pressed forward they reach at least as far as the eye; muzzle rather long and pointed; fur rather long, sometimes spiny, and very variable in colour. Usually it is brown above and more or less pure white below; but in Europe it is black, and this black form—the so-called Old English Black Rat—is most often found in India in seaports, having evidently been re-imported. As the Sewer-rat may also be black, the name is not a good one.

The Roof-rat, as this species is best called, is essentially a climbing rat, and when shifting for itself commonly lives and builds its nest in trees, though it sometimes also lives in burrows in the ground. Its climbing habits lead it especially to frequent roofs, and thus it is particularly a house-rat, and the species mainly influential in spreading plague through infection carried by its fleas. The same climbing habit evidently favours it in getting access to ships and maintaining itself there, and is leading to its re-establishment in Europe, whence it had been to a great extent driven by the Sewer-rat, owing to the advantage it takes of the numerous overhead wires in towns. Although omnivorous, it is less addicted to animal food than the Sewer-rat, and less savage generally; it is also less prolific, the litters not usually exceeding nine in number. Both species breed several times in the year, and, with the common Field-rat or Mole-rat, are the especial pest-rats of India, the most noxious of our small mammals.

LITTLE BURMESE RAT

Other Names.—Scientific: *Mus concolor.*

Habitat.—Pegu and Tenasserim.

Description.—General shape and proportions of ears and tail as in the common Roof-rat, but size much smaller, the head and body only measuring 4 in. in length. Fur brown throughout, coarse, spiny above.

This species shows the close connection between the larger "rats" and the small "mice"; it especially frequents the thatch of houses.

PERSIAN LONG-TAILED FIELD-MOUSE

OTHER NAMES.—Scientific: *Mus arianus, erythronotus.*

HABITAT.—Central Asia to Gilgit.

DESCRIPTION.—A large mouse, while the last is reckoned by Blanford as a small rat. It is of about the same size and general proportions as the last, but with much larger ears, more instead of less than ½ in. long, and has the under-parts white or very pale, and the upper lip and under-side of tail white. It is the eastern form of the Long-tailed Field-mouse of Europe, and is a true field-mouse in summer, though in winter it will come into houses.

COMMON HOUSE-MOUSE

OTHER NAMES.—Scientific: *Mus musculus, urbanus.* Native: *Lengtia-indur*, Bengali; *Mesuri, Músi, Chuhi*, Hindi; *Manei buduga*, Canarese; *Kusetta-miyo*, Cingalese; *Shintad-gandu*, Wadari.

HABITAT.—Nearly throughout our area and most of the rest of the world as well; Blanford says "it is difficult to say whether this species is indigenous or introduced" with us—probably because it is chiefly found in houses but sometimes in gardens and fields near villages and towns. A variously-coloured domestic breed is well known as a pet and subject for research.

DESCRIPTION.—The original typical mouse, with large ears, ½ in. long, and tail generally longer than head and body, which may reach 3 in. in a large specimen. Fur short and soft, brown above, grey below, almost absent on tail, which is all dark.

Sterndale says: "I have kept these mice in confinement for considerable periods. . . . Their activity in running up and down the wires of a cage is marvellous. They have also an extraordinary faculty for running up a perpendicular board, and the height from which they can jump is astounding. One day, in my study, I chased one of these mice on to the top of a bookcase. Standing on some steps, I was about to put my hand over him, when he jumped on to the marble floor and ran off. I measured the height, and have since measured it again, 8 ft. 9½ in.

"I consider this species the most muscular of all mice of the same size. I have had at the same time in confinement an English mouse (albino), a Bengal field mouse, and house mice from Simla of another species, and none of them could show equal activity. I use, for the purpose of taming mice, a glass fish-globe, out of which none of the other mice could get, but I have repeatedly seen specimens of *M. urbanus* jump clear out of the opening at the top. They would look up, gather their hind-quarters together, and then go in for a high leap. They are much more voracious than the Simla or other mice. The allowance of food given would be devoured in less than half the time taken by the others, and they are more given to gnawing. What sort of mothers they are in freedom I know not, but one which produced four young in one of my cages devoured her offspring before they were a week old. I have two before me just now as I write, and they have had a quarrel about the highest place on a little grated window. The larger one got the advantage, so the other seized hold of her tail, and gave it a good nip."

Mice are, as most people know, born blind and naked (as indeed are most rodents); a litter may number as many as eight, and breeding occurs about four times a year. Sterndale says he kept the albino above mentioned for three years—a great age for a mouse.

This mouse is absent from most of North-Western India, where its place is taken by the next species. It is so irresistibly attracted by canary seed that grass seed is evidently its natural food, though in practice it is omnivorous. Paper is a favourite nesting material, and important papers should always be enclosed in tin boxes, even where there is no danger from white ants.

PERSIAN HOUSE-MOUSE

OTHER NAMES.—Scientific: *Mus bactrianus.*

HABITAT.—Egypt east through Asia to North-Western India.

DESCRIPTION.—Similar in size and form to the common House-mouse, but with the tail usually shorter than the head and body, which may be larger than in the last. Colour fawn, shading into white below.

This may turn out to be the "wild" or independent form of the common House-mouse, though also a house species, the colouring bearing much the same relation to that of the common kind as does that of the Alexandrine rat to that of the "Black rat," or that of the brown Musk-shrew to that of the grey species. Its habitat also suggests this.

Sterndale says: "Dr. Anderson got, not long ago, two of these mice in a box from Kohat. . . . Whilst we were talking about them, we noticed an act of intelligence for which I should not have given them credit, had I not seen it with my own eyes. They were in a box with a glass front; in the upper left-hand corner was a small sleeping chamber, led up to by a sloping piece of wood. The entrance of this chamber was barred by wires bent into the form of a lady's hair-pin, and passed through holes in the roof of the box. The mice had been driven out, and the sleeping chamber barred, for they were having their portraits taken. Whilst we were talking we found, to our surprise, that one mouse was inside the chamber, although the bars were down. There seemed hardly space for it to squeeze through; however, it was driven out, and we went on with our conversation, but found, on looking at the cage again, that our little friend was once more inside, so he was driven out again, and we kept an eye on him. . . . We saw him trot up his sloping board, put his little head on one side, and seize one of the wires, which worked very loosely in its socket, give it a hitch up, when he adroitly caught it lower down, hitched it up again and again till he got it high enough to allow him to slip in underneath. . . . He had only been in the box two days, so he was not long in finding out the weak point."

INDIAN FIELD-MOUSE

OTHER NAMES.—Scientific: *Mus buduga, Leggada lepida.* Native: *Chitta-burkani, Chit-yelka, Chitta-ganda, Shintad-phurka, Shintad-bhurka,* Wadaris; *Chitta-yelka,* Yanadis.

HABITAT.—Southern India and Ceylon.

DESCRIPTION.—About size of house-mouse, but tail decidedly shorter than head and body, fur sandy to dark drab above, white below, often mixed with fine transparent spines. Ears smaller than in House-mouse, not extending to eye when laid forward as in that species.

Although occasionally found in houses, this mouse is generally an out-door species, and is found not only in fields, but in gardens and woods; it is, in fact, the common "country mouse" of India. It lives in pairs in burrows, these being marked by a little heap of stones near the entrance, and must be a favourite prey of the Roller or "Blue-jay," as bird-catchers use it for a bait in catching the birds.

BROWN SPINY MOUSE

OTHER NAMES.—Scientific: *Mus* or *Leggada platythrix.* Native: *Legyáde, Kal-yelka, Legad-gandu, Rálelagan-gandu,* Wadaris; *Gijeli-gandu,* Yanadis; *Kal ilei,* Canarese.

HABITAT.—Southern India and Ceylon, north to Sind, but not as far east as Bengal.

DESCRIPTION.—Larger than the House-mouse, with a thick rather hairy tail shorter than the head and body, which are over 3 in Fur very spiny, dark brown, with under-parts white.

The Legyade lives in pairs in burrows in red gravel soil, shutting up its hole when at home with small pebbles, of which a stock is kept outside; the living-chamber is also bedded with small pebbles.

METAD RAT

OTHER NAMES.—Scientific: *Mus mettada*, *Golunda mettada*. Native: *Mettád*, *Mettangandu*, Wadaris; *Metta-yelka*, Yanadis; *Kera ilei*, Canarese.

HABITAT.—Sind to Southern India.

DESCRIPTION.—Size of a small rat, with the tail about the length of the head and body, which measure 5 in. Ear $\frac{3}{4}$ in. Fur drab above, white below, thick and soft in quality.

The Mettad is a rat of cultivated land, and very casual in its habits; it is a poor burrower, and often shelters in heaps of stones, old field-rat burrows, or even cracks caused by the heat. It lives in small parties—very likely families, of about half a dozen, as well as in pairs; but the female has up to eight young at a birth. The collapse of earth-cracks when the rain comes on seems to be the great check on rats of this species, which then perish in numbers, for Elliot, from whom the above details are gleaned, states that when the rainfall was short in the 1826 monsoon, these rats increased so much as to become a plague, ravaging the grain-fields to such an extent that farmers could not pay their rents. They hired the Wadaris to destroy the rats, but though thousands were killed there was no perceptible diminution.

The Bush-rat occupies a genus to itself (*Golunda*) among our rats, the characters of which can be given under our only Indian species.

INDIAN BUSH-RAT OR COFFEE-RAT

OTHER NAMES.—Scientific: *Golunda ellioti*. Native: *Gulandi*, Canarese; *Gulat-yelka*, Wadaris; *Sora-pauji-gadur*, Yanadis; *Utu-elli*, Tamil; *Cofee-watee-meyo*, Cingalese—a name which, as Sterndale says, seems a corruption of "Coffee-rat."

HABITAT.—Sind to Southern India and Ceylon, but not Bengal; said to be migratory at times.

DESCRIPTION.—A small round-headed rat with a tapering coarse-haired tail decidedly shorter than the head and body, which measure about 5 in. Fur of coarse and stiff quality, yellowish-brown grizzled with black above, grey or dirty white below. Ears rather more than $\frac{1}{2}$ in. long.

The Gulandi is a wood-rat, making a round or oval nest of grass and herb-stalks in a bush or on the ground. It is solitary and diurnal, and feeds much on grass roots, but has also proved a pest in coffee plantations, where it fed on the buds and blossoms of the coffee. In spite of this power of climbing, which is, after all, a usual accomplishment in rats, it is a clumsy animal, slow and with little power of jumping, and thus easily caught. Malabar coolies, Tennant noted, were so fond of fried or curried coffee-rats that they preferred

Coffee-rat.

districts which were overrun by them. When an estate has been invaded by these rats under pressure of hunger more than a thousand have been killed in a day, according to Kelaart.

It is to be hoped that missionary workers will be careful not to discourage the habit of eating such animals among their converts—rather should they encourage them to regard the creatures as a provision for the poor.

Another representative of a distinct genus of mice (*Vandeleuria*) may be characterised under its single known species. This is the

LONG-TAILED TREE-MOUSE

OTHER NAMES.—Scientific: *Vandeleuria oleracea, Mus oleraceus.* Native: *Marad ilei*, Canarese; *Meina-yelka*, Yanadis.

HABITAT.—India east to Yunnan, and Ceylon.

DESCRIPTION.—About the size of the House-mouse or a little larger, with a very long tail, more than an inch longer than the head and body; ears large, and inner and outer toes on all feet rather widely separable and with nails instead of claws. Fur soft and chestnut-coloured above, white below and on the feet; tail hairy and dark-coloured.

This very pretty little animal is a climber, living and nesting in trees, and sometimes in the roofs of houses. It is lively and hard to catch. Blanford found three and four young in a nest, and Jerdon eight or ten apparently full-grown ones.

The Voles or Meadow-mice (*Microtus*) are thickset, short-eared little animals with rather short tails and thick fur. They are familiar in temperate climates, and with us are only found high up in the Himalayas. Only one needs notice here.

SIKKIM VOLE

OTHER NAMES.—Scientific: *Microtus sikkimensis*. Native: *Phalchua*, Nepalese; *Chikyu*, Karanti; *Sing phuchi*, Tibetan.

HABITAT.—Sikkim, above 7,000 ft. up to 10,000 ft.

DESCRIPTION.—Tail about a third the length of the head and body, which measure nearly 5 in.; ear ½ in. Fur brown, dark to golden-brown above, much paler beneath.

The Sikkim Vole lives in forests and nests in hollow trees or under roots; it is also found under stones.

The Hamsters (*Cricetus*) represent a further development of the chubby vole type, much resembling guinea-pigs, except that they have short but noticeable tails. The only species we have is found in Gilgit.

GREY HAMSTER

OTHER NAMES.—Scientific: *Cricetus phæus, fulvus, isabellinus.*

HABITAT.—Central Asia to Gilgit.

DESCRIPTION.—Fur soft and grey above, sometimes with a sandy tinge, white below; tail about a quarter as long as the head and body, which vary from less than 4 to more than 5 in. In fact, the animal may be described, as far as size goes, as a small rat or a large mouse in its two extreme forms, and there is an intermediate one of 4½ in. in head and body length. These three varieties are treated as species by Blanford, under the three names given above, *phæus* being the smallest and known for over a century. He says, however: "It is somewhat doubtful whether these three forms of *Cricetus* should be considered species or only varieties. . . . The different forms occur in several places [Gilgit included], but this is not in favour of their being distinct." Many naturalists will probably agree that there is here a similar problem to that presented by the two forms of the leopard, and lump the lot. In the case of these little vegetable feeders, however, it should be possible easily to solve the problem by breeding and cross-breeding the three forms in captivity.

Hamster.

The true Mole-rats (*Spalacidæ*) contain only one Indian genus, the Bamboo-rats (*Rhizomys*) which, if not nearly so mole-like as some non-Indian members of the family, are nevertheless big-headed, sausage-bodied, very short-legged animals with very small eyes and ears, and tails not more than a third of the length of the head and body, so that they are at least much more like moles than the Field-rats of the genus *Nesocia* called Mole-rats by Blanford, which have tails more than half of the head and body length, and conform generally to the ordinary rat type except for their blunt muzzles. The Bamboo-rats, of which we have only three species, are all Eastern animals and powerful burrowers. They have five toes on all feet, though the first toe of the fore-foot is very small, and their incisors are particularly large and powerful. They are used as food by the hill-men of Burma.

BAY BAMBOO-RAT

Other Names.—Scientific : *Rhizomys badius*. Native : *Yukron*, Kakhyen ; *Khai*, Burmese.

Habitat.—Eastern Himalayan Terai east through Burma to Siam, and the ranges above Burma.

Description.—About the size of the Sewer-rat, but with the tail less than 3 in. long and the little ears hidden in the thick fur, which is not always bay or chestnut, but sometimes drab.

M

The Bay or Chestnut Bamboo-rat burrows in high grass or under roots of trees and lives on shoots and roots, coming out of its

Bay Bamboo-Rat.

burrow to feed, when it is easily caught, being slow and fearless, though savage.

HOARY BAMBOO-RAT

Other Names.—Scientific: *Rhizomys pruinosus.*

Habitat.—Hill ranges south of Assam, Kakhyen Hills, Karennee, Cambodia, and South China.

Description.—Much larger than any ordinary rat, the head and body being about 1 ft. long, while the tail is only 4 in., and the ears, as in the last, hidden in the fur, which is grizzled dark brown, the white hairs being more numerous below. Old females have pale brown faces, a peculiar case of the assumption of a special colouring in age by their sex, though old male mammals often show distinctive colour.

The female of this Bamboo-rat, at any rate, is not very prolific, the litter not exceeding four.

LARGE BAMBOO-RAT

Other Names.—Scientific: *Rhizomys sumatrensis.* Native: *Pwe*, Burmese; *Tikus bulo*, Malay, which is very like the name for *Gymnura*, and perhaps only means any large rat-like animal.

Habitat.—From Moulmein and Karennee south-east to Siam and the Malay Peninsula.

Description.—Bigger even than the Bandicoot, the head and body being about 18 in. long, though the tail is not more than 6 in. The fur is very variable in colour, slate, drab, fawn, or buff, grizzled with coarse pale hairs, and in young animals bright rusty-red on the cheeks. It is thin, and allows the ears to be seen, small though they are.

At the opposite extreme to these clumsy animals come the pretty and graceful hopping Jerboas (*Dipodidæ*), of which the characters of the one species which just comes within our limits may be given under its heading.

AFGHAN JERBOA

OTHER NAMES.—Scientific: *Alactaga indica*. Native: *Khani*, Afghan.

HABITAT.—From South-Eastern Persia to the plains south of Quetta.

DESCRIPTION.—Like a very small rat on stilts, with fore-limbs shorter than the rather long rabbit-like ears and a long thin brush-tipped tail. The legs below the hock are very long and spindly, and of the five toes only the three central ones touch the ground; the little fore-feet are five-toed with the inner toe very small. Colour fawn above, white below, with the tail-brush first black then white. Head and body very compact, less than 4 in. long; tail about twice that, and leg from hock to claws over 2 in.

The Afghan Jerboa, like its kind generally, is an active leaper and travels at great speed in this way; no doubt when going slowly it walks with alternate steps, like the Egyptian Jerboa so often kept as a pet, and never uses the fore-legs in progression at all. It is a good burrower, although so different in shape from most mining animals, and goes to ground from October to April, being a hibernator; even during its active period it does not come out by day. A captive specimen ate green wheat and other herbage, potatoes and grain, and would drink, although Major Money, who records this, said that it appeared not to need water when wild. The Egyptian Jerboa in captivity drinks by lifting water to its mouth with the paws; perhaps these little animals brush up dew in this way when at large.

The Porcupines (*Hystricidæ*) are very different from all the other rodents we have been describing; they are very much larger, and their spines are much better developed in length than in any other of our mammals, being in fact commonly called quills; the spines, however, are not so fully developed over the body as in the Hedgehogs among the Insectivores. They have five toes on all feet, though the first toe on the fore-foot is small. They are more exclusively vege-table feeders than most rodents, and their young are well advanced at birth, not being blind, naked, and helpless as usual, nor is the litter numerous. All our species are terrestrial and nocturnal.

The large typical Porcupines (*Hystrix*) are blunt-nosed, stout, thick-set animals of very large size for rodents, weighing over a stone and even at times over two. The hinder part of the back and upper flanks are covered with long sharp spines so stiff and stout as to be used as penholders, and these grade off into shorter spines and hairs, while a few long thin bristle-like spines occur on the back. The tail is short, and covered with short spines, ending in a brush of peculiar quills with narrow roots and blunt open ends. These appear to act as a rattle, and the quills rustle as the beast moves, for he fears enemies little, being an unpleasant animal to interfere with.

Sterndale says: "The porcupine attacks by backing up against an opponent or thrusting at him by a sidelong motion. I kept one some years ago, and had ample opportunity of studying his mode of defence. When a dog or any other foe comes to close quarters, the porcupine wheels round and rapidly charges back. They have also a sideway jerk which is effective." Under these circumstances the spines are erected, and are dangerous not only from the wounds they produce—a goat tethered as a bait for a carnivore has been killed thus—but still more from the fact that some are always loose and liable to be left in the wound, when, unless removed at once, they work further in and cause worse trouble. Owing to this it is advisable and usual to call dogs off the scent of a porcupine, which they follow eagerly.

Porcupines are dainty feeders, and very destructive in gardens and forests; they often live in colonies, as many as fifteen having been killed in a set of burrows by poison gas. It is a pity, however, to waste them, as their flesh is about the best afforded by Indian mammals. being very like delicate pork.

All our species are very much alike in general appearance, dark brown or black, with a whitish half-collar below the neck, and more or less white on the long bristles, back-spines, and tail.

COMMON INDIAN PORCUPINE

OTHER NAMES.—Scientific: *Hystrix leucura.* Native: *Kanta-sahi*, *Sáyi*, *Sáyal*, *Sarsel*, Hindi; *Sájru*, Bengali; *Chotia-dumsi*, Nepalese; *Saori*, *Chaodi*, Guzrati; *Salendra*, Mahratti; *Yed*, Canarese; *Ho-igu*, Gondi; *Hitava*, Cingalese; *Sinkor*, Sindhi; *Sikhan*, Baluchi; *Shkunr*, Pushtu; *Jekra*, Korku; *Jiki*, Ho-Kol; *Yeddu pandi*, Telegu; *Malánpani*, Tamil.

HABITAT.—India and Ceylon, including Kashmir, but not

extending far up the hills in the Eastern Himalayas. Blanford thinks the West-Asiatic Porcupine is most likely only a race of this species.

DESCRIPTION.—The largest of our Porcupines, over 2 ft. in length of head and body, ranging to 2 ft. 8 in., and weighing up to thirty pounds; tail without spines shorter than head. The main distinction from the others, however, is the very long crest and mane of bristles, which may be 1 ft. or more in length, and are at least 6 in. long. The weapon-quills are also overhung by long bristle-spines. The

Porcupine.

tail-quills are white, but in some specimens these, and the white rings on the long weapon-quills of the back, are more or less orange instead of white, though this colour may disappear after a moult in confinement.

Sterndale says: "The Indian porcupine lives in burrows, in banks, hill-sides, on the bunds of tanks, and in the sides of rivers and nullahs. . . . In the jungle its food consists chiefly of roots, especially of some kinds of wild yam (*Dioscorea*). I have found porcupines in the densest bamboo jungles of the Central Provinces, where their food was doubtless young bamboo shoots and various kind[s] of roots. . . . The Gonds of Seeonee were always on the look out for a porcupine. I described in my book on that district the digging out of one.

"The entrance of the animal's abode was a hole in a bank at which the dogs were yelping and scratching; but the bipeds had gone more scientifically to work by countermining from above, sinking shafts downwards at various points, till at last they reached his inner chamber, when he scuttled out and, charging backwards at the dogs with all his spines erected, he soon sent them flying, howling most piteously; but a Gondee axe hurled at his head soon put an end to his career, for a porcupine's skull is particularly tender."

The leopard, being quick-pawed and quick-witted, is said sometimes to bring the porcupine to book by a sudden blow on the head.

The female produces from two to four young, which are born with their eyes open. Their bodies are covered with short soft spines, which, however, speedily harden. "It is said," says Sterndale, "that the young do not remain long with their mother, but I cannot speak to this from personal experience. I have had young ones, but not those born in captivity."

The voice of the porcupine is a grunt, and it has a habit of gnawing bones or elephant tusks which it may find in the jungle.

BENGAL PORCUPINE

OTHER NAMES.—Scientific: *Hystrix bengalensis.* Native: *Sajru*, Bengali; *Phyu*, Burmese.

HABITAT.—Sikkim, and Lower Bengal east to Arakan.

DESCRIPTION.—Not so large as the common species on the whole, but still over 2 ft. in length of head and body. Mane-bristles not more than 6 in. long, and the crest scanty. Tail black and white. Only a few long spiny bristles among the quills; body spines very flat and grooved.

CRESTLESS HIMALAYAN PORCUPINE

OTHER NAMES.—Scientific: *Hystrix hodgsoni, longicauda.* Native: *Anchotia-sahi*, *Anchotia-dumsi*, Nepalese; *Sathung*, Lepcha; *O-e*, Limbu; *Midi*, Cachari; *Subon-dem*, Manipuri; *Suku*, Kuki; *Sisi*, Daphla; *Tuigon*, *Soke*, *Liso*, *Vikhá*, *Sekru*, Naga.

HABITAT.—Nepal to Assam, not ascending the Himalayas to more than about 5,000 ft.

DESCRIPTION.—The smallest of the large porcupines, being

barely 2 ft. in length of head and body, though the tail is as long as that of the large species, 8 in. with the spines. Mane absent or very feebly developed, body-spines flat and grooved, long spiny bristles among the weapon-quills scanty. Tail-quills partly black and partly white.

Hodgson says that this species is monogamous, and produces two young in spring. It breeds readily in confinement, and is, he says, eaten even by high-caste Hindus.

The only Indian species of the other genus of Porcupines found with us (*Atherura*) can be characterised under its name.

BRUSH-TAILED PORCUPINE

OTHER NAMES.—Scientific: *Atherura macrura.* Native: *Landak*, Malay.

HABITAT.—Burma east to Borneo.

DESCRIPTION.—Not so peculiar-looking as the other porcupines, being like a huge, spiny, brush-tailed rat—in fact, it is sometimes called Porcupine-rat—the spines as a whole not being long enough to obscure the outline of the head and body, which are rat-like, and the tail being nearly half as long as these, which measure from 1½ to nearly 2 ft. A few very long bristle-spines project on the hinder back, and the brush at the end of the tail is mostly made up of curious flat bristles strongly contracted at short intervals. Colour brown for the most part, more or less pure white below, on the long bristles and the brush.

In spite of its very different appearance and far less massive build, this animal is said to have the same habits as the typical porcupines just described. Its very close African ally, *Atherura africana,* is said to be a staple article of food with the natives of the island of Fernando Po.

In the sub-order of Double-toothed Rodents (*Duplicidentata*) there are, as before remarked, a pair of little incisors behind the ordinary large ones in the upper jaw. Young animals at birth have a third pair, but these soon disappear. The incisors in the present sub-order of rodents are not so large as in the others, and the animals have five toes on the fore- and four on the hind-feet, well covered with fur even below. Their eyes are usually large and they have no eyelids. The size is always fair or large as rodents go, and the feeding habits strongly vegetarian. They live on the ground and never have long tails.

Of the two families of this group, the Hares (*Leporidæ*) are the best known of all rodents, owing to the common rabbit being one of them, so that their characteristics, long ears and hind-legs and short upturned tail or "scut," are familiar to every one.

Most of our hares, however, have longer hind-legs and ears than the rabbit, and the young are born with their eyes open and are well covered with fur, not blind and naked like most young rodents. Hares live upon herbage, and generally do not burrow. Most of our species are much alike, but easily distinguishable by certain special points, particularly the colour of the tail. The flesh in most is dark in colour, not white like the rabbit's. Tame rabbits, by the way, thrive well in India, but there seems to be no instance of their being established wild. Eight species of hares are found with us.

COMMON INDIAN HARE

OTHER NAMES.—Scientific: *Lepus ruficaudatus.* Native: *Khargosh*, *Khará*, Hindi; *Sásra*, Bengali; *Malol*, Gondi; *Kulhai*, Kol and Sontali; *Koarli*, Korku; *Manya* at Rajmehal.

HABITAT.—Central and eastern parts of Northern India, but not in the South-West Punjab, or in Sind or Western Rajputana. It does not ascend the hills.

DESCRIPTION.—A foot and a half or a little more in length of head and body; ears decidedly longer than the tail, which is 4 in. with the fur. The female, as in the rabbit, is the larger animal, and may weigh five pounds.

Fur of coarse quality, reddish-brown mixed with black above, without black on chest, legs, and upper-side of tail; throat, belly, and under-side of tail white.

Sterndale says: "The Indian hare is generally found in open bush country, often on the banks of rivers, at least as far as my experience goes in the Central Provinces. Jerdon says, and McMaster corroborates his statement, that this species, as well as the next, take readily to earth when pursued, and seem to be well acquainted with all the fox-holes in their neighbourhood, and McMaster adds that they seem to be well aware which holes have foxes or not, and never go into a tenanted one [no doubt warned by scent]. The Indian hare is by no means so good for the table as the European one, being dry and tasteless, and hardly worth cooking." Blanford, however, says "much of the usual inferiority is probably due to cookery. When jugged this hare is by no means unpalatable." The editor found that in Dehra Dun there was a notion—probably well-founded—that hares found near a station were not desirable as food, being presumably foul-feeders, as so many Indian creatures are near native habitations; and this may account for the hare being unclean in Mosaic law. Blanford says that more than once he has found only a single young one in a pregnant female, though Hodgson says two are usually born.

BLACK-NAPED HARE

OTHER NAMES.—Scientific: *Khargosh*, Hindi; *Malla*, Canarese; *Musal*, Tamil; *Kundeli*, Telegu; *Hava*, Cingalese; *Lassa*, Mahratti.

HABITAT.—India south of the Godavari, and including the Nilgiris; also Ceylon.

DESCRIPTION.—Easily distinguished from the last and all our other hares by the conspicuous patch of black velvety fur on the back of the neck; otherwise similarly coloured, and also coarse-furred. Size about the same, but weight sometimes more, especially in the Nilgiris, where it may even reach eight pounds.

The Black-naped Hare, on the Nilgiris at any rate, often takes to hollow trees when hunted. It breeds there from autumn to the beginning of spring, producing one or two young, and is often, if well kept and cooked, nearly as good eating as our British hare. According to Jerdon it has been introduced into Java and Mauritius.

SIND HARE

OTHER NAMES.—Scientific: *Lepus dayanus*. Native: *Lassa*, *Saho*, *Seher*, Sindih.

HABITAT.—Most of the Indian desert east of the Indus, Sind, and Cutch; Blanford, who gives these details, thinks it also occurs in the Deraját in the Punjab.

DESCRIPTION.—A little smaller than the common Indian hare, and with soft instead of harsh fur; colour much more greyish above, and —the most marked distinction—upper-side of tail blackish-brown, its under-side, with the throat and belly, white.

This hare chiefly affects desert districts.

BURMESE HARE

OTHER NAMES.—Scientific: *Lepus peguensis*. Native: *Yung*, *Phu-goung*, Burmese.

HABITAT.—Burma, but not in deep forest or coastland.

DESCRIPTION.—A little larger than the common Indian hare, and with large black tips to the ears and the top of the tail black; all under-parts clearly defined, white. Head and body 21 in., but ears only 4¼ in. as against 5 in. in the common Indian species.

This hare is apparently not at all well known, for Blanford says:

"I am indebted to Major [later Colonel] Bingham for a good skin of this species, of which there was till recently no specimen in Europe."

AFGHAN HARE

OTHER NAMES.—Scientific: *Lepus tibetanus.*

HABITAT.—Afghanistan, Baluchistan, and Upper Indus Valley.

DESCRIPTION.—About the size of, or rather less than, the common Indian hare, but with soft fur and the ears broader in proportion to their length of 5 in. Weight, according to Blanford, three and a half pounds. Colour often more greyish than in the common animal, and tail marked above with a broad black stripe. The broad ears (3 in., laid flat) will distinguish it from the last two species. Although a mountain animal, it is found as low as 500 ft. above sea-level in Baluchistan.

WOOLLY HARE

OTHER NAMES.—Scientific: *Lepus oiostolus.* Native: *Rigong*, Tibetan.

HABITAT.—Tibet and Sikkim.

DESCRIPTION.—Larger than our common hares and with shorter ears in proportion, the ears being well furred, not nearly naked as in the ordinary species. Body fur more or less curly, especially in the young, soft in texture, thick and woolly, fawn-colour with some admixture of dark brown. Throat and belly white, rump grey, tail white. Young sometimes grey. Ears nearly 5 in. long, while the head and body measure 22 in. Hind-foot to hock 4½ in.

This hare, according to Blanford, may ultimately prove, with the next, to be a variety of the widely-ranging Blue or Scotch Hare, but does not turn white in winter like that species.

UPLAND HARE

OTHER NAMES.—Scientific: *Lepus hypsibius.*

HABITAT.—Ladak and Rukshu, at high elevations.

DESCRIPTION.—The largest of our hares, measuring 2 ft. in head and body length, at least in skins, but with short ears for its size, 4½ in. in the skin, less than the hind-foot, which is 5 in. Darker above and with longer and woollier fur than the last; tail all white, whereas in the last there are a few grey hairs at the root.

Blanford, however, hints that this may be only a variety of the woolly hare, which seems likely.

HISPID HARE

OTHER NAMES.—Scientific : *Lepus hispidus, Caprolagus hispidus.* " Black Rabbit " of Dacca sportsmen.

HABITAT.—Himalayan Terai, ranging south to Dacca.

DESCRIPTION.—The most distinct of our hares, with the ears decidedly shorter than the head, instead of at least equal to it, small eyes, comparatively short hind-legs, and harsh, even bristly fur much mixed with long black hairs and of a general dark rusty grey or brown in colour above, dirty white below, with the tail altogether brown. Size about equal to the common hare, but the ears less than 3 in., and tail about 2 in. The general appearance is very rabbit-like, so it might just as well be called " Rough Rabbit " as " Hispid Hare " ; and it may fairly form a distinct genus.

It also burrows like the rabbit, but is not social ; its flesh is said to be white like a rabbit's, but the condition of the newly-born young is not known. In fact, very little is known about it at all, though native accounts credit it with living on roots and bark. It also frequents tree and grass cover. The more powerful teeth and claws in this animal would be enough to make one suspect a difference between its habits and those of ordinary hares.

The Pikas (*Lagomyidæ*) are also called Piping or Calling Hares, or Mouse-hares, but they look more like Guinea-pigs than anything else, owing to their short legs, small size, short round ears, and the complete absence of a tail. In the character of their coats and the furry feet, however, they are hare-like, and resemble rabbits in their way of living, being social burrowers. They feed on herbage, and live at high elevations among rocks. Their piping call is in strong contrast to the general silence of their allies the hares. We have five species, all much alike, and none exceeding a guinea-pig in size.

HIMALAYAN PIKA

OTHER NAMES.—Scientific : *Lagomys roylei.* Native : *Rang-runt, Rang-duni*, in Kunawar ; *Gumchen*, Bhutia.

HABITAT.—Kashmir eastwards to North-East Tibet and Kansu. Range from 11,000 to 16,000 ft. in our hills.

DESCRIPTION.—About the size of a small rat, the head and body being 6½ in. Colour some shade of brown, with now and then a collar of paler tint, which is, however, narrow, not broad like the collar of the Red Pika presently to be noticed. The toe-pads of this species are exposed, and its ears of moderate size.

Although this Pika most commonly occurs among rocks, it is found in steep pine-forests in the Eastern Himalayas. Four young have been found in a pregnant female, but there seems to be no other information about the breeding of this or any of our other Pikas.

HODGSON'S OR CURZON'S PIKA

OTHER NAMES.—Scientific: *Lagomys curzoniæ.* Native: *Abra*, Tibetan.

HABITAT.—The Chumbi valley; Blanford believes Sikkim also, at high elevations.

DESCRIPTION.—Rather larger than the last, with broad pale borders to the ears, which are also of moderate size in this species; in the last, if there is a pale border to the ears, it is narrow. Colour pale sandy; toe-pads concealed by hair. This is a rare animal, nearly related to the last.

LARGE-EARED PIKA

OTHER NAMES.—Scientific: *Lagomys macrotis, auritus.*

HABITAT.—North of the Kuenlun range, and Gilgit, in the latter case at a wide range of elevation, from 7,500 to 13,000 ft.

DESCRIPTION.—About 7 in. in length, thus being intermediate in size between the last two species; ears large for a Pika—1 in. long, whereas in the last two they are not more than $\frac{3}{4}$ in.; toe-pads visible. Colour from dirty buff to reddish- or darkish-brown, with the feet white, whereas in the Himalayan species they are brown, and in Hodgson's dirty white.

The Large-eared Pika is locally abundant on open stony ground near the snow-line.

RED PIKA

OTHER NAMES.—Scientific: *Lagomys rufescens.*

HABITAT.—Persia, Afghan Turkestan, Afghanistan, and the neighbourhood of Quetta.

DESCRIPTION.—Size about that of the Himalayan Pika, and ears barely longer, toe-pads also exposed; but distinguished by a broad band of whitish hue across the nape; general colour pale reddish-brown, becoming redder behind the pale collar in summer coat, especially in front of the shoulders. This Pika ranges lower than the others, even down to 5,000 ft.

LADAK PIKA

OTHER NAMES.—Scientific: *Lagomys ladacensis.* Native: *Zabra, Karin, Phise Karin*, Ladakhi.

HABITAT.—High elevations in Eastern Ladak and Rukshu, above 14,000 ft.

DESCRIPTION.—The largest of our Pikas, about 9 in. long, and with comparatively large ears, at least 1 in. long. Toe-pads hardly visible in winter, but bare in summer, when also the back is reddish, the general colour of the fur being pale yellowish-brown, often redder on the face.

ORDER UNGULATA

The Ungulata or Hoofed Mammals are animals of good to very large size—our smallest being as big as a wild rabbit, a large animal for a rodent—and of very varied form. All our species have the toes encased at the tips with hoofs or nails as opposed to claws; and the limbs themselves are adapted solely for progress on the ground, not for grasping or digging. The toes are generally less than the primitive number of five, and the wrist and heel raised above the ground—these joints are usually called knee and hock, the true knee in the hind-leg being generally tucked up close to the body. The body is usually bulky and comparatively short and stiff, the tail always thin and often short, and the legs, as has been well remarked, reduced to jointed sticks; the back teeth are broad and specialised for grinding vegetable food, which is the sole diet of most. The other teeth are often more or less deficient, but may be developed into tusks in the males. These also often bear horns, and may differ much in appearance from the females, while the young are also often different from either in colour; but they are born perfect and active, and closely resembling the parents in form, though generally with longer limbs, as they soon take to travelling. The hair of Ungulates is coarse and often thin or deficient; the animals are, so to speak, campers on the surface of the ground rather than dwellers in dens. They are generally social and polygamous, and have keenly developed senses, being especially conspicuous for long-distance scenting powers.

They are seldom directly dangerous to men, but often very destructive to crops. They are valuable for food and are the most important of game animals, besides furnishing the most important domestic species.

Three easily distinguished sub-orders are found with us—the *Proboscidea*, including the elephant only; the Odd-toed Ungulates (*Perissodactyla*), in which the chief and sometimes the only toe is the third—the middle toe of the complete five-toed foot; and the Even-toed Ungulates (*Artiodactyla*), in which there are two main toes, the third and fourth being evenly developed and flattened on their inner surfaces so as to fit like one split hoof, whence these animals are often called cloven-hoofed.

The Proboscidea contain only one family, the Elephants (*Elephantidæ*), and we have one of the only two living species, the characters of which are given below.

INDIAN ELEPHANT

Other Names.—Scientific : *Elephas indicus, maximus*. Native : *Hathi* (male), *Hathni* (female), Hindi ; *Hasti, Gája*, Sanskrit ; *Gáj*, Bengali ; *Ani*, Southern Indian languages ; *Fil*, Persian ; *Allia*, Cingalese ; *Gája*, Malay ; *Tsheng*, Burmese ; *Yani*, Gondi ; *Tengmú*, Lepcha ; *Lángchen, Lamhoché*, Bhotia ; *Mongma, Naplo*, Garo ; *Miyung*, Cachari ; *Atche*, Aka ; *Sotso, Supo, Chu, Tsu*, Nága ; *Sitte*, Abor ; *Tsang*, Khámti ; *Magui*, Singpho ; *Saipi*, Kuki ; *Amieng, Mányong*, Mishmi ; *Sámú*, Manipuri ; *Tsing*, Talain ; *Tsan*, Shan ; *Káhsa*, Karen.

Habitat.—India east to Borneo, and Ceylon, not ranging high in the Himalayas, but up to several thousand feet in the southern hills. Elephants are confined to forest districts, and their range has become much restricted within the last few centuries.

Description.—The largest of our land animals, and well known to everybody by the long trunk, at the end of which the nostrils are placed, with a finger-like process above and a lip-like one below them, which are used as finger and thumb, while the whole trunk serves as an arm. Lower lip small, pointed and spout-like. Head very large and neck short, body bulky, sloping from shoulders to croup, though the limbs, which are thick and very straight, are of about equal length ; wrist and ankle low down, and knee also set low, so that the limbs resemble those of the primates more than those of other Ungulates. All the five toes are also present, and joined into one pad, but only four bear nails in the hind-foot, and sometimes in the fore, which is larger and rounder. Tail thin and long, with a row of very coarse bristles on each side near the end ; with the exception of these, some long, thin, straggling hairs on the lower lip, and the well-developed eyelashes, the animal is usually almost hairless. Young elephants, however, have a good deal of hair, which may be quite thick on the head, and Bishop Heber records a small female " almost as shaggy as a poodle-dog," evidently a reversion to a hair-clad ancestor very like the extinct Mammoth, which was nearly related. Eyes very small and ears large and flat.

Colour of skin slaty, the head and ears often with flesh-coloured patches speckled with black ; hairs black as a rule, but there is a red-haired race in Burma, and the white elephants, which are commoner, or, rather, less rare, in the eastern part of the animal's range, have the hairs sandy, the skin being flesh-coloured. The only one the editor has seen, exhibited recently in the London Zoo, also had the iris white instead of brown as usual.

No teeth in the fore-part of the jaws except one pair of incisors, short and not noticeable in females, young, and some males known as *maknas*, which are vastly in the majority in Ceylon ; but the ordinary male or tusker has these incisors in the form of very long, continually growing ivory tusks. A tusk of 8 ft. is recorded.

Grinders very long, composed of alternating plates of harder enamel and softer ivory : only one and a half are in use at a time, for these teeth are being cut during all the animal's lifetime, moving forwards from the back, so that the half-tooth may be either one that is nearly worn out or about to be shed, or one that is coming into use.

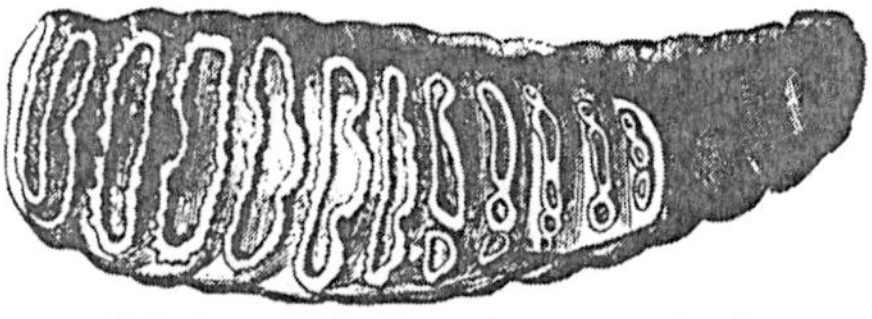

Grinder of Elephant (upper surface).

The total number is six for each side of each jaw, and the part of the tooth exposed is but a small portion of its total depth. Sterndale says : "In the wild state, sand and grit, entangled in the roots of plants, help in the work of attrition, and, according to Professor Boyd Dawkins, the tame animal, getting cleaner food, and not having such wear and tear of teeth, gets a deformity by the piling over of the plates of which the grinder is composed. An instance of this has come under my notice. An elephant belonging to my brother-in-law, Colonel W. B. Thomson, then Deputy Commissioner of Seconee, suffered from an aggravated type of this malformation. He was relieved by an ingenious mahout, who managed to saw off the projecting portion of the tooth, which now forms a paper-weight. In my account of Seeonee I have given a detailed description of the mode in which the operation was effected.

The skull of the elephant possesses many striking features quite different from any other animal. The brain in bulk does not greatly exceed that of a man, therefore the rest of the enormous head is formed of cellular bone, affording a large space for the attachment of the powerful muscles of the trunk, and at the same time combining lightness and strength. This cellular bone grows with the animal, and is in great measure absent at birth. In the young elephant the brain nearly fills the head, and the brain-case increases but little in size during growth, but the cellular portion increases rapidly with the growth of the animal, and is piled up over the frontals for a considerable height, giving the appearance of a bold forehead, the brain remaining in a small space at the base of the skull, close to its articulation with the neck . . . the brain itself is highly convoluted. The nasal aperture or olfactory fossa, is very large, and is placed a little below the brain-case. Few people who are intimate with but the external form of the elephant would suppose that the bump just above the root of the trunk, at which the hunter takes aim for the 'front

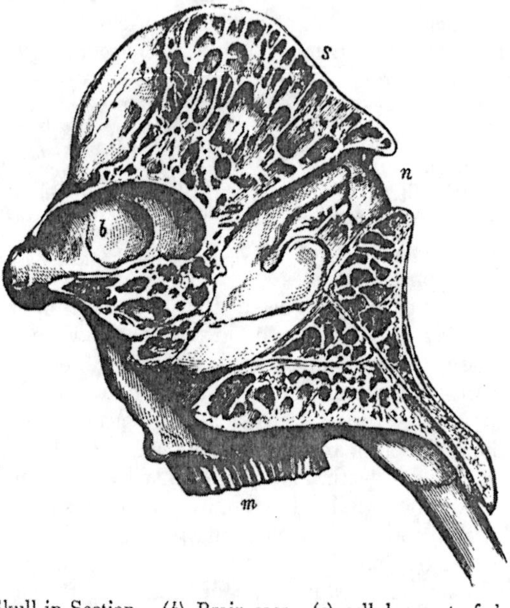

Elephant's Skull in Section. (*b*) Brain-case; (*s*) cellular part of skull; (*n*) nasal opening; (*m*) grinder.

shot' is really the seat of the organ of smell, the channels of which run down the trunk to the orifice at the end."

"As regards the size of elephants," Sterndale says, "few people agree; the controversy is as strong on this point as on the size of tigers. I quite believe few elephants attain to or exceed 10 ft., still there are one or two recorded instances, the most trustworthy of which is Mr. Sanderson's measurement of the Sirmoor Rajah's elephant, which is 10 ft. 7½ in. at the shoulder—a truly enormous animal. I have heard of a tusker at Hyderabad that is over 11 ft., but we must hold this open to doubt till an accurate measurement, which I have applied for, is received. Elephants should be measured like a horse, with a standard and cross-bar, and not by means of a piece of string over the rounded muscles of the shoulder. Kellaart, usually a most accurate observer, mentions in his *Prodromus Faunæ Zeylanicæ* having measured a Ceylon elephant nearly 12 ft. high, but does not say how it was done."

The elephant is liable to malformations of the tusks. "I have heard," says Sterndale, "of their overlapping and crossing the trunk in a manner to impede the free use of that organ." The editor well knew an elephant, Jingo, formerly shown in the London Zoo, which had precisely this defect.

Neither Sterndale nor Blanford mentions the individual differences in elephants by which Indians divide them into different castes: the Koomeriah, a massive majestic animal; the Mirga, the opposite extreme, a long-legged weed; and the Dwasala, the average middle-class elephant, such as most specimens are.

The habits of elephants have long been well known, and need only a brief summary here. They frequent high grass as well as forest, and feed on grass as well as on leaves, twigs, bark, and fruit. They usually drink twice a day, filling the last foot or so of the trunk with water, and then squirting it into the mouth. Tame animals eat loose grain in the same way. They require a very large quantity of food, Sanderson having found six or seven hundred pounds of green fodder to be only a day's supply for one.

The females and young are gregarious, but males are often solitary, not only young animals which have not gained a position as herd-bull, but the old bulls themselves, which do not always stay with their herds, and often become dangerous "rogues," so that the idea that such noxious animals are soured by expulsion by a rival is not always correct. It is said to have been noticed that rogues became more common during the Great War—when, of course, little shooting went on—and a recent writer states that probably any male elephant over a certain age is a dangerous animal for an unarmed man to meet. Rogues have a price set on their heads, but otherwise elephants are protected in our Eastern empire. The leader of the herd is never the herd-bull, but a female.

Elephants are fond of bathing as well as wallowing, when the weather is hot; they also squirt water over themselves, and even, when none is available procure it by thrusting the trunk into the mouth. The editor has seen an animal in the London Zoo behave thus when heated, and noticed that the water was full of particles of bread, etc., so that it is evidently the fluid contents of the stomach that are thus utilised, rather than some internal secretion, though such a secretion may form part of it. At any rate the elephant has no water-storing arrangement in its interior such as is found in the stomach of the camel. Elephants are fond of shade, and will often take up dust, etc., to cover their backs when exposed to the sun. They are restless animals, but remain quiet during the middle hours of the day and night. They lie down when sleeping, but are seldom seen thus. When kneeling down, they extend the fore-legs in front, and really kneel on the two knees behind, the feet extending backwards; they go down steep hills in this way, resting on the wrists or fore-"knees" when going up such places. They will also use their feet to make footholds where possible, and owing to this adaptability of limb are remarkably good climbers for their huge bulk and weight. They can only walk or trot—or rather shuffle, being, it is said, so incapable of any sort of spring that they cannot cross a trench 6 in. beyond the length of their stride, which in a large specimen is 6½ ft. This is attributed to the straightness of their limbs, and if disabled in one hind-leg they are helpless, no doubt for the same reason, so that the tiger sometimes captures an unwary young one by tearing out its hind-leg tendons with his claws and then waiting till the herd has at last left it. Elephants are powerful and enduring but very slow swimmers, and support their young, if very small, at such times with their trunks—calves rather older ride on their dams' backs in the water.

At birth the calf is only 1 yd. high, with the trunk 1 ft. long and not very flexible; it begins to eat grass at about six months old. Usually only one is born, though twins occur at times, and the gestation period is from eighteen to twenty-two months. While quite small, the calf runs under its mother's body; it sucks with the mouth like other young mammals, but the teats of the parent are not placed as in other ungulates, but in the arm-pit—another resemblance to the primates. Calves are usually born from September to November; they are rarely produced in captivity in most places, but not uncommonly in Burma, and quite regularly in Siam.

Elephants are not mature till after twenty-five years, and are supposed to live till 150; captive ones have been known to exceed a century. The adult male becomes periodically *mast* or mad, and is then dangerous, but warning of the attack is given by an exudation from small holes in the temples; and Sanderson observed this in some females also.

The most acute sense of the elephant is smell, but the trunk has a well-developed sense of touch, and the skin generally is more sensitive and easily injured than would be expected from its thickness.

The animal is highly-strung and emotional, and has even been known to shed tears when forced to leave its home, while large specimens when caught and tied will even die at times from shock. It is natural that the beast should be nervous of soft ground, as it is in great danger of getting bogged in such circumstances. Many are also timid with other animals, and not every one is suitable for shikar by any means.

Besides the "trumpeting" and a roar, the elephant emits an alarm-call by blowing through the trunk while rapping it on the ground, besides rumbling in the throat if discontented, and squeaking through the trunk in pleasure.

About the intelligence of the elephant there is much difference of opinion. Sterndale says: "I think one as often sees instances of decided stupidity on the part of elephants as of sagacity, but I think the amount of intelligence varies in individuals. I have known cases where elephants have tried to get their mahouts off their backs—two cases in my own district; in the one the elephant tried shaking and then lying down, both of which proved ineffectual; in the other it tried tearing off the rafters of a hut and throwing them over its back, and finally rubbing against low branches of trees, which proved successful. The second elephant, I think, showed the greatest amount of original thought; but there is no doubt that the sagacity of the animal has been greatly overrated. . . .

"On the other hand, we do hear of wonderful cases of reasoning on the part of these creatures. I have never seen anything very extraordinary myself; but I had one elephant which almost invariably attempted to get loose at night, and often succeeded, if we were encamped in the neighbourhood of sugar-cane cultivation—nothing else tempted her; and many a rupee have I had to pay for the damage done. This elephant knew me perfectly after an absence of eighteen months, trumpeted when she saw me, and purred as I came up and stroked her trunk. I then gave her the old sign, and in a moment she lifted me by the trunk on to her head. I never mounted her any other way, and, as I used to slip off by a side rope, the constant kneeling down and getting up was avoided."

On this subject, Blanford remarks that the elephant is remarkably docile, no other known mammal being capable of domestication when adult to the same extent, and that docility in animals is frequently confounded with intelligence.

This is true, but it must be remembered that docility alone will not enable an animal to learn much—it must have some intelligence to grasp what is required of it, and elephants from ancient times have been known as capable of being taught very many tricks. Also individual differences in intelligence must be taken into account, as well as the highly-strung nature of the elephant, nervousness often inhibiting intelligence even in man. The propensity of an elephant to put anything it can seize under its fore-legs when in danger of being bogged, which makes it then so dangerous to its riders, seems to indicate intelligence, and also the cunning of "rogues." Napier, imported with other elephants into the Andamans for timber-work, was at large for fourteen years, and was so cunning that he would never return from an excursion by the same route as that by which he had gone out. Trainers and keepers who work with elephants are, the editor believes, impressed with the sagacity of the animals, and they would seem to be the best qualified to judge; in any case, this subject is perhaps the most interesting connected with this wonderful animal.

A few lines may be added on the one living relative of our elephant and on its ancestry. The African elephant differs from the Indian in being taller and slighter, with an evenly rounded forehead like the young of our species, in having two lips at the end of the trunk, and no finger, and only three nails on the hind-feet; while there are tusks in both sexes, and the pattern of the grinders is different. But the most conspicuous difference is in the ears, which in the African animal are enormous, meeting on the nape above, and reaching down to the throat below. In size it is at its best larger than the Indian animal, but it varies much locally, and a pigmy race exists in West Africa in which a full-grown male is not bigger than a dray-horse. The species also appears less docile in captivity and fiercer when wild, as well as less sensitive to sun and less dependent on the neighbourhood of water.

The remains of various ancestral elephants lead from the Mastodons, best known from America, to various proboscideans disinterred in Egypt by that admirable naturalist the late Dr. Andrews, and end in a form about the size of a hog with a very short trunk and several incisors, the upper outer ones rather enlarged and pointing downwards, which afterwards changed direction and became the tusks, while the front teeth of the lower jaw disappeared in time, the jaw ultimately shortening and the whole skull becoming high and short.

The limbs, however, were from the first very much the same as they are at present, having merely become elongated while the body became shorter.

These early forms were no doubt well covered with hair, of which the Mammoth had a plentiful coat; and, as we have seen, remains of this occur in our species to-day.

The *Perissodactyla*, or Odd-toed Ungulates, contain three families, with but a single genus in each—the Horses, Tapirs, and Rhinoceroses. The Horses (*Equidæ*) are distinguished by having but a single toe on each foot, with a large rounded hoof; the Tapirs (*Tapiridæ*) by being odd-toed only behind, where there are three toes on each foot, while the fore-feet are four-toed, though here also the third toe is the biggest; the Rhinoceroses (*Rhinocerotidæ*) by having three toes on all feet.

We have only one species of the Horse family, which, in spite of their notoriously noisy gait, are the most confirmed tip-toe walkers of all animals, going on the end of one toe only.

Asiatic Wild Ass.

THE ASIATIC WILD ASS

OTHER NAMES.—Scientific: *Equus hemionus, onager*. Native: *Ghor-khar*, Hindi; *Ghour, Kerdecht*, Persian; *Koulan*, Kirghiz; *Kiang, Dzightai*, Tibetan.

HABITAT.—Western Asia east to Central Asia and south to North-West India to Bikanir and the Rann of Cutch.

DESCRIPTION.—Stands from 11 to 12 hands at the shoulder, which is lower than the croup, and in general form resembles a mule, with the ears longer than in the horse but shorter than the ass's, and the tail more bushy than the ass's, but less so than that of the horse. Mane short and erect, "chestnuts" present on the fore-legs but not on the hinder pair. Colour dun or chestnut, sometimes sandy grey, with the muzzle, legs, and under-parts white, and the mane, tail-tuft, and a stripe down the back dark brown.

There are two well-marked varieties, the Southern or Onager, which is lighter in colour, and the Kiang or Central Asian, which is darker and redder, with a rather thick coat in winter. This is often the larger, and looks more horse-like—in fact, some writers have actually called it a horse, while from ancient times the other has always been called an ass or a "wild mule." The two forms have often been, and are still sometimes, ranked as distinct species, but such good all-round naturalists as Blyth and Blanford have united them, and in zoological matters it is generally the most scientific policy to follow the "lumpers" rather than the "splitters" where species are concerned. The Asiatic Wild Ass lives in herds of very various sizes—as few as four or as many as a thousand having been seen together, but a score would probably represent the average. It frequents dry or actually desert open country, generally plains, but also takes to the hills, where it is a fine climber like the mule. It feeds on grass and other herbs, and has an incredible power of thriving on little food; a writer in the *Geographical Journal*, Colonel Meinertzhagen, in 1927 relates how he found some grazing, and on going to the spot and gathering every plant to be found in an area of 100 yards by 10, got not enough to make a meal for a guinea-pig!

This creature is the swiftest of all wild equines, and can rarely be fairly run down by one rider, though Blanford relates that some have been ridden down and speared on the Rann of Cutch. He believes, however, that these specimens were mares in foal—in which case the act was a most brutal one. The foals are supposed to be born, in our trans-Indus territory, from June to August. Some foals are captured by being ridden down by relays of horsemen, and the animal is well known in captivity, both in the East and at home. Sterndale says: "I remember we had a pair of these asses in the Zoological Gardens at Lahore in 1868; they were to a certain extent tame, but very skittish, and would whinny and kick on being approached. I never heard of their being mounted."

Some met with by Colonel Waddell at Lhasa made friends at once with the British forces' mules, and two which were being taken home —of which only one arrived, the other having been drowned *en route*—

though they would not bear being mounted, could be handled, and consented to wear ponies' rugs at night.

Some of the ancients could go further than this with them, for Herodotus says that the Indian contingent of Xerxes' great army had chariots drawn by wild asses.

The Onager race has always been esteemed for sport and even for food, being, curiously enough, lawful meat for Mohammedans at the present day.

The Kiang is regarded by sportsmen in Tibet rather as a nuisance than anything else, its curiosity and noisy galloping antics scaring off game which they desire to shoot.

There is a difference of opinion as to whether the Asiatic ass neighs or brays, some observers crediting it with the one noise and some with the other. Apparently "the brays have it."

As so many people in India are interested in horses, it may be worth while to mention that the real original wild horse—as opposed to the "feral" descendants of escaped stock such as the American mustangs—is now known to exist in Western Mongolia. It was originally described as a new species, *Equus prjewalskii*, but is a most obvious hog-maned, switch-tailed, black-pointed dun pony, only differing from some tame horses in having no forelock, and the first few inches of the tail short-haired. In winter the coat is thick, and bay rather than dun. The foal has mane, legs and tail nearly all dun.

The Tapir family, most of the very few species of which are American, has also only one representative with us.

MALAYAN TAPIR

Other Names.—Scientific: *Tapirus malayanus*, *indicus*. Native: *Tara-shu*, Burmese; *Kuda ayer*, *Tennu*, Malay.

Habitat.—Tenasserim to Sumatra.

Description.—A thick-set animal of pony size, standing from 9 to over 10 hands, and recalling both a pig and a pony in appearance; the snout is longer than a pig's and much more flexible—a short trunk, in fact; the ears are small and rounded, and the tail very short. The four toes of the front feet and the three of the hind all bear hoofs, but the weight is also partially borne on foot-pads behind these. Coat very short and close throughout, with no trace of the short hog-mane of the American Tapirs. Colour very remarkable; in the adult white on most of the body, black on the limbs and the whole forequarter except the tips of the ears, which are white; in the young, until about five months old, black, boldly streaked and spotted with pale markings, which are buff on the upper and white on the lower parts; the trunk is also much shorter than in the adult, and the coat so close that the little animal looks as if painted. Young American Tapirs are also like this, though the adults are utterly unlike our species in their colour, which is brown.

The Tapir has a well-developed set of incisors in both jaws, like the horses, but the teeth are mostly smaller, and have not the "mark" on the crown. The outer upper pair are canine-like, and indeed

Malayan Tapir.

bigger than the small canines. The grinders are tubercled, more like primate than ungulate teeth.

The Tapir is a shy forest animal, fond of water, and feeding on succulent vegetation. It is easily tamed, but not very common in captivity; in fact, no Tapir is abundant, nor have any ever been so, judging by the rarity of fossil remains. Yet this family have a wider range over the globe than the more active and abundant horses. Their feet are particularly interesting as showing a stage through which ancestral horses passed. The coloration also, although so different in the young and adult states, is protective in both cases, in our species at least, for the young animal is said to be invisible when lying down in cover in the hot hours, its spots on the dark background simulating sun-flecks, while the adult, when living near rocky streams, is similarly protected by resembling when in repose a grey boulder. The animal is fond of water, and is said to be able to walk along the bottom when out of its depth.

The Rhinoceroses (*Rhinocerotidæ*) are the only mammals with three toes on all feet. They are large—generally huge—beasts with naked or very sparsely hairy skins, long bulky bodies, short legs—in which the joints are placed as in ordinary quadrupeds, not as in elephants—and large heads on short necks, the profile being concave or "dished" till the nose is reached, which is decidedly arched, and ends in a lip pointed in all our species. The eyes are small, and the ears oval and moderate. The three hoofs of the feet do not support the whole weight, which rests in part on a pad behind them. The tail is thin and short. The skin in all our species—but not in the African two—is thrown into more or less marked folds.

What has given these animals celebrity, however, is the horn—or pair of horns—if one can speak of a pair when the two horns, when present, are set tandem fashion, not abreast as in other two-horned animals.

The single horn is always on the bulged bones of the nose, as is the first of two, the second being on the forehead about above the eye. These are the only horns which are genuinely horny all through, those of cattle, antelopes, etc., being composed of a bony core with a mere plating of horn, like claws and hoofs, while the horns of deer are pure bone.

This "genuineness" of the rhinoceroses' horns may have been the reason why the horns were so much esteemed in olden times for the manufacture of drinking-cups, the legend being that any poison poured therein would split them. The Chinese still value them as medicine, and Indians consider the urine medicinal.

This idea has had some effect in reducing the numbers of these animals in Asia at any rate; while their flesh is also good eating and their thick hide was much used for shields, being capable of turning even a bullet when dried, though not on the living animal when fired at direct.

In any case, however, they are solitary and not conspicuous with us even where they do occur, frequenting high grass or forest, where they feed on the local vegetation, and being silent animals. They are fond of water and of wallowing in mud; and although so unwieldy can trot and even gallop freely.

Their grinders are well developed, but the teeth in the fore-part of the jaws deficient; but in the lower jaws there are in our species two short sharp tusks variously regarded as canines or outer incisors, which are used in attack. Our three species are easily distinguished by the special characters of their skins, of which the two main folds, common to all, are found, one behind the shoulder, and the other in front of the haunch. They have one young at a birth, but estimates of the gestation period vary, from over to under a year.

Great One-horned Rhinoceros.

GREAT ONE-HORNED RHINOCEROS

OTHER NAMES.—Scientific: *Rhinoceros unicornis.* Native: *Gainda, Genra, Gargadan,* Hindi; *Gonda,* Bengali; *Gor,* Assamese.

HABITAT.—Low country of Assam. The distribution has long been in process of reduction; in the nineteenth century the animal extended along the Terai to Nepal and Sikkim, and in the sixteenth ranged even to Peshawar according to the Emperor Baber, who, like so many of our own soldiers of repute, was an excellent practical naturalist.

DESCRIPTION.—The largest of our rhinoceroses and the fourth largest land mammal, the other three being the African and Indian elephants and the African Square-lipped or "White" Rhinoceros. The record height at the shoulder is 5 ft. 9 in., but the horn rarely exceeds 1 ft. There is no difference in its length, or indeed any other obvious difference, in the two sexes. Skin very strongly tubercled and thrown into heavy folds, which form collars round the throat, the last of which is deepest and forms a conspicuous horizontal dewlap in front of the chest; on the shoulder a fold runs back from a fold which crosses the nape, but dies away before it reaches the shoulder-fold. Colour of skin slate; it only bears hair on the ears and tail.

The great Indian rhinoceros, now so sadly restricted in range, is the most celebrated of all, the single horn and mailed appearance of the skin having much impressed the ancients, who did not know much of the other species. It lives chiefly in grass jungle, where the height of its cover secures it from observation. It is believed to be a grass-feeder, and to live for a hundred years—at any rate it has lived for about half that time in captivity, more than once. A pair lived forty-five years in the Barrackpore Park, and Blanford cites fifty or sixty years. The only voice of the beast recorded is a grunt. It has a curious habit of forming piles of dung by depositing it in the same spot, and in captivity has a trick of grinding its horn down flat against any available hard surface.

Old writers made much of the supposed enmity of the rhinoceros to the elephant, and elephants themselves believe in it still, and so do their mahouts. Blanford says the animal is quiet and harmless as a rule, but it is quite possible that it has not always been so, since it is obvious that in animals capable of inflicting harm those that are also willing and anxious to do so are most likely to come into conflict with man and be killed off, which must in time have its effect on the race. Elephants, we know, are very nervous, but if any wild animals were inclined to attack them it would be a "rogue" rhinoceros, if such existed or still exist, since they are the most obvious rivals. In any case this fine beast should never be shot now unless it shows vice or on the rare occasion of a royal visit, for which it is worthy game. It could quite possibly be domesticated and used for haulage or ploughing; the editor when in India heard of one which was used as a pack-animal to carry a rajah's ladies' attire to be washed, and the old rulers of India used to put rhinoceroses into the battlefield with iron tridents fastened to their horns, a use which implies some amount of discipline.

All rhinoceroses, however, are rare in captivity; in seven years in India the editor, though constantly in touch with Calcutta dealers, never saw one on sale. Not only their scarcity, but the fact that, compared with the elephant, they are a poor show and of little use, accounts for this and for their high price, governed by the small demand.

Outlines of Burmese Rhinoceros (above) and Indian Rhinoceros (below) to show difference in skin-folds.

BURMESE OR LESSER ONE-HORNED RHINOCEROS

Other Names—Scientific: *Rhinoceros sondaicus.* Native: *Gainda*, Hindi; *Kyeng, Kyan-tsheng*, Burmese; *Kunda, Kedi, Kweda*, Nága; *Bádák*, Malay.

Habitat.—Locally from the Sundarbans east to Borneo, and except, of course, in the first-named locality, on hilly ground up to perhaps 7,000 ft.

Description.—The name Lesser One-horned Rhinoceros is not very appropriate, as the difference in size is not apparently very great, a specimen of the present animal of 5 ft. 6 in. high being on record; while Blanford, though saying its head is much smaller than that of the last, gives the same basal length—23 in.—to the skulls of both, while assigning less than 2 in. difference in width, though breadth of skull is, as he notes, a variable character in rhinoceroses.

Skin tessellated, but not tubercular, and showing a little hair on the upper parts; throat-fold before the shoulder not hanging below the anterior ones, and folds generally less heavy. Fold proceeding from the nape-fold running nearly straight up and forming a second nape-fold, just before the shoulder, so that the nape-skin is bounded by folds at each end. Colour of skin as in the last; horn shorter, and apparently not found in the female, which is commonly hornless.

This rhinoceros, which may just as well be called Burman as Javan —so many Indian animals having Burman representatives—is not only different in haunts and food from the last, but is said to be more gentle in disposition; not much, however, is on record about it, though it is so much more widely distributed than the other.

Hairy Two-horned Rhinoceros. In distance Burmese Rhinoceros (above) and Indian Rhinoceros (below).

HAIRY TWO-HORNED RHINOCEROS

OTHER NAMES.—Scientific: *Rhinoceros sumatrensis, lasiotis.* Native: *Kyan-shaw*, Burmese; *Bádák*, Malay.

HABITAT.—Tipperah east and south to Siam and Borneo; rare in Assam.

DESCRIPTION.—Considerably smaller than any other rhinoceros, barely reaching 4 ft. 6 in. at the shoulder; but the first of the two horns this species possess is far longer than the horns of our others, reaching 32 in. The second horn is quite short. Skin with a thin coat of hair something like a buffalo's, the ears and tail particularly hairy; skin-folds not so well marked as in the other species, and that before the haunches dying out before it reaches the back. Colour of skin some shade of brown, with the hair either brown or black. The amount of hair is also variable, the so-called Hairy-eared or Ear-fringed Rhinoceros, once regarded as a species, being merely an especially hairy and reddish variety.

The Hairy Rhinoceros is particularly interesting, as exhibiting some remains of the full coat which invested the Woolly Northern Rhinoceros of the Stone Age, and also as forming a link between the other Asiatic species and the smooth-skinned, two-horned African kinds.

Like the last species, it is a forest animal and goes some distance up the hills. The type of the Hairy-eared variety was caught in Chittagong in 1868 owing to getting bogged in a quicksand. It was noticed that when approached by elephants when tied up she roared with fright, and when conducted to a river could not swim, but only paddle enough to keep her head above water, so that she had to be towed. Anderson, however, heard of a rhinoceros being seen swimming in the sea in the Mergui Archipelago. The Chittagong rhinoceros above alluded to made the record price for a wild animal, the London Zoological Society having paid £1,250 for her.

Mason says the Karens are afraid of a "fire-eating" Rhinoceros, the animal being supposed to attack fire. Blanford doubts this, but Mason quotes an African author on the propensity of one of the African species to do so. Rhinoceroses have poor sight, but good hearing, and their scent is keen. They are touchy animals in some cases, and there would be nothing more wonderful in such a beast charging on the scent of fire and glare than in most mammals being scared by these; reaction to a strange stimulus need not necessarily be the same in all.

Of the even-toed ungulates we have, counting the domesticated camel, five families:

The Pigs (*Suidæ*) differ from all our other hoofed mammals in their long conical snout terminating in a vertical disk in which the nostrils are pierced; the Camels (*Camelidæ*) in having two toes only, padded rather than hoofed, the two small back ones being absent.

The Chevrotains or Mouse-deer (*Tragulidæ*) are like tiny hornless deer, not reaching a yard in total length, but have the mouth more deeply cleft than in deer, approaching the carnivores in this respect. All our other even-toed ungulates are over a yard in length.

Of these, the Hollow-horned Ruminants (*Bovidæ*) are distinguished, in the case of the males and of most females, by having horns consisting of a bony core encased in a horny sheath. Oxen, goats, sheep, and antelopes belong to this group, the most varied of all mammalian families.

In the Deer (*Cervidæ*) the males, except the Musk-deer, distinguished by his long tusks, have in all our species branched horns (properly called antlers) which really have no horn in them at all, but are, as above remarked, pure bone; they are also not permanent, but shed and renewed regularly. Female deer cannot be distinguished by any general character from hornless female antelopes, but only by knowledge of the particular species; however, as no one has any business to be shooting either, this does not matter so much. Possibly the two families ought really to be united.

Pigs (*Suidæ*) are among the most distinct of animals in appearance; in addition to the peculiarity of their snouts above-mentioned, their heads are large, their eyes and ears small, their necks very short, their bodies heavy and their legs comparatively small. The back hoofs are better developed than in most of the even-toed group, and in all the feet all the foot-bones are perfect and separate, as in mammals with paws. The mouth is deeply cleft as in carnivores.

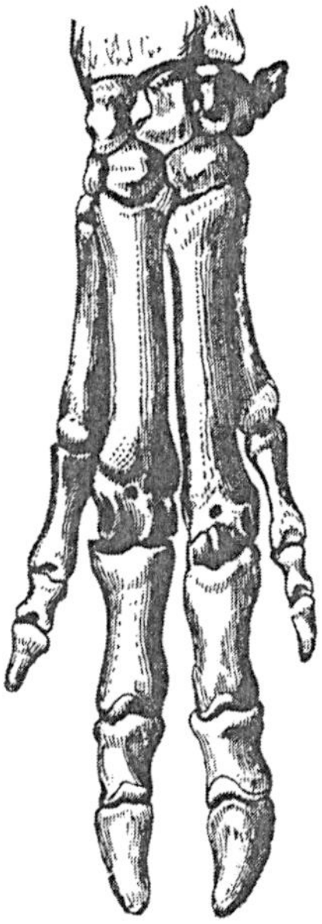

Bones of Pig's Foot.

Pigs have also a full set of teeth; the lower incisors are peculiar in projecting forwards, and the canines in the males project out of the mouth as tusks, the upper as well as the lower pair inclining upwards. These teeth grow continually like the incisors of rodents, and are so placed as to wear each other to an edge, being used in attack for ripping. The short-tusked sows bite like most other mammals, a rare action in even-toed ungulates.

The grinders are adapted for more or less succulent food, rather like our own, and not so much for consuming harsh grass and twigs. Pigs, as all know, are omnivorous, and freely eat any animal food they can get, while in their vegetable diet, though eating grass, herbs, and shoots, they show a strong liking for such articles as roots and fruits both hard and soft. In fact, their diet is practically the same

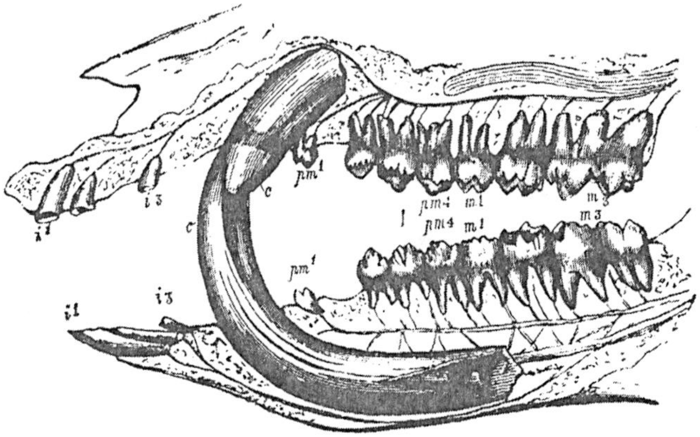

Teeth of Boar.

as that of the bears among the carnivores; but while the bears dig for hidden food with their claws, the pigs "root" it up with their strong gristly snouts They use their fore-feet in feeding, however, to hold down food. Their coats are thin, harsh, and bristly, and the young porkers differ much from the adult, being striped. The tail is small, and poorly covered.

Several are born in a litter, and are not so active and independent at first as most young hoofed animals, being concealed in a nest for a few days.

Although much valued as food wherever religion does not prohibit their use, pigs are in some respects most noxious animals, owing to their destructiveness to crops of various kinds; the males are also often dangerous. On the other hand, they destroy snakes, etc.

They are cunning and very courageous, keen-scented, and far more active than would be expected from their heavy build. Their habits are sociable, though the herds are not very large as a rule, and greatly attached to cover, where they pass the day.

They are fond of water, and delight in wallowing in mud; but they are not naturally dirty animals, their bad reputation in this respect being derived from unfortunate tame pigs kept in close captivity.

Only three species are found in our area.

Wild Boar.

INDIAN WILD BOAR

Other Names.—Scientific: *Sus cristatus, indicus.* Native: *Suar, Bura-* or *Bad-janwar*, Hindi; *Dúkaru*, Mahratti; *Paddi*, Gondi; *Pandi*, Telegu; *Handi, Mikka, Jenadi*, Canarese; *Kis*,

Rajmehal; *Tau-wet*, Burmese; *Walura*, Cingalese; *Gúrág*, *Kuk*, Persian; *Katu-pani*, Tamil; *Bir Sukri*, Ho Kol; *Sukaram*, Malabarese; *Banel*, Nepalese; *Ripha*, *Phák*, Bhotia; *Sarao*, Daphla; *Bali*, *Techim*, Mishmi; *Sniang*, Khaso; *Vák*, Garo; *Omar*, *Hono*, Kachari; *Kubak*, *Tharo*, *Kashag*, *Mengi*, *Vák*, Naga; *Eyeg*, Abor; *Mu*, Khámti; *Ok*, Manipuri; *Vu*, Kuki; *Wa*, Singpho; *Kalet*, Talain; *Hto*, Karen; *Mu*, Shan; *Babi utan*, Malay.

Some of these names, where several are in use in one place, presumably indicate differences in age or sex, like our words "boar," "sow," and "porker" or "pig."

HABITAT.—Indian Empire generally, including Ceylon, but not the outlying island groups. In the hills this boar ranges up to 15,000 ft.; but Blanford thinks the species inhabiting Afghanistan and Baluchistan may be the European form (*Sus scrofa*), which is stouter in build and has a woolly under-coat, and the last grinders smaller.

DESCRIPTION.—Height from about a yard at the shoulder, or even an inch or two more, in males, down to about 2 ft. in the small Malay Peninsula race. Coat coarse, developed into a crest on the spine, becoming thinner downwards. Tail thin, fringed at the tip, barely reaching the hocks. Colour grizzly or rusty grey, blacker in the younger animals, the mane, ears, and feet black; some specimens are dull brown. First coat of young pigs dark brown striped lengthways with buff.

Tusks of full-grown male up to 9 in. long, though a foot, including the root portion, is on record. Where feeding is good, in Bengal, the swine are heavier in build than in less fertile tracts; a boar may weigh four maunds.

Sterndale says: "It is gregarious, living in herds, usually called *sounders*. . . . An old boar is generally the chief, but occasionally he gets driven from the herd and wanders solitary and morose, and is in such a case an awkward customer to tackle. An old boar of this kind is usually a match for a tiger, in fact few tigers, unless young and inexperienced, would attack one. I have known two instances of tigers killed by boars; one happened a few miles from the station of Seeonee, to which place we had the animal carried. On another occasion, whilst on tour in the district, a deputation from a distant village came into my camp to beg of me to visit them, and shoot a large boar which had taken possession of a small rocky hill, and from it made his nightly forays into their ricefields, and was given to attacking those who approached him. I went and got the boar out and shot him, but lost a tiger, who also sneaked out and broke through a line of beaters; these two were the sole occupants of this small isolated knoll, and lived evidently on terms of mutual respect. The boar was the largest I had ever seen or killed, but, as the sùn was getting fierce, and I had far to ride to camp, I regret I left him to the villagers without taking any measurements. It is allowable to shoot hogs in some hilly part of India where riding is out of the question, otherwise the shooting of a boar in riding country is deservedly looked upon as the crime of vulpicide would be in Leicestershire—a thing not to be spoken of. The boar possesses a singular amount of courage; he is probably the most courageous of all animals, much more so than the tiger, but unless irritated he is not prone to attack at first sight, except in a few cases of solitary individuals, like the one above mentioned. I was once rather ludicrously and very uncomfortably held at bay by a boar who covered the retreat of his family. One evening, after dismissing my *amláh*, I took up a shot-gun, and, ordering the elephant to follow, strolled across some fields to a low scrub-covered hill where I thought I might pick up a few partridges or a pea-fowl before dusk. On entering the bush which skirted the base of the hill I was suddenly brought up by a savage grunt, and there in front of me stood an old boar with his bristles up, while the rest of his family scampered off into the thicket. I remembered Shakespeare's (the poet's—not the gallant shikari general's) opinion:—

> 'To fly the boar, before the boar pursues,
> Were to incense the boar to follow us,'

and therefore stood my ground, undergoing the stern scrutiny of my bristly friend, who cocked his head on one side and eyed me in a doubtful sort of way, whilst he made up his mind whether to go for me or not, whilst I on my part cogitated on the probable effect at close quarters of two barrels of No. 6 shot. However, he backed a bit, and then sidled to the rear a few paces, when he brought up with another grunt, but, finding I had not moved, he finally turned round and dashed after his spouse and little ones. . . . I believe a wild pig will charge at anything when enraged. I had an elephant who, though perfectly staunch with tigers, would bolt from a wild boar. The period of gestation is four months, and it produces twice a year; it is supposed to live to the age of twenty years, and, as its fecundity is proverbial, we might reasonably suppose that these animals would be continually on the increase, but they have many enemies, whilst young, among the felines, and the sows frequently fall a prey to tigers and panthers. Occasionally I have come across in the jungles a heap of branches and grass, and at first could not make out what it was, but the Gonds soon informed me that these heaps were the nests or lairs of the wild pigs, and they invariably turned them over to look for squeakers. . . . Many castes of Hindus, who would turn with abhorrence from the village pig, will not scruple to eat the flesh of the wild boar. On the whole it is probably a cleaner feeder, but it will not hesitate to devour carrion if it should come across a dead animal in its wanderings."

BANDED OR ISLAND PIG

OTHER NAMES.—Scientific: *Sus vittatus*, *andamanensis*. Native: *Babi utan*, Malay.

HABITAT.—Malay Peninsula and islands east to Flores; Andamans and Nicobars.

DESCRIPTION.—The Banded Pig is better called Island Pig, as it mainly inhabits islands, and is in some races self-coloured, without the tan band along the muzzle which commonly distinguishes it; the hair along the spine is black, the body dark brown and tan. The Andaman and Nicobar race is all black, and of small size, Andamanese specimens being only about 20 in. at the shoulder, though Nicobar ones are rather larger, with noticeably larger grinders. The last of these teeth is shorter than the two preceding ones taken together, while in the common Indian boar it is longer in the lower jaw, and generally in the upper also.

The tail in the Island Pig is short, and in the Nicobar race covered scantily with long hairs; the young are striped with buff and brown as usual.

The editor had an opportunity of bringing two young boars of the Andaman race, still showing stripes, from the Andamans to the Calcutta Zoological Gardens, and one of them bred with a sow which had been there some time. Although she looked like a very hairy domestic pig, the young were fully striped, and very lively and playful. In the Andamans this pig is a favourite game animal of the native pigmy hunters, who always dock the tail of those they kill.

Mr. Miller, the American naturalist, though, as Lydekker states in his Catalogue of the Ungulate Mammals in the British Museum, referring the Andaman pig to the Banded or *Sus vittatus* group, yet emphasises its relationship to the Tenasserim form of the Indian boar, which looks as if it might be ancestral to both, and appears to connect the two.

PIGMY HOG

OTHER NAMES.—Scientific: *Sus salvanius*, *Porcula salvania*. Native: *Sano banel*, Nepalese.

HABITAT.—Himalayan Terai.

DESCRIPTION.—The smallest pig known, less than 1 ft high at the shoulder. Upper tusks short, tail very short, and naked like the ears; snout shorter than in the large pigs. Coat very coarse and scanty, some shade of brown in colour; young striped brown and buff.

The Pigmy Hog goes in herds of about a dozen, comprising both sexes; it is seldom met with, and, owing perhaps to unfamiliarity with man, is remarkably fierce, the males attacking readily. It is extremely good eating, and, as it is too small to be seriously dangerous or destructive, is worthy of a wider distribution. It is very rare in captivity; the

Pigmy Hog.

editor has only seen one living specimen, and that not in India, but in the London Zoological Gardens.

The Ruminants, to which all the remaining Ungulate families belong, all have the incisors wanting, or nearly so, in the upper jaw, where there is a hard pad against which the lower incisors bite; the lower canines are generally incisor-shaped, and lie close up against the true incisors. Their characteristic act of rumination, or chewing the cud—*i.e.* the food they have hastily swallowed—is connected with their complex stomach, which always has three, and generally four, compartments: the very large paunch, which comes first, and is a storage bag like the crop of some birds; the honeycomb-bag (*reticulum*) lined with hexagonal cells; the reed or true digestive stomach (*abomasum*) which comes last, and the third compartment, not present in all the families, which is lined with folds like the leaves of a book, and is called the manyplies (*psalterium*). When enough food has been collected in the paunch, the animal seeks repose, and, often lying down, chews over again the food, which rises up in boluses into the mouth, and again swallows it. Thus the food, gathered without loss of time, is made the most of at leisure.

Of the two families in which the stomach lacks the third compartment or manyplies, the Camels (*Camelidæ*) are only represented with us by the tame

ONE-HUMPED CAMEL

OTHER NAMES.—Scientific: *Camelus dromedarius.* Native: *Unt.*

HABITAT.—Only known in the domestic state, chiefly in Northern Africa, east to Arabia, and Northern India, though escaped animals have reverted to the wild state in Spain and in Australia.

DESCRIPTION.—This is hardly necessary, but some structural peculiarities may be noticed. The outer incisors are present in the upper jaw, and the young have the full set; there are normal canines in both jaws, and the first grinders are canine-like; thus the beast has a formidable set of pointed teeth, and fights by biting, unlike other ruminants. The first and second compartments of the stomach both have water-storage cells which can be closed, but the well-known power of abstaining from water is largely a matter of training, and in any case is only for a few days, and is not to be compared with that of many other mammals not provided with storage arrangements.

The equally well-known hump, which is mostly composed of fat, absorbed in time of dearth, is very variable, and little developed in the fast camel or dromedary breed; there is no sign of it in the skeleton. The curious two-toed padded feet, with blunt claws rather than hoofs, are supposed to be especially adapted to traversing sand; and camels are, indeed, mostly used in dry countries, and are apt to slip and dislocate the hind-legs—unless the hocks are tied—when brought on to muddy ground. But camels bred on such land can traverse it, and the wild camels of Spain inhabit marshes. Camels can subsist on very coarse vegetation and are very destructive in forests; the males are also very savage in the rutting season, when they blow out the soft palate like a red bladder. They lie down squarely, tucking the limbs under them like carnivores, not sideways as most ungulates do, and there are horny pads on the breast and on the true knee or stifle—which is let down very low—to support the weight.

The Chevrotains, Deerlets, or Mouse-deer (*Tragulidæ*) form the other family without the manyplies compartment of the stomach, and exhibit a considerable approach to the pigs in structure, though looking like small hornless deer. They were formerly classed mistakenly with the Musk-deer. They have the deep mouth of a pig, and the front grinders are narrow with cutting edges, though the lower canines are incisor-like, and the upper incisors wanting, as in the typical ruminants. The upper canines are developed into long tusks in the males, and project from the mouth, but downwards in the ordinary way, not outwards as in boars. The feet, though like those of deer or antelopes outwardly, and especially slender, have the bones of the small outside toes fully developed as in pigs, running right up under the skin to the wrist or knee, and heel or hock. The hind-quarters of the little animals are high, and the tail and ears short; they lie down as camels do, and also sit up like carnivores. They are solitary and secretive, live in forests, feeding on more or less succulent vegetation and fallen fruit, and have one or two young at a time. They are particularly interesting as survivals from a time when all ruminants were hornless. We have only four species, all belonging to the genus *Tragulus*, about the size of hares or rabbits, and with short close-lying coats, coloured alike in adults and young. In captivity these animals should be fed on salad and sliced roots and fruit, and be well bedded down or kept, if in cages for transport, on a cane-barred floor, as a hard uniform floor results in swollen and enlarged hocks. They have bred in captivity, and are sometimes, but rarely, brought to Europe.

Indian Chevrotain.

MEMINNA OR INDIAN CHEVROTAIN

OTHER NAMES.—Scientific: *Tragulus meminna*. Native: *Pisari*, *Pisora*, *Pisai*, Hindi; *Mugi*, Central India; *Turi-maoo*, Gondi;

Jitri-haran, Bengali; *Gandwa*, Uria; *Yar*, Kol; *Wal-muha*, Cingalese; *Kuru-pandi*, Telegu; *Kuram-pandi*, Tamil; *Kúr-pandi*, Canarese.

HABITAT.—Southern India and Ceylon.

DESCRIPTION.—Tail very short, hardly half length of head; throat and backs of legs hairy as in most ungulates; colour olive with lines of more or less pure white spots along the body, throat striped with white. Height up to 1 ft. at shoulder, length a little over 18 in.

Sterndale, who kept some young specimens, says: "They are timid and delicate, but become very tame, and I have had them running loose about the house. They trip about most daintily on the tips of the toes, and look as if a puff of wind would blow them away." In spite of this fairy-like attribute, the gait is stiff, and Indians believe, as Europeans used to about the elephant, that they have no knee-joints. At large the Meminna takes refuge and spends the heat of the day in crevices in rocks, and here the young—usually twins—are brought forth at the end of the rains or the beginning of the cold weather. The rutting-season is about the middle of the year, and then only are the pair found together. The voice is a weak bleat.

It is said that the animal fears to go about much when leaves are falling, lest these, being pierced by its little hoofs, should act as clogs.

The last one the editor saw alive, at the shop of Mr. G. Palmer, in London, was so tame that it could be handled and nursed by children.

KANCHIL OR LITTLE MALAY CHEVROTAIN

OTHER NAMES.—Scientific: *Tragulus javanicus, kanchil.* Native: *Kanchil*, *Pelandoc*, Malay; *Yun*, Burmese.

HABITAT.—Tenasserim east to Java; Cambodia and Cochin China.

DESCRIPTION.—The smallest of our hoofed animals, only about 18 in. in length of head and body; tail more than half as long as head, throat and backs of all legs below knee and hock naked. Colour brown, nape and back mostly black; three white longitudinal stripes on throat.

This little animal, famed in Malay folk-lore for its cunning, like the fox in ours, is said to abound in Malay mangrove-jungle. Like the last species, it will breed in captivity, though also timid and delicate. The young may be single or twins.

Probably these minute ungulates really are very cunning, otherwise they could not have survived through long ages, being defenceless and not prolific. The present one is the most abundant and widely distributed species, and so is very likely the best able to look after itself.

Larger Malayan Chevrotain.

NAPU OR LARGER MALAY CHEVROTAIN

OTHER NAMES.—Scientific: *Tragulus napu.* Native: *Napu,* Malay.

HABITAT.—Tenasserim to Borneo.

DESCRIPTION.—The largest of our species, over 1 ft. at the shoulder, and more than 2 ft. long. Tail about as long as head, throat and backs of lower hind legs bare. Coat coarser than in the small species, and colour much greyer and not so reddish, especially on the flanks. Five white stripes on the throat, not always distinct.

The Napu is not nearly so common an animal as the Kanchil, and is not credited with so much acuteness.

RED OR STANLEYAN CHEVROTAIN

OTHER NAMES.—Scientific: *Tragulus stanleyanus.*

HABITAT.—Malayan Peninsula and islands.

DESCRIPTION.—Intermediate in size between the Kanchil and the Napu, but distinguishable from both by its brighter and more uniform chestnut coloration, with little or no black along the neck.

The typical Ruminants, with incisiform lower canines, and complete ruminant stomach but incomplete foot-bones to the small side toes, are divided into the two families of Deer or Antlered Ruminants (*Cervidæ*) and the hollow-horned and very varied *Bovidæ.*

The latter, containing such very different types as the buffaloes and gazelles, are hard to describe generally except by the character of the hollow bone-cored horns, absent in some females. In size, shape, length of tail, and character of coat there is very great variation, and also in habits.

One curious trait is, however, to be noted, the tendency for the females to develop greater speed than the males, though this is found in deer also.

The Sheep (genus *Ovis*) are short-tailed animals, with fairly long legs and short, blunt, compact hoofs, with the small back hoofs much reduced so as not to be readily noticeable. The wild forms may have a woolly under-coat, but no wool is to be seen on the surface, the visible coat being composed of close-set hair, mostly short. In fact, the animals would look more like deer than sheep were it not for the horns, which are very characteristic, thick at the base, and rapidly tapering and arching outwards and downwards, with a spiral tendency. In the females, however, they are much shorter and tend more to a simple backward curvature. Sheep may be ruffed, but are never bearded on the chin like goats, nor have the males the strong odour of those animals. In all the feet there are gland-pits between the two large front hoofs.

Sheep are hill animals, and good climbers, but do not usually frequent such broken and difficult ground as goats; they also live mostly on herbage, not being so fond of browsing. They are swift of foot and keen of scent and sight, so that the open and comparatively easy ground they often frequent makes them all the harder to stalk. They are perhaps the best of all game animals, affording plenty of scope for skill, a fine trophy and the finest of mutton, while at the same time doing no harm, which cannot be said of all game.

In stalking sheep, as in the case of all mountain game, it is important to get above them, as they look out for danger chiefly from below.

We have three species, two of which vary much locally.

ARGALI

OTHER NAMES.—Scientific: *Ovis ammon, hodgsoni, poli.* Native: *Nyan* or *Nyanmo* (female), *Hyan, Nyang, Nyand,* Tibetan; *Kuchkar, Mesh* (female), Wakhan.

HABITAT.—Central and Northern Asia from Bokhara to Western

Kamtchatka. There are nearly a dozen local races, of which two come into our area—the Tibetan race, *hodgsoni*, in North Ladakh, and the Pamir race, *poli*, in Hunza. Both are high-level animals, the Tibetan in summer ranging about 15,000 ft.

DESCRIPTION.—The largest of known sheep, reaching nearly

Argali (Pamir or *poli* race).

12 hands at the shoulder in the Tibetan form, the Pamir variety being rather smaller, but still over 40 in. Ewes are but little smaller than rams. Tail very short, only 3 in. with the hair. A short mane down the back of the neck, and in our races at least, a ruff on the front and sides of it, in old rams. Colour brown above, white on the limbs, muzzle, ruff, and stern; mane black or blackish, but wanting

in ewes, which also are less pure and distinct in the white parts. There is a gland-pit below the eye. Horns of rams of huge size and strongly wrinkled, in the *hodgsoni* race extremely thick at the base, describing nearly a circle and then turning out a little. A length of 57 in. round the curve is recorded, and a basal girth of 19 in. Ewes' horns are said to reach 2 ft., but are generally 6 in. less. The *poli* race has less massive but much longer horns, describing the full circle and then turning outwards and backwards for about half as much; such horns have even reached 75 in., and, though 17 in. is the record girth, are naturally far more imposing in appearance than the more massive Tibetan type. About 3 ft. for a ram of this race, and 4 ft. for a Pamir *poli* ram, would be fair measurements. The more western typical Argali, found outside our limits, has measured 62 in. in length of horn and 20 in. in basal girth.

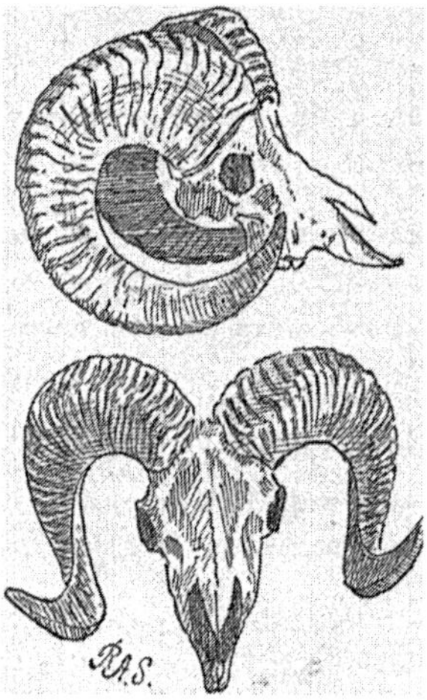

Horns of Argali (Tibetan race).

Although many game animals exceed this giant sheep in size, its gallant carriage and splendid horn-curves give it unsurpassed dignity,

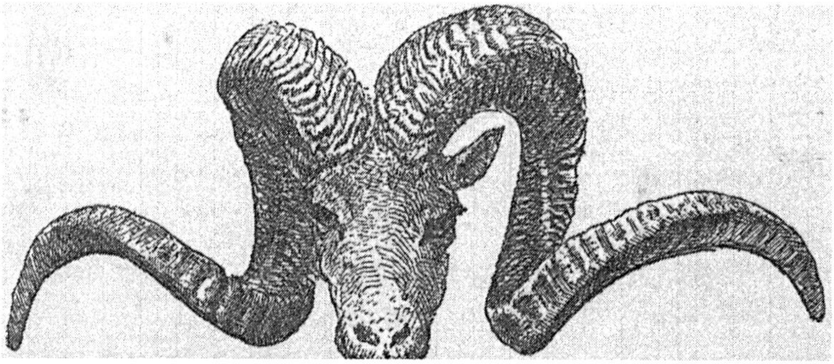

Horns of Argali (Pamir or *poli* race).

and its high speed, which is not affected by the rarefied atmosphere which tries other animals so severely, and keen sight and scent, are worthy of its appearance.

In summer rams associate in small flocks by themselves; they are often difficult to find, even where numerous, as they are so local in their habits that one may range over a good deal of country and be within a mile or two of a flock without knowing it.

When found, too, the ground they are on is often too open to give a chance of stalking such vigilant animals successfully, while attempts to drive them result in scaring them off altogether. Thus the hunt resolves itself into waiting till the animals shift their ground into a locality which gives the stalker a chance, a combination of circumstances which has given the Argali the reputation of being one of the hardest of game animals to bring to book.

Its chief natural enemies are the large Tibetan wolves, which account for many in winter, and should always be killed off anywhere near sheep ground, if possible.

There was a report that the *poli* sheep were much reduced in numbers, but a recent American expedition to the Pamirs reported coming across, altogether, about a thousand rams and six hundred ewes.

The rutting-season is in mid-winter, and the young are born about mid-summer.

These giant sheep appear to be exceedingly rare in captivity; the editor has only seen one captive Argali, a male specimen exhibited in the London Zoological Gardens some years before the war. This was of the Ammon type.

URIAL

Other Names.—Scientific: *Ovis vignei*, *cycloceros*. Native: *Urial*, Punjabi; *Koch*, *Gad*, *Garand* (female), Baluchi and Sindhi; *Sha*, Ladakhi (with suffix *po* for ram and *mo* for ewe); *Urin*, Astor; *Kar*, *Gad* (female), Brahui; *Koh-i-dumba*, Afghan.

Habitat.—Central Asia from Turkestan, east to North-West India, descending to sea-level locally in Sind and the Punjab. The Tibetan race or Sha (*vignei*) used to be considered distinct from the Baluch and North-West Indian Urial (*cycloceros*), and the two represent local races of the species, which has other local forms elsewhere.

Description.—Of about ordinary sheep size, seldom over 1 yd. at the shoulder in the Ladak race or Sha, which is the larger. Tail absolutely as well as relatively longer than in the Argali—4 in. No mane, but a ruff in full-grown rams, in two halves on the throat.

Colour, pale reddish-brown in summer, drab in winter, limbs, belly and stern white in adult rams, ruff black, or in old animals black and white; a more or less black patch behind the shoulder; ewes and young nearly uniform brown. A gland-pit below the eye is present.

Horns of ram wrinkled, describing nearly a circle, about 2 ft., but ranging up to a length of $37\frac{3}{4}$ in. round the curve, and a basal girth of $11\frac{1}{2}$ in., a more ordinary girth being 10 in. The horns of the Sha form are the more massive, but its ruff is said to be poorer. Ewes have but short and slightly curved horns.

The Urial differs from all other wild sheep in having a wide range in elevation and a corresponding tolerance of climate from the cold of Tibet, at 14,000 ft., to the heat of Indian low levels.

Urial (the hair below the chin is a neck-ruff, not a beard).

Its haunts are also varied, from open valleys in Ladak to rocky hill-sides in the Salt Range; it sometimes enters scrub-jungle, and may be found on bleak and barren mountains or on grassy ground below forest. It is fond of salt, and hence often found near salt-mines.

The herds vary from three to ten times that number, and generally contain both sexes, though in the summer rams often associate away from the ewes. In the Punjab Urial mate in September, but as in

Astor the lambs are born early in June, the inference is that the mating is later there, unless the gestation period be more than six months, which seems unlikely—it has been variously given as seven and four. Domestic sheep go about five months with young. Urial will sometimes associate with these, and have bred with them freely. This is probably a case of species-crossing, as tame sheep are evidently derived from the European Mouflon (*Ovis musimon*), which has a most tame-sheepish face and "baa," while the Urial is said by Blanford to have "a kind of bleat," implying that the note is not quite the same. It also utters an alarm-whistle.

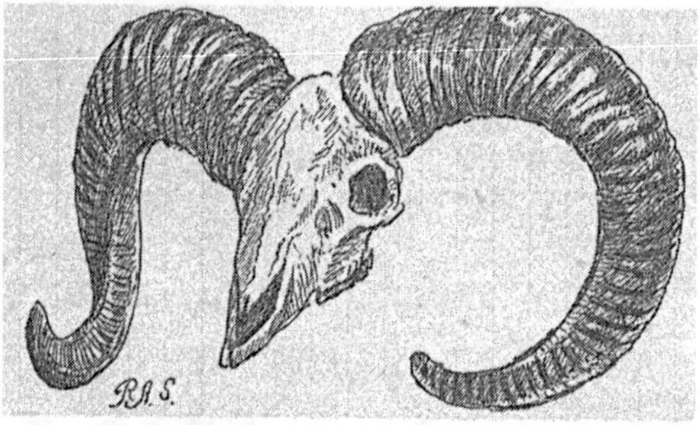

Skull of an Argali-Urial Hybrid (once named as a species, *Ovis brookei*).

A very interesting case of the rare crossing of species of wild mammals has been recorded of this species by Sterndale, but in the *Proceedings of the London Zoological Society*, and not in his book on Indian mammals. A male Argali, it seems, took and kept possession of a flock of Urial ewes in Zanskar for some time, and sired many lambs before wolves killed him in one winter. The hybrids proved fertile and bred back to the Urial, and the flock thus reverted to the Urial type. The half-bred Argali-Urial, which the natives also called Nyan-sha, were rather large animals with white ruffs; the quarter-Argali-Urial, of the second generation, were more like Urial, with some black on the neck, but more massive horns. A hybrid between Argali ewe and Urial ram has also been found with a flock of Argali.

The Urial at its western limit, the Kopet Dagh range dividing Turkestan from Persia, is, according to Lydekker, large in size—the horns sometimes measuring nearly 4 ft. round the curve—and very white in the ruff, thus approaching the smaller races of the Argali, some of which inhabit regions not far removed. This seems to show there had been interbreeding at some period; as sheep are easily driven away from a region, gaps in the distribution might well occur; or possibly it was in this region that Urial and Argali began to be differentiated. The Red Sheep (*Ovis orientalis*) of Asia Minor is said to approach the Urial type locally, while on the other side it is connected with the Mouflon; and in Eastern Kamtchatka we get a race of the American Bighorn (*Ovis canadensis*), an animal which comes next to the Argali in size and is even more variable locally. It looks very much as if all the sheep of the most typical kinds—Argali, Urial, Mouflon, etc.—were, like their age-long enemies the wolves, varying races of one species distributed all round the Northern Hemisphere.

Bharal.

BHARAL OR BLUE SHEEP

OTHER NAMES.—Scientific: *Ovis bharal*, *nahura*. Native: *Bharal*, *Bharut*, Hindi; *Na*, *Sha*, Tibetan; *Nervati*, Nepalese; *Gnao*, Bhutanese; *War*, on the Sutlej.

HABITAT.—Yarkand and Tibet to Moupin and Kuenlun, and along the axis of the Himalayas—sometimes south of it, but always at levels of about 10,000 ft. up to 16,000 ft.

DESCRIPTION.—About ordinary sheep size, rams about 1 yd at shoulder, but ewes decidedly smaller. Tail much longer than in our other two species—7 in. in rams; no ruff or mane. Colour very distinctive, grey, bluer in winter and browner in summer; belly and stern white, as are the limbs, except for black marks down the front. The tail-end is also black, and the ram has a black face, fore-neck, and flank-stripes separating the grey and white portions.

Horns of ram much smoother than in our other sheep, arching outwards at first, but then turning back; thus they look like ordinary sheep horns in front, but from the side are rather like an S, whereas in the others they form a C or Q, according to length. They have been known to reach over 30 in. (32·1 and 30·5) with a girth of 13 in., but 2 ft. for the length and 11-in. girth are the more usual thing. Ewes have small diverging horns shorter than the head. No gland-pit below the eye.

In this and several points the Bharal is more like a goat than a sheep, and, especially in form of horns, comes very near the Caucasian goat *Capra cylindicornis*, but it has neither beard nor scent, does not resemble any goat in colour, and certainly looks sheepish, not at all goat-like, in general appearance. In its habits, however, it is partially goat-like, frequenting precipitous and humanly inaccessible ground as well as undulating country; it avoids even bush-cover and keeps to levels above forest. It is very hard to see when lying down among rocks, as it often does; and even captive specimens in the London Zoological Gardens, where the species bred well, were, as the editor can testify, often quite hard to make out on the rockwork in the enclosure they occupied some years ago.

The herds are sometimes large, even up to a hundred animals, the sexes associating except, generally, in summer. This species is equally good as mutton as the others; but it will not breed with tame sheep as Urial do, so far as is known—another proof of its goat affinities, for it is very doubtful if goats ever breed with sheep even when both are tame, much less produce fertile hybrids with them, though there is a very ancient belief that they do, possibly founded on the existence of hairy tame sheep of various kinds.

The goats (genus *Capra*) are generally similar to sheep, but have no gland-pits below the eyes or between the large hoofs of the hind-feet, while they carry their tails, which are never so short as in some sheep, more jauntily, and, in the male sex at any rate, have chin-beards and a strong scent. Their coats often show some long hair, and they may be with or without woolly under-fur. Their horns, in the males, are very different from those of sheep, less massive, cork-screw- or scimitar-shaped, not at all C-like.

In habits, too, they differ considerably, having less speed, but being far better climbers, frequenting precipitous and broken ground, and often entering cover. Thus they are more easy to stalk in some cases, but their pursuit is dangerous on account of the bad ground.

They browse much as well as feeding on herbage, and like a greater variety of food than sheep; hence they can more easily pick up a living. The females are good eating, but the males too rank for European tastes, though natives like the meat.

Markhor (race with open-spiral horns).

MARKHOR

OTHER NAMES.—Scientific: *Capra megaceros, jerdoni, falconeri.* Native: *Márkhor*, Afghan, Panjabi, and Kashmiri; *Ráche*, Ladakhi;

Rezkuh, *Matt* (male), *Hit*, *Haraf* (female), Brahui; *Pachin*, *Sara* (male), *Buzkuhi* (female), Baluchi.

HABITAT.—Mountain ranges in Afghanistan, south of Kashmir, east to the Chenab, Baltistan, Astor, Gilgit, Hazara, and near Quetta.

Markhor (race with screw-spiral horns).

DESCRIPTION.—A very variable animal—the most so of all goats and perhaps of all ruminants—but distinguished by the horns of the male always being like some kind of screw, and by the female unlike those of other wild goats, being bearded on the chin. Coat with no under-fur or hardly any, brown in summer and grey in winter, nearly white in old males in summer. These are not only well bearded on the chin, but very shaggy down neck and breast as well; the front of the beard is black, and the tail and front of the lower part of the legs also dark, while the kids, which are drab, have a dark streak down the spine.

Horns of males vary greatly according to locality, the spiral, which turns outwards at first, being like that of a corkscrew in Pir Panjal specimens, and even more open in those from Astor and Baltistan. This is the *falconeri* form. The Cabul form, *megaceros*, has the horns much straighter, but with the open twist. The Suleman Range form, *jerdoni*, looks very different, the horns being more like an ordinary screw than a corkscrew, with a close spiral running round a straight core. The various forms, however, though once considered distinct species, run into each other, but the last is smaller than the rest—some of which may be about 3 ft. 6 in. at the shoulder in males—and less fully bearded. Femaleshave short twisted horns. The best horns of the open-spiral variety may measure over 5 ft. round the curves, and nearly 15 in at the base, but horns 4 ft. when thus measured are good; and this measurement would be near the record for the straight, close-spiralled form, 49 in. being the limit. Measured straight from base to tip the dimensions are naturally much less.

The Markhor frequents the most difficult and dangerous ground of any game, being a splendid climber, the best of all this agile group, and keeps to forest wherever this exists, though in summer the does range above it. Owing to its want of under-fur, it is comparatively sensitive to cold, and comes down to the valleys when snow falls on the heights.

The young may be twins or single, and are produced in May and June, at any rate in Astor and Gilgit. The animals will breed in captivity in Europe, and have crossed with tame goats.

The editor has seen a case in which a Markhor buck in the London Zoological Gardens was worsted in a fight with a much smaller Mouflon ram, but possibly in the open the result might have been different.

HIMALAYAN IBEX

Other Names.—Scientific: *Capra sibirica*. Native: *Sakin*, *Skin*, *Dabmo* (male), *Danmo* (female), Ladakhi; *Buz*, Kunawar; *Kail*, Kashmiri; *Tangrol*, Kulu; *Skiu*, Balti.

Habitat.—Altai to Himalayas as far as the source of the Ganges.

Description.—A thickset goat of large size, but not so big as the largest Markhor, and more heavily built. Coat with no long hair except the full chin-beard, confined to the male, which has also a coarse mane on the spine. Colour brown in summer coat, very dark but diversified with whitish back-patches in old bucks; in winter dirty white. Extremities and the beard and mane of bucks dark.

Ibex (Western form).

Under the winter coat is a thick growth of wool. Buck's height about 40 in. at shoulder; does much smaller, in fact, a third less. Horns broad in front, knobbed at intervals, narrow behind; they curve backward in scimitar shape. Four feet round the curve is very good, but 6 in. more is on record. Does have horns about 1 ft. long, rough, and oval in section, not triangular like the bucks'.

Our Ibex, which is hardly more than a large, fine full-bearded race of the well-known European Ibex (*C. ibex*)—now only found in a few places in Piedmont—is an animal of high elevations at all seasons, its thick coat enabling it to stay more or less near the snow-line even in winter, when it takes to steep places where much snow cannot lie. The rutting-season is at this time, and the sexes then associate; but in summer old bucks go to the steepest places at great elevations, where they spend most of the day, coming down to feed in the mornings and evenings.

The young, single or twins, are born in May and June. Ibex set sentries when feeding, which warn the herd by a whistle. Wary as they are, however, the nature of their haunts renders stalking fairly easy. They are much shot for the under-wool, or *pashm*; but this is a wasteful way of obtaining the article, and it would be wiser to obtain male kids to rear and experiment in crossing them with tame goats, as the hybrid would probably be fertile, and the fine *pashm* could be bred into the tame stock, some breeds of which have such a coat already.

PASANG OR WILD COMMON GOAT

Other Names.—Scientific: *Capra ægagrus, hircus.* Native: *Pasang* (male), *Boz* (female), or *Boz-Pasang*, Persian; *Borz*, Afghan; *Sair, Sarah, Phashin, Pachin, Borz-Kuhi* (last for male), Baluch; *Chank* (male), *Hit, Haraf* (female), Brahui; *Ter, Sarah*, Sindhi. Often called Sind or Persian Ibex by sportsmen, but the name Ibex is best kept for the last species only, leaving Pasang for the present one.

Habitat.—High ground from Western Asia to Sind. With us it does not extend east or north of the Bolan Pass and Quetta, near which place it meets the Markhor, and hybrids have been found.

Description.—Extremely like many of the tame goats descended from it; but the female is beardless, while tame she-goats usually have a small thin beard. Beard of male full, but confined to chin; a neck-mane in winter. Coat bright brown in summer, greyer in winter. Old bucks have the face, spine, tail, and beard black, and black stripes down the legs; and their coat is lighter than the does'. In winter, if in a cold climate, there is an under-coat. Height of a buck about 1 yd. at shoulder; does are smaller.

Horns with the same curve as in the Ibex, but very different otherwise, the fronts being sharp-edged and jagged and the backs rounded; anything much over 1 yd. along the curve is good, but 52½ in. is on record; but the girth of these at the base was only 7 in., as opposed to over 11 in. in record horns of the Ibex. Female horns are small, nearly upright, and oval in section. Doe Pasang can be distinguished from doe Ibex also by being white underneath, Ibex being pale brown there.

The Pasang, which is simply the ordinary goat in its original wild state, and might be called Wild Goat if the name were not so indefinite, is found low down in our limits, but haunts cliffs and crags, and is extraordinarily active. Its young number from one to three, and Blanford thinks they are born early in spring in Sind, having seen a very young kid caught on March 11th. With regard to tame goats, Sterndale says: "Mr. Blyth some years ago pointed out that a hind-quarter of goat with the foot attached can always be told from the same piece of mutton by the absence of the feet-pits in the goat. . . . I noticed in 1880 at Simla herds of goats with horns quite of the Markhor type, and one old fellow in a herd of about one hundred, which was being driven through the station to some rajah's place in the vicinity, had a remarkably fine head, with the broad flat twist of the Markhor horn. I tried in vain to get a similar one; several heads were brought to me from the bazaar, but they were poor in comparison. Goats are more prolific than sheep. The power of gestation commences at the early age of seven months; the period is five months, and the female produces sometimes twice a year, and from two to occasionally four at a birth. The goat is a hardy animal, subsisting on the coarsest herbage, but its flesh and milk can be immensely improved by a selected diet. Some of the small domestic goats of Bengal are wonderful milkers. I have kept them for years in Calcutta for the use of my children, and once took two of them with me to Marseilles by the 'Messageries' steamer. I prefer them to the larger goats of the north-west. My children have been singularly free from ailments during their infancy, and I attribute the immunity chiefly to the use of goats' milk drawn fresh as required."

With regard to the resemblance of some tame goats' horns to those of Markhor, Kinloch has pointed out that the spiral runs in a different direction in the two cases, turning outwards in the Markhor and inwards in the tame goat when screw-horned. There are, however, exceptions to this, and the fact that Pasang and Markhor have been known to interbreed, as noted above, and that Markhor breed readily with tame goats, indicates that there may be a Markhor strain in some, if the hybrid be fertile. As, however, there is a screw-horned breed of tame sheep in Eastern Europe, and in this case Markhor admixture is out of the question, it is on the whole probable that tame goats are practically pure Pasang.

The Tahrs (genus *Hemitragus*) are effeminate-looking, short-horned, beardless goats, but have as strong an odour as the more ordinary kinds, and resemble them in other respects. We have two of the three known kinds.

HIMALAYAN TAHR

OTHER NAMES.—Scientific: *Hemitragus jemlaicus*, *Capra jemlaica*. Native: *Tehr*, *Jehr*, near Simla; *Jharal*, Nepalese; *Krás*, *Jagla*, Kashmiri; *Jhula* (male), *Tahrni* (female), Kunawar; *Esbu* (male), *Esbi* (female), on Sutlej above Chini; *Kart*, Kulu and Chamba.

HABITAT.—Himalayas.

DESCRIPTION.—A yard or a little more at the shoulder in the buck, the doe much smaller. Colour, brown of various shades, generally dark, darkest in old bucks, drab in the young. Coat all round the neck very full in old bucks, forming a shaggy mane down to shoulders and knees. Tail carried low. Horns compressed, sharp-edged in front, diverging and bending backwards, and only about 1 ft. long even in bucks, though 16½ in. is on record. Female horns are not much shorter than the average buck's, and may measure 10 in. The female has four teats, whereas she-goats generally have only two.

Tahr.

The Tahr likes high levels, but seldom goes above forest, as it likes cover, especially in the case of the male; the ground it frequents is nearly as bad as Markhor country—in fact, the two on the Pir Panjál are found together, according to Kinloch, who says that Tahr ground proper has one advantage over Markhor ground in that there is usually something to hold on to if one slips. Oak and ringal are the favourite cover.

Tahr become very fat in autumn, and Indians then like even the old buck, although it smells much worse than other goats.

Mr. R. I. Pocock has observed, in the case of specimens kept in the London Zoological Gardens, where the species has lived and bred well, that the smell, which is only perceptible at certain seasons, is not the usual goat odour, but resembles that of cormorants. The female is good eating even for Europeans, like she-goats generally. Does go with young for six months, and generally produce one only, in June or July. Hodgson, who gives these details, apparently on native evidence, found that no young were produced when tame Tahr in his possession paired with domestic goats; yet he records a case in which a male Tahr paired with a female spotted deer, and the latter produced offspring, which grew up into a fine animal more resembling the dam than the sire. Sterndale accepts this account without comment, but Blanford doubts it, and in view of the apparent inability of Tahr to breed with goats, it certainly seems unlikely. Hybridism, however, is a very curious thing, and unexpected results often are chronicled; thus, cattle do not breed with buffaloes, and yet produce offspring, and fertile offspring at that, with the American bison, which seems a more remote animal; and pea-fowl have never bred with turkeys, but have done so with guinea-fowl and common poultry.

NILGIRI TAHR

OTHER NAMES.—Scientific: *Hemitragus hylocrius.* Native: *Warri-ádú*, *Warri-átú*, Tamil; *Mulla-átú*, Malabarese; *Kard-ardu*, Canarese.

HABITAT.—Southern Indian hill-ranges—Nilgiris, Anamalais, and Western Ghats.

DESCRIPTION.—A more leggy and shorter-bodied animal than the Himalayan Tahr, with a short coarse coat and no hairy development even in the buck except a short mane on the ridge of the neck and shoulders. Height up to 42 in. at shoulder in bucks, does about 1 yd. Colour dark brown, darkest in old bucks, which have a whitish saddle. Does and kids greyer. Horns like those of the northern Tahr, but convex outside instead of flat, and running a little longer sometimes, up to 16 in. in bucks, while 17 in. is on record, and doe horns may be 11 in.

This goat, though the tallest of our species, is the least imposing, having neither beard nor the large mane of its Himalayan relative, and very ill deserves the name of Ibex given it by sportsmen; it would be better to use the native name *Warri-átú*, as the buck's horns are commonly only 1 ft. long—the length of a doe's in the true Ibex. It keeps as a rule at heights of from 4,000 to 6,000 ft., but may come lower, and haunts crags or grassy slopes, spending the middle of the day on rocky ledges. The does, which have but two teats like other she-goats, not four like the northern Tahr, produce twin kids at almost any time during the year; they are good eating, but the male is rank-scented, and it would be interesting to know the character of the odour in this species, which has never been sent to England in captivity. It is much troubled by leopards, which should wherever possible be killed down near its haunts, as the species, though not a particularly attractive one, is interesting from its living so far away from other goats, stranded, as it were, on our southern hills.

The typical Goat-Antelopes or Capricorns (*Nemorhædus*), devoid of beard and scent, and with short, black, ringed horns, look rather like coarse she-goats. Their tails are short, and their general habits goat-like, except that they are not nearly so social as true goats are. We have but two species.

SEROW

OTHER NAMES.—Scientific: *Nemorhædus bubalinus, sumatrensis.* Native: *Sarao*, in the North-West Himalayas; *Aimu*, in Kunawar; *Ramu*, *Halj*, *Salabhir*, Kashmiri; *Nga*, Leeshams of Sanda Valley; *Paypa*, Shans; *Shanli*, Chinese of Burmo-Chinese frontier; *Goa*, Chamba; *Yamu*, Kulu; *Thar*, Nepali; *Gya*, Bhutanese; *Sichi*, Lepcha; *Tau-tschiek*, *Tau-myin*, Burmese; *Kambing-utan*, Malay.

Serow.

HABITAT. — Kashmir, east to Yunnan and south to Sumatra; the eastern form *sumatrensis* is treated as distinct by Blanford, but he expresses doubt on the subject.

DESCRIPTION. — A coarse-looking, leggy, large-headed animal about 1 yd. at the shoulder, with large ears, a gland-pit under the eye, and a coarse coat developed into a slight mane down the back of the neck. Horns short, sharp, slightly curved back, and ringed except at the ends; usually less than 1 ft. in length in males, though

13½ in. is recorded. The record female horns are 8¾ in. The sexes on the whole differ remarkably little, but the general colour is very variable individually and locally. The western form is black, with tan flanks and white stockings; the eastern may be all tan except a black spinal stripe. There is a white-maned species in China.

The Serow is, as shown by its many native names, a well-known animal, but is nowhere abundant, and is very shy.

It frequents thick forest or rocky hillsides, at between 6,000 and 12,000 ft., and is generally solitary; but the pair must be more or less attached, as Kinloch heard of a case in which an unwounded male charged when his mate had been shot. The Serow is, indeed, remarkable for courage, and will fight to the death with wild dogs; the same quality makes it dangerous to man when wounded.

It is as awkward in gait as in appearance, but a very fine climber, and Kinloch considered it probably the best performer of the difficult feat of going down steep hills. Like a carnivore, it has a lair or den in some sheltered spot, very often a cave. Its alarm-note is a combination of snort, scream, and whistle, just as its appearance suggests the cow, donkey, pig, and goat. Kinloch, who makes this comparison, says that he has heard Serow screaming when they had not apparently been alarmed, so that they may call to each other in this way.

There is difference of opinion about the time of the birth of the kids, which may apparently take place either in spring or in autumn. One only is born, and the gestation is said to last eight months. The flesh of the Serow is coarse, and, as its horns and skin are poor trophies, the only inducement it offers to the shikari is that of difficulties to overcome.

GORAL

Other Names.—Scientific: *Nemorhædus goral*, *Cemas goral*. Native: *Goral*, North-West Himalayas; *Pij*, *Pijur*, *Rai*, *Rom*, Kashmiri; *Sah*, Sutlej Valley; *Suh-ging*, Lepcha; *Ra-giyu*, Bhutanese; *Deo Chágal*, Assamese.

Habitat.—Himalayas, Siwaliks, and Naga Hills.

Description.—Much like a drab she-goat, rather over 2 ft. at shoulder, with white throat and dark spinal and leg-stripes; tail also black. Horns nearly parallel, about 6 in. long in bucks, for which the record is 9¾ in., the does' record being 7¾ in. Coat rather coarse; no face-glands.

The Goral is the least interesting of our ruminants in appearance, but must have a good idea of looking after itself, for it is a common animal between 3,000 and 8,000 ft., often lives near habitations, and is not easily driven away by shooting.

Although not herding like a true goat, it is often found in pairs or small parties of about half a dozen, feeding in morning and evening, and frequenting various situations, either rocky, wooded, or grassy. The young are said to be born in spring after half a year's gestation.

Goral.

The alarm-note is a hissing snort. Goral are not very shy, and Kinloch considers their pursuit excellent training for beginners, as it is "like miniature ibex shooting."

The other member of the Capricorn group we have forms a very distinct genus (*Budorcas*), little known till of recent years.

Takin.

TAKIN

OTHER NAMES.—Scientific: *Budorcas taxicolor.* Native: *Takin* (pronounced "takhon," nasally).

HABITAT.—Mishmi Hills and Eastern Tibet.

DESCRIPTION.—A heavy, clumsy-looking animal of about 10 hands at the withers, which are high; tail very short, limbs short and stout, with unusually large back hoofs. Head large and neck short, so that the general appearance is something between a bull and a goat; the profile, however, is arched like a ram's, and the horns are rather like those of the Gnus of Africa, thick, rising close together, curving sharply outwards for a little almost at once, and then turning equally sharply backwards for the rest of their length, which may be 2 ft. in bucks, and in does half as much. Sterndale well says that the front view resembles a trident with the central prong removed. Coat long and thick, varying much locally, with the extremities generally black, and a mixture of black in the yellowish or reddish-brown body-colour. There is a very handsome variety in which the colour is golden throughout; possibly this beast was the "ram with the golden fleece" secured by Jason in the old Greek Argo-legend.

The Takin may be solitary or associate in herds; it frequents steep, bushy, and difficult ground at high elevations, and not much is known of it at present, though two living specimens have been exhibited at the London Zoological Gardens, of which one was on view at the time this revision was being written.

The Gazelles (*Gazella*) are quite in accordance with the popular idea of an antelope, very graceful, slender, goat-sized creatures with long slim necks and legs, and large beautiful dark eyes. Their coats are smooth, their tails rather short, and their horns—often absent in females—ringed and slightly bent backwards and outwards in males. They frequent dry open country and are sociable and remarkable for speed. In all our species the main colour is fawn or sandy.

Indian Gazelle (male and female).

INDIAN GAZELLE

Other Names.—Scientific: *Chinkára*, *Chikára*, *Kal-punch*, Hindi; *Kal-sipi*, Mahratti; *Tiska*, *Budari*, *Mudari*, Canarese; *Barudu-jinka*, Telegu; *Porsya* (male), *Chari* (female), Baori; *Ask*, *Ast*, *Ahu*, Baluch; *Khazm*, Brahui; *Sank-hulé*, Mysore.

Habitat.—From the eastern shore of the Persian Gulf through Baluchistan south to Central India and Mysore; not found in the Western Ghats and Konkan, or east of Palamow and Western Sirguja, or of Seonee and Chanda in the Central Provinces, or much south of the Kistna.

Description.—About the size of a small goat, a buck being little over 2 ft. at the shoulder, and weighing about 50 lb. (does weigh less by 10 lb. or more). Knees with tufts of hair; tail decidedly longer than a goat's or wild sheep's, over 8 in. A small gland below the eye. Horns of buck but slightly curved, turning slightly outwards, backwards, and forwards at the tip, with one or two dozen rings; generally they are less than 1 ft. long, 14 in. is the record. Horns of does are straight, generally smooth, and quite short, the record being only 8 in. Blanford once got a dark-faced doe with ringed horns 7¼ in. long in Baluchistan, which he at first considered a distinct species, and called it *Gazella fuscifrons*, but it later turned out to be only a variety. Generally the face is not much darker than the general pale chestnut of the upper parts; the white of the lower body does not reach up to the tail in this species, and there are no light side-stripes, though these are found on the sides of the face.

Sterndale says: "This pretty little creature, miscalled 'ravine-deer,' is familiar to most shikaris. How it got called a *deer* it is difficult to say, except on the principle of 'rats and mice and such small deer.' The Madras term of 'goat-antelope' is more appropriate. I remember once, when out on field service with the late Dr. Jerdon in the Indian Mutiny, a few *chikara* crossed our line of march. A young and somewhat bumptious ensign, who knew not of the fame of the doctor as a naturalist, called out 'There are some deer, there are some deer!' 'Those are not deer,' quietly remarked Jerdon. 'Oh, I say,' exclaimed the boy, thinking he had got a rise out of the doctor, 'Jerdon says those are not deer!' 'No more they are, young man, no more they are; much more of the goat—much more of the goat.'" In justice to the frivolous youth, it may be said that most antelopes do look very like deer in general form, and the term "goat-antelope" is wanted and was used by Sterndale for the capricorns we have just been considering, which are "much more of the goat" than gazelles, albeit gazelles and goats are both hollow-horned ruminants; moreover, deer as a family differ little from these except in the antlers of the males.

"This gazelle," proceeds Sterndale, "frequents broken ground, with sandy nullahs bordered by scrub-jungle, and is most common in dry climates. It is unknown, I believe, in Bengal, and, according to Jerdon, on the Malabar coast, but is, I think, found almost everywhere else in India. It abounds in the Central Provinces, and I have found it in parts of the Punjab, and it is common throughout the north-west. It is a restless, wary little beast, and requires good shooting, for it does not afford much of a mark. When disturbed they keep constantly shifting, not going far, but hovering about in a most tantalising way. Natives it cares little for, unless it be a shikari with a gun, of which it seems to have intuitive perception ; but the ordinary cultivator, with his load of wood and grass, may approach within easy shot ; therefore, it is not a bad plan, when there is no available cover, to get one of these men to walk alongside of you, whilst, with a blanket or horse-cloth over you, you make yourself look as like your guide as you can. A horse or bullock is also a great help. I had a little bullock which formed part of some loot at Banda—a very handsome little bull, easy to ride and steady under fire—and I found him most useful in stalking blackbuck and gazelle. When alarmed, the *chikara* stamps its foot and gives a sharp little hiss. It is generally found in small herds of four or five, but often singly. Jerdon, however, says that in the extreme north-west he had seen twenty or more together, and this is corroborated by Kinloch."

Blanford says that he believes this gazelle never drinks. He also states that the doe is often seen with two fawns, and that the flesh is excellent.

Persian Gazelle.

PERSIAN GAZELLE

OTHER NAMES.—Scientific : *Gazella subgutturosa*. Native : *Ahu*, Persian.

HABITAT.—Persia and Central Asia to the Gobi Desert, entering our territory north of Quetta. Common in Afghanistan.

DESCRIPTION.—About the same size as the last, and with horns similarly ringed, but turning inwards at the tips, and a little longer at their maximum, 14·7 in. Female without horns. Tail moderate. Colour much as in the last, sandy above, white below, the white, however, extending up the stern to the root of the tail. Knee-tufts present, and pale side- and face-stripes.

The Persian Gazelle is said by Blanford to be more strictly a desert animal than the *chikara*, though he states that this is most abundant in the Indian Desert.

TIBETAN GAZELLE

OTHER NAMES.—Scientific: *Gazella picticaudata*. Native: *Goa*, *Rágao*, Tibetan.

HABITAT.—Tibet, Ladakh, and north of Nepal and Sikkim.

DESCRIPTION.—About the same size as the others, but lower on the legs, which have no knee-tufts; face-glands only indicated by bare patches, and ears shorter than in the others; tail a mere stump. Horns longer than in the others, commonly 13 in., while 15¾ in. is recorded. Rings of horns more numerous than in the other species, over two dozen, but less distinct; the curve of the horns is also different, as they bend strongly backwards, though the tips curve forward as in the Chikara.

In this species also the female has no horns. Winter coat full and fine, and forming a sort of moustache round the mouth, grizzled fawn at this season, but curiously enough with a grey shade in summer. White under-parts not so clearly defined as in the last two, but white on stern including the tail, which has a black tip; no light and dark streaks on the face.

The Goa keeps at high elevations—between about 13,000 and 18,000 ft.—associating in small parties, and being often found singly in summer. It is not very shy or easily frightened even by noise or human scent.

Allied to the Gazelles is a peculiar Tibetan antelope, which forms a genus of its own (*Pantholops*).

CHIRU

OTHER NAMES.—Scientific: *Pantholops hodgsoni*. Native: *Chiru*, Nepalese, and Tibetan; also called in the latter language *Tsús* (male), *Chus* (female).

HABITAT.—Tibet, Ladakh, north of Kumaon and Sikkim.

DESCRIPTION.—About the same size as the common Blackbuck,

$2\frac{1}{2}$ ft. at shoulder, but more heavily built, with a puffy and slightly bearded muzzle, and longer tail, which measures 9 in. Horns with the fronts well ringed, erect, long, slender, and nearly straight, but turning a little inwardly after diverging at first. They are unusually uniform in size, generally 2 ft. or an inch or two over, but a length of $27\frac{1}{2}$ in. is known. Coat exceedingly dense, woolly at roots, very pale brown, with the face and streaks down the legs black in bucks; in the does, which have no horns, these dark markings are absent also. Horns of buck black.

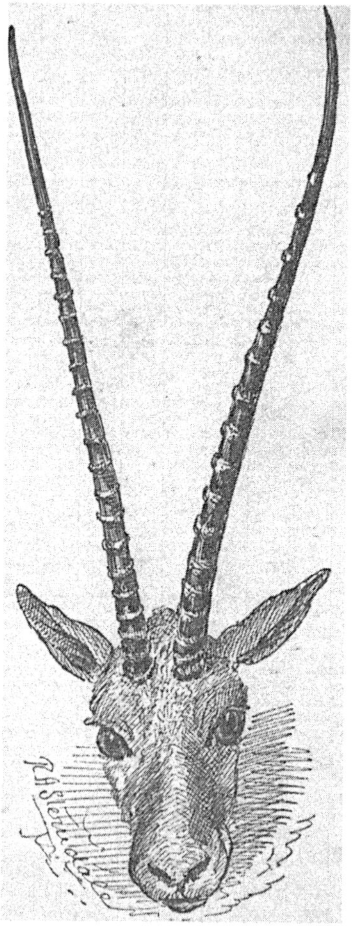

Chiru.

The Chiru is an animal of high elevations, between 12,000 and 18,000 ft. Unlike the Goa, it is shy and wary, and though sometimes found alone or in small parties, it may collect in herds of hundreds. In summer the sexes separate; pairing is said to take place in winter, and the gestation period to be six months, one fawn being born. When lying down for the day the Chiru has a peculiar habit, according to Kinloch, of scraping out lairs or beds deep enough to conceal its body, presumably for protection against wind, as the long horns, which are still visible, would betray it to enemies. In Chang Chenmo he found many bucks, but only saw one doe in three visits.

Our Common Antelope is the only member of the genus *Antilope* as now restricted, and so can claim to be *the* Antelope *par excellence*.

Blackbuck.

BLACKBUCK

Other Names.—Scientific: *Antilope cervicapra, bezoartica.* Native: *Mirga, Ena* (male), Sanskrit; *Haran, Harna* (male), *Harni, Kalwit* (female), *Mrig*, Hindi; *Kala* (male), *Goria* (female), Tirhoot; *Kalsar* (male), *Baoti* (female), Behar; *Bureta*, Bhagalpur; *Baraut, Sasin*, Nepalese; *Phandayat*, Mahratti; *Báhmain-haran*, Uriya; *Chigri, Húlé-kara*, Canarese; *Irri* (male), *Sedi* (female), *Jinka*, Telegu; *Alali* (male), *Gondoli* (female), Baori; *Bádú*, Ho Kol; *Kutsar*, Korku; *Veli-man*, Tamil.

Habitat.—India, generally, but not ascending the Himalayas, and not found in Burma or Ceylon, the Gangetic delta, or the Malabar coast south of Surat. Commonest in the north-west and Deccan.

DESCRIPTION.—A singularly elegant and well-proportioned animal, about 32 in. at shoulder in the male; tail short, about 7 in. Does are smaller, and generally hornless. Horns of male well ringed and spiral, varying much in number of turns and in degree of divergence. Measured straight, they are generally under 2 ft., but there is a record of 28¾ in. Does, when horned, have smooth, backward-turning horns; such does are very rare, Blanford having only met with one, while Sterndale mentions none at all. Coat close and short, mostly black in old bucks, with white underparts, eye-rings, and muzzle, and back of neck fawn. Does and young bucks fawn, white below. Old bucks become gradually blacker with age, but in some cases at any rate reassume the fawn coat for a certain time every year. The longest horns are to be got in the north-west.

The Blackbuck is one of the most beautiful of existing animals; beside it gazelles look spindly, and most other animals unfinished or coarse. The buck has a peculiar courting pose in which he shows off as distinctly as any bird, turning his head well back and his tail forward, so that the brown nape is concealed and the white underside of the tail exposed, while the large gland-pits under the eye are widely opened. He is extremely polygamous, for though pairs may be found, any number of does from ten to fifty are generally appropriated by one old male, who may tolerate a few young brown ones, or drive them off to herd by themselves. Great herds, even of thousands, of both sexes may, however, sometimes be found, including both adult and immature bucks. They do not avoid cultivation, but are not found in any sort of high cover, and rarely even among bush, nor do they frequent either hills or swamps. Grassy plains are their usual haunts, and grass their ordinary food. Blanford thought they never drank, though he had been told they did, and pointed out that they abound between the salt Chilka Lake in Orissa and the sea, where a well supplies the only fresh water; but since his time they have been observed in this locality at the edge of the water, with lowered heads as if drinking, so that they can probably safely drink salt water, as oceanic birds are known to do.

When alarmed, the herd bound into the air, one after another, when starting to run; they are very fast, especially the does, and as a general rule can escape from greyhounds, except on heavy sand, fine pasture, or heavy soil in the rains. The Cheetah, however, can often run into them, the buck, which brings up the rear, being generally taken. They are clever at hiding. Sterndale says: "In my book on Seeonee I have given a case of a wounded buck which I rode down to the brink of a river, when he suddenly disappeared. The country was so open and I was so close behind him that it seemed impossible for him to have got out of sight in so short a space of time; but I looked right and left without seeing a trace of him, and, hailing some fishermen on the opposite bank, found that they had not seen him cross. Finally my eye lighted on what seemed to be a couple of sticks projecting from a bed of rushes some 4 or 5 ft. from the bank. Here was my friend submerged to the tip of his nose, with nothing but the tell-tale horns sticking out.

"This antelope attaches itself to localities, and after being driven away for miles will return to its old place. The first buck I ever shot I recovered, after having driven him away for some distance, and wounded him, on the very spot I first found him; and the following extract from my journals will show how tenaciously they cling sometimes to favourite places: 'I was out on the boundary between Khapa and Belgaon, and came across a particularly fine old buck, with very wide-spreading horns; so peculiar were they that I could have sworn to the head amongst a thousand. He was too far off for a safe shot when I first saw him, but I could not resist the chance of a snap at him, and tried it, but missed; and I left the place. My work led me again soon after to Belgaon itself, and whilst I was in camp there I found my friend again; but he was very wary; for three days I hunted him about, but could not get a shot. At last I got my chance; it was on the morning of the day I left Belgaon. I rode round by the boundary, when up jumped my friend from a bed of rushes, and took off across country. I followed him cautiously and found him again with some does about two miles off. A man was ploughing in a field close by; so, hailing him, I got his bullocks and drove them carefully up past the does. We splashed through a nullah, and waded through a lot of rushes, and at last I found myself behind a clump of coarse grass, with a nullah between me and the antelope. They jumped up on my approach, and Blacky, seeing his enemy, made a speedy bolt of it; but I was within easy range of him, and a bullet brought him down on his head with a complete somersault. Now this buck, in spite of the previous shot at him, and being hunted about from day to day, never left his ground, and used to sleep every night in a field near my tent.

"This antelope has been raised by the Hindoos among the constellations harnessed to the chariot of the moon. Brahmins can feed on its flesh under certain circumstances prescribed by the 'Institutes of Menu,' and it is sometimes tamed by fakirs. It is easily domesticated, but the bucks are always dangerous when their horns are full grown, especially to children. The breeding season begins in the spring, but fawns of all ages may be seen at any time of the year. The flesh of this species is among the best of the wild ruminants."

The doe has a hissing alarm note, and the buck grunts when excited, as when displaying. The animals live and breed well in captivity, in England as well as in India.

The Nilgai also has a genus of its own.

Nilgai.

NILGAO OR NILGAI

OTHER NAMES.—Scientific: *Portax pictus*, *Boselaphus tragocamelus*. Native: *Nilgao* (male), *Nilgai* (female), *Lilgao*, *Lilgai*, *Rojh*, *Rojhra* (male), *Rooi* (female), Hindi; *Gúraya* Gondi; *Maravi*, *Mairu*, *Kard-kadrai*, *Mánú-potú*, Canarese; *Murim* (male), *Susam* (female), Ho Kol.

HABITAT.—Indian Peninsula, but not ascending the Himalayas or ranging south of Mysore. It does not reach the Indus, and is commoner in the north-west and Central Provinces than the south.

DESCRIPTION.—A large animal, about 13 hands at the shoulder, and recalling an ill-shaped horse in form, with withers higher than croup, tail tufted and reaching to hocks, carried tucked in like a donkey's. Neck with a short hog-mane at the back, and a tuft of hair on the throat of the bull. Small face-glands, but a moist ox-like muzzle. Horns normally present only in male, short and smooth, slightly curved forward at the tips. Coat smooth, blue roan in the male, with the long hairs and ear-tips black, and throat-patch, two cheek-spots, and two fetlock-rings white. Cows and calves light chestnut. Gelding males have this colour, but possess horns, and horned cows are on record The record for the horns is only $11\frac{3}{4}$ in., and they are usually about 8 in.

The Nilgao used often to be called Blue bull, and though Nilgai is used by Blanford and most modern writers, this name really applies to the female, which is not blue, and Nilgao, which Sterndale uses, is more correct. He says: "The nilgao inhabits open country with scrub or scanty tree jungles, also, in the Central Provinces, low hilly tracts with open glades and valleys. He feeds on beyr (*Zizyphus jujuba*) and other trees, and at times even devours such quantities of the intensely acrid berries of the *aonla* (*Phyllanthus emblica*) that his flesh becomes saturated with the bitter elements of the fruit. This is most noticeable in soup, less so in a steak, which is at times not bad. The tongue and marrow-bones, however, are generally as much as the sportsman claims, and in the Central Provinces at least, the natives are grateful for all the rest.

"He rests during the day in shade, but is less of a nocturnal feeder than the sambar stag. I have found nilgao feeding at all times during the day. The droppings are usually found in one place. The nilgao drinks daily, the sambar only every third day, and many are shot over water. Although he is such an imposing animal, the blue bull is but poor shooting, unless when fairly run down in the open. With a sharp spurt he is easily blown, but if not pressed will gallop for ever. In some parts of India nilgai are speared in this way. I myself preferred shooting them either from a light double-barrelled carbine or large-bore pistol when alongside; the jobbing at such a large cow-like animal with a spear was always repugnant to my feelings. They are very tenacious of life. I once knocked one over as I thought dead, and putting my rifle against a tree, went to help my shikaree to *hallal* him, when he jumped up, kicked us over, and disappeared in the jungle; I never saw him again. A similar thing happened to a friend who was with me, only he sat upon his supposed dead bull, quietly smoking a cigar and waiting for his shikarees, when up sprang the animal, sending him flying, and vanished. On another occasion, whilst walking through the jungle, I came suddenly on a fine dark male standing chest on to me. I hardly noticed him at first; but, just as he was about to plunge away into the thicket, I rapidly fired, and with a bound he was out of sight. I hunted all over the place and could find no trace of him. At last, by circling round, I suddenly came upon him at about 30 yds. off, standing broadside on. I gave him a shot and heard the bullet strike, but there was not the slightest motion. I could hardly believe that he was dead in such a posture. I went up close, and finally stopped in front of him; his neck was stretched out, his mouth open and eyes rolling, but he seemed paralysed. I stepped up close and put a ball through his ear, when he fell dead with a groan. I have never seen anything like it before or since, and can only suppose that the shot in the chest had in some way choked him. . . .

"The nilgao is the only one of the deer and antelope in India that could be turned to any useful purpose. The sambar stag, though almost equal in size, will not bear the slightest burden, but the nilgao will carry a man. I had one in my collection of animals which I trained, not to saddle, for such a thing would not stay on his back, but to saddle-cloth. He was a little difficult to ride, rather jumpy at times, otherwise his pace was a shuffling trot. I used to take him out into camp with me, and made him earn his grain by carrying the servants' bundles. He was not very safe, for he was, when excited, apt to charge; and a charge from a blue bull with his short sharp horns is not to be despised. In some parts the Hindoos will not touch the flesh of this animal, which they believe to be allied to the cow." In this belief they are unconsciously right, for the nilgao is one of the animals which connect the antelopes with the oxen; but it is a pity they are so scientific in this point, for it is one of the worst crop-destroyers in the country, being a grazer as well as a browser, and not at all averse to cultivated country. The cow, although decidedly smaller, is faster than the bull, and, Kinloch says, cannot be ridden down by one man. She produces a single calf or twins after a gestation of eight or nine months. Nilgao breed well in captivity, either in India or at home, and have long been very well-known menagerie animals. They have been trained to draught, but are said to be almost impossible to stop if they bolt.

The last of our antelopes is another sole member of its genus, and very different from all the rest.

FOUR-HORNED ANTELOPE

OTHER NAMES.—Scientific: *Tetraceros quadricornis*. Native: *Chousingha*, *Chouka*, *Doda*, Hindi; *Bhir-kura* (male), *Bhir* (female), Gondi; *Bhirul*, Bheel; *Kotari*, in Chutia Nagpur; *Kurus*, *Kotri*, Gondi (Bastar); *Kond-guri*, *Kaulla-kuri*, Canarese; *Jangli bakri*, in the Deccan; but Sterndale says he has heard this name, and *Bhirki*, which Blanford gives as used at Saugor, applied to the Barking Deer presently to be mentioned.

HABITAT.—India generally, except the plain of the Ganges and the Madras part of the Malabar coast; not Ceylon or Burma.

DESCRIPTION.—A small animal with narrow muzzle. Croup higher than the withers, where the male measures only about 1 in. over 2 ft., the female being still smaller. She is hornless, whereas the male has one or two pairs of short straight horns, the longer placed in the usual position between the ears, the shorter, which vary much in development, between the eyes. The longer horns are generally not more than $4\frac{1}{2}$ in. long, and commonly 3 in.; the record for the front horns is $2\frac{1}{2}$ in., and 1 in. is more usual; but an animal with a fore horn of 3 in. and a hind one of $7\frac{1}{4}$ in. was recorded in the Bombay Natural History Society's *Journal* in 1928. The fore horns may be absent in fully adult animals in the Madras Presidency; but Blanford points out that they develop comparatively late, a male from Nimar that he knew not having developed them till the third year, though early in the second the back pair were well developed. Tail rather long, 5 in.; coat short and coarse, light brown with dark stripes down the legs, but varying a good deal in shade.

Four-horned Antelope.

The Four-horned Antelope is a denizen of bush and thin forest, solitary or at most found in pairs. Sterndale says it is "very shy and difficult to get, even in jungles where it abounds. It was plentiful in the Seeonee district, yet I seldom came across it, and was long before I secured a pair of live ones for my collection. It frequents, according to my experience, bamboo jungle. . . . It is an awkward-looking creature in action, as it runs with its neck stuck out in a poky sort of way, making short leaps; in walking it trips along on the tips of its toes like the little mouse-deer (*Meminna*). . . . It is not good eating, but can be improved by being well larded with mutton-fat when roasted." Blanford, however, thinks it better than that of most Indian deer, though not equal to antelope or gazelle. He says it pairs in the rains, the single or twin young being born in the beginning of the year, after, according to Hodgson, a six months' gestation.

Blanford also states that this antelope is easily tamed; but small though it is, it can, like most horned animals, be dangerous. A native keeper in the Calcutta Zoological Gardens told the editor that it would attack with a spring; and even 3-in. or 4-in. horns are not pleasant to receive in one's stomach!

The Cattle (genus *Bos*) are large, heavily-built animals with longer tails than our other ruminants, a large, moist, naked muzzle, and horns in both sexes. The back hoofs are fairly developed, but there are no foot- or face-glands. The Indian Empire is exceedingly rich in species of these fine animals, far more so than any other region.

They are social, and for the most part grass-eaters and fond of water and of salt. The species are markedly different in appearance and habits; yet all are easily recognisable as oxen. Although sometimes dangerous and destructive, they are, on the whole, the most valuable of all mammals. They very rarely bear more than one calf at a birth.

ZEBU

Other Names.—Scientific: *Bos indicus*. Native: *Gai*, Hindi. It is unnecessary to give other native names, as this is simply the common domestic ox of India, and readers will know the names applied to cattle in their district.

Habitat.—Africa and South-East Asia; always as a tame animal, except in a few localities in India where it has become "feral," *i.e.* run wild. Blanford gives as these localities Oudh, Rohilkund, Surat, Mysore, Nellore, Char Sidhi, the mouth of the Megna, etc.

Description.—Differs from European cattle, the descendants of *Bos taurus*, the Aurochs, now extinct as a wild animal, in its less divergent and more backwardly-directed horns, its deeper dewlap extending forward to the chin, its rounded instead of square-cut hind-quarters, its longer legs, and often in the possession of a fatty hump. The colour varies much, as in taurine cattle, and sometimes resembles theirs; but generally is less variegated, and in a very common form the adult bull is blackish, shading into iron-grey, the cow pale iron-grey, and the calves of both sexes white. Iron-grey males, however, are very common also. The size of the breeds varies much more than in taurine cattle, the large Guzerat cattle being larger than any European breed, and the small Gainis about the size of sheep.

Compared with European cattle, Zebu are very silent, and when they do low the voice is different; they are more active, often trotting freely even when not of the specialised long-legged Mysore trotting breed; they do not seek shade or stand in water like taurine cattle, and their beef has not the distinctive flavour of the meat of these, but does not taste stronger than mutton.

When wild, they can exist in spite of the presence of tigers, which are so destructive to the tame stock. Jerdon says of their habits when wild near Nellore, "The country they frequent is much covered with jungle and intersected with salt-water creeks and back-waters, and the cattle are as wild and wary as the most feral species. Their horns are very large and upright, and they were of large size. I shot one there in 1843, but had great difficulty in stalking it, and had to follow it across one or two creeks." The term "feral" here is wrongly used, as it properly means secondarily wild or "run wild," but Jerdon's meaning is obvious. It would be interesting to know exactly where wild Zebu are to be found now, and what their colour is. The name Zebu, by the way, is not Indian, and its origin is unknown; possibly it may be derived from Zebu or Cebu in the Philippines, if such cattle are kept there, for some specimens early brought to Europe may have come thence.

The evidence above given is in favour of Zebu being a distinct species from taurine cattle, and so nearly all naturalists have regarded them; but Mr. R. I. Pocock has very ably argued that they are only a highly-specialised race of taurine cattle. In favour of this view it may be stated that no ancestral form has been found among the several fossil species found in India, and that the Aurochs, the ancestor of taurine cattle, survived in Europe down to the seventeenth century, so that it seems strange, if Zebu were ever a wild species, that they should have become extinct in India, and yet now thrive there as feral animals.

It is possible that Zebu have a cross of the Banting, presently to be noticed, and that their presence in Africa may be due to very early importations from Asia. Cattle which display a combination of taurine and zebuine characters may be of mixed blood, or the resemblances may be due to the principle of "analogous variation," whereby one species takes on some character of another independently, as when the ass shows a drooping mane like the usual domestic horse (though both are equally hog-maned when wild), or the horse displays an ass character by having no hind "chestnuts." In this case, crossing cannot have come into play, the ass-horse mule being almost always sterile.

Cattle hybrids, by the way, are remarkable for fertility, as will shortly be seen.

Gaur.

GAUR OR GAYAL

OTHER NAMES.—Scientific: *Bos gaurus, frontalis, Gavæus gaurus, frontalis.* Native: *Gaur, Gaurigai,* Hindi; *Gáyál,* Orissa; *Gaor* (male), *Gaib* (female), *Chutia Nagpur; Pera-mao,* Southern Gonds; *Gaviya,* Mahratti; *Karkona, Karti, Kardyenuné, Kard-korna, Daddu,* Canarese; *Katu yeni, Katu erimai,* Tamil; *Pyoung,* Burmese; *Saladang,* Malay; *Mithan,* Assamese.

In various parts of Peninsular India, the names *Ban-boda, Ban-parra, Ran-hila, Ran-pads, Jangli-khulga, Ban-bhainea,* and *Arna,* are used, according to Blanford, who points out that all these names mean "wild buffalo," so that Indians miscall the beast as persistently as the European sportsmen who call it Bison; the real Bisons of Europe and North America being very different animals, shaggy, bearded, and short-horned.

HABITAT.—Peninsula of India, east and south through Assam and Burma to the Malay Peninsula and Siam, but only where large forest areas exist. It does not ascend the Himalayas, and is now extinct in Ceylon, though it seems formerly to have existed there; possibly it was exterminated by some cattle disease, to which danger it is always liable.

DESCRIPTION.—A very large massive ox with high-ridged fore-back, and deep carcase, but comparatively fine limbs and small compact hoofs. Tail reaching hocks; coat close and short, becoming very scanty above in old bulls, which are nearly black. Younger animals are browner, cows and quite young bulls often redder; an almost chestnut cow was in the Indian Museum in the editor's time. Both sexes have white stockings, and the poll pale grey, drab, or nearly white. Calves have a black spine-stripe.

The lighter animals are found in the drier parts of the country, and the colour tends to be lighter in the cold weather. Horns nearly C-shaped, curving first outwards and then inwards, and with a slight backward bend at the tip; on the whole not very unlike those of European cattle except for the want of forward inclination. The colour is also somewhat similar, pale greenish or yellowish with black tips. Two feet round the curve is ordinary for a bull's horn, and a record for a cow's; the bull record is 39 in. with a basal girth of 19 in., though 22 in. have been measured as girth in 32-in. horns. Very large bulls may be 6 ft. at the shoulder, but cows are not over 5 ft.

Sterndale says: "The Gaur prefers hilly ground, though it is sometimes found on low levels. It is extremely shy and retiring in its habits, and so quick of hearing that extreme care has to be taken in stalking to avoid treading on a dry leaf or stick. I know to my cost that the labour of hours may be thrown away by a moment of impatience. In spite of all the wondrous tales of its ferocity, it is as a rule a timid, inoffensive animal. Solitary bulls are sometimes dangerous if suddenly come upon. I once did so, and the bull turned and dashed up-hill before I could get a shot, whereas a friend of mine, to whom a similar thing occurred a few weeks before, was suddenly charged, and his gun-bearer was knocked over. The Gaur seldom leaves its jungles, but I have known it do so on the borders of the Sonawani forest, in order to visit a small tank at Untra near Ashta, and the cultivation in the vicinity suffered accordingly.

"Hitherto most attempts to rear this animal in captivity have failed. It is said not to live over the third year. Though I offered rewards for calves for my collection, I never succeeded in getting one." Blanford, however, mentions a bull from the Malay Peninsula exhibited in the London Zoological Gardens in the early 'nineties. This the editor saw, and noticed what had been recorded, that the breath of the animal was even sweeter than that of ordinary European cattle, recalling the odour of violets. Recent correspondents of *The Field* stated that the Gaur has a great dislike for the buffalo, and may kill tame ones. As an inhabitant of hill forests, however, it must seldom meet this rival, though it is sometimes found in long grass cover on the flat, and its ordinary food is grass, occasionally varied by leaves and bark.

Gayal.

A domestic form of the Gaur, the Gayal or Mithan, formerly classed as a distinct species (*Bos frontalis*), is kept by various tribes in the hill-tracts from Assam to Chittagong, and is known as *Sandung* by the Manipuris, *Shel* or *Shio* by the Kukis, *Jhongnua* by the Mughs, *Bui-sang* or *Hui* by the Nagas, *Phu* by the Akas, *Siha* by the Daphlas, and *Nuni* in Burmese. The names *Gáyál* and *Mithan*, as we have seen, are applied to the wild Gaur also, and Mr. E. C. Stuart Baker has proved that the two forms are not distinct, but intergrade.

Typical Gayal look decidedly different from Gaur. The colour is the same, unless they are white, pied, yellow, or black-stockinged, but the horns are merely slightly-curved cones, all black, except in albinistic specimens, and the poll between them is straight, not transversely arched as in Gaur, nor is the forehead concave as in that form, while the head is shorter and broader, the back-ridge lower, the legs shorter, and the whole animal smaller. There is also a decided dewlap on the fore-neck, which is wanting in the Gaur.

These animals are not worked, but occasionally a bull is killed for meat. The milk is said to be used, but Blanford doubts this, on the ground that the Indo-Chinese tribes who own Gayal do not drink milk. It is possible, however, that they may use more or less solid preparations of it.

Gayal shift for themselves by day, but spend the night at the village, to which they are much attached. They are much hardier than Gaur, and are fairly well known in captivity. They will breed with Zebu, and a Gayal-Zebu hybrid bred at the London Zoological Gardens in the 'eighties produced offspring with an American Bison, this being apparently the first recorded instance of a double hybrid.

BANTENG

Other Names.—Scientific: *Bos sondaicus*, *Gavæus sondaicus* Native: *Tsaing*, Burmese; *Sapi-utan*, Malay; *Banteng*, Javanese.

Habitat.—Burma east to Bali.

Description.—Very like the Gaur, but smaller and slighter, with longer head, legs, and tail, which last reaches below the hocks, shorter horns and lower back-ridge. There is also a dewlap, and a white stern-patch as well as the white stockings, while the body-colour is generally chestnut, though bulls are often black, especially in localities east of Burma, where bay is more usual. Calves have a black spine-stripe, but no white stockings. The forehead is not concave, nor the poll between the horns transversely arched; in old bulls it is here covered with callous horny skin.

The horns of the bull turn out and up, and then back and in, and rather resemble some Zebu horns; 2 ft. 6 in. in length have been measured, with a basal girth of 17 in., but usually they are considerably smaller, and those of cows in the eastern domestic form at any rate—for Banteng are domesticated in Java and Bali—are short and directed straight back, thus also resembling some Zebus. The largest Burmese bull recorded was 16 hands at the shoulder, but a Javan bull has measured 5 ft. 9½ in., which would be about the ordinary height for a Gaur.

The Banteng, however, is a less ponderous animal, and, if less imposing, is more elegant, especially when the bull is black and contrasts with the red cows. Wild Banteng affect grass-jungle rather than hill forest. They are largely bred in Bali for export, and supply beef to Singapore. They have bred in captivity in the Calcutta Zoological Gardens, where the editor noticed the young bull in the family he watched became black as soon as full-sized; and the great Dutch naturalist, Mr. F. Blaauw, has bred them freely at his park at Gooilust in Holland.

With regard to the possible descent of the Zebu, more or less, from the Banteng, the hump of the former cannot have anything to do with this, as has been suggested; because the hump of the Zebu, when present, is, like that of the camel, not correlated with any peculiarity of the backbone, which is quite normal in these animals. The ridge of the fore-back of the white-stockinged bovines we have been discussing is quite different in character, being less abrupt and formed by the prolongation of the dorsal spines of the vertebræ. Banteng, like Gayal, will breed with ordinary cattle.

YAK

OTHER NAMES.—Scientific: *Bos grunniens*. Native: *Banchour*, Hindi; *Yak, Bubul, Soora-goy, Dong, Brong-dong, Pegu*, Tibetan; *Boku* (old bull). *Dong* and *Brong-dong* mean the wild animal and *Pegu* the tame one.

HABITAT.—North Ladak and Tibet to Kansu.

DESCRIPTION.—A massive, short-legged animal, with the coat thick but short except on the chest, flanks, shoulders, and thighs, along which parts it is very long and forms a sort of flounce. Tail very bushy, more so than a horse's, reaching the hocks. Bull from between 5 ft. and 6 ft. at shoulder. Horns more like those of European taurine cattle than in any other species, having a forward as well as outward and upward inclination. Anything over 2 ft. is good, the record being 40 in., with a basal girth of nearly 19 in. Cows have smaller horns and are decidedly less in dimensions altogether. Colour black in the wild race, often variegated with white or all white in the tame, which is not nearly so large and is sometimes hornless.

Wild Yaks live in the bleakest situations on the mountains, and range up to 20,000 ft. in summer, when cows and young collect in herds, larger at times than those formed by our other cattle, even up to a hundred animals or more, bulls being found alone or in quite small parties, except in pairing-time, in winter, when each associates with a few cows. These large animals can subsist on a diet of coarse grass, and are such inveterate herbage-eaters that tame ones will not eat grain, a habit often productive of much inconvenience, as where they are kept they are often the only baggage-animals obtainable. Generally speaking the tame Yak serves in Tibet all the uses of oxen elsewhere, as a worker and provider of milk and meat. It is a fine climber, and can plough through snow in a remarkable way. Snow is eaten in winter by these animals, which are in every way well adapted to a cold region, and have been introduced into Canada. They are well known in captivity in Europe. In the Himalayas they are crossed with the Zebu, the hybrid being known as *Zo*.

The tame Yak is notorious for its grunting, having indeed been called the Grunting Ox, as well as Horse-tailed Buffalo; the Wild Yak is said not to grunt, but can probably do so; only, being its own master, it seldom has anything to grunt about. The tame animal is often vexatiously stupid and obstinate; its aversion to grain might perhaps be overcome by mixing this at first with chaffed grass or hay.

Wild Yaks are timid, but, as might be expected, will charge at times if wounded.

Buffalo.

BUFFALO

OTHER NAMES.—Scientific: *Bos bubalus*. Native: *Bhains* (the tame race), *Arna* (male), *Arni* (female), *Arna-bhainsa*, *Jangli bhains*, Hindi; *Mang*, Bhagalpur; *Mains*, Bengali; *Gera erumi*, Gondi; *Karbo*, Malay; *Mi Harak*, Cingalese; *Bir*, *Biar*, Ho Kol; *Moh*, Assamese; *Siloi*, Kuki; *Gubui*, *Rili*, *Ziz*, *Le*, Naga; *Misip*, Cachari; *Iroi*, Manipuri; *Kywai*, Burmese; *Pana*, Karen.

HABITAT.—In the wild state, the plains of Eastern and Central India, south to about the Godavari and Pranhita. The wild buffaloes of Burma and the Malay Peninsula are suspected by Blanford of being feral or descendants of escaped animals; perhaps the same may be suggested with regard to the buffaloes which are common in North Ceylon, as there are no wild ones in Southern India; moreover, buffaloes have run wild in the Philippines and on Melville Island off the northern coast of Australia.

Tame buffaloes are kept throughout India generally, even on the mountains; they are also largely found in the countries further east as far as China, and the islands of the Malay Archipelago, while on the west they are kept in Asia Minor, Egypt, South-Eastern Europe, and even as far west as Italy.

DESCRIPTION.—A long-headed, short-legged ox with large hoofs and straight back. Tail about reaching hocks, coat coarse and very thin, allowing the skin to be seen. Horns peculiar, transversely ridged and triangular in section, running backwards and inwards, and with a varied curvature, some strongly curved, almost into a circle, others nearly straight except where they turn up at the ends. Unlike what obtains in our other oxen, cows generally have longer horns than bulls, though the latter's horns are more massive. The record horn-length is no less than $78\frac{1}{2}$ in., which, as Blanford says, would give an outside sweep of 14 ft. if a pair of this size were measured round from tip to tip; this is often done with buffalo horns, though there is no reason why they should be measured differently from those of other animals, unless in order to show sensational figures. The beast itself is said to exceed 6 ft. at the shoulder at times, which would make it larger than the Gaur when of the same height, as the Buffalo is longer in the body and lower on the leg. Colour dark slate with the hair black as a rule; but some have whitish legs, and some a dun coat; the dun wild buffaloes of Assam have also noticeably shorter muzzles.

Tame buffaloes are often white-stockinged like Gaur and Banteng; an interesting case of one species assuming the character of another without crossing, for the Buffalo never crosses with other oxen. Some tame buffaloes are dun, and some white with flesh-coloured skins, but apparently they are never pied, although the editor once saw a pair at the London Zoological Gardens with the tail-tuft white and white hair on the poll.

Sterndale says: "The buffalo never ascends mountains like the bison, but keeps to low and swampy ground and open grass plains, living in large herds, which occasionally split up into smaller ones during the breeding season in autumn. The female produces one, or sometimes two, in the summer, after a period of gestation of ten months. . . . I have known cases of the domestic animal absconding from the herd and running wild. Such a one was shot by a friend of mine in a jungle many miles from the haunts of men, but yet quite out of the range of the wild animal. Probably it had been driven from a herd. Domestic buffalo bulls are much used in the Central Provinces for carrying purposes. I had them yearly whilst in camp, and noticed that one old bull lorded it over the others, who stood in great awe of him; at last one day there was a great uproar; three younger animals combined, and gave him such a thrashing that he never held up his head again. In a feral state he would doubtless have left the herd and become a solitary wanderer. . . . The buffalo is, I should say, a courageous animal, at least, it shows itself so in the domesticated state. A number of them together will not hesitate to charge a tiger, for which purpose they are often used to drive a wounded tiger out of cover. A herdsman was once seized by a man-eater one afternoon a few hundred yards from my tent. His cows fled, but his buffaloes, hearing his cries, rushed up and saved him.

"The attachment evinced by these uncouth creatures to their owner was once strongly brought to my notice in the Mutiny. In

R

beating up the broken forces of a rebel Thakoor, whom we had defeated the previous day, I, with a few troopers, ran some of them to bay in a rocky ravine. Amongst them was a Brahmin who had a buffalo cow. This creature followed her master, who was with us as a prisoner, for the whole day, keeping at a distance from the troops, but within call of her owner's voice. When we made a short halt in the afternoon, the man offered to give us some milk; she came to his call at once, and we had a grateful draught, the more so as we had had nothing to eat since the previous night. That buffalo saved her master's life, for when in the evening the prisoners were brought up for court-martial and sentenced to be hanged, extenuating circumstances were urged for our friend with the buffalo, and he was allowed to go, as I could testify he had not been found with arms in his hands; and I had the greatest pleasure in telling him to be off, and have nothing more to do with rebel Thakoors."

The Buffalo is certainly the most courageous of our oxen, and a wild animal has been known to charge an elephant and knock it over; unfortunately its courage is often unpleasantly displayed, for it will often invade cultivation and keep off the owner, and solitary bulls often charge unprovoked, though herds seldom do so. Tame buffaloes are also dangerous to strangers, though controlled even by small native children whom they know. They often have wild blood, as wild bulls frequently mate with tame cows. This makes for physical improvement, as the wild animal is larger and less scraggy than the tame one. The chief food of buffaloes is grass, and they are so fond of water that they may be called semi-aquatic, often passing the heat of the day in lying down in any that is available. As draught animals they are very powerful, but also very slow; they presumably will not bear tail-twisting, as one does not see this brutality applied to them. The cows are valuable milch animals.

The Deer (*Cervidæ*) when horned, as they almost always are when males, have horns of a completely different character from those of other ungulates. There is really no horn in them, for they are a temporary bony growth, periodically shed and renewed. After shedding, two raw patches are seen, marking the tops of their permanent bony supports, the pedicels; these scab over, and then swellings appear, which, still covered by a soft downy skin, the velvet, go on enlarging till at length they assume the complete form. A knotty ring, the burr, then forms at the junction with the pedicel; the velvet dries, splits, and is rubbed off by the animal, leaving the bony antlers, as they are properly called, bare and hard. When growing they are full of blood, warm, and tender, and no doubt at this time the animal is forced to acquire the skill in managing its head that enables it to pass through timber without entangling its branched weapons. While without these, and during the earlier stages of their growth, the beast is mild and harmless, but becomes savage as its armament matures, and if tame, is dangerous to man.

The development in size depends to some extent on the quality of the feed the stag has had previously; but in any case there is much individual variation, and young stags only bear a single spike at first,

Stag with Growing Antlers.

other branches coming by degrees after shedding this. Senile stags "go back," the antlers becoming poorer after each shedding In cold and temperate climates the antlers are shed at regular times each year, but in India the time is more irregular in some cases, no doubt depending on the time of the individual stag's birth; and it is said that in some cases the antlers may be retained for two or three years. The first prong above the pedicel is called the brow-antler.

Where the antlers are absent or small, the males have well-developed upper canine tusks; the females also usually have small upper canines, which are absent in the last family. All our deer have short tails and slim legs and fairly long necks, while the back hoofs are sufficiently large to be noticeable if not serviceable; and most have eye-pits. They are generally social, and in many cases destructive to crops; their flesh is, however, always esteemed, and they are valuable game animals. The Indian Empire is richer in species of deer than any other area of the same size, and the various kinds are easily distinguished.

The Musk-deer has a genus to itself, and is our only hornless species, in fact; there is only one other hornless deer, the Chinese Water-deer (*Hydrelaphus inermis*).

Musk-deer.

MUSK-DEER

Other Names.—Scientific: *Moschus moschiferus*. Native: *Kastura*, *Múshk*, Hindi; *Ráos*, *Rous*, Kashmiri; *La*, *Láwa*, Tibetan; *Ribjo*, Ladakhi; *Bena*, in Kunawar; *Masak nába*, Pahari.

Habitat.—A mountain animal, found in Central Asia, Siberia, Tibet, and along the Himalayas above 8,000 ft., ranging up to 12,000 ft. in summer.

Description.—The smallest of our deer, being less than 2 ft. at the croup, which is considerably higher than the shoulder; legs long, especially the hinder, with a bend at the pastern which brings the back hoofs, which are larger than in other ungulates, low enough to touch the ground. Coat long and thick, presenting a uniform surface, and soft and springy to the touch, though the hairs are exceptionally coarse and brittle. Tail 2 in. or less, naked, except at the tip in the buck, which also has downward-projecting canines in the upper jaw, sometimes 3 in. long, and a pouch or "pod" on the abdomen containing the musk in the form of a crumbly paste.

Colour extremely variable, generally speaking a grizzly brown with brindled markings, but sometimes nearly white or black, orange-tinted below and more or less above, or pale-spotted. Young distinctly spotted, as in most deer.

The Musk-deer is a very peculiar animal in every way; it is in its habits very like a hare, unsocial, and lying in a lair or "form" when not feeding. It lives in cover on steep places, and progresses by bounds, showing great sure-footedness, to which the peculiar formation of its feet, almost like four-pronged pincers, no doubt contributes. It feeds on herbage, flowers, and lichens, and is good eating, the flesh not having any musky taste even in the case of the buck.

It pairs at the beginning of the year, and the young are born in June, after a gestation of 160 days; twins are sometimes produced, but a single fawn is more usual. As the young breed before they are twelve months old, it is a prolific animal, and to this, and probably to the fact that the male has been most sought after by hunters, may be attributed its survival after many centuries of persecution, the scent-pouch or musk-pod having been for ages an important article of trade. When captured it screams harshly like a hare, but seems to have no other call. There is hardly any musk in the pouch except at the breeding season, but then it contains about 1 oz. The animal does well in captivity, and has bred; it would be worth while to attempt its domestication, for it would probably be found possible to express the musk without injuring the animal, and thus obtain it less wastefully than at present. The smell of the drug when fresh is very strong and not at all pleasant; its value in perfumery is like that of a mordant in dyeing, to fix and give permanency to more pleasant and delicate odours. It is also used in medicine.

The Musk differs from our other deer not only in having no horns, but in having no face-glands, while it possesses a gall-bladder, which is wanting in all other deer, though present in the hollow-horned ruminants.

The Muntjacs (*Cervulus*) are small, short-legged, high-rumped deer with long conspicuous horn-pedicels, half as long as the head, and with small two-pronged antlers and large projecting upper canine teeth in the males. There are two converging bony ridges on the face, running up into the pedicels in the buck, and marked at their upper ends by two tufts of hair in the doe. Owing to this the animals are sometimes called rib-faced deer; they are unsocial, and frequent cover.

Muntjac.

INDIAN MUNTJAC

Other Names.—Scientific: *Cervulus muntjac.* Native: *Kákar*, *Jangli-bakri*, Hindi; *Maya*, Bengali; *Ratwa*, Nepalese; *Karsiar*, Bhotia; *Sikku*, Lepcha; *Gutra* (male), *Gutri* (female), *Bherki*, Gondi; *Bekra*, *Bekar*, Mahratti; *Kánkari*, *Cháli*, Canarese; *Kuka-gori*, Telegu; *Gyi*, Burmese; *Kidang*, Malay; *Weli*, *Hula-*

muha, Cingalese; *Kalai*, *Katu-ardu*, Tamil; *Hugeri*, Assamese. The name Muntjac, commonly found in natural history books, is Sundanese; and the names of Barking Deer, Rib-faced Deer, and Jungle Sheep are also current in India, though perhaps Kakar is oftenest used. In Ceylon the name Red Deer is used—rather absurdly, as this is the name of the large stag of Europe.

HABITAT.—Hill-forests of India, Ceylon, and Burma, extending east to Malaysia, Hainan, and Borneo. It seldom goes higher than 6,000 ft. in the Himalayas.

DESCRIPTION.—About 1 yd. long and 2 ft. at the shoulder in the buck, does being smaller. Tail about as long as head; hairy pedicels of horns of male 3 or 4 in., bearing antlers of about the same length, with a brow-tine inclining sharply upwards; the main beam is seldom over 5 in., though 11 in. is on record, but perhaps the pedicel was, wrongly, included in this measurement. A specimen with extra little single-tined antlers growing from the sides of the pedicels is on record.

Coat close and very sleek, bright bay, with black streaks along the face-ridges inside, extending up the pedicels in the buck; throat, groin, and under-side of tail white. Dark brown or even greyish-black varieties are found in the hills, and the editor has seen in the London Zoological Gardens a snow-white, pink-eyed albino. Fawns are pale-spotted.

Sterndale says: "The rib-face is a retiring little animal, and is generally found alone, or at times in pairs. Captain Baldwin mentions four having been seen together at one time, and General McMaster mentions three; but these are rare cases.

"It is very subtle in its movements, carrying its head low, and creeping, as Hodgson remarks, like a weasel under tangled thickets and fallen timber. In captivity I have found it to be a coarse feeder, and [it] would eat meat of all kinds greedily. . . . Its call is a hoarse, sharp bark, whence it takes its name of barking deer. What Jerdon says about the length of its tongue is true; it can certainly lick a good portion of its face with it."

Although the canine teeth are short compared with those of the musk, the Muntjac uses them freely when at bay, and may hurt dogs badly. They have some power of motion in the socket. The bark is freely uttered both as a sexual call and as an alarm-note. The flesh is exceptionally good, and the coat scents the hand with a peculiar gamy smell when stroked. A buck kept tame in England has been known to search for hens' eggs and eat them, and the animal may be somewhat omnivorous, though no doubt leaves, herbage, and other vegetable products are its usual food. It pairs in Northern India in the beginning of the year, and the young, single or twins, are born about midsummer, the gestation being for six months. Some young, however, may be found at all seasons, the rutting-time being evidently irregular.

Muntjac are well known in captivity, and have bred in the London Zoological Gardens. They produce, either with the mouth or with the feet, a peculiar rattling sound when running.

FEA'S MUNTJAC

OTHER NAMES.—Scientific: *Cervulus feæ.*

HABITAT.—Muleyit Mountain and Tenasserim-Siam frontier.

DESCRIPTION.—Apparently rather smaller than the Common Muntjac, with a shorter tail and with a tuft of hair between the pedicels. Top of head yellow, rest of coat mostly dark brown speckled above with yellow; under-parts light brown; tail white with a black band along the top; a white band up each thigh and white rings above the hoofs.

This is now classed as a dark variety of the common Muntjac.

Typical deer (*Cervus*) have no face-ridges, but the horn-pedicels short, never more than 1 or 2 in. high, and are generally large animals. Their antlers are also well developed, with at least three points in the adult. We have no less than six species of this fine group, generally social animals. Although graceful in their movements, deer are not so remarkable for speed as many antelopes, and Blanford thought most could be ridden down with fair ease.

SAMBAR OR RUSA

OTHER NAMES.—Scientific: *Cervus unicolor*, *Rusa aristotelis*. Native: *Sámbar*, *Sámar*, Hindi; *Jarao* (male), *Jarai* (female), Nepalese; *Maha* in the Terai; *Merú*, Mahratti; *Ma-ao*, *Mauk*, Gondi; *Kadavé*, *Kadaba*, Canarese; *Kennadi*, Telegu; *Gous*, *Gaoj* (male), *Bholongi* (female), Eastern Bengali; *Tshat*, Burmese; *Gona Rusa*, Cingalese; *Sáram*, Ho Kol; *Kadumai*, Tamil; *Khát-khowa-pohu*, Assamese; *Sacha*, Daphla; *Takhau*, *Hseukhau*, *Kheu*, Karen; *Rusa*, *Rusa-etam*, Malay. Called "Elk" in Ceylon.

HABITAT.—South-East Asia and the islands of the Malay Archipelago, but chiefly confined to hill-forest, ranging as high as 10,000 ft. in the Himalayas, and in Southern India and Ceylon to the hill-tops. It is not found where there is no forest, as in parts of the Punjab and north-west.

DESCRIPTION.—A very variable species, in India a large animal, stags ranging up to 4½ ft. at the shoulder, and more massively built than our other deer. Tail about three-fourths as long as head, and conspicuously bushy. Coat coarse, and on the stag's neck long. Ears about half as long as head.

Antlers large and particularly massive and rugged, normally with three points; a large brow-tine curving forwards and upwards, and two tines, varying in relative length, at the end of the "beam" or main shaft. A yard is a very good length for a horn, but 4 ft. is recorded; a girth at mid-beam of 8½ in. is the record for thickness, but the length in this case was only 41 in., the longer horns, as in the

Sambar.

Argali, being the less massive. The best horns are found in Central India and Bengal. Burmese horns have the inner upper tine shorter than the outer, while in Malay heads the reverse is the case; this Malay form and the Burmese also have longer brow-tines. The Malay form is sometimes ranked as a distinct species under the name of Rusa.

Ceylon Sambar are smaller than Indian, and some of the races from small eastern islands are very small, even down to 2 ft. at the shoulder.

The horns are not very apt to produce extra points, but Sterndale had a fine pair over 40 in. long and 7½ at mid-beam, with an extra tine 9 in. long near the top of the right one; and in the Indian Museum in the editor's time was a fine pair with nine points, so well-shaped that the asymmetry was not noticeable. He has also recorded a pair with flattened ends somewhat as in the Fallow Deer.

Colour dark brown, reddish in hinds and fawns, darker or even blackish or slate-colour in some old stags. The editor has seen one pale-spotted fawn, though fawns in this species are usually unspotted, and one very red one, about the hue of the Muntjac.

Head of Sambar.

"No sportsman," says Sterndale, "could wish for a nobler quarry than a fine male sambar. As I write, visions of the past rise before me, of dewy mornings ere the sun was up; the fresh breeze at day-break, and the waking cry of the koel and peacock, or the call of the painted partridge; then, as we move cautiously through the jungle that skirts the foot of the rocky range of hills, how the heart bounds when, stepping behind a sheltering bush, we watch the noble stag coming leisurely up the slope! How grand he looks! with his proud carriage and shaggy, massive neck, sauntering slowly up the rise, stopping now and then to cull a berry, or to scratch his sides with his wide sweeping antlers, looming large and almost black through the morning mists, which have deepened his dark brown hide, reminding one of Landseer's picture of 'The Challenge.'

"Stalking sambar is by far the most enjoyable and sportsmanlike way of killing them, but more are shot in *battues*, or over water when they come down to drink. According to native shikaris the sambar drinks only every third day, whereas the nylgao drinks daily; and this tallies with my own experience; in places where sambar were scarce I have found a better chance of getting one over water when the footprints were about a couple of days old. An exciting way of hunting this animal is practised by the Bunjaras, or gipsies of Central India. They fairly run it to bay with dogs, and then spear it. I have given in *Seonee* a description of the *modus operandi.*

"When wounded or brought to bay the sambar is no ignoble foe; even a female has an awkward way of rearing up and striking out with her fore-feet. A large hind in my collection at Seeonee once seriously hurt the keeper in this manner."

Blanford thinks that the Sambar drinks daily, and says it certainly travels long distances to its drinking-places at times. Probably both he and Sterndale are right; the quality of the fodder must vary, and the power of individuals or of local families of resisting thirst probably does so also, whether through constitution or involuntary training. Sambar browse much as well as grazing; they feed mostly at night, and seek shade during the day. They affect wild country, though visiting cultivation when it occurs amongst this; and they are only moderately sociable, even herds numbering a dozen or less, and hinds as well as stags being often solitary. The latter fight much. The male's call is a rather metallic bellow, the female's a low grunting low. Pairing takes place in spring in the Himalayas, but in late autumn in the Peninsula; the gestation period is eight months, and the young are usually born singly. The horns are usually, but not always, shed in spring; and it is of this species that it has been asserted, by Forsyth, that the antlers are not always shed annually, he having known stags which retained them for years.

Sambar are hard to kill, and their meat is coarse, but of good flavour. They have been introduced into New Zealand, and the Rusa race into Mauritius, the Bonin Islands, and probably into some of the eastern ones of the Malay Archipelago, some of which seem rather far out of the range of most ruminants.

Needless to say, they do well in captivity, and they will breed in that condition, both in India and Europe, but in Britain must not be allowed to range in woodland, as they are so inveterately attached to cover that they will remain in it all day in winter and contract fatal chills.

A pigmy stag described to the editor by the late W. Rutledge, an excellent observer of long experience in the animal trade, may have been an extremely dwarf form of eastern island sambar; it was no bigger than a Chevrotain, but had three-pointed antlers.

Spotted Deer.

SPOTTED DEER

Other Names.—Scientific: *Cervus axis*, *Axis maculatus*. Native: *Chital*, *Chitra*, *Chitra-jank* (male), Hindi; *Chatidah*, Bhágalpur; *Boro Khotiya*, Rungpore Bengali; *Buriya*, Gorakhpur; *Sáraga*, *Sárung*, *Jati*, *Mikka*, Canarese; *Dupi*, Telegu; *Lupi*, *Kars*, Gondi; *Tic Muha*, Cingalese; *Pali-man*, Tamil, Malabarese.

Habitat.—India, except Sind and the Punjab plains, not going up the Himalayas above the foot-hills, but found up to 4,000 ft. in places in Southern India. Also found in Ceylon, and introduced in New Zealand.

Description.—Very like the home Fallow Deer in form and colour of coat. Size moderate, a yard or a little more at the shoulder in bucks, considerably less in does. Tail longer than in our other deer, tapering, as long as head. Coat smooth throughout, light chestnut, spotted with white in both sexes and at all ages and seasons. A blackish variety occasionally occurs, which shows only faint traces of the spots. The ordinary specimens have a black line all along the spinal column from the nape to the tip of the tail, which last is white underneath, as are the throat and belly.

Horns of the Sambar type, with only a brow-tine and two branches at the tip of the beam, which is, however, smooth, thin, and far longer proportionately than in the Sambar, horns of 30 in. being common, while a pair of 38 and 38¾ in., with a 4-in. girth at the centre of the beam, is on record. The outer top tine is always much longer than the inner. Where the brow-tine and beam meet small extra points often occur, and in the Bombay Natural History Society's Journal (vol. xxix, 1924), an account and figure were given of a specimen which had a large branch projecting from the back of the beam and dividing into points in both horns. A shed pair were found, and then their owner was shot bearing a new pair of like character. This was a great pity, as it would have been of great scientific interest to note if his stock perpetuated his peculiarity.

Spotted Deer are smaller in South India, Ceylon, and Lower Bengal than elsewhere, and have smaller horns.

Concerning their habits, Sterndale says: "This deer is generally found in forests bordering streams. I have never found it at any great distance from water; it is gregarious, and is found in herds of thirty and forty in favourable localities. Generally, spotted deer and lovely scenery are found together, at all events in Central India. The very name *chital* recalls to me the loveliest bits of the rivers of the Central Provinces, the Nerbudda, the Pench, the Bangunga, and the bright little Hirrie. Where the bamboo bends over the water, and the *kouha* and *saj* make sunless glades, there will be found the bonny dappled hides of India's fairest deer. There is no more beautiful sight in creation than a *chital* stag in a sun-flecked dell."

The herds may be larger than mentioned above, even including hundreds of animals, according to Blanford.

Chital are gregarious at all seasons, and pairing and the production of young may occur at any time, as does the shedding of the horns. The gestation is variously given as six or eight months. Spotted Deer have no objection to plains or to the neighbourhood of man, provided broken ground or forest is available for a refuge, and when deer damage is complained of in India and Ceylon, this beautiful species is, it is to be feared, generally the culprit. However, its venison is good if kept till tender, and the skin is eminently suitable for rugs, so that there is no excuse for letting it become a pest. The note is a hoarse bark.

Spotted Deer live and breed particularly well in captivity, both in India and in Europe, and are well known in menageries by the name of Axis.

Hog-Deer.

HOG-DEER

Other Names.—Scientific: *Cervus porcinus*, *Axis porcinus*. Native: *Párá*, Hindi; *Khar Laguna*, Nepalese; *Nutrini haran*, Bengali; *Wil-muha*, Cingalese; *Dodar* in Rohilkund; *Darai*, *Dayai*, Burmese.

Habitat.—Plain country, watered by the Indus and Ganges system, and eastwards through Burma to Tenasserim; also Ceylon, but only between the Kaltura River and Madura, where it is supposed to have been introduced.

Description.—A small, rather short-legged deer, about 2 ft. at the shoulder, with horn-pedicels noticeably elevated above the skull, and tail nearly as long as head. Coat short and smooth throughout, brown in winter, in summer paler and yellower and generally more or less marked with white or pale spots above. According to Jerdon the old buck assumes a slaty hue at this time, but as Blanford does not mention this, it probably is not general. Under-side of tail white; fawns white-spotted for their first half-year.

Antlers small, generally about 1 ft. long, with a brow-tine slanting sharply upwards, and two top tines of which the inner is much the smaller; altogether much like those of a young Chital. The record length is not much over 20 in.

Sterndale says: "This animal is seldom found in forest land: it seems to prefer open grass jungle, lying sheltered during the day in thick patches, and lies close till almost run upon by beaters or elephants. Its gait is awkward, with some resemblance to that of a hog, carrying its head low; it is not speedy, and can easily be run down by dogs in the open. McMaster writes: 'Great numbers of these deer are each season killed by Burmans, being mobbed with dogs.' The meat is fair. Hog-deer are not gregarious like *chital;* they are usually solitary, though found occasionally in pairs."

The horns are shed about April, and the rutting season is September and October. This species and the Spotted Deer have interbred, and the hybrid progeny survived.

À propos of a supposed wild hybrid reported in the *Field* a year or two ago, it was noted that Hog-deer and Spotted Deer interbred so persistently in the Duke of Bedford's park at Woburn Abbey, that they had to be separated to keep the species pure. The hybrid character of the above specimen was doubted, and certainly the skin photographed was well spotted, and the horns on the skull also figured might have been poor or young chital horns; but as the horn-pedicels were distinctly intermediate in height, the animal probably really was a hybrid. The case is of interest, not only because wild hybrid mammals are so rare, but because in several points, as will have been seen, the Hog-deer differs from all our other typical deer and approaches the muntjacs, though it has no upper canine teeth at all. Chital, however, seldom have these teeth, and this readiness on the part of the two to interbreed may perhaps be taken as a further proof of the close alliance of the two species. Blanford states that when ridden for spearing they generally give a good run. At bay, in spite of its small size, the Para shows much courage and will charge in a determined manner.

This deer goes with young eight months. It does well in captivity, but owing to its comparatively unattractive appearance is not very popular either in India or Europe.

BARASINGHA OR SWAMP-DEER

OTHER NAMES.—Scientific: *Cervus duvauceli*, *Rucervus duvauceli*. Native: *Bárasingha*, *Máhá*, Hindi; *Baraya*, *Gour*, *Ghos*, Nepalese; *Jhinkar*, Kyarda Dun; *Potiya haran*, Monghyr; *Goin*, Sindhi; *Goinjak* (male), *Gaoni* (female) in Central India; *Báranerwari*, *Sál-sámar*, Mandla; *Bhelingi pohu*, Assamese.

HABITAT.—India only, and there local, the range being given by Blanford as "along the base of the Himalayas from Upper Assam to the Kyarda Dún, west of the Jumna, throughout Assam, in a few places in the Indo-Gangetic plain from the Eastern Sundarbans to Baháwalpur and to Rohri in Upper Sind, and locally throughout the area between the Ganges and Godávari as far east as Mandla." Sterndale says: "I have found it in abundance in the Raigarh Bichia tracts of Mandla. . . . In the open valleys, studded with sal forest, of the Thanwur, Halone, and Bunjar tributaries of the Nerbudda, may be found bits reminding one of English parks, with noble herds of this handsome deer. It seems to love water and open country."

DESCRIPTION.—Smaller than the Sambar and more slightly built, with a long head and long narrow muzzle; tail about half the length of head. Coat rather fine and woolly, forming a mane on the neck; brown in winter, often pale; chestnut in summer, with, as a rule, white spots along the spine at least. The hinds are lighter in colour than the stags, and the fawns white-spotted. Height of a stag 11 hands or a little over. Horns with a brow-antler coming straight out and then curving upwards slightly, a long, straight, smooth beam, and two diverging branches at the top, which are subdivided, the inner into two, and the outer into three points, so that the total number of points in the pair is twelve, whence the name "twelve-tined deer," sometimes used; this is not, however, very appropriate, as many other points are often thrown off from these top branches, a pair of horns with over twenty being recorded. An ordinary length is 30 in., and the record 38 in. with a girth of 5¼ in. at mid-beam. There are often small points on the brow-tine.

The Bárasingha is chiefly a grass-deer, and avoids thick forest; it feeds mostly on grass, and by day, though resting at noon. Its main food is grass; and it would be interesting to know why it has such a liking for sál timber, Forsyth having noticed that its range in the Central Provinces corresponded with that of this tree, as did that of red jungle-fowl. At one time a much isolated patch of sál near Panchmarhi was noted for holding these two very different kinds of game, but according to Mr. J. W. Best, writing in the *Field* for 1927 (p. 505), this is unfortunately no longer the case, both having been extinct for many years. The name of Swamp-deer, often given to this species, is not justified by the animal's usual habits, though Anderson observed that a captive stag liked to lie in water in the hot weather.

In the cold weather large herds associate, numbering even hundreds where the species is common; pairing takes place after October, and in Assam at any rate stags with growing horns are found singly at the end of March, so that shedding, as Blanford remarks, must take place about February. The Bárasingha does well in captivity, but is not very common in that state. The call of the stag is unpleasant, being described as something between the braying of an ass and the squeaking, grinding sound of a native oil-press.

THAMENG

OTHER NAMES.—Scientific: *Cervus eldi*. Native: *Thameng*, Burmese; *Sangnai*, *Sangrai*, Manipuri.

HABITAT.—Flat alluvial country in Manipur and south through Burma to the Malay Peninsula, Cambodia, and Hainan.

DESCRIPTION.—A long-muzzled species much resembling the last in general appearance, but smaller, the stag being about 45 in. at the shoulder, and the hind 3 in. less. The tail also is short and the coat coarse and in the cold season shaggy, and forming a neck-mane in the stag. Colour, in winter, very dark brown in the stag; in summer, pale chestnut above, white below, hinds being paler than stags. Tail with a black mark along the top. Fawns are spotted. Horns very peculiar, the lower portion forming a hook, owing to the brow-tine, which is very large, being perfectly continuous with the beam and curving gradually up. The beams of the two antlers diverge strongly, and at the top, which bends forwards, bear small branches varying from two to ten on each; the two horns seldom match, and there are commonly some small points on the brow-tine. In young stags the horn, as yet unbranched at the top, looks like a letter C, fixed by its back on the head. The length is usually rather under 1 yd., reckoning in the usual way from burr to tip; but 38¼ in. is said to have occurred. There seems no reason to take in the brow-antler in the measurement, as is sometimes done; and the name "brow-antlered deer" sometimes used is hardly distinctive, since all our deer but the hornless musk have the brow-antler.

The Thameng is really more or less of a swampdeer, inhabiting swamps as well as grassy plains, and, like the Bárasingha, is decidedly gregarious, fifty or more being sometimes found in a herd. Generally it keeps in the open, and though more often seen on wet ground than our other deer, is found locally in places where no fresh water is to be had in the hot weather, so that it is unlike other deer, and like some antelopes, in being able to do without this. In swamps it often feeds on wild rice and other marsh-plants, elsewhere presumably on grass. Shedding takes place about midsummer in Manipur, and at the beginning of autumn in Lower Burma. Pairing in Burma is in

Wapiti.

spring, the fawns being born in late autumn. Stags are in their prime at seven years, but breeding may begin at eighteen months. The hind has a short barking grunt, the stag a lower and longer call. The Thameng is not very common in captivity.

In the Manipur Valley, which is swampy throughout, there is a peculiar local race in which the hind pasterns are covered with a horny instead of hairy skin, and touch the ground in walking.

Blanford thought that Schomburgk's Deer (*Cervus schomburgki*), a Siamese species, might possibly prove to inhabit the South Shan States. It is a good-sized brown species, rather shaggy-coated in winter, with very peculiar antlers; the beam is very short, only about the length of the brow-tine, and divides into two branches, which subdivide into so many and often so long points that the general effect is that of a twiggy bush and quite unlike anything to be seen in other deer. The horn-length is usually above 2 ft., and the record 33 in.

HANGAL

OTHER NAMES.—Scientific: *Cervus cashmirianus.* Native: *Hangal*, *Honglu* (male), *Minyamar* (female), Kashmiri; *Bárasingha*, Hindi.

HABITAT.—Kashmir.

DESCRIPTION.—A large deer, 12 or 13 hands at the shoulder in the stag, but not so robust as the Sambar; tail short, not a third the length of head. Coat close, except on the fore-neck of the breeding stag, where it is long and shaggy. Colour brown, drab, or liver in winter, light chestnut in summer, with the under-parts dark brown in the stag and whitish in the hind. Mouth white and ears and a stern-patch whitish. Fawns spotted till three or four years old. Horns with a large upward-curved brow-tine, a bez (bay) or second brow-tine close to this, and a tres (tray) tine about the middle of the beam, which last divides into at least two tines at the top. There are thus normally ten points, and there may be more, up to even as many as eighteen, on the pair of horns. The length is usually well over 1 yd., and there is a record of 55 in. with a mid-beam girth of 7 in. The bez, or second brow-tine, is usually considerably longer than the first.

The Hangal is closely related to the American Wapiti (which also inhabits North-East and Central Asia), and, like that animal, has a general resemblance to the red deer at home. Its challenge call, like that of the Wapiti, is a loud metallic squeal, not a roar like the red deer's. It frequents pine forests, especially where there are grassy glades near a water supply, and wanders a good deal. In winter it is found in herds, but only a few are seen together in summer, when the stags are usually solitary. The horns are shed in spring and new-grown in October, when pairing takes place, the fawns appearing next April, which gives a half-year's gestation-period. The Hangal is rarely seen in captivity.

SHOU

Other Names.—Scientific: *Cervus wallichii, affinis.* Native: *Shou*, Tibetan.

Habitat.—Tibet, Sikkim in the Chumbi Valley, and Bhutan.

Description.—Similar to the Hangal, but running considerably larger, with the antlers bent sharply forward at mid-beam just above the tres tine; they are generally five-pointed, and the bez-tine is often not larger than the brow. The record length is 57¾ in.

It seems doubtful if this stag is really fully distinct from the Hangal, and, indeed, whether both are not simply some of the Asiatic races of the Wapiti, considering the great variability of the antlers in stags of the red-deer type.

ORDER EDENTATA

The order Edentata, or toothless mammals, is represented in India by only one family, the Pangolins (*Manidæ*), and all our three species belong to the only genus, *Manis.* They are really toothless (which is not the case with all so-called Edentates), and differ from all our other mammals in looking like large lizards; they are almost earless, have long tails, very thick at the base, and are covered with scales except on the under-parts and the inside of the limbs, the tail being scaly even on the under-side. The scales are, however, much larger than is usual in reptiles, and are sometimes interspersed with a few hairs, while there is a scanty growth of hair on the scaleless parts. The head is small, with a narrow muzzle and small mouth; the tongue long, extensible, and worm-like, and the stomach muscular like a bird's gizzard. All the feet bear five toes with strong claws, those on the fore-feet being larger than those behind, and the middle claw in all the feet is the largest of all. The fore-claws are especially adapted for digging, and their points are preserved by the peculiar pose of the fore-foot in walking; the claws are turned inwards, and the animal treads on the backs and outsides of the outer toes. The hind-feet are generally plantigrade, treading on the soles. In walking the back is arched.

When attacked, Pangolins roll themselves into a ball, the sharp projecting edges of the overlapping scales then serving for offence as well as defence. They are very strong, though slow, and are powerful burrowers, digging up the nests of ants and termites, the so-called "white ants," on which they feed, by means of the long tongue, which is well lubricated by large salivary glands. Stones are often found in the stomach, either swallowed to aid digestion, as by birds, or accidentally with the insect food. Pangolins are nocturnal as a rule, hiding by day either in rock-crevices or in burrows made by themselves. They are apparently monogamous, and have only one or two young at a time.

Indian Pangolin.

INDIAN PANGOLIN

Other Names.—Scientific: *Manis pentadactyla.* Native: *Bájra-Kit*, Sanscrit; *Bájrakapta, Silu, Sakunphor, Sál sálu, Surajmukhi*, Hindi; *Shalma*, Bauri; *Armú*, Kol; *Kauli-mah, Kaulimanjra, Kassoli-manjur*, Mahratti; *Alawa*, Telegu; *Alangú*, Malabarese; *Banroku*, Deccan; *Keyot-much*, Rangpore; *Katpohu*, Bengali; *Kabalaya*, Cingalese; *Kishaur*, Rishtu; *Challa, Mirún*, Sindhi.

Habitat.—India (except the Himalayas) and Ceylon.

Description.—About 2 ft. in length of head and body; tail 18 in. Ceylon specimens have the tail rather longer in proportion, and females are smaller than males. Fore-claws very long, the middle one twice the length of the corresponding hind-claw. About a dozen rows of scales round the body. Colour light fawn or olive, under-parts fleshy.

Sterndale says: "This species burrows in the ground to a depth of 12 ft., more or less, where it makes a large chamber, sometimes 6 ft. in circumference. It lives in pairs, and has from one to two young ones at a time in the spring months. Sir W. Elliot, who gives an interesting detailed account of it, says that it closes up the entrance to its burrow with earth when in it, so that it would be difficult to find it but for the peculiar track it leaves. . . . I have had specimens brought me by the Gonds, but found them very somnolent during the day. . . . The first one I got had been kept for some time without water, and drank most eagerly when it arrived, in the manner described by Sir Walter Elliot, 'by rapidly darting out its long extensile tongue, which it repeated so rapidly as to fill the water with froth.' The only noise it makes is a faint hiss. It sleeps rolled up, with the head between the fore-legs, and the tail folded firmly over all. The natives believe in the aphrodisiac virtues of the flesh."

Blanford says that a female kept by Mr. W. Daly in the Shevroy Hills produced a young one weighing 1 lb. on July 11; this weight indicates a very small size for the newly-born specimen, as a female weighs about 20 lb.

Pangolins are rare in captivity, and said to be hard to feed; Blyth found that one died soon after a meal of chopped raw meat and cooked egg and rice, which it ate at night. Repletion was no doubt the cause of death, as suggested, for such food would be suitable. It would have been better to give raw egg beaten up in milk at first, or water thickened with satoo, the latter being the method of Indian bird-fanciers with insectivorous birds, more satoo being added till the bird is eating paste. The Pangolin soon gets tame, and has a peculiar habit of standing up on the hind-legs in a stooping position.

Blanford doubts whether it drinks frequently or at all when wild, as it is often found where no water can be had; but the fact that it knows how to drink, and does so readily in captivity, surely indicates that it takes water when available, though, like so many mammals, able to dispense with it.

EARED OR HILL PANGOLIN

Other Names.—Scientific: *Manis aurita.* Native: *Bájarkit*, Hindi; *Sálak*, Khasi; *Kwengnya*, Newári.

Habitat.—Moderate heights in the Himalayas from Nepal east, and through Assam, and the north Bhamo Hills to Karennee, South China, Hainan, and Formosa.

Description.—Fore-claws much longer than hind as in the last, but slenderer and considerably smaller body; ears large enough to be noticeable; hairs between the scales more numerous. Head and body under 2 ft., tail little more than 1 ft. Scales much smaller than in the Indian Pangolin, forming about seventeen rows. Colour, dark brown, the bare under-parts fleshy. Young specimens sometimes show pale bands on the scales.

MALAY PANGOLIN

OTHER NAMES.—Scientific: *Manis javanica.* Native: *Theng-khwe-khyat*, Burmese; *Pangoling*, *Tanjileng*, Malay.

HABITAT.—Burma, east to the Malay countries to Celebes, south to Cochin China and Cambodia, west to Sylhet and Tipperah.

DESCRIPTION.—About the same size as the Eared Pangolin, but more slenderly built still and with the tail longer. Ears rudimentary and hairs between the scales scanty as in the Indian species. Fore-claws much shorter than in the other two, not nearly twice the length of hind ones. Scales usually in seventeen rows, dark brown or sometimes variegated, longer than in the others, and often keeled. Bare skin whitish. Head and body about 20 in. long, tail nearly as much.

This Pangolin differs somewhat in habits from the last two, for though it burrows, it rarely frequents rocks, and in Java and Borneo, at any rate, climbs trees and hides in their crevices. It also sometimes turns the hind-claws inwards as well as the front ones, probably an adaptation to the climbing habit.

REPTILIA OF INDIA

THE Reptiles are cold-blooded, air-breathing vertebrates without hair, and possessing either scales or claws, or both. They reproduce generally by laying eggs, which are hard- or soft-shelled, but always white and elliptical or round, and sometimes by bringing forth live young; these bear a close general resemblance to their parents, but commonly differ in some details, such as proportions and colour; the head is generally larger, the tail longer, and the hues more varied and brilliant. In any case the newly-born young have teeth when these are present and shift for themselves from the first.

Reptiles never have long limbs, and are generally more sluggish than mammals, but are capable of spurts of great activity. In cold weather or prolonged drought they become torpid. They are generally animal feeders, and the teeth, when present, as they usually are, are more uniform in structure than in most mammals, and are not confined to two sets, but are continually being lost and reproduced Their skins are generally shed in masses, not as scurf. They are probably more abundant than mammals in most parts of India, being essentially animals of warm climates, and particularly abundant forms of life in such. In the larger species growth continues long, and its limits are unknown.

In dealing with them I shall follow the same plan as with the mammals, mentioning only the important forms, such as are likely to attract attention, or deserve notice on account of their peculiarities or harmful nature; most reptiles, however, are either indifferent, or useful insect destroyers.

The reptiles of our Indian Empire belong to three orders, distinguished as follows:—

The Tortoises (*Chelonia*) by having the body enclosed in a shell or case, and horny cutting edges to the jaws instead of teeth.

The Crocodiles (*Emydosauria*) resemble giant lizards, but can be distinguished from any true lizards even when young and small, by the exposure of the teeth even when the mouth is closed, and by the peculiar crest of horny plates on the tail, which is single at the end and splits into two diverging portions on the upper-part.

The Lizards and Snakes (*Squamata*) are the ordinary reptiles with none of the above peculiarities.

ORDER EMYDOSAURIA

In addition to the special peculiarities mentioned above, crocodiles have five more or less webbed toes on the fore and four on the hind feet, only the three inner of which bear claws. The tongue is broad, and so attached to the floor of the mouth that it cannot be protruded. The tail is compressed, and is the propeller in swimming, the creatures being mainly aquatic. It is also used as a fighting weapon as well as the jaws. The scales of the back, which are very thick and prominent, are underlaid by a bony armour, so that a rifle-bullet is apt to glance off, and the fatal spots are the eye and just behind the arm. The hide of the under-parts, in Indian species at any rate, has no underlying armour, and is the part valued by leather-dressers.

Although the brain is very small, crocodiles are wary and cunning, and in some cases dangerous, while they are generally destroyers of useful animals. They swallow stones and other hard substances, no doubt to aid digestion.

Their eggs are numerous and very small for the size of the parent, being about the size of a goose's. They are hard-shelled and elliptical in form, and are buried by the parent in the sand at the water-side.

Young crocodiles are more brightly coloured than adults, which are very dull, and grow to a larger size than any other reptiles ; they are also internally the most highly developed, and approach birds and mammals.

The mouth, generally deep in reptiles, is especially so in crocodiles, the knuckles on which the lower jaw articulates being the hindermost parts of the skull, while the ends of the jawbone are prolonged further back still. In consequence of this structure the crocodile appears to move the upper jaw when it opens its mouth, instead of the lower as is really the case.

Crocodiles have a peculiar habit of lying on shore with the mouth open. Owing to a valve in the throat also they are able to keep it partly open under water without this entering the lungs, and use this faculty in drowning air-breathing prey. Their eyes are small, and light-coloured with a vertical pupil in our species ; it is said that thrusting one's finger into the eye is the way to make a crocodile release one if seized. The eyes and nostrils both project above the general level of the head, and thus the reptile can keep watch and breathe while otherwise submerged, to sink at will and come up near a victim on the bank. Where large crocodiles exist it is unwise to stand within a yard of the water, as there is a risk of being swept in by the reptile's tail brought suddenly round.

The presence of crocodiles is often perceptible by the musky odour they emit from two glands under the chin.

Crocodiles in India are often called alligators, but the true alligators, though members of the same family, are American and Chinese; the characters in which they differ from crocodiles are unimportant compared with those which separate both alligators and crocodiles from garials, of which we have one species, forming a genus of its own.

GARIAL

Other Names.—Scientific: *Gavialis gangeticus*. Native: *Garial*, Hindi; *Gavial* and *Gavialis* originated in an error, *r* having been mistaken for *v*.

Habitat.—A few Indian and Burmese rivers, the Indus, Ganges, Brahmaputra, Mahánadi, and Koladyne, and the larger tributaries of the first three.

Description.—A very large crocodile, growing to 20 ft., and it is said even to nearly 30 ft. Muzzle very long, narrow and parallel-sided, enlarging at the tip, which bears a hump in old males; more than two dozen teeth on each side of each jaw. Colour olive, dark in the adults, light in the young, which are also spotted or barred with dark brown. The muzzle in the young is also longer proportionately than in the adult, its length being about five times its breadth at the base, whereas in the adult it is less than four times.

The Garial is a fish-eater, and is supposed to be harmless, but in the stomach of a large specimen, the skeleton of which was exhibited in the Calcutta Museum in my time, there had been found a native woman's ornaments. These may have been picked up and swallowed by the reptile as stones are, or it may have fed on a corpse, but their occurrence is worth remembering, as it may indicate that the Garial is not always harmless. Compared with other crocodiles the Garial is rare in captivity.

Our two typical crocodiles (genus *Crocodilus*) have wedge-shaped snouts with the outline of the upper jaw uneven, and less than twenty teeth on each side of each jaw, more uneven in size than those of the Garial. Young specimens have well-defined foreheads and shorter muzzles than adults.

COAST CROCODILE

Other Names.—Scientific: *Crocodilus porosus, pondicerianus.* Native: *Magar*, Hindustani.

Habitat.—Coasts of Eastern India, and of Ceylon and Burma, east to North Australia and even Fiji and the Solomons.

Description.—The largest of crocodiles, and, indeed, of living reptiles, growing to 11 yds. Muzzle rather long, about twice as long as its breadth at the base just in front of the eyes, and marked by two prominent converging ridges; a square formed by four large scales on the nape, flanked by one or two small ones, and either none or only a few small irregular ones between this and the head. Four to eight rows of scales down the back. Colour olive, dark in the adult, pale in the young, which have large black spots.

The coast crocodile is often found far out at sea, and, though it ascends rivers, is not known definitely to penetrate them far above the tideway. It is a very fierce reptile and a dangerous man-eater.

COMMON INDIAN CROCODILE

Other Names.—Scientific: *Crocodilus palustris.* Native: *Magar.*

Habitat.—India, Ceylon, Burma, and the Malay Peninsula and islands.

Description.—Much smaller than the coast crocodile, but said to exceed 12 ft. in length at times. Muzzle shorter and broader than in that species, its length much less than twice its breadth at the base, not more than one and a half times; no ridges, though the surface is rough.

There is the same square of four shields on the nape, with one smaller one on each side; but between these and the head there is a line of four distinct scales. Lines of scales down the back fewer than in the last species, usually four, or at least not more than six. Colour olive, dark in the adult, pale with black spots in the young.

This is the commonest crocodile in India; it is sometimes called Marsh Crocodile, but frequents rivers and ponds as well as marshes. It is not so dangerous as the coast species, but should not be trusted.

ORDER CHELONIA

In addition to their shell and horny-edged instead of toothed jaws, tortoises are noticeable by reason of the peculiar structure of their fore-legs, in which the humerus or upper arm-bone turns forwards instead of backwards as in other quadrupeds, and forms a sort of knee with the bones of the forearm; hence the awkward gait of land-tortoises, which are much in the minority, though among our species may be found all gradations between active carnivorous swimmers and slow terrestrial passively-resisting vegetarians. The bony foundations of the shell may be overlaid by horny plates or leathery skin, and the head and limbs may be withdrawn under it more or less completely in some cases. The tail in our species is nearly always short and little noticeable.

Tortoises can give a very severe bite, and the larger freshwater kinds are at times dangerous.

The eggs vary according to the group, being either hard- or soft-shelled, round or elliptical. They are buried by the female in the ground.

The order with us contains five families, distinguished as follows :—

The ordinary Tortoises and Terrapins (*Testudinidæ*) by having a horn-coated shell, short toes and tail, and at least four claws on each foot, generally five.

The Snapper (the only species of the *Platysternidæ*) by having a quite long tail, about as long as the small shell.

The Soft-shells (*Trionychidæ*) by having no plates, but a soft skin everywhere, and three claws on each foot.

The Sea-Turtles (*Chelonidæ*) by having the fore-limbs in the form of wing-like flippers, horny shell-shields, but only one or two claws.

The Leathery Turtle (the only species of the *Sphargidæ*) by having wing-like flippers, but neither claws nor, except on the head, any horny shields, while at the same time the shell has several conspicuous ridges.

The Soft-shells, besides being covered with soft skin throughout, have lips deceptively covering a very vicious beak, and the nostrils at the end of a soft fleshy snout or short proboscis. The shell is very flat, the neck long, and the feet large and very fully webbed; the three claws are on the inner toes, and well developed. These creatures are very active swimmers, generally carnivorous, and spend nearly all their time in the water. Dr. Boulenger thinks the larger species may grow to 5 ft. in length of shell, and it is obvious that the bite of an individual of this size is serious; in fact, no one should enter water where large Soft-shell tortoises are found, as they often attack; and even small ones should be handled with care, as the American species at any rate can snap backwards as far as the middle of their backs. The head can be drawn right into the shell, and darted out with great rapidity. The Indian species appear not to be esteemed as food, which is strange, as the Americans prize theirs highly. The eggs of the Soft-shells have hard but brittle shells, and the young are often handsomely variegated. The typical Soft-shells belong to the genus *Trionyx*, which includes most of the largest and most formidable species.

LARGE-HEADED SOFT-SHELL

OTHER NAMES.—Scientific : *Trionyx subplanus, güntheri.*

HABITAT.—Mergui to Java.

DESCRIPTION.—Head very large and shell very flat, with broken ridges in young. Colour brown, with the under-parts, sides of neck and dots on it and the head yellowish.

GANGES SOFT-SHELL

OTHER NAMES.—Scientific : *Trionyx gangeticus.*

HABITAT.—Ganges and its tributaries.

DESCRIPTION.—Head medium-sized ; colour olive above, yellowish below ; a black streak from crown to nape giving off back-slanting side-streaks ; back of young finely pencilled with black.

SOUTHERN SOFT-SHELL

OTHER NAMES.—Scientific : *Trionyx leithii.*

HABITAT.—Rivers Kistna and Nelambar.

DESCRIPTION.—Similar to the last, but snout longer, and young with two or more pairs of eye-spots on the back.

BROWN SOFT-SHELL

OTHER NAMES.—Scientific : *Trionyx hurum, gangeticus.*

HABITAT.—Ganges and its tributaries.

DESCRIPTION.—Head medium-sized ; colour, olive-brown below as well as above, with light dots on the extremities and the edge of the shell, and black spots or pencillings on the head. Young with large yellow spots on the head and two or three pairs of large eye-spots on the back, which also bears rows of little warts.

BURMESE SOFT-SHELL

OTHER NAMES.—Scientific : *Trionyx formosus.*

HABITAT.—Rivers Irrawaddy, Sittoung, and Salween.

DESCRIPTION.—Head medium-sized, thickly spotted with black above, white below like rest of under-parts ; upper parts olive-brown. Young with black-edged yellow markings on head, and two pairs of large eye-spots on back, which bears rows of little warts.

PHAYRE'S SOFT-SHELL

OTHER NAMES.—Scientific: *Trionyx phayrii.*

HABITAT.—Pegu to Sumatra.

DESCRIPTION.—Head medium-sized, with muzzle a little longer than the last.

MALAY SOFT-SHELL

OTHER NAMES.—Scientific: *Trionyx cartilagineus, ornatus.*

HABITAT.—Pegu east to Java and south to Siam and Camboja.

DESCRIPTION.—Head medium-sized, muzzle rather long; upper parts and chin olive-brown, head and chin thickly spotted with yellow, rest of under-parts white. Young with light spots, and generally a few large dark ones, on the back.

The next species has a genus of its own (*Pelochelys*).

COAST SOFT-SHELL

OTHER NAMES.—Scientific: *Pelochelys cantoris.*

HABITAT.—Burma, Malay Peninsula, Borneo, the Philippines, and in India the Ganges.

DESCRIPTION.—Head medium-sized, with very short, broad muzzle, and eyes far forward; weaker jaws than in *Trionyx*. Colour olive above, sometimes with dark spots; under-shell whitish. Young with warty back and throat white-speckled on an olive ground.

This species differs from the others in entering salt water as well as living in rivers.

The next species also has a genus to itself (*Chitra*). It is a large, formidable reptile.

CHITRA

OTHER NAMES.—Scientific: *Chitra indica.*

HABITAT.—Ganges and Irrawaddy.

DESCRIPTION.—Muzzle very short, with eyes very near its end; head altogether small, jaws weaker than in *Trionyx;* colour green or olive, whitish below, and with dark stripes on the head. Young with dark pencilling on back.

The Box Soft-shells (genus *Emyda*) are distinguished by a flap of skin at the back of the under-shell, which can be shut over the hind legs when drawn in; the jaws are strong and head medium-sized with short snout They do not grow very large, and are less completely aquatic than other soft-shells, being sometimes found at a distance from water. Ordinary *Trionyx* are easily hurt by crawling over a hard surface, which grazes the soft skin on the under-shell, and if kept in captivity should always have a soft mat fastened over their landing-place. The Box Soft-shells are vegetable feeders and said not to be savage.

COMMON BOX SOFT-SHELL

OTHER NAMES.—Scientific: *Emyda granosa.*

HABITAT.—Fresh water in country watered by Indus and Ganges.

DESCRIPTION.—Brown with an olive tinge and yellow spots; border of upper-shell, and whole of under-shell, cream-coloured. Young with spots more distinct and back skin ridged. A yellow variety was recorded in the *Journal* of the Bombay Natural History Society for 1928.

SOUTHERN BOX SOFT-SHELL

OTHER NAMES.—Scientific: *Emyda vittata, ceylonensis.*

HABITAT.—Southern India and Ceylon.

DESCRIPTION.—Like the last, but without spots, and sometimes with dark bands. Its distinctness is doubtful.

BURMESE BOX SOFT-SHELL

OTHER NAMES.—Scientific: *Emyda scutata.*

HABITAT.—Irrawaddy River.

DESCRIPTION.—Spotted or pencilled with a darker colour on a brown ground.

The ordinary Tortoises and Terrapins (*Testudinidæ*) comprise the majority of the order and include the few land forms besides many aquatic or amphibious species; the latter are the Terrapins, but it is often hard to draw the line between Tortoises and these, though as a whole they have longer toes and claws, more or less webbed, and flatter shells. All can draw the neck and limbs in under the shell, which is always covered with horny plates or shields.

Our Indian species are mostly vegetable feeders, and do not grow so large or show such ferocity as some soft-shells. Their eggs are hard-shelled.

Our typical Tortoises—often distinguished as Land-tortoises—are heavily built, with high strong shells, and have short club feet with coarse scales and strong blunt nails. There are only two joints in the toes instead of the usual three. They walk on the toes of the fore-feet and on the soles of the hind-feet, and are thus higher in front than behind; their pace is proverbially slow, and the movement of the fore-feet very awkward, the curious arrangement of the upper arm being adapted to swimming rather than walking, though these tortoises have as a rule a very poor idea of the former exercise.

They are the most harmless of the group, and rely on the protection given by their extremely strong shells. Their food is herbage and fruit, possibly at times varied with such few forms of small animal life as cannot get out of their way, for Anderson saw one in captivity eat some dead prawns and fish procured to feed soft-shells, and I have seen one eat raw meat. All our species are under 2 ft. long.

CLAW-TAILED TORTOISE

OTHER NAMES.—Scientific: *Testudo elongata.*

HABITAT.—From Chaibassa in Bengal east through Burma to Camboja and Cochin China.

DESCRIPTION.—Shell flattish for a land-tortoise, its depth being less than half its length, which may exceed 10 in.; spinal region particularly flat. No thigh-spurs, but a claw-like tip to the tail. Colour greenish yellow, more or less heavily and distinctly blotched with black, each shield above and below having its own blotch or patches.

LEITH'S TORTOISE

OTHER NAMES.—Scientific: *Testudo leithii.*

HABITAT.—Lower Egypt, Western Syria; said also to inhabit Sindh.

DESCRIPTION.—Shell strongly humped, its depth being more than half its length, which is 5 in.; scales of fore-legs very large. Colour yellow, each upper shield with a dark-brown border except behind, and each lower one with a dark-brown triangle.

Although the original specimen, described in 1869, was said to have come from Sind, the species has not been found there since.

INDIAN STARRED TORTOISE

OTHER NAMES.—Scientific: *Testudo elegans.*

HABITAT.—India and Ceylon, except Lower Bengal.

DESCRIPTION.—Shell strongly humped, its depth being about half its length of 10 in.; upper back-shields prominent; scales of limbs prominent, forming short spurs on the thighs and heels. Colour black, with a yellow star of about a dozen rays on each central shield; marginal shields and under-shell shields also star-marked with yellow.

This is the common land-tortoise of India, frequenting dry grassy hills; its habits were studied by Hutton, who found that in the cold weather it pushed itself into cover, but did not actually become torpid, though remaining quiescent. Specimens he kept were fond of wallowing in water in hot weather; the males fought by pushing against each other with heads drawn in, each trying to overturn his rival, who had great difficulty in getting right side up again if thrown on his back. A female in two hours dug a hole 6 in. deep and 4 in. wide in which she laid and buried four eggs.

BURMESE STARRED TORTOISE

OTHER NAMES.—Scientific: *Testudo platynota.*

HABITAT.—Burma.

DESCRIPTION.—Differs from the last in being flat along the top of the back, in having a yellow under-shell with black blotches but no star-marks, and in the rays of the stars on the upper shields being broader and only about six in number. The scales on the limbs are also less prominent, and there are no heel-spurs.

BROWN TORTOISE

OTHER NAMES.—Scientific: *Testudo* or *Manouria emys.*

HABITAT.—Assam, east to Sumatra.

DESCRIPTION.—The largest Indian land-tortoise, reaching 18 in. in length of shell, which is more than twice as long as deep and rather flat. Scales of limbs large and pointed, forming spurs on thighs and heels. Colour dark brown in adults, yellowish-brown with dark brown marks in young.

This tortoise is said to be partly aquatic in its habits, thus forming the first link with the Terrapins.

These differ in having distinct toes, more or less webbed, with the usual three joints, and ordinary claws. They comprise the majority of the family and the largest species in it, and are more or less aquatic. Those which are most so are often very flat and have broad paddle-like paws, thus approaching the Soft-shells, from which, however, they are easily distinguished by the horny-shielded shell, to say nothing of having more than three claws and no proboscis snout.

The Land-Terrapins (*Geoemyda*) are more or less terrestrial, and most resemble land-tortoises, being distinguished by the different feet and by having the head covered with uniform skin, not with shields. The toes are only slightly webbed.

SPINOUS LAND-TERRAPIN

Other Names.—Scientific: *Geoemyda spinosa.*

Habitat.—Tenasserim to Borneo.

Description.—Decidedly flat, especially along the spine, where, however, there is a low blunt keel; upper-shell notched both before and behind. Colour brown, with radiating streaks on each shield of the under-shell, and a yellow spot on each side of the neck. Young redder, with a more strongly arched and keeled upper-shell, strongly notched all round, the bordering shields forming spines, and short spines also on the side-shields. Shell about 8 in. in adult.

LARGE LAND-TERRAPIN

Other Names.—Scientific: *Geoemyda grandis.*

Habitat.—Burma to Siam.

Description.—About twice as large as the last species. Shell vaulted or roof-shaped, with a blunt but well-marked keel; only hinder edge notched. Colour much as in the last, but darker, the inter-spaces between the yellow rays below being black, and the upper-shell dark brown.

FLAT LAND-TERRAPIN

Other Names.—Scientific: *Geoemyda depressa.*

Habitat.—Akyab Hills.

Description.—Shell decidedly flat, especially behind, where it is broadened; only hinder edge notched. Colour light brown above, yellow below, the shields here star-marked with few and broad black bands. Head grey, neck and legs light brown.

The Three-keeled Terrapins (*Nicoria*) are also more or less terrestrial, but look more distinct from land-tortoises, owing to the three-keeled shell. The head is uniformly covered with skin.

COMMON THREE-KEELED LAND-TERRAPIN

Other Names.—Scientific: *Nicoria trijuga, thermalis, edeniana.*

Habitat.—Punjab southwards, Ceylon, and Burma.

Description.—Not very flat; toes with a short but distinct web. Colour variable locally; shell brown to black, with the edge of the breast-plate more or less yellow, and sometimes the keels of the back; head more or less marked with yellow. Size from 9 in. in the Indian to 16 in. in the Burmese race.

Common Three-keeled Land-Terrapin.

BENGAL THREE-KEELED LAND-TERRAPIN

OTHER NAMES.—Scientific: *Nicoria tricarinata.*

HABITAT.—Bengal.

DESCRIPTION.—Shell distinctly arched; toes hardly at all webbed. Colour brown to black above with the keels and under-shell yellow, and the head distinctly streaked with yellow. This appears to be more terrestrial than the last.

The Box-Terrapins (*Cyclemys*) are a third semi-terrestrial group, apparently always small, the shell not reaching nearly 1 ft. in length. The beak is hooked, and the head uniformly covered with skin; the toes more or less webbed. But the most important peculiarity is the soft hinge in the middle of the under-shell, which allows of its being shut up behind when the hind-legs are drawn in. None of the species are found west of the Bay of Bengal. The hinge of the shell is not distinctly developed in the young, though they would seem to need it most, as it ensures better protection for the soft parts.

BROAD BOX-TERRAPIN

OTHER NAMES.—Scientific: *Cyclemys platynota.*

HABITAT.—Mergui to Borneo.

DESCRIPTION.—Hinder edge of shell notched, spine with blunt broken keel; beak also notched; toes well webbed. Colour reddish or yellowish brown, star-marked with darker on the back; shields of under-shell spotted with brown on a yellow ground, or brown with yellow along their junctions. Neck brown streaked with yellowish. Young marked with black spots on the back, the spots paired along the spine.

DHOR BOX-TERRAPIN

Other Names.—Scientific: *Cyclemys dhor, oldhamii.*

Habitat.—Pegu, south and east to Malay Islands, Siam and Camboja.

Description.—Shell with a continuous blunt keel; hinder end and beak notched; feet well webbed. Colour brown, darker below and with darker spots above; neck streaked. Young with the under-shell light brown or even yellowish, streaked or spotted with dark brown.

FREE-TOED BOX-TERRAPIN

Other Names.—Scientific: *Cyclemys* or *Pyxidea mouhoti.*

Habitat.—Cachar, Siam, and Cochin China.

Description.—Shell flat, three-keeled, and notched at hinder end; beak with a strong hook, not notched; toes hardly webbed at all. Colour brown above, yellowish below, sometimes with dark brown patches. Young with yellow spots on neck.

BLUNT-BEAKED BOX-TERRAPIN

Other Names.—Scientific: *Cyclemys* or *Cuora amboinensis.*

Habitat.—Burma and Siam, east to Moluccas.

Description.—Shell well arched, not notched behind, one keel sometimes present; beak barely hooked, toes fairly well webbed. Colour some shade of brown above; under-side, including that of head and neck, yellow, breast-plate with black blotches or brown with the seams between shields yellow. Two yellow stripes along side of head. Young with all the centre of the under-shell black, and three keels on the upper-shell.

The next is our only species of its genus (*Bellia*), and is also small.

THICK-NECKED TERRAPIN

Other Names.—Scientific: *Bellia crassicollis.*

Habitat.—Tenasserim to Sumatra.

Description.—Shell rather flat, especially along the spine in the male, indistinctly keeled, notched behind; toes very well webbed; head large, with small shields at the back, muzzle short, beak not hooked. Colour, dark brown or black, with eight large yellow spots on the head, and the under-shell with its sides or the seams between its shields yellowish, or all variegated with yellowish. Young with three distinct keels, and head-spots more distinct than in adult.

This species is semi-aquatic, as is the next, which also is the only species in its genus, in our area at least, and is also small.

HAMILTON'S TERRAPIN

OTHER NAMES.—Scientific: *Damonia hamiltonii.*

HABITAT.—Bengal and Northern India.

DESCRIPTION.—Shell well humped, with three rows of knobs; hind end slightly notched. Head very short-muzzled, with a notch in the beak, and large shields in front and small behind, rather large for the body; toes very well webbed. Colour dark brown or blackish spotted with yellow throughout, the shell streaked as well as spotted.

The remaining genera are all aquatic and vegetable feeders. Their feet are very fully webbed, and the edges of the jaws toothed.

The Eyed Terrapins (*Morenia*) have one shield covering the muzzle and crown, followed by a wrinkled skin. The shell is rather flat, plain-edged behind, and the size small.

BURMESE EYED TERRAPIN

OTHER NAMES.—Scientific: *Morenia ocellata, Emys ocellata.*

HABITAT.—Burma.

DESCRIPTION.—Shell with an interrupted keel, head medium-sized, short-muzzled, with beak notched in front as well as along the sides; lower jaw more markedly saw-edged.

Colour, brown, each shield eyed in black and yellow; under-shell yellow; head with two yellow streaks along each side on an olive ground. Young with keel more strongly developed. Male's shell 6 in. and female's 8 in. long.

BENGAL EYED TERRAPIN

OTHER NAMES.—Scientific: *Morenia ocellata.*

HABITAT.—Bengal.

DESCRIPTION.—Smaller than the last—the shell an inch shorter in both sexes, which differ in size similarly—muzzle longer and sharper. Colour black, with yellowish streaks on the spinal shields and yellow-edged eyes surmounted by yellowish loops on the side ones; head with three yellow streaks instead of two.

The next two species are large and each is the only one in its genus, and highly aquatic.

THURGI

OTHER NAMES.—Scientific: *Hardella thurgi.*

HABITAT.—Ganges and Indus and their tributaries.

DESCRIPTION.—Shell rather flat, broken-keeled, plain-edged; snout short, lower jaw more strongly serrated than upper. Colour dark brown, or black, under-shell often yellowish with black blotches. Females grow to 18 in. in length of shell, but the males are considerably inferior in size.

BATAGUR

OTHER NAMES.—Scientific: *Batagur baska.*

HABITAT.—Bengal, east to Malay Peninsula.

DESCRIPTION.—Shell rather flat, feet broad and rather paddle-shaped with only four claws, nose tip-tilted and pointed. Colour olive-brown above, yellowish below.

The Batagur and several others of these very aquatic terrapins are used as food by some castes of Indians, and the name Batagur is used by some writers to include all the saw-jawed species, including those of the next genus (*Kachuga*), which have also been called Pangshures.

The species in this genus are more numerous than in any other genus of our tortoises, and vary much in form and size; they are saw-jawed and have broadly-webbed feet, and their outstanding characteristic is the unusual length of the fourth shield of those along the spine,* which is at least as long as any of the others.

RED-STREAKED KACHUGA

OTHER NAMES.—Scientific: *Kachuga lineata*, *Batagur lineata.*

HABITAT.—Burma and the north of the Indian Peninsula.

DESCRIPTION.—A large species, growing to 15 in. in length of shell, which is markedly convex. Edges of upper jaw broad, with a ridge nearer the outer than the inner side; lower jaw in front as wide as the eye-socket. Colour brown, with red streaks along the neck; underparts yellowish. Young considerably different in form, the shell being well keeled with a notched hinder margin, this and the central keel disappearing with age, the keel at first breaking up into lumps.

* The first shield, over the neck, is not reckoned; it is called the nuchal, those following being the vertebrals.

IRRAWADDY KACHUGA

OTHER NAMES.—Scientific: *Kachuga trivittata.*

HABITAT.—Tenasserim and Irrawaddy from Bhamo downwards.

DESCRIPTION.—Apparently grows larger than the last, the shell measuring up to 22 in.; upper jaw much narrower along the edges, with a ridge nearer the inner margin, lower jaw in front not so wide as eye-socket. There are sometimes three black bands down the shell, apparently in adult males only.

DHONGOKA

OTHER NAMES.—Scientific: *Kachuga* or *Batagur dhongoka.*

HABITAT.—Ganges and Indus; perhaps also Poona.

DESCRIPTION.—Shell fairly large—attaining 14 in.—and very flat, with a knob on each of the first few spinal shields; hinder edge undulated. Colour brown with three dark streaks down the back; under-parts yellowish. Young with distinct keels.

SMITH'S KACHUGA

OTHER NAMES.—Scientific: *Kachuga* or *Pangshura smithii.*

HABITAT.—Upper reaches of Ganges and Indus river-systems.

DESCRIPTION.—Apparently small, the shell, which is very flat and slightly keeled, only slightly exceeding 8 in. Colour light brown, usually blackish along the spine; shields of lower surface dark brown with yellow edges.

SYLHET KACHUGA

OTHER NAMES.—Scientific: *Kachuga sylhetensis.*

HABITAT.—Sylhet and Assam.

DESCRIPTION.—A small species, 7 in. in length of shell, which is high and roof-shaped, with a keel ending in a blunt spike on the third spinal shield and reappearing on the last two as a ridge, and strongly notched hinder border. Colour brown, the keel usually pale; shields of breastplate brown edged with yellow.

BLANFORD'S KACHUGA

OTHER NAMES.—Scientific: *Kachuga intermedia.*

HABITAT.—Hasdo and Godavari rivers.

DESCRIPTION.—Shell high and roof-shaped, with a keel ending in a lump on the third spinal shield; colour brown, head olive with five rusty spots across the back of it, most distinct above the eyes;

shields of under-shell black, yellow-bordered except at their hinder ends.

This is a rare terrapin, not having been seen by Dr. Boulenger at the time of the publication of the Reptile volume of the Fauna of British India in 1890; the length of shell—4½ in.—there given probably does not indicate that it never grows larger.

COMMON ROOFED TERRAPIN

OTHER NAMES.—Scientific: *Kachuga tectum*, *Pangshura tecta.*

HABITAT.—Ganges and Indus and their tributaries.

DESCRIPTION.—Shell up to about 9 in. long, high and roof-shaped, with hinder edge plain or nearly so and a half-keel ending in a lump on the third spinal shield. Colour olive, usually red or yellow of some shade on the under-shell, which may, however, be brown with the shields bordered with yellow except at their hinder ends; head striped with orange, neck with yellow, limbs spotted with yellow. Young with an orange spinal stripe, yellow border, and black spots on the upper-shell. This is the brightest of Indian Terrapins and is the quickest mover on land of any tortoise I have seen.

The Snapper, which looks like a cross between a tortoise and a lizard, is the sole member of the family *Platysternidæ*, which connects the typical tortoises with the great American Snappers (*Chelydridæ*) and most resembles the latter, though a small reptile.

ASIATIC SNAPPER

OTHER NAMES.—Scientific: *Platysternum megacephalum.* Also called Casqued Terrapin and Long-tailed Terrapin.

HABITAT.—Burma, most common in the south, Siam, and South China.

DESCRIPTION.—Distinguished from all our tortoises by the length of the tail, which is as long as the shell or even slightly longer. Shell oval, small, and very flat. Toes only slightly webbed, with strong sharp claws on all except the outer one. Head very large, especially swollen behind the eyes, covered above with one large shield (whence the name Casqued Terrapin), and with a strongly-hooked beak. The head and neck together are half as long as the shell, which measures 6 in., the total length being about 15 in. Colour brown, paler below. Young spotted with black above, with the head striped and the upper-shell edged with yellow; under-parts yellow with black central stripe. Little is known about this curious little reptile, except that it inhabits streams; it should, in spite of its small size, be handled with care, as the big American Snappers are dangerous animals, and will bite and hold on like bull-dogs. Like them, our species is no doubt carnivorous.

The typical Turtles (*Chelonidæ*) are large sea-tortoises with a flat heart-shaped shell covered with horny shields, and flipper-like limbs with no outward indication of toes, while only the first one or two claws are present. The hind flippers are short, broad, and rounded, the fore ones very long and wing-like; they are used in swimming very like the wings of a bird, and in captivity at any rate turtles are extraordinarily active and restless, more so than most warm-blooded animals, in fact. In the wild state they only leave the sea to deposit their eggs, which are round, soft-shelled, and very numerous. The female buries them in the sand in a hole dug out with her hind-flippers. The eggs are always good food, but the same cannot always be said of the flesh. With the exception of the Green Turtle, they are carnivorous. All the known species, which are found in all warm seas, occur with us.

The Green and Hawk's-bill Turtles (*Chelone*) are distinguished by having heads of moderate size, and not more than four shields in each costal row—the costals being the rows on each side of the central or vertebral series.

GREEN TURTLE

OTHER NAMES.—Scientific: *Chelone mydas*, *Chelonia virgata*. Also called Edible Turtle.

HABITAT.—Warm seas, sometimes straying into colder waters. Not common in the Bay of Bengal.

DESCRIPTION.—Muzzle very short and blunt, descending perpendicularly from the nostrils, with no sign of hook; one claw on each flipper. Shields of back not overlapping. Colour of upper-shell marbled olive, lower surface paler and plain. The length of shell reaches 4 ft. Young with a slight keel along the spine, and sometimes with a second claw on each flipper. Colour black above, white below, the contrast being retained more or less till the shell is a foot long.

This is the turtle so celebrated for its excellence as food; it has, however, been known to be poisonous on occasion.

The fat is green, whence the name of the species; the meat of the upper-shell is known as calipash, that of the lower as calipee.

When turned on its back the creature is helpless and unable to right itself, and in transport has to be kept in this position, otherwise, as we have seen in the case of cetacean mammals, it will be suffocated by its own weight when out of water for any length of time.

It is generally stated to be herbivorous and is known to live largely on marine plants, but it feeds so readily on fish and raw meat in captivity that it is evidently omnivorous, and perhaps even carnivorous by preference. Possibly the occasionally deleterious nature of its flesh may be due to a diet of carrion or of some poisonous marine organism.

HAWK'S-BILL TURTLE

OTHER NAMES.—Scientific: *Chelone imbricata.*

HABITAT.—Same as the last; especially common off the Ceylonese coasts and those of the Maldives with us.

DESCRIPTION.—Muzzle projecting well in front of the nostrils, the beak well marked off from the head, altogether more like a bird's than that of any other tortoise. It is, however, more like a finch's or a fowl's than a hawk's, the hook not being much developed, in spite of the name. Two claws on each flipper. Back-shields overlapping except in aged specimens; hinder end notched, whereas in the Green Turtle it is plain or nearly so. Colour tortoise-shell—marbled brown and yellow—above, yellow below; shields of extremities brown bordered with yellow. Young with three keels on the upper shell, which is light brown, the lower being darker. Size smaller than in other turtles, the shell not exceeding a yard in length.

The Hawk's-bill's flesh is unfit for food, though its eggs are good eating; but it is of great value as the producer of tortoise-shell, this being the trade name for the horny shields of the shell. It is an animal feeder.

The only member of the other genus (*Thalassochelys*) may have its characters given under the species heading.

LOGGERHEAD TURTLE

OTHER NAMES.—Scientific: *Thalassochelys caretta, Caouana olivacea.*

HABITAT.—Mediterranean as well as warmer seas, not infrequently straying north. The common turtle of the Bay of Bengal.

DESCRIPTION.—Head large, with strong jaws projecting slightly but decidedly in front of the nostrils, and hooked; back-shields not overlapping. One or two claws on each flipper. Costal or side-shields at least five, often more, up to eight. Colour brown, under-surface yellowish. Young with three keels and a notched hind-margin to the shell; colour dark all over. The adult reaches 4 ft. in shell-length.

The Loggerhead is an animal feeder, living mostly on shell-fish.

Its flesh is very like beef, and has been known to be mistaken for it when cooked even by a butcher, according to Mr. Hornaday.

The Leathery Turtle, the only member of the family *Sphargidæ*, is very distinct from the other turtles, and differs from them and from all other tortoises in having the backbone and ribs free from the bony shell, which is composed of numerous small plates and covered with skin. It has no horny shields except on the head, and no claws; but its general form is like that of the typical turtles, except that it is not so flat and that the shell bears many keels at all ages, while the hind-flippers are square-cut, not rounded. It is the largest of all turtles, reaching 5 ft. in length of shell.

LEATHERY TURTLE

OTHER NAMES.—Scientific: *Dermochelys, Dermatochelys*, or *Sphargis coriacea.* Also known as Luth.

HABITAT.—Tropical seas, sometimes straying into cooler waters, even as far north as Scotland.

DESCRIPTION.—Head blunt, beak with double hook; shell with seven knotty keels above, five below. Colour, dark brown, sometimes with yellow markings or light under-surface. Young with longer fore-flippers than adult, equalling length of shell; they and the keels have light borders at this stage.

The Leathery Turtle has the usual habits of turtles and is an animal feeder: it is able to utter a loud noise. It has only once tried to breed in our limits, at the mouth of the Yé in Tenasserim, and is everywhere rare. It is unfit for food, and should never be killed, even for a specimen, as even a blind man could identify it by the peculiar shell. It is a curious fact that medium-sized specimens have never been seen—only adults and a few infantile ones.

ORDER SQUAMATA

The Lizards and Snakes comprise the vast majority of reptiles in our region as elsewhere, and only the most important from their peculiarities, abundance, or noxious character can be dealt with here. The order is divided into three suborders, readily enough distinguished.

The Chamæleon (*Rhiptoglossa*) by the peculiar grasping feet, with the toes bound up by skin into two opposing sets.

The Snakes (*Ophidia*), which have no feet at all, by the lower jaw having no bony union at the chin.

The Lizards (*Lacertilia*) comprise all the ordinary four-footed reptiles, besides some legless snake-like species, distinguished from snakes by the peculiarity above-mentioned. The distinction between lizards and crocodiles has been given above, and though it may not always be convenient to examine a snake's chin, its tongue, which is long-forked and sheathed at the base, is a more ready distinction ; for though the Monitors among the Lizards have a quite similar tongue, they have very well-developed limbs. Another snaky point in these is the length of their necks, which are longer than in other lizards—longer than the head, in fact—and the way in which they hold them up. Thus their family (*Varanidæ*) is easily recognised.

Of the seven other families of lizards found here, our representatives may be distinguished as follows :—

The Geckos (*Geckonidæ*), such as our familiar house-lizards, by having large eyes with no eyelids—a snake-point again—by the broad, hardly-notched tongue, broad flat head, and moderately long tail. Altogether they look much like miniature alligators. (See specimen figured along with Long-snouted Whip-Snake.)

The Eyelid-Geckos (*Eublepharidæ*) are generally similar, but have eyelids.

The Agamids (*Agamidæ*), such as the common garden-lizard, have eyelids, a short high head, and generally a very long thin tail.

The Slow-worms (*Anguidæ*) are snake-like in form, but with eyelids and a short-forked tongue.

The Beaked Slow-worm (*Dibamidæ*) is known by being also snake-like, but with no visible eyes and a beak-like snout.

There remain the typical Lizards (*Lacertidæ*) and the Skinks (*Scincidæ*) which have no specially striking points as a rule. The Skinks are, however, particularly smooth and cylindrical in form, the head, neck, body, and tail passing insensibly into each other, while the scaling is much alike all over. Some Skinks have very tiny or imperfect limbs, and some none at all ; these last can be distinguished from snakes by having eyelids, and from the Slow-worm by lacking the groove along the side of the latter.

The typical Lacertine Lizards are not numerous or familiar in India ; they are very like the ordinary Skinks but with the head more distinct and the body less round, while the upper parts generally have smaller scales than the lower, and the temples have a patch of minute scales ; the body is not so round—in a word, they look more lively and less " slinky."

The tails of most Geckos, Skinks, and Lacertine lizards are fragile, and come off at once if the animal wriggles on being seized thereby ; a new tail grows, but has a gristly rod inside instead of vertebræ, and much smaller scales beginning abruptly from the point of fracture; thus, if a Lizard's tail comes off at once, or if it is obviously a second edition, the owner must belong to one of the above-mentioned families.

Nearly all our lizards are mainly insectivorous and lay eggs, which are round and hard-shelled, but their habits vary much otherwise. They are nearly always solitary, however, and, except the Geckos, lovers of sunshine.

Geckos usually have expanded toes, and can run on any sort of surface, and even upside down. They are the most familiar of all Indian vertebrate animals, inasmuch as some are very commonly found indoors, and, though supposed to be nocturnal, are often in evidence in the daytime, while they have no objection to artificial light. Most species, however, are out-door animals, frequenting rocks and trees. They generally have soft skins with very small wart-like scales.

Our one member of the genus *Alsophylax* may be found either indoors or out.

NARROW-TOED HOUSE-GECKO

OTHER NAMES.—Scientific: *Alsophylax tuberculatus*.

HABITAT.—Persian Gulf through Baluchistan to Sind.

DESCRIPTION.—A small Lizard, about 4 in. long, of which the tail is about half. Much like the common house-lizards in form, but with a slimmer tail and ordinary narrow toes. Pupil of eye vertical. Colour pale brown with cross-lines of dark spots, and a dark streak along each side of the head.

The genus *Calodactylus* contains only our single species.

GOLDEN GECKO

OTHER NAMES.—Scientific: *Calodactylus aureus*.

HABITAT.—Tirupati Hills.

DESCRIPTION.—Size reaching nearly 7 in.; head large and well marked off, tail very thin, and not so long as head and body. Toes with square-tipped expansions, one at the end of each, and one a little above it, except on the inner toes. Pupil vertical. Colour golden, dotted or pencilled with brown.

Although so local, this Gecko is likely to attract attention by its beautiful colour; it haunts rocks in dark nullahs.

Our commonest House-Geckos all belong to the genus *Hemidactylus*; they are small, not reaching more than about 6½ in. Their toes are flat, expanded till the last joint, which is narrow; the expanded portions bear suction-plates divided in the middle. The tail is about equal to the head and body, and the pupil vertical. They are very frail little creatures, with a skin so soft that it tears if they be not handled with great care; the tissues are so transparent that the two eggs which are all that the female produces at one laying may be seen within her body when ripe, and if a profile view of the head be obtained against the light, one can see right through it from one ear-hole to the other. The male has a row of pores on the inner side of each thigh.

These are very bold and greedy little creatures, devouring not only insects, but each other if the size renders this possible; the young specimens are therefore very nervous. I have even seen a gecko on the inside of the window of a closed shop, in broad daylight, beating another of about half its own size, which it held by the middle, on the glass, and evidently intending to devour it.

They have retreats in crevices or behind pictures or furniture, and lay their eggs, which are round and hard-shelled, in suitable crannies. In spite of their fragility, I once saw one fall down the well of a staircase of four storeys on to a stone floor, land flat on its stomach with an audible smack, and scamper off, apparently quite unhurt.

Although not at all aquatic, if dropped into water they will both swim and dive. Once one ran up my leg under the trousers, causing me some alarm till I danced it down, as I thought it might be a centipede, and was wearing no pants, it being the hot weather.

COMMON HOUSE-GECKO

Other Names.—Scientific: *Hemidactylus gleadovii, maculatus.*

Habitat.—India, east to South China; also Ceylon.

Description.—The smallest and roughest of our common species, not reaching 5 in., and with about twenty rows of keeled warts running down the back. About seven suction-plates under the middle toe (each counted as one, in spite of the central divisions); large scales bordering the upper lip about nine in number. Male's thigh-pores numbering about twenty on the two legs. Colour light-brown with irregular dark spots, and a dark eye-streak.

This is the commonest of our species; no doubt its small size favours it, just as, to a much greater degree, the house-mouse has the advantage over the two common house-rats.

ASIAN HOUSE-GECKO

Other Names.—Scientific: *Hemidactylus coctæi.*

Habitat —All across Asia from Arabia to the Malay Peninsula; but not Ceylon. Also found in Abyssinia.

Description.—Length a little over 6 in.; tail slightly longer than head and body. Ear-hole oblique. Skin generally smooth, with uniformly minute granules, but sometimes with warts here and there on the flanks. About twelve suction-plates under each middle toe, and about thirteen large scales along the upper lip. Male's thigh-pores about a dozen on the two legs. Colour grey, with the markings, if present, feeble.

This is apparently our next commonest Gecko

VARIED HOUSE-GECKO

OTHER NAMES.—Scientific: *Hemidactylus leschenaultii.*

HABITAT.—India, Malay Peninsula, and Ceylon.

DESCRIPTION.—The largest of our common species, reaching about 6½ in.; skin either smooth and minutely granular, or diversified with scattered warts; ear-hole vertical. Only about half a dozen suction-plates under each middle toe; large scales on upper lip about nine in number. Male's thigh-pores about twenty-eight on the two legs. Colour much more variegated than in the last two, though the pattern is not at all uniform. The ground is grey, and the dark markings may be either wavy crossbars, longitudinal stripes, or a chain of diamond-spots down the spine, a streak runs from eye to shoulder.

This species seems to be the scarcest of the three. All may apparently often be present in the same house, meeting in the search for prey, but choosing lairs in different parts of the building.

The typical genus (*Gecko*) of the family has three large species with us, one very familiar in Burma. In these the suction-plates of the toes are undivided, and the last joint is very short.

TUCKTOO

OTHER NAMES.—Scientific: *Gecko verticillatus, guttatus.*

HABITAT.—Eastern Bengal to South China and the Malay Islands.

DESCRIPTION.—Our largest Gecko except the next species, reaching a length of a little over a foot. Tail a little shorter than head and body. Skin granulated, with about a dozen rows of warts running down the back. Colour, grey, spotted or pencilled with red; tail with dark and light rings. Young with cross-rows of pale spots.

This Gecko is a familar house-lizard in the eastern parts of our area, but is also found on trees. Its loud call, imitated by its name, is well known. It can bite hard, and will put up a long and plucky fight when seized by a snake

GIANT GECKO

OTHER NAMES.—Scientific: *Gecko stentor.*

HABITAT.—Chittagong, east to Borneo; also the Andamans.

DESCRIPTION.—Reaches a length of over 14 in.; tail a little shorter than head and body, which, like the limbs, are longer than in the Tucktoo. Skin granulated, with about eleven rows of warts. Colour drab or brown, with marblings of a darker colour, often with pale spots in the adult as well as the young.

TWIN-SPOTTED GECKO

OTHER NAMES.—Scientific: *Gecko monarchus.*

HABITAT.—Malay Peninsula and Islands; also Ceylon.

DESCRIPTION.—Grows to over 7 in.; tail decidedly longer than head and body. Skin granulated, with scattered pointed warts. Colour, grey or brown with dark spots, which always form two rows down the spine. It is a very noisy reptile, constantly repeating a cry of "Tok."

A curious Parachuting Gecko has a genus to itself.

FLYING-GECKO

OTHER NAMES.—Scientific: *Ptyçhozoon homalocephalum.*

HABITAT.—Southern Burma, east to Borneo; Nicobars and Loo Choo Islands.

DESCRIPTION.—Feet webbed, legs fringed with flaps of skin, and flanks with much wider flaps, broadest in the middle; tail nearly as long as head and body, with a row of small flaps along each side, and a large one at the end. Colour, olive-green above, brown at sides, with wavy dark cross-bars; cheek-flaps pink spotted with blue. Length a little over 7 in.

This very curious Gecko lives in trees, and is supposed to take long flying leaps, supported by its skinny parachutes and toe-webs.

The next genus contains only one species in our area.

GREEN GECKO

OTHER NAMES.—Scientific: *Phelsuma andamanense.*

HABITAT.—Andamans.

DESCRIPTION.—Five inches long; tail equal to head and body. Toes clawless, the inner ones minute and rudimentary, the others with broadly expanded rounded tips. Colour beautiful leaf-green, generally marked with orange. The colour of this Gecko is so remarkable in this family that it deserves mention in spite of its very local habitat;

it frequents trees, and is diurnal; the pupil of the eye is round, not vertical as in the other Geckos previously dealt with.

The Eyelid-Geckos (*Eublepharidæ*) only number two species with us. They have the general appearance of ordinary Geckos, except that the toes are thin, not dilated, and that eyelids are present. The tail is bulged and carrot-shaped, the skin granular and thickly studded with warts, the pupil vertical. Indians regard these Geckos as poisonous, and call them Biscobra, as they do young Monitors.

SOUTHERN EYELID-GECKO

OTHER NAMES.—Scientific: *Eublepharis hardwickii.*

HABITAT.—Bengal and Central and South India.

DESCRIPTION.—Grows to 8 in.; form thick-set, with short legs and toes. Warts on body large, bigger than the spaces which separate them. Colour cream, with the head, two very broad bands across the back, and three broad tail-rings rusty; the latter colour predominates. Upper lips cream, these cream markings meeting on the nape.

NORTHERN EYELID-GECKO

OTHER NAMES.—Scientific: *Eublepharis macularius.*

HABITAT.—Sind and the Punjab; also found at Nineveh.

DESCRIPTION.—Much larger than the last, reaching nearly a foot in length; body and toes longer, warts less abundant and smaller than the spaces between them. Tail about as long as body without head. Colour whitish, spotted or pencilled with rusty and more or less banded with this colour. Young with five broad rusty bands on the back, and the tail also ringed with rusty bands, this colour predominating over the pale background.

The Agamas (*Agamidæ*) are mostly very wiry, athletic-looking lizards, generally clad in overlapping scales; the upper part of the head is covered with small scales, not large plates; the males often differ much from the females, an unusual case among reptiles. Many are good climbers and live on trees and bushes.

The Flying Dragons (*Draco*), are small lizards with very long tails, three wattles on the throat, and a parachute-web on each side of the body, supported by the long hinder ribs. These are usually carried folded and not noticeable, but when the lizard makes a long leap are spread out, and look like short rounded wings, though they cannot be flapped. These little creatures are, in proportion to their size (less than 5 in. in length of head and body), far better parachutists than our gliding mammals, for they can glide for about 10 yds. at a flight. Sometimes they expand their wings, which are handsomely coloured, when in repose, as many butterflies do. As might be expected, they live on trees. They are said to be very delicate in confinement, and have hardly ever been brought to Europe alive; but there must be some way of keeping them, and they are so curious that they are well worth taking trouble over.

They are well distinguished by their wing-markings.

BLACK-SPOTTED DRAGON

OTHER NAMES.—Scientific: *Draco maculatus.*

HABITAT.—Assam to Singapore; also Yunnan.

DESCRIPTION.—Male with the central wattle very large, much exceeding the head in length; female also with a large but less developed central wattle. Tail one and a half times as long as head and body. Colour greyish, variegated with darker; wings speckled with round black spots; two blue spots flanking the large central wattle at the base. Total length nearly 8 in.

MARBLED-WINGED DRAGON

OTHER NAMES.—Scientific: *Draco blanfordii.*

HABITAT.—Tenasserim.

DESCRIPTION.—The largest of the dragons, growing to nearly 14 in. Large central wattle of the male longer than the head, large-scaled, but thin. Tail nearly twice as long as head and body. Colour drab with dark speckling; wings with dark-brown marblings and spots and pencillings of a pale tint; a red patch on the greenish throat.

PALE-SPOTTED DRAGON

OTHER NAMES.—Scientific: *Draco dussumieri.*

HABITAT.—Southern India, near the western sea-board.

DESCRIPTION.—Male's central wattle much longer than the head; tail more than one and a half times length of head and body. Colour drab with ring-spots down the back; throat with dark mottling; wings purple-black with round pale spots. Total length nearly 8 in.

BAND-WINGED DRAGON

OTHER NAMES.—Scientific: *Draco tæniopterus.*

HABITAT.—Tenasserim to Siam.

DESCRIPTION.—Male's central wattle large-scaled, only a little longer than the head; tail nearly twice the length of head and body.

Colour shining brownish or greyish, with no definite markings; wings with five broad curved black bands. Total length 8 in.

The next genus (*Sitana*) has only one species.

FAN-THROATED LIZARD

OTHER NAMES.—Scientific: *Sitana ponticeriana, minor.*

HABITAT.—India generally, except Sind and Western Bengal; also Ceylon.

DESCRIPTION.—Remarkable for having only four toes on hind-foot, the outer toe being absent; legs remarkably variable in length, the hinder if pressed forward sometimes extending only to the eye, sometimes well beyond the end of the muzzle. Tail at least once and a half the length of head and body, often twice their length. Back with rows of large sharp-edged scales. Male with a large dewlap reaching all down the neck and chest, folded back in repose. Colour olive-brown, diamond-marked down the back; male's dewlap in the breeding season gaily coloured with red, black, and blue. Total length nearly 8 in.

Although inhabiting woods as well as open country, this is a ground-lizard, not a climber.

The curious Rhinoceros-Lizards (*Ceratophora*) are all confined to Ceylon; they have peculiar soft horns on the snout.

NAKED-HORNED RHINOCEROS-LIZARD

OTHER NAMES.—Scientific: *Ceratophora stoddartii.*

HABITAT.—Mountains of Ceylon.

DESCRIPTION.—Male with a naked pointed horn on the snout, absent or very short in the female; in the male it may equal the length from muzzle-tip to eye, but is variable in size. Tail more than twice as long as head and body; total length nearly 10 in. Colour olive, more or less cross-barred with darker; horn pale-coloured.

BLUNT-HORNED RHINOCEROS-LIZARD

OTHER NAMES.—Scientific: *Ceratophora tennentii.*

HABITAT.—Ceylon.

DESCRIPTION.—Horn scaly, flattened at the sides and blunt, well developed in both male and female. Tail not quite twice as long as head and body; total length just over 10 in. Colour olive and brownish; young more distinctly variegated, with a crooked bar across the face.

Blunt-horned and Naked-horned Rhinoceros-Lizards

SMALL RHINOCEROS-LIZARD

OTHER NAMES.—Scientific: *Ceratophora aspera.*

HABITAT.—Ceylon.

DESCRIPTION.—Horn on nose of male large, scaly, but round and tapering to a point; in female only rudimentary or wanting; tail barely longer than head and body; total length about $3\frac{1}{2}$ in. Colour brown, marked with a lighter and a darker shade; male with a white throat-mark.

The genus *Lyriocephalus* contains only one species.

LYRE-LIZARD

OTHER NAMES.—Scientific: *Lyriocephalus scutatus.*

HABITAT.—Kandian district of Ceylon.

DESCRIPTION.—A fairly large lizard, measuring 14 in. though the tail only equals the head and body. Head with a knob on the nose, and two curved bony ridges running over the eyes converging in front to form a lyre-shape, and ending at the back in short spikes. Male with a large dewlap. Colour greenish. Young without the nasal knob. When excited this lizard gapes, displaying the scarlet lining of its mouth.

The genus *Calotes* contains our common garden-lizard, and seventeen other species, all more or less climbers. They have a crest of spines down the neck and back; the tail is very long.

COMMON GARDEN-LIZARD

OTHER NAMES.—Scientific: *Calotes versicolor.* Sometimes called "Bloodsucker."

HABITAT.—Indian Empire generally, Cochin China and Southern China.

DESCRIPTION.—Head large and high, snout short and pointed; mane of spines very well marked in adult male; scales keeled and rough; tail slender, more than twice as long as head and body. Colour, brown, with more or less distinct dark or light markings, especially in females and young. The colour is changeable, and the male's head often blushes red, whence the name Bloodsucker. The total length may reach 20 in.

This lizard is difficult to describe accurately, but it is well known, as it is one of the commonest and most familiar of Indian animals; it passes much of its time lying on boughs and twigs, basking or waiting for insects, on which it springs; but it is also often seen on the ground. It can swim well if necessary. Butterflies are often found

Long-tailed Green Calotes.

bearing the marks of its bite on the wings of both sides, seized as they met in repose; the injury is like a child's bite out of a piece of bread-and-butter, not like the notch made by a bird's bill. I found on experimenting with specimens that this lizard will eat even those butterflies which are most distasteful to birds, the "White" *Delias eucharis* with the red-and-yellow under-side to the hind-wings, and the black-and-scarlet "Swallow-tail" *Papilio aristolochiæ.*

I once had a hand-reared Pied Kingfisher free in the Indian Museum compound, and used to feed it on small fish thrown on the grass. A garden-lizard would often take these, and once when the bird had seized the fish just before it, it caught its feathered rival by the tail in its vexation. Years after I read of an exactly similar instance, recorded in the Journal of the Bombay Natural History Society, except that the kingfisher in this instance was a wild one of the White-breasted species.

The garden-lizard buries its eggs in holes in the ground.

LONG-TAILED GREEN CALOTES

OTHER NAMES.—Scientific: *Calotes ophiomachus.*

HABITAT.—South India, Ceylon, and Nicobars.

DESCRIPTION.—Larger than the common garden-lizard, the head and body measuring more than 5 in., whereas in the other they are barely this. Tail very long, nearly four times the length of head and body. Mane of spines well developed in male; scales larger than in the common species and smoother on the back. Colour green, often broadly cross-banded with darker green.

MALAYAN GREEN CALOTES

OTHER NAMES.—Scientific: *Calotes cristatellus.*

HABITAT.—Tenasserim, south-west to Malay Islands.

DESCRIPTION.—Also a green, very long-tailed species, but with the tail barely more than three times the length of head and body, which are about 5 in. Scales much smaller than in the two last, mane of spines on neck short, on back very short indeed.

MOUSTACHED CALOTES

OTHER NAMES.—Scientific: *Calotes mystaceus.*

HABITAT.—Burma, Ceylon, Siam, and the Nicobars.

DESCRIPTION.—About the size of the common garden-lizard, but with shorter tail, about twice the length of the head and body; scales keeled and rough, particularly large above; mane of spines well developed in the male, higher on the neck than the back. Colour olive, with the lips yellow, back often boldly cross-barred with red.

The typical genus *Agama* that gives this family its name contains lizards with rather flattened bodies, not compressed as in the garden-lizard genus, and heads heart-shaped above; there is no spiny mane or hardly any, and the tail is comparatively short for this family, seldom twice the length of the head and body. There is a crease across the throat. These are barren-ground lizards, generally seen on rocks, and only found with us in the North-West.

They are extraordinarily active, so much so that, according to Lydekker, the best way to get specimens is to lash at them with a riding-whip.

BLUE-FLANKED AGAMA

OTHER NAMES.—Scientific: *Agama isolepis.*

HABITAT.—Persia, east to Baluchistan and the Punjab; also Egypt.

DESCRIPTION.—Tail about one and a half times the length of head and body, its scales not arranged in regular rings; legs moderately developed. Colour light drab or brown, sometimes with dark cross-bars, and a chain of pale diamond-marks down the back. Male with a small dewlap, and the throat and flanks blue at breeding-time. Total length nearly 1 ft.

This Agama is found both on plains and hills, and on shrubs as well as rocks.

SPOTTED AGAMA

OTHER NAMES.—Scientific: *Agama tuberculata.*

HABITAT.—Kashmir and Western Himalayas.

DESCRIPTION.—A little larger than the last, with stronger limbs, very coarsely and roughly scaled, and longer tail, very flat at the root. Colour brown with dark and sometimes light spots. No dewlap in male, whose throat when breeding is light-spotted blue.

This lizard ranges high for a reptile, up to 12,000 feet.

The Toad-heads (genus *Phrynocephalus*) are a sort of exaggeration of the Agamas, with decidedly flat bodies, very broad, flat, rounded heads much like a toad's, and tails generally shorter in proportion. They are all small and found in the North-West, living in sandy places, and supposed to produce live young. One only needs mention here.

THEOBALD'S TOAD-HEAD

OTHER NAMES.—Scientific: *Phrynocephalus theobaldi.*

HABITAT.—Turkestan to Upper Indus Valley.

DESCRIPTION.—Tail flat at the base, a little longer than head and body; scales of back small and smooth; colour grey, with plain or leopard-like spots; below white, the male distinguished by black on the throat, the belly, and the end of the tail.

Next come two very remarkable lizards, each typifying a different genus, and not at all resembling each other in appearance except for their very small body-scales, but agreeing, and differing from all our other lizards, in being vegetable-feeders, living on herbage and fruit. Both are ground-livers, and make burrows as retreats. The first is the only member of its genus anywhere.

BELL'S BORDERED LIZARD

OTHER NAMES.—Scientific: *Liolepis belliana.*

HABITAT.—Burma, east to the Malay Peninsula and Southern China; also South Canara in India.

DESCRIPTION.—A lizard at first sight of ordinary lizard-shape, with long tapering tail nearly twice the length of head and body, and rather long legs and toes; head rather small and Roman-nosed. Sides with an expansible flounce of skin supported by elongated ribs somewhat as in the Dragons. Ground-colour above variable, some shade of grey with yellow black-edged markings; flanks boldly barred with black and orange. Total length 20 in.

This peculiar lizard is able to take short skimming flights along the surface of the ground by expanding its flounces, somewhat as the Dragons do from tree to tree. It also expands them under excitement as the Cobra does its hood.

The other vegetarian lizard is a member of a well-known genus (*Uromastix*) which contains several other species found in dry parts of Asia and Africa.

SPINY-TAILED LIZARD, OR MASTIGURE

OTHER NAMES.—Scientific: *Uromastix hardwickii.*

HABITAT.—Baluchistan and North-West India.

DESCRIPTION.—Head high and very short, much like a land-tortoise's; body broad, limbs short and stout. Tail stout, nearly one and a half times the length of head and body, covered above with cross-bands of very strong spiny scales, contrasting strikingly with the very small body-scales. Colour, sandy, often speckled with darker, and with a black inner-thigh patch. Total length 1 ft.

The Mastigure inhabits very dry, almost desert country. Other species of the genus are used for food by natives of the countries they inhabit, including one found in Mesopotamia. The spiny tail is used as a weapon.

The Indian Slow-worm's characters can be given under its specific heading, as it is the only one of its family (*Anguidæ*) found with us.

INDIAN SLOW-WORM OR GLASS-SNAKE

OTHER NAMES.—Scientific: *Ophisaurus apus.*

HABITAT.—Hill-ranges of Eastern India (Khasi Hills and Himalayas), extending east to Yunnan, and south to Eastern Bengal and Rangoon.

DESCRIPTION.—Snake-like in appearance, but with eyelids and small ear-holes, and the tongue not nearly so deeply forked as in a snake; a crease along each side of the body, which, with the head, is not more than half the length of the tail.* Colour, brown, darker along the sides; often spotted with blue and black. Total length nearly 2 ft.

This is a relative of the European Slow-worm, and is still nearer the Glass-Snake, so well known in animal-dealers' shops at home; the latter feeds on small animals of various kinds, including snails, and has a brittle tail. It ranges east to Afghanistan. The rest of the family (*Anguidæ*), which is quite numerous, are American.

The Monitors (*Varanidæ*) are often called Iguanas by Europeans in India, but except for their large size, do not resemble the typical American Iguanas, which are more like some of our Agamids, with spiny crests, and are largely vegetable feeders. There is only one genus, *Varanus*, and all the species are large, 2 ft. or more, with long tails, not fragile, and unusually long necks for lizards, longer than the head, a point which is noticeable even in small young specimens. The scales are small, even on the head. Their long-forked, completely snake-like tongue is also noticeable, and may account for the name *gho-samp* given to the young. They are formidable reptiles, biting hard, lashing with the tail, and scratching very vigorously with their powerful claws. I have even known a specimen of an African species reach out backwards and scratch me with its hind claws as I held it by the neck and the base of the tail—a thing I fancy no mammal even would have thought of doing. Indians call them *Gorpad*, and native burglars sometimes use large specimens as living grapnels, tying a rope round the reptile's loins and sending it up a wall in which there is a convenient crevice at the right height.

* Snake-like reptiles look nearly all head and tail—the true tail is the portion behind the vent.

The lizard enters this, and holds on fast enough to support the weight of a man scaling the rope—an otherwise inaccessible Mohammedan fort was once taken by Mahrattas using this device.

The larger Monitors are undoubtedly destructive animals, feeding as they do on fairly large prey such as ground-birds and their eggs; but they are also useful in destroying noxious mammals and reptiles, so should not be destroyed unless actually doing damage. We have no less than six species, easily enough distinguished, one peculiar point being the remarkable difference in the position of the nostril, which is not always near the end of the snout as usual. The bite of a Monitor seems to be more or less poisonous, as a dog's head has been known to swell seriously after being bitten. The great "Dragon Lizard" of the little Malayan island of Komodo is a monitor, and grows large enough to be really dangerous to man.

DESERT MONITOR

Other Names.—Scientific: *Varanus griseus.*

Habitat.—North Africa, east to North-West India.

Description.—Nostril much nearer to eye than to end of muzzle, which is flat; tail nearly one and a third times as long as head and body. Colour sandy or greenish grey in adult, sometimes more or less cross-barred with brown; young distinctly so barred and also spotted with yellow. Length up to a little over 4 ft.

This monitor lives in deserts, inhabiting burrows, and shunning the midday sun in summer.

BARRED MONITOR

Other Names.—Scientific: *Varanus flavescens.*

Habitat.—Northern India, east to Malay Peninsula.

Description.—Tail one and a fifth times as long as head and body. Nostril nearer to end of muzzle, which is short and rounded, than to eye. Toes short. Colour greenish or yellowish brown, irregularly cross-barred above with darker; lower parts yellowish, rather faintly cross-barred with brown. Young darker, irregularly crossed-barred with yellow, underparts more distinctly barred on a yellow ground. Total length about a yard.

This is a land-monitor like the last species.

LARGE LAND-MONITOR

Other Names—Scientific: *Varanus bengalensis.* Native: *Tallagoya,* Cingalese.

Habitat.—India generally, and Ceylon.

DESCRIPTION.—Tail about one and a third times as long as head and body, compressed and keeled; nostril about midway between eye and end of muzzle, which is high and arched. Colour speckled with black on a variable ground, olive, yellowish, or brownish. Young with pale ring-spots and often cross-barred with blackish; in older but still immature examples these bars may remain. Total length 6 ft.

Being the ordinary land-monitor of India, this is the species to which the name *Gorpad* especially applies.

MARBLED MONITOR

OTHER NAMES.—Scientific: *Varanus nebulosus.*

HABITAT.—Bengal, east and south to Malay Peninsula.

DESCRIPTION.—Tail nearly twice as long as head and body, compressed and keeled; nostril midway between eye and end of muzzle, which is rather high. Eyebrow-scales large. Colour marbled and speckled with light and dark on a greenish or brownish ground; throat with blackish marbling or bars. Young with yellow ring-spots above, blackish marbling below, and two V-shaped blackish bars on upper surface of neck. Total length a little over 3 ft.

BROAD-BARRED MONITOR

OTHER NAMES.—Scientific: *Varanus dumerilii.*

HABITAT.—Tenasserim to Borneo.

DESCRIPTION.—About the same size as the last; nostril about midway between eye and end of muzzle, which is flattened; tail keeled and compressed. Nape- and back-scales large for a monitor, especially the former. Colour dark brown, barred with light brown on the back and spotted with yellow on the limbs. Head and neck light brown with dark brown markings.

WATER-MONITOR

OTHER NAMES.—Scientific: *Varanus salvator.* Native: *Kabaragoya*, Cingalese.

HABITAT.—Bengal, east to Malaysia and South China; also Ceylon.

DESCRIPTION.—The largest of our monitors, reaching more than 7 ft. in length, of which the tail is about half. Nostril much nearer to the end of the muzzle, which is long and flattened, than to the eye. Tail keeled and decidedly compressed. Eyebrow-scales enlarged. Colour very dark brown, marked with ring-spots or plain spots of yellow, the pattern being brightest in young specimens.

This large monitor frequents swamps and often climbs trees near water, to which it readily takes. A large specimen, quite 6 ft. long, used to frequent the island in the lake in the Calcutta Zoological Gardens in the 'nineties; it was not feared by the waterfowl—Ruddy

Water-Monitor.

Sheldrakes and Purple Moorhens—kept there, probably getting enough to eat in the shape of frogs, fish, and fresh-water crabs, and so not molesting them. It may grow to a much greater size, rivalling the Komodo "Dragon," for a writer in one of our best papers some years ago described reptilian monsters more than 12 ft. long, with heads as big as Rugby footballs, coming to feed on a boar's carcase in the Sunderbunds, which could not have been anything else but giant examples of this monitor. In this little-frequented region it may be nearly free from mammalian competition, as the Komodo monitor certainly is, and so have a chance to grow to a gigantic size.

The typical or Lacertine lizards (*Lacertidæ*) are not very important in India, though so familiar in Europe. Their head-scales are large plates, and their body-scales usually different in size below and above; the tongue is rather deeply forked, and the tail long, rounded, and brittle. There is no keel or crest on the back or head. They are very active, and like the sun. Only a few need mention here.

LONG-TAILED LIZARD

OTHER NAMES.—Scientific: *Tachydromus sexlineatus.*

HABITAT—Eastern Himalayas, south-east to Southern China and Borneo.

DESCRIPTION.—The longest-tailed lizard we have, the tail measuring considerably more than four times the length of the head and body, which are only 2½ in. Body-scales keeled. Colour shining brown or green, with a black streak or streaks along the sides, light-bordered above. This lizard runs on the tops of long grass, supported by its tail trailing behind, and diving down when alarmed.

SAND-LIZARD

OTHER NAMES.—Scientific: *Acanthodactylus cantoris.*

HABITAT.—South-East Persia to North-West India.

DESCRIPTION.—Tail rather more than twice as long as head and body, which are nearly 3 in. Back-scales keeled, noticeably enlarged on the hind back. Toes fringed with projecting scales. Colour sandy or greyish, sometimes dark-speckled; young with a pink tail and pale stripes and pale-spotted dark ones.

This is a very active sand-lizard; the fringed toes are an adaptation for travelling on sand.

SNAKE-EYED LIZARD

OTHER NAMES.—Scientific: *Ophiops jerdonii.*

HABITAT.—South to Central India, and Madras.

DESCRIPTION.—Eyelids fused and transparent; tail at least one and a half times as long as head and body, which are less than 2 in.; back-scales keeled. Legs shorter in the female than in the male, the hinder one pressed forward not reaching the arm-pit, whereas in the male it reaches or passes the shoulder. Colour coppery, with two gold-and-black streaks along the sides.

The Skinks (*Scincidæ*), as remarked above, are very sleek-looking lizards with plated heads, but the scales pretty uniform all over the body as a rule, and head, neck, body and tail passing imperceptibly into each other. The tail is fragile. They generally live on the ground, and some display various gradations towards the snake-like form, the limbs being much reduced or even absent. Unlike our other lizards, they generally produce living young.

COMMON STRIPED SKINK

OTHER NAMES.—Scientific: *Mabuia carinata.*

HABITAT.—India, Burma, and Ceylon.

DESCRIPTION.—A thick-set lizard with tail about one and a half times as long as head and body, and limbs rather short. Colour brown, with a pale stripe along each side of the upper parts from eye to tail, and in the breeding male a scarlet one along the flank. Total length about 14 in.

This is one of our commonest lizards in the plains, and in spite of its heavy build a fairly good climber, ascending several yards above the ground.

COMMON HILL-SKINK

OTHER NAMES.—Scientific: *Lygosoma indicum.*

HABITAT.—Eastern Himalayas to Burmese hills.

DESCRIPTION.—Smaller than the last and with a longer tail, which is nearly twice as long as the head and body, which measure 3½ in. Colour brown, usually light-spotted, and darkest on cheeks and flanks, which have a light border above.

BLUE-TAILED SKINK

OTHER NAMES.—Scientific: *Lygosoma laterimaculatum.*

HABITAT.—Hills of Southern India.

DESCRIPTION.—A small lizard, barely 2 in. in length of head and body when adult; tail about one and three-quarters their length, blue in young specimens. General colour bronze, with a dark and light streak from head to tail on each side, with rows of black spots above and below it.

THREE-TOED SKINK

OTHER NAMES.—Scientific: *Ophiomorus tridactylus.*

HABITAT.—Eastern Persia to the Punjab, Sind, and Cutch.

DESCRIPTION.—A long, thin, almost snake-like lizard with short limbs bearing only three toes on each. Tail much shorter than head and body; muzzle pointed, projecting above in front of the mouth. Colour cream, sometimes with rows of little brown spots above. Total length about 6 in.

This is a sand-lizard and a burrower.

The characteristics of our one representative of the *Dibamidæ* may be given under its heading:

BEAKED SLOW-WORM

OTHER NAMES.—Scientific: *Dibamus novæ-guineæ.*

HABITAT.—Nicobars, Malay Peninsula, and New Guinea.

DESCRIPTION.—A small snake-like lizard, growing to a little over 6 in. Eyes under the head-shields and hardly noticeable. Muzzle bluntly pointed, covered with three large shields, one above and one on each side, or even with only a uniform covering, the three having fused; one large lip-shield on each side covering the lower jaw. Scales of body similar all over; no limbs in the female, in the male two flaps at sides of vent. Tail very short, about a ninth of total length. Colour brown throughout with a purplish tinge.

Dr. Boulenger considers this curious little burrowing lizard to be probably a degenerate skink. It differs from all our other snake-like lizards and snakes by the great development in size of the few muzzle- and lip-shields, forming a sort of beak. It lays hard-shelled eggs, and the only specimen known from the Malay Peninsula was found, in an egg got from a dead tree-trunk, as an embryo.

The Chamæleons (*Chamæleontidæ*) are such a distinct family that they have a sub-order (*Rhiptoglossa*) to themselves. We have only one species, a member of the typical genus.

INDIAN CHAMÆLEON

OTHER NAMES.—Scientific: *Chamæleon calcaratus.*

HABITAT.—India south of the Ganges, and Ceylon.

DESCRIPTION.—A very remarkable reptile with longer limbs than usual, a large bony head raised behind into a helmet-like crest, and a prehensile tail, exceeding head and body in length. Body compressed, with a granulated skin, and a crest of spines below reaching up to the chin. Toes divided into two sets, inner and outer, bound together with skin, so as to show hardly more than the claws separate; in the fore-limb there are three toes in the inner set and two in the outer; in the hind-limb two in the inner and three in the outer. Eyes large and prominent, but covered almost entirely by the lids, so that only the pupil can be seen, in the middle. Colour changeable, depending on the state of mind—fear, anger, etc.—of the creature, also on warmth

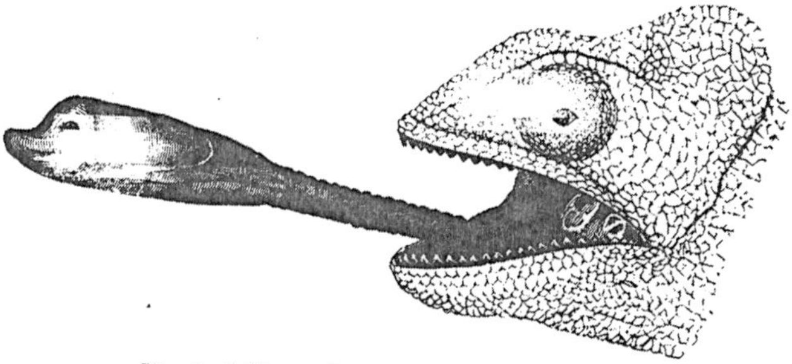

Head of Chamæleon with tongue protruded.

or cold, sleep or waking, or the surroundings. Total length 15 in. Male with spurs on the hind feet.

The Chamæleon is only found in wooded country; it is a climber, and, though it stands up well on its legs like a mammal, very slow in its movements. The eyes move independently, and when both are focussed on its insect prey, this is captured by the shooting out of the very long, club-tipped, sticky tongue.

The common Chamæleon of the Mediterranean region, well known to pet-keepers at home, only drinks drops of water from leaves as a rule, and probably the habits of our species are the same.

The Snakes (sub-order *Ophidia*) are, as above remarked, distinguished from the lizards by having the two halves of the lower jaw only united by ligament. The absence of limbs is paralleled by some of the lizards; so also is the absence of eyelids and ear-openings, and so is the characteristic long-forked tongue with a sheath at the base. Their body varies a good deal in length and thickness, and their tail, which may be distinguished as the portion behind the vent, is of very

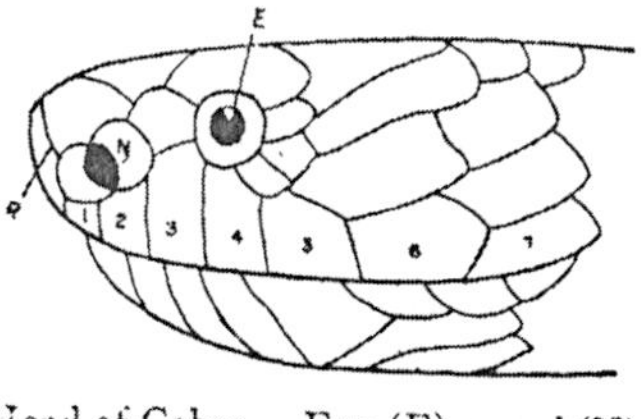

Head of Cobra. Eye (E), nasal (N), rostral (R), and lip (1-7) shields.

variable length, but never so long as the body, and sometimes a mere stump, shorter than in any lizard. Their head is usually covered with large shields, and in most the belly has a single row of large, shallow, but broad scales, connected with the ends of the ribs. The ribs being movable, these scales can be raised, so as to give a grip on the surface over which the snake is moving; but the main impulse is given by a wavy motion of the body from side to side. They also swim in this way, and many are more or less aquatic in their habits; many are also climbers, and some both arboreal and aquatic.

They generally feed on vertebrate animals, and are often strongly specialised in diet, preying chiefly or exclusively on some special group of animals, often a restricted one.

Their powers of gorging relatively large prey are generally very great, owing to the loose union and power of independent motion in the bones of the upper as well as the lower jaw, so that such snakes seem to pull themselves over the prey as a stocking is pulled over the leg. The victim is sometimes swallowed alive, and sometimes first killed by constriction in the coils of the snake, or by its poison. In spite of the backward inclination of the teeth, they can disgorge prey readily.

Poison-glands and their accompanying fangs are developed in two quite distinct families of snakes; in the Vipers (*Viperidæ*), all of which are poisonous, and in some of the ordinary or Colubrine snakes (*Colubridæ*), most of which are harmless. The poison of the two groups differs in its properties, and though a viperine can poison a colubrine, or *vice versâ*, the poison is without effect on members of the same family as its possessor.

The poison-gland is situated between the eye and the upper jaw, and may extend down the body; its secretion is like saliva in appearance and also limited in amount, so that the oftener a snake bites the less virulent the bite will be, unless it be given time to secrete more poison. The poison-fangs are grooved, or, if the edges of the groove meet, perforated; if they be pulled out, the snake is harmless for a time, but not for long, as new fangs will soon grow up in their places.

Poisonous snakes are not usually vicious and aggressive; in fact, some are less ready to bite than are some of the harmless species. There is also no hard-and-fast rule for distinguishing any poisonous from any harmless snake; but the poisonous species are much in the minority, and nearly all the most dangerous kinds are easily recognisable. The colours of snakes are often variable, but individuals cannot change their colour as so many lizards do.

When changing their skins, snakes generally slough off the whole epidermis at once, unlike lizards, whose slough comes off in pieces;

they become dull-coloured as the old skin loosens, and the fixed transparent eyelid becoming loose at the same time obscures their sight, so that at this time they are nervous and particularly apt to bite.

Most snakes lay eggs, which are elliptical and soft-shelled; but many, far more than among the lizards, produce living young, including nearly all our vipers.

We have species of all the nine known families of snakes in India, which may be distinguished as follows :—

The Worm-Snakes (*Typhlopidæ*) are small worm-like snakes with no teeth in the lower jaw and a stump-tail either conical or ending in a spine.

The *Glauconia* or Hip-snake (*Glauconiidæ*), the only species of its family found with us, has no teeth in the upper jaw, but is otherwise very like the last family. All our other snakes have teeth in both jaws.

The Boas (*Boidæ*), including the giant Pythons and the ordinary-sized Sand-boas, have vestiges of hind-limbs consisting of a spur on each side of the vent; moreover their heads, at least behind the eyes, are covered with small scales, not large shields. The tail is of fair length.

The Ilysiids (*Ilysiidæ*) have the vent-spurs, but the tail is a mere blunt stump.

The Earth-Snakes (*Uropeltidæ*) are recognised by their peculiar tails, very short and ending in a large flat or convex shield or a small double-pointed, square, or single-pointed one. If the last, the large head-shields back of the eye and larger and more distinct eye will distinguish them from the Worm-Snakes.

The Rainbow-Snake, the sole member of the family *Xenopeltidæ*, is remarkable for its beautiful iridescence; this is also found in some of the Earth-Snakes, but in the Rainbow-Snake the tail is not peculiar in form, and is more than a stump, measuring a tenth of the snake's length.

The Night-Snakes (*Amblycephalidæ*) are noticeable for their large prominent eyes and short broad snouts, the width of the eye being about equal to its distance from the end of the muzzle. Their necks are narrow, and on the whole they are very like some of the Colubrines, but distinguished by having no groove on the chin.

The Vipers (*Viperidæ*), with the exception of the very rare Deceptive Viper (*Azemiops*), which can be recognised, as will be seen later, by its colour, are very easily distinguished; they have the head broad at the back, and covered above with small scales, except in one genus in which large plates are found as in most other snakes, but this belongs to the Pit-Vipers, and shows a pit between the eye and the nose, not found in any other shield-crowned snake.

All our other snakes belong to the great family *Colubridæ*, which is as numerous as all the rest put together. While not presenting the special peculiarities of the families above mentioned, the individual groups are often more easily recognised; the Cobras, for instance, by their expansible neck or "hood," and the poisonous Sea-Snakes by their flat paddle-like tails.

In most cases only a selection of species can be made here.

The Worm-Snakes (*Typhlopidæ*), besides the worm-like shape with no distinct neck and absence of teeth in the lower jaw,* have the eyes under the head-shields, and so not very distinct; the shield at the tip of the nose (rostral) is very large, and the belly shields are like those of the back, not specialised in size and breadth as in most snakes. Those little snakes burrow, and live on worms and insects; they lay but few eggs, very large for their size.

COMMON WORM-SNAKE

OTHER NAMES.—Scientific: *Typhlops braminus.*

HABITAT.—Africa below the Equator, east through Arabia and South-East Asia to the Malay Islands. Also found in Mexico.

DESCRIPTION.—A very small snake, only growing to 7 in., with rounded snout and stumpy spine-tipped tail barely longer than it is broad. Colour dark brown or nearly black, with whitish extremities as a rule. A flesh-pink variety is found in Southern India.

The Common Worm-Snake is one of the commonest of Indian animals, though seldom seen on account of its burrowing habits; sometimes it causes a surprise by getting into water-pipes, and is sometimes found in numbers in rotten wood, where, no doubt, it goes after white ants, its usual food. The wood-burrowing habit, favouring dispersal in drift-timber, may have had something to do with the remarkably wide distribution of this little creature, one of our feeblest vertebrates. I once gave one to a Whip-Scorpion (*Thelyphonus*), which had no difficulty in killing it, and soon chewed and sucked it into a pellet.

DIARD'S WORM-SNAKE

OTHER NAMES.—Scientific: *Typhlops diardi.*

HABITAT.—Bengal, east to Burma and Cochin China; also Sikkim.

DESCRIPTION.—Scales smaller than in the common species (twenty-four or more, instead of twenty, round the body) and tail shorter, at least as broad as long. Colour, olive-brown, with light cross-streaks on each scale; size up to 17 in.

* A lens is necessary to make this out.

HOOK-NOSED WORM-SNAKE

OTHER NAMES.—Scientific: *Typhlops acutus.*

HABITAT.—Deccan southwards in India.

DESCRIPTION.—The giant of these little snakes, growing to 2 ft.; scales smaller than in the last two, about thirty round the body; tail at least as broad as long, spine-tipped. Nose sharp and hooked; rostral scale extending back well beyond the eyes, which is not the case with the last two. Colour, light-brown, with pale cross-streaks on each scale.

Our single species of the next family (*Glauconiidæ*) may be called the

HIP-SNAKE

OTHER NAMES.—Scientific: *Glauconia blanfordi.*

HABITAT.—Sindh.

DESCRIPTION.—Like a Worm-Snake in most respects, but with the upper jaw toothless and not the lower; the upper jaw projects considerably, the lower barely reaching beyond the level of the eye. Scales alike above and below, but much larger than in worm-snakes, there being only fourteen round the body, while our worm-snakes never have less than eighteen. Tail longer than in worm-snakes, about one-thirteenth length of body; colour, light brown. Length $9\frac{1}{2}$ in.

The peculiarity from which I venture to give this snake the name of hip-snake is that it has the pelvis or ring of hip-bones more developed than in any other snake; there is also a rudimentary thigh-bone. In worm-snakes there is only one bone on each side to represent the hip-girdle. The present species is very rare, only five specimens being on record.

The Boas and Pythons (*Boidæ*) seem the greatest contrast possible to the little burrowers above mentioned, but that is because one usually thinks of the sensational giant members of the family, of which we have two. Our other two species form a link with their humbler kin. As in the last family, there are rudiments of a hip-girdle, and the vestige of thigh-bone ends in this case in a spur or claw which can be seen on each side of the vent. In boas the scales of the body are small, and the head is not covered above with large shields, or only partially.

In the Pythons (genus *Python*) there are pits on some of the lip-shields, and the upper part of the head to about its centre is covered with large shields, the rest with small scales, and the scales of the body are very small. The broad shallow ventral shields are present, but narrower than in most snakes; the tail is fairly long, and prehensile. The pupil of the eye is vertical, and these snakes are largely nocturnal; they prey mostly, at any rate when adults, on mammals and birds, which they seize with the jaws and suffocate by constricting them with the coils of the body, which is flung round the victim as quickly as a lash of a whip. Though quick in seizing and coiling, they are not very swift movers on the ground; they climb well, and are fond of water, often lying in it for long periods. Their strength is enormous, their contraction breaking bones even of large animals, and probably the largest specimens could overpower any animal; but, as with other large cold-blooded vertebrates, their exact limit of size is not known. They lay eggs, and incubate them by coiling round them when collected in a pile; at this time, although supposed to be "cold-blooded," their temperature rises. They have great powers of fasting, and can live a year without food.

INDIAN PYTHON

OTHER NAMES.—Scientific: *Python molurus*. Native: *Adjigar*, Hindi; *Periya pambu*, Tamil; *Pimbera*, Cingalese.

HABITAT.—Indian Peninsula, Rajputana, Bengal, Malay Peninsula, and Java; also Ceylon.

DESCRIPTION.—Shields of lower lip less than twenty on each side; shields below tail less than eighty; pits on two of the front upper-lip shields on each side. Colour buff or drab, with a row of large blotches, inclining to an oblong shape, along the back, these being chestnut with black edges; smaller spots along the sides. Head with a spear-mark above, an eye-stripe along the side, and a cross-stripe below the eye, all brown in colour. Length usually about 4 yds., but some specimens reach 20 ft. and, it is said, several feet more.

The Indian Python is rare in the extreme south-eastern part of its range, but otherwise well-known for a large snake, and is not uncommon in captivity. It is sometimes known as Rock-Snake, but prefers forest to bare rock. A snake of this kind has been known to kill and swallow a full-grown leopard, another to eat worms and berries.

MALAY OR RETICULATED PYTHON

OTHER NAMES.—Scientific: *Python reticulatus*. Native: *Ular sawa*, Malay.

HABITAT.—Burma, east through the Malay Islands.

DESCRIPTION.—The largest snake known except the American

Anaconda, reaching 10 yds. Lower-lip shields over twenty on each side, shields under tail over eighty; four of the front upper-lip shields on each side pitted. Colour brown or buff, marked above with large diamond-shaped or round black figures edged with yellow; head plain brown except for a black streak along the middle of it above.

The skin shows a beautiful rainbow sheen when the snake has newly sloughed, and the late W. Rutledge told me he once had a specimen in which the usual yellow borders of the black pattern were replaced by scarlet. I once saw one myself in his possession which had the iris of the eye yellow instead of the usual light brown, which gave it a very fierce look. This magnificent snake, the most splendid and imposing of modern reptiles, is well known in captivity.

DWARF PYTHON

OTHER NAMES.—Scientific: *Python curtus.*

HABITAT.—Malaysia and Sumatra.

DESCRIPTION.—Resembles the Indian Python in having but two upper-lip shields pitted, but has a far smaller number of shields below the tail—not over thirty-two. It is stoutly built, but only reaches 3 yds. Colour brown or dull red, with pale spots down the back and grey ones edged with black along the sides. Head with a black line down the middle, and cheeks dark with a pale streak behind the eye.

This Python feeds largely on rats, and should presumably be classed as a useful animal.

The Boas are mostly American, but we have two Indian species, one occupying a genus to itself, and one the only member of its genus with us.

SAND-BOA

OTHER NAMES.—Scientific: *Gongylophis conicus*

HABITAT.—Northern India.

DESCRIPTION.—A thick-set snake with short tail, one-twelfth of the length of the head and body, which measure only 2 ft. Head covered above with small scales; body-scales small and keeled; tail-scales strongly keeled; eye very small. Colour grey above, tinged with yellow or brown; a row of large dark-brown joined patches on the spine, edged with black, and a spear-mark on the back of the head; under-surface white.

The Dwarf Boa feeds on mice, and Dr. Boulenger found that one he kept had a fierce temper. In its small-scaled head, stout build, and style of marking it rather recalls a viper, and if the ferocity is general, this behaviour may be part of a form of defensive mimicry of a dangerous species.

INDIAN ERYX

OTHER NAMES.—Scientific: *Eryx johnii.*

HABITAT.—Central and Southern India.

DESCRIPTION.—A thick-set snake, with the head passing gradually into the neck, and the tail, which is only one-twelfth of the length of the head and body, which measure 1 yd., very blunt, so that the reptile looks much alike at both ends. Rostral scale large and broad, making the muzzle blunt-ended; body-scales only slightly keeled. Colour pale drab or brown, sometimes more or less plainly cross-barred, especially behind. Young specimens are often quite handsome, light coral-red.

The Eryx is confined to sandy tracts, and lives on small mammals and on worms. It is a night-snake, and is a favourite with snake-charmers—to its cost, for these worthies cruelly cut the end of its tail so as to produce the appearance of a mouth there, and exhibit it as a two-headed snake.

The Ilysiid Snakes (*Ilysiidæ*) should probably be classed in the last family, as Dr. Boulenger regards them as degraded boas. We have only two species, thickset snakes with the neck as big as the head—which has large shields as far as the small eyes—very short blunt tails, and ventral scales not twice as large as the rest. They are burrowers, and oviparous. We have only two species.

RED-TAILED SNAKE

OTHER NAMES.—Scientific: *Cylindrophis rufus.*

HABITAT.—Burma, east to the Malay Islands.

DESCRIPTION.—Grows to nearly 2½ ft.; only five to ten scales beneath the tail. Colour brown or shining black, sometimes pale-cross-barred, and cross-barred with black and white below; underside of tail often scarlet.

This snake has a large appetite, taking eels and snakes as large as itself; when alarmed it, like the next, hides its head and raises and curves its hinder parts, so that they appear like a head.

SPOTTED CYLINDROPHIS

OTHER NAMES.—Scientific: *Cylindrophis maculatus.*

HABITAT.—Ceylon.

DESCRIPTION.—About the size of the last; four to six scales under tail. Black-edged chestnut spots above; white below.

The Earth-Snakes (*Uropeltidæ*), in addition to the shielded tails above-mentioned, have the eyes generally situated inside—but not beneath—one shield instead of surrounded by several as in most snakes. Their bodies show no neck, and are cylindrical and but little flexible, their snouts usually pointed, and the teeth, though present in both jaws as in most snakes, neither large nor numerous. Their ventral scales are comparatively small, but twice as large as the others or less. They are always small, and live mostly underground, feeding on earth-worms; but they may also be found under stones or logs, or among grass high up on the hills, or even, in wet weather, on roads.

Truncate Earth-Snake.

They produce living young. Considering their mostly hidden life, their often unusually brilliant colours, red, yellow, purple, and iridescent black, seem surprising; but these may have a "warning" significance, and it would be interesting to know if these harmless, helpless creatures are unpalatable. If not, the bright hues are evidently due to variation unchecked by natural selection, owing to the sheltered lives the snakes lead; and, after all, all "warning colours" must have been in the first place incidental. The earth-snakes are confined to the Indian Peninsula and Ceylon, and usually to hills, but they may be found in forests at the foot of these. The number of species is extraordinary—no less than forty—distributed among seven genera; and, even allowing for possible over-division by specialists, the concentration of so many in a restricted area is remarkable enough. It is obviously only possible to notice a few here.

TRUNCATE EARTH-SNAKE

OTHER NAMES.—Scientific: *Uropeltis grandis.*

HABITAT.—Central Provinces of Ceylon.

DESCRIPTION.—Tail as it were obliquely docked, the cut portion rounded and warty. Muzzle sharp, the large rostral shield running back above halfway to the level of the eyes. Colour dark brown, sometimes yellow-spotted; lower parts yellow, sometimes brown-spotted. Grows to 18 in.

RED-BELLIED EARTH-SNAKE

OTHER NAMES.—Scientific: *Rhinophis sanguineus.*

HABITAT.—Hills of Southern India.

DESCRIPTION.—Tail shielded and rough at the end, but convex, not truncate; muzzle sharp, shield of tail not so long as head. Colour blue-black, under-parts and lower flanks scarlet with black spots. Grows to 16 in.

OCELLATED EARTH-SNAKE

OTHER NAMES.—Scientific: *Sibybura ocellata.*

HABITAT.—Nilgiris and Anamallays, also Tinnevelly Hills.

DESCRIPTION.—Shield at end of tail small, ending in two tiny points on the same plane; eye so small that it barely takes up a third of the shield containing it. Colour brown or buff, with many black-eyed yellow markings disposed as cross-bars; below, yellow and brown. The ocellated cross-bars may be absent. Length up to 20 in.

The sole member of the family *Xenopeltidæ* is the

RAINBOW-SNAKE

OTHER NAMES.—Scientific: *Xenopeltis unicolor.*

HABITAT.—Trichinopoly only in India; Burma, east to the Malay Islands; and Indo-China.

DESCRIPTION.—Neck as thick as head; tail a tenth of total length, which reaches rather over 1 yd.; head covered with large shields above; ventral scales large. Eyes small. Colour brown or black, the scales light-edged, with an extremely fine iridescent gloss; under-parts white or yellow, lips yellow; young yellow-headed and yellow-naped.

The Rainbow Snake is a fierce-tempered burrower, feeding on small mammals and on other snakes.

The Night-Snakes (*Amblycephalidæ*), in addition to the peculiarities noted above, are remarkable for not having the mouth dilatable to the extent found in most snakes; they are insectivorous, so do not take large prey which involves jaw-stretching. Their bodies are fairly slim and tails fairly long. One of our species may be noted.

HILL NIGHT-SNAKE

OTHER NAMES.—Scientific: *Amblycephalus monticola.*

HABITAT.—Eastern Himalayas to Naga Hills.

DESCRIPTION.—Grows to about 2 ft. 6 in.; head covered with very large shields; scales along back six-sided and of large size. Tail about a quarter of total length. Colour brown, the sides cross-barred with black; two black lines running back from the eye; under-parts yellow, and brown-speckled.

The Vipers (*Viperidæ*) are as a rule as easy to recognise as the Boas, and the more or less heart-shaped head being generally so characteristic, and, Vipers being the only European poisonous snakes, they are largely responsible for the general idea of what a venomous reptile ought to look like. Their eyes are set far forward, nearer the tip of the nose than the corner of the mouth; whereas in the Boas, which resemble them in generally having the head covered with small scales, the eye is set about midway between these two points. Vipers' tails are rather short, and taper abruptly from the body.

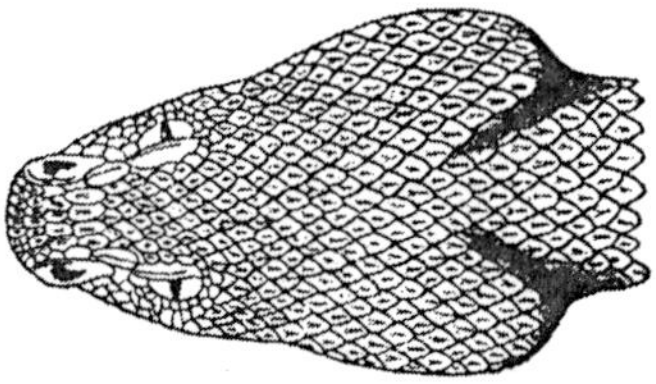

Head of Russell's Viper.

All our Vipers are land-snakes, and produce, as a rule, living young. All are poisonous, but in only a few is the poison deadly to man, the ill-effects in the case of the bite of most being slight. The fangs are large compared with those of most of the poisonous snakes, and the canal conducting the poison is closed, so as to produce the effect of a perforated tooth. In biting, the Vipers strike or stab rather than grip. The characteristic action of the poison is the effect it has on the blood, causing oozing from the mucous membranes and under the skin. The genera of the Viper family are usually very distinct, and easily recognisable by an amateur naturalist.

The first species we have to deal with, however, presents no very striking characteristics, and, in fact, does not look like a Viper at all. It is the only member of its genus, and may be called the

DECEPTIVE VIPER

Other Names.—Scientific: *Azemiops feæ.*

Habitat.—Kakhyen Hills.

Description.—Head oval, covered with large shields; eyes nearer to end of snout than to corner of mouth; nostrils about as wide apart as their distance from the eyes. Tail rather more than an eighth of the total length. Colour dark grey, the scales black-edged, the body with more than a dozen white cross-bars. Head yellow, with a triangular black patch on the crown, divided by a yellow line which runs a little way down the neck, a black stripe running back from the eye to the lip, and another running down from the eye vertically to it. The general appearance is that of an ordinary harmless snake, but the peculiar combination of black and yellow head with dark white-barred body ought to distinguish the snake easily if met with. The length is 2 ft.

Nothing is known about the habits of this snake, of which only one specimen is on record, and it is only mentioned here to draw attention to it.

The typical genus *Vipera*, to which our Adder at home belongs, has the head covered with small scales, which, like those of the body, are keeled. Vipers are sluggish or obstinate snakes, and hence liable to cause accidents, as they are not so much inclined to get out of the way as others, and are irritable in temper. We have but two species.

DABOIA OR RUSSELL'S VIPER

Other Names.—Scientific: *Vipera russellii.* Native: *Daboia*, Hindi; *Tic polonga*, Cingalese.

Habitat.—India east to Burma and Siam; also Ceylon.

Description.—Six or eight rows of scales on the head between the supraoculars, or eyebrow-scales, which are narrow; rostral scale measuring about the same in breadth and depth. Tail about an eighth of the total length, which may be 4 ft. Colour light brown, with a row of black rings down the back, with lighter edges, and a row of similar rings along each side; in young specimens the colour inside the rings is darker and redder than the general ground, and the spinal row of rings touch each other. Some individuals have no pattern at all, but indistinct dark markings.

The Daboia is one of the best-known Indian poisonous snakes, and is particularly deadly owing to its large size and especially long fangs; it is also disinclined to move. The old snake-keeper at the Calcutta

Russell's Viper.

Zoo in my time, who was one of the professional charmer class, said that a cobra would get tame in time, but that the present species could never be trusted.

It ranges up the Himalayas to 6,000 ft.

WESTERN DABOIA

OTHER NAMES.—Scientific: *Vipera lebetina.*

HABITAT.—North Africa east to Kashmir, also Cyprus and Milo.

DESCRIPTION.—Generally similar in detail to Russell's Viper, but growing larger, with the scales on the forehead smaller, there being at least nine rows between the eyes and often twelve, while the supra-ocular shield is often absent; rostral shield shallower, its depth not equalling its length. Colour different from that of most Indian Daboias, being drab with faint markings or none when adult; young specimens are plainly cross-barred or spotted with darker.

The next genus contains only one species with us.

PHOORSA OR SAW-SCALED VIPER

OTHER NAMES.—Scientific: *Echis carinata.* Native: *Phoorsa,* Hindi.

HABITAT.—North Africa east to India; not Ceylon nor south of the Carnatic and the Concan in the Peninsula.

Description.—A small snake, only reaching 2 ft.; tail about a tenth of total length. Head covered with small scales; body-scales keeled, the keels of the scales on the flanks saw-edged. Colour light-brown to cream, or tinged with grey or red, with a cross- or broad-arrow-shaped mark on the head and a row of spots down the spine, all these marks being pale with dark edgings; a further row of spots along each flank.

The colouring is the best guide to identifying this snake, the saw-like character of the keels of the flank-scales requiring a close examina-

Phoorsa or Saw-scaled Viper.

tion, though their presence is indicated to the ear by the rasping sound the snake makes with them by rubbing its coils against each other. It frequents open sandy dry country, and is fierce and deadly poisonous.

All our other vipers are Pit-Vipers, *i.e.* have a pit on the side of the muzzle between eye and nostril; they are not generally dangerous, though the deadly American Rattle-snakes belong to this group.

Those of the genus *Ancistrodon* have large scales on the crown, as in most snakes, but unlike most of this family. We have only two.

HIMALAYAN PIT-VIPER

Other Names.—Scientific: *Ancistrodon himalayanus.*

Habitat.—North-Western Himalayas east to Sikkim; apparently also Khasi Hills.

Description.—Grows to nearly 1 yd.; large shields on upper surface of muzzle as well as on crown; body-scales well keeled, in over twenty rows. No lip-shield touches the facial pit. Colour brown, spotted or cross-barred with black; a pale-bordered black band along side of head.

This Viper is usually abundant, at temperate elevations, but ranges up to 10,000 ft.

KARAWALA

OTHER NAMES.—Scientific : *Ancistrodon hypnale.*

HABITAT.—Western Ghats and Ceylon.

DESCRIPTION.—Grows to a little over $1\frac{1}{2}$ ft. ; tail about an eighth of the head-and-body length. Scales of snout small, unlike shields of crown ; second lip-shield touching face-pit ; body-scales not strongly keeled, in less than twenty rows. Colour plain or spotted and cross-barred with dark brown, or marked with small jet-black twin-spots. Ground very variable, buff, brown, or drab ; cheeks commonly dark-brown, light-edged above.

This snake's bite is rarely fatal.

The remaining Pit-Vipers (*Trimeresurus* or *Lachesis*) have the head covered with small scales as in *Vipera* and *Echis*, from which the facial pit distinguishes them ; they also have the head much broader behind than in any other of our Vipers, presenting the " ace of spades " type in perfection. Some of them are climbers, and have prehensile tails ; it is not necessary to mention all.

Large-spotted Pit-Viper.

LARGE-SPOTTED PIT-VIPER

OTHER NAMES.—Scientific : *Trimeresurus* or *Lachesis monticola.*

HABITAT.—Eastern Asia from Tibet to Sumatra.

Description.—Grows to 2 ft., of which the tail is about a seventh; eyes small, not half the size of eyebrow-shields; only five to eight rows of scales between these. Colour brown or buff, with a row or two of big angular dark-brown spots down the spine, and smaller ones down the sides.

This Pit-Viper is found up to 8,000 ft. elevation. It differs from our other Vipers in laying eggs.

PURPLE PIT-VIPER

Other Names.—Scientific: *Trimeresurus* or *Lachesis purpureomaculatus.*

Habitat.—South-Eastern Asia from the Himalayas to Sumatra, also the Andamans and Nicobars.

Description.—Grows to a little over a yard; tail about a sixth of total length. Twelve or more rows of scales between eyes. Body-scales well keeled, in more than two dozen rows. Colour purple, more or less variegated with green, especially on the sides; sometimes all green, except for a row of pale spots along the sides.

GREEN PIT-VIPER

Other Names.—Scientific: *Trimeresurus* or *Lachesis gramineus.*

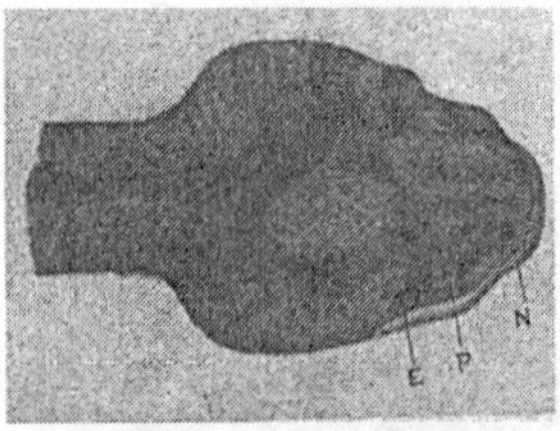

Head of Green Pit-Viper, showing pit (P) between eye (E) and nostril (N).

Habitat.—South-Eastern Asia from the Himalayas to the Malay Islands.

Description.—Grows to $2\frac{1}{2}$ ft.; tail prehensile, between a fifth and a sixth of total length. Scales not strongly keeled, in less than twenty-four rows round the body. Colour usually green, but sometimes buff, drab, or purplish, sometimes with spots of various colours; when resembling the last species in colour, the less-keeled and less numerous scales will distinguish it.

This is a tree- and bush-snake.

LARGE-SCALED PIT-VIPER

Other Names.—Scientific: *Trimeresurus* or *Lachesis macrolepis.*

Habitat.—Anamalais and Pulneys.

Description.—Grows to a little over 2 ft., and has remarkably large scales, well keeled, and in not more than fifteen rows round the body. Colour green or olive, with a pale line along the sides.

WAGLER'S PIT-VIPER

Other Names.—Scientific: *Trimeresurus* or *Lachesis wagleri.*
Habitat.—Malay Peninsula and islands.
Description.—Remarkable for its large head, nearly as broad as long, and gay colour, green cross-barred with black and yellow, or black cross-barred with yellow; young even brighter, green marked with blue or purple as well as yellow or white; grows to nearly 1 yd.

A slow snake found on trees or on the ground; though not Indian or Burmese, so striking a near neighbour deserves mention.

All our other snakes belong to the great family of *Colubridæ*, which includes the majority of snakes, showing great diversity among themselves. While all the previous families are non-venomous, except the vipers, which are all so, the Colubrines may be called a semi-venomous family, falling as they do into three sections—the *Aglypha*, which have ordinary solid teeth and are harmless; the *Opisthoglypha*, or back-fanged snakes, in which some of the back teeth are enlarged and grooved, to carry a poison which is fatal to small animals; and the *Proteroglypha*, or front-fanged snakes, which have grooved or canal-bearing fangs in the front of the jaw, and are venomous to man, though in practice there is little danger from some.

Each section is divided into terrestrial and aquatic sub-families.

It will be as well here to take the last section (*Proteroglypha*) first, so as to keep all our poisonous snakes together, it being understood that this does not imply any relationship between the vipers and the poisonous snakes of the present family. The venom of these is, as has been remarked above, of different quality; it acts, so far as is known, by paralysing respiration; and they wound by a true bite with the two jaws rather than by a stab like the vipers. All these snakes have large head-shields and the neck as thick as the head.

The land Colubrine poisonous snakes form the subfamily *Elapinæ;* and the most notorious of these are the Cobras (genus *Naia*), of which we have two species. When lying or crawling undisturbed they do not look peculiar, but on any excitement they rear the fore-part of the body and expand the upper neck, of which the skin is distensible and supported on long ribs, into the so-called hood, and thus are extremely conspicuous. Like most colubrine snakes, they lay eggs.

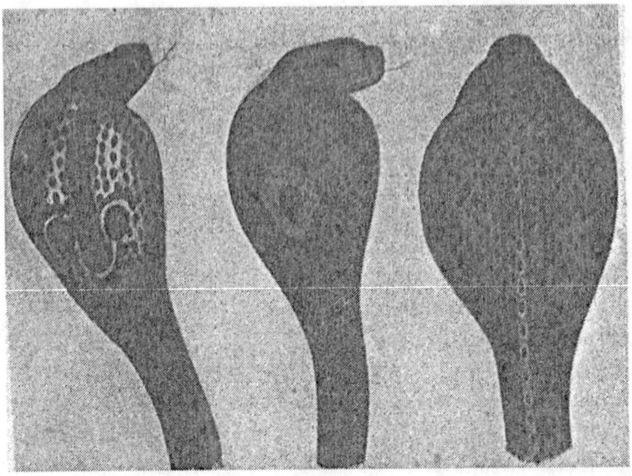

Cobra Hoods, showing (1) full spectacle-mark, (2) single ocellus, and (3) non-ocellate variety.

COMMON COBRA

OTHER NAMES.—Scientific: *Naia tripudians*. Native: *Nag*, Hindi.

HABITAT.—Asia generally from Persia to the Malay Archipelago; also the Andamans and Ceylon.

DESCRIPTION.—Grows to over 2 yds. About two dozen rows of scales across the neck, and about twenty across the middle of the body. Colour extremely variable, generally some shade of brown, but sometimes black, or even bright yellow. Some varieties have the "spectacle-mark"—a pair of ocelli connected by a U-shaped band, on the back of the hood; but there may be only a single ocellus or only the U-shaped mark, especially in south-eastern varieties. The London Zoological Gardens recently exhibited a red-eyed white specimen, and the Indian Museum has one with two heads, a well-known monstrosity in snakes.

The Cobra is a particularly well-known snake in India, found up to temperate elevations in the hills as well as in the plains, and with an unfortunate habit of coming about houses. As is well known, it is very deadly; in the Malay States it is said to spit instead of biting, and to be a good marksman up to 8 ft. This habit is sufficiently unpleasant, as snake-poison in the eye is dangerous; bathing with milk is said to afford relief. Besides rats, mice, frogs, and toads, it will eat other snakes, and seeks its prey at night. It can be tamed, and is, as is well known, a favourite with snake-charmers.

KING COBRA OR HAMADRYAD

OTHER NAMES.—Scientific: *Naia bungarus.*

HABITAT.—India eastwards through South-Eastern Asia and its islands to the Philippines; found in the Andamans, but not Ceylon.

DESCRIPTION.—Grows to thrice the length of the common Cobra, but has the hood much narrower in proportion; scales larger, in not more than twenty-one rows across the neck, or fifteen in the middle of the body. Colour also variable, but not so much so as in the other species; fawn or olive, usually cross-barred with darker, but never with any form of spectacle-mark on the hood. Young most often black, barred or finely speckled with yellow.

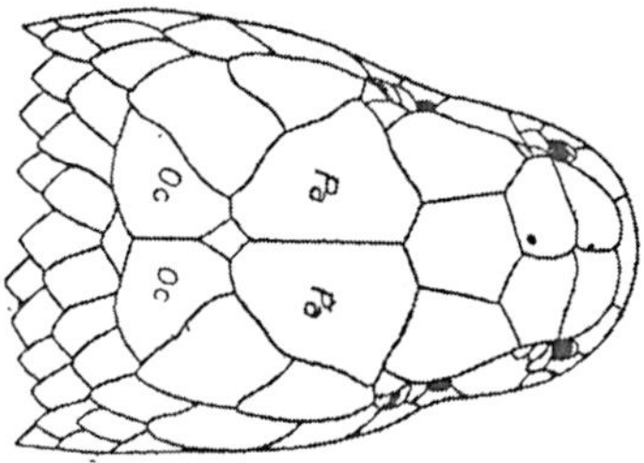

Outline of head of King Cobra, showing details of shields. The pair of large "occipital" shields (Oc) behind the parietals (Pa) are wanting in the common Cobra.

The King Cobra is in India, though not in Malaya, rarer than the common species, and keeps to jungle; it is fierce, and will sometimes attack unprovoked. Although deadly, it has not quite such virulent poison as the common Cobra. It feeds chiefly on other snakes, presumably including the common Cobra, since the first one ever shown at the London Zoo had devoured all its companions of this kind when received. According to Mr. Ditmars of the New York Zoo, it is very intelligent, and discriminates between poisonous and harmless snakes of species new to it, whatever their appearance—possibly guided by scent.

The Kraits (genus *Bungarus*) are snakes with no striking peculiarity of appearance, but generally cross-barred in marking. They are ground-snakes, very venomous, but only two are common enough to need mention.

COMMON KRAIT

OTHER NAMES.—Scientific: *Bungarus cœruleus, candidus.*

HABITAT.—India east to Malay Islands.

DESCRIPTION.—Grows to 1½ yds.; colour blue-black, narrowly cross-barred with white, the bars often broken up into little spots.

The Krait is very common in India, and much given to entering dwellings. More deaths from snake-bite are due to this species than to any other, for although it is peaceable and not anxious to bite, it

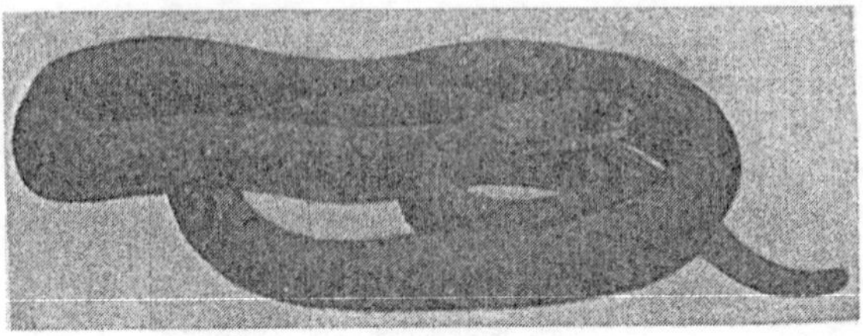

Common Krait.

may often be trodden on, and its venom is very powerful, four times as much so as that of the Cobra. The female incubates her eggs.

It feeds on mice, frogs, toads, and especially on other snakes. East of India it is rare, and in Ceylon is replaced by a very similar species, the Ceylon Krait (*Bungarus ceylonicus*).

Banded Krait

BANDED KRAIT

OTHER NAMES.—Scientific: *Bungarus fasciatus.* Native: *Ráj-sámp*, Hindi.

HABITAT.—India east to Java.

DESCRIPTION.—Perhaps the most easily recognisable of our snakes, owing to its striking coloration, black and yellow in broad subequal cross-bars; back decidedly keeled. It grows to over 2 yds., but its venom is not nearly so powerful as that of the small common Krait, not equalling that of the King Cobra in power, to say nothing of the common Cobra's.

The Banded Krait is chiefly a snake-eater, though it also takes other animals, even taking to water for fish. It has been observed to incubate its eggs. I observed that snakes put in with it for food, in the Calcutta Zoo showed a great desire to escape, the only instance in which I have witnessed alarm in live animals offered for a snake's consumption.

The Coral-Snakes (*Callophis*) are small, bright-coloured snakes closely allied to the Kraits, but with shorter tails. Their mouths are small and they are not free biters, so that, although their venom is strong, and they live on the ground, they are not very dangerous. Only one need be particularised.

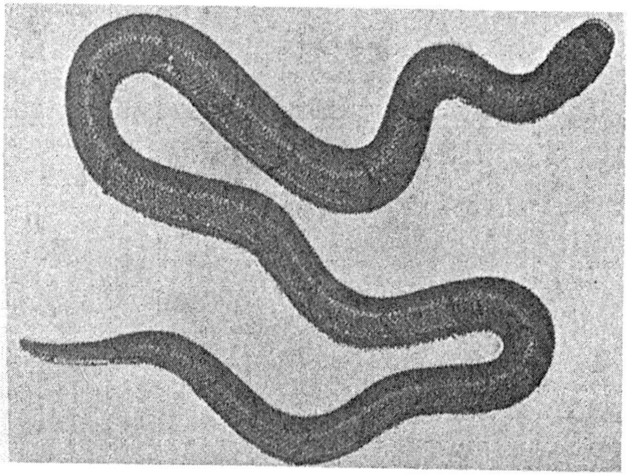

Cross-barred Coral-Snake.

CROSS-BARRED CORAL-SNAKE

OTHER NAMES.—Scientific: *Callophis maclellandii.*
HABITAT.—Nepal east to South China.
DESCRIPTION.—Grows to rather over 2 ft.; tail about a tenth of

total length. Thirteen rows of scales round body. Colour reddish-brown, distantly cross-barred with black; head with two black cross-bars and a yellow one between them; under-parts yellow, cross-barred or spotted with black, the spots being square. In Sikkim is found a variety with no cross-bars or only some spots in their place, and a black stripe down the spine.

The two known Large-Gland-Snakes (*Doliophis*) are like the Coral-Snakes, except for an internal peculiarity—the enormous development of the poison-glands, which extend down the fore-third of the body, so that the heart is shifted back, causing an enlargement at this point. What the use of this extraordinary arrangement for venom-storage may be is a puzzle; the snakes are not wasteful of it, for no one, apparently, has seen them bite a man, and they feed on other snakes, although such victims seem not to require special provision for over-powering them.

COMMON LARGE-GLAND-SNAKE

OTHER NAMES.—Scientific: *Doliophis* or *Adeniophis intestinalis*.

HABITAT.—Burma and the Malay countries.

DESCRIPTION.—Does not grow to half the size of the next; less than thirty-four shields under tail. Colour very variable, but only the tail red; the belly pale yellow, both cross-barred with black; general colour some shade of brown, with a stripe down the back ranging from orange to red. This snake is very common in the Malay Peninsula, and is abroad both by day and night.

RED-HEADED LARGE-GLAND-SNAKE

OTHER NAMES.—Scientific: *Doliophis* or *Adeniophis bivirgatus*.

HABITAT.—Burma and the Malay countries.

DESCRIPTION.—The most brilliant of our reptiles, shining steel-blue with the head, tail, and belly scarlet, and pale-blue stripes along the sides. Grows to about 5 ft. Thirty-four or more scales under the tail.

The Sea-Snakes (*Hydrophiinæ*) are closely related to the above poisonous Colubrines, especially to the Kraits, and hardly deserve the subfamily rank which has been given them. They have compressed bodies, and broad, blunt, compressed tails serving as a paddle; generally their scales are small below as well as above, but some have broad ventral shields. They are viviparous, feed on fish and crustaceans, and slough their skins in pieces like lizards.

Their colour is usually olive or grey, cross-barred with black; in some the fore-part of the body is extraordinarily slender and the head very small. When out of water they are usually nearly blind and very helpless, and their fangs are short, so that, although their venom is very strong, accidents are seldom caused by them.

There are many species, divided into several genera, but only three need noticing here.

AMPHIBIOUS SEA-SNAKE

OTHER NAME.—Scientific: *Platurus colubrinus.*

HABITAT.—Bay of Bengal to South Pacific.

DESCRIPTION.—Grows to 5 ft.; head and neck not conspicuously small and slender; broad well-developed belly-shields. Colour grey or olive, cross-barred with black, most distinctly in the young.

This snake has been found a day's journey inland in Sumatra, and I caught two, a good-sized and a small specimen, coiled together on the stonework foundations of a boat-house on Ross Island in the Andamans. There are other records of snakes of this genus found ashore, and it would be of interest to know if they feed when on land.

CHITTUL OR BLUNT-NOSED SEA-SNAKE

OTHER NAME.—Scientific: *Distira cyanocincta.*

HABITAT.—Asian seas from Persian Gulf to Japan.

DESCRIPTION.—Grows to over 2 yds.; no special peculiarity of form of head and neck, nose bluntly rounded, corner of mouth turned up. Colour olive, more or less distinctly cross-barred with black. This is one of the commonest sea-snakes.

HOOK-NOSED SEA-SNAKE

OTHER NAME.—Scientific: *Enhydrina valakadien.*

HABITAT.—Eastern seas from Persia to Papua.

DESCRIPTION.—Grows to over 4 ft.; end of snout curved and hooked, the rostral shield extending below the lip; fore-parts not tapering, and colour black-barred olive or grey, adults sometimes plain slate-colour; ventral shields very small, almost like the others.

This Sea-Snake is very common, more so, apparently, than any land-snake, judging from the numbers caught in fishing-nets; its venom is far the most powerful among those of our poisonous snakes, so that it is unsafe to take risks with it or other sea-snakes. It invades fresh water even up to 80 miles from the sea.

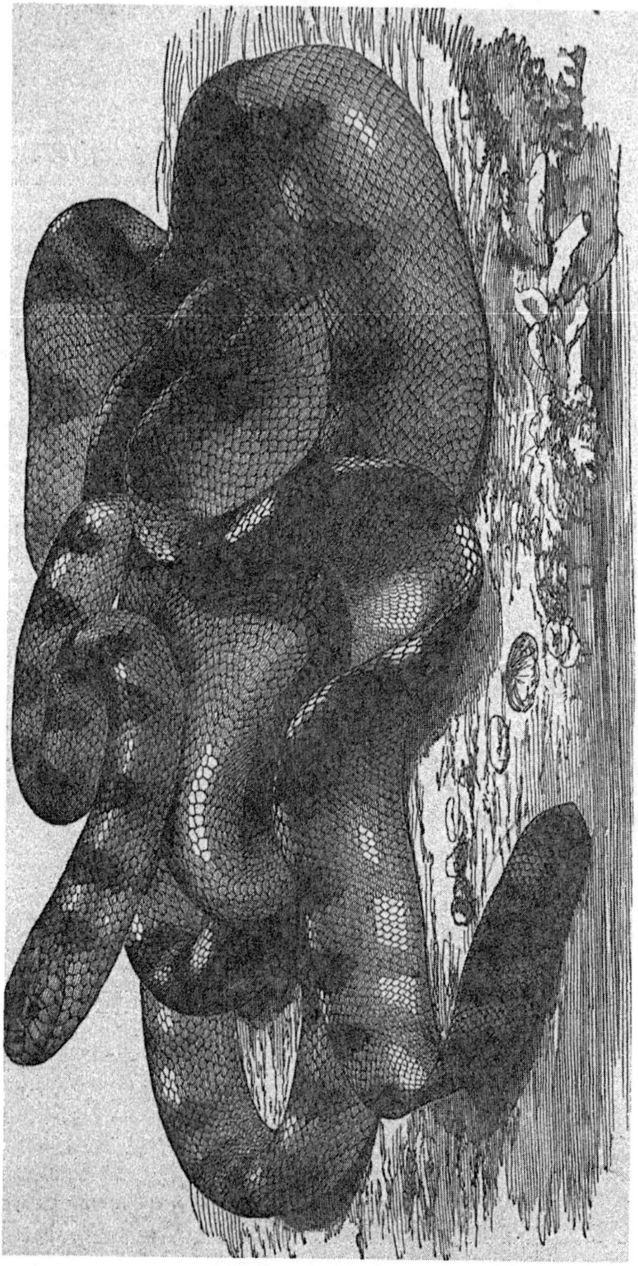

Chitul or Blunt-nosed Sea-Snake.

The *Opisthoglypha*, or back-fanged snakes, are taken as harmless; it is quite difficult for them to get a fair bite at a human being, owing to the position of their poison-teeth in the back of the mouth, but it might be as well to avoid putting one's little finger into the mouth of a large specimen to give it a chance, as will be seen. Their heads are generally covered with large shields, and the neck usually slender. It is not necessary here to go into subfamily details, but only to mention the species most likely to attract attention.

The Whip-Snakes (*Dryophis*) are very elegant slender reptiles, with tails longer than in other snakes; they live on trees, high grass, and bushes, feeding on birds, lizards, etc., and are viviparous and inclined to be fierce.

COMMON WHIP-SNAKE

Other Names.—Scientific: *Dryophis prasinus.*

Habitat.—South-Eastern Asia from the Himalayas to the Malay Islands.

Description.—Snout pointed and rather long, but not soft at the end. Colour, green or brown, with a yellow stripe along each side. Grows to 5½ ft., of which the tail is more than a third.

LONG-SNOUTED WHIP-SNAKE

Other Names.—Scientific: *Dryophis mycterizans.*

Habitat.—From the Deccan east to Burma and south to Ceylon.

Description.—Generally like the last, but with a projecting soft appendage to the nose, and the tail a little longer in proportion; also found either green or brown, and a pink variety is on record. Grows to over 2 yds.

This snake is said by natives to strike at the eye, and I proved by experience that it does so, the snake having left its mark on both lids; no pain resulted, but bites on the hand have been known to give trouble for a few days.

FLOWER-SNAKE

Other Names.—Scientific: *Chrysopelea ornata.*

Habitat.—India east to the Malay Islands; also Ceylon.

Description.—A snake of ordinary form except for the flat square-tipped muzzle; grows to 4½ ft., of which the tail is about a quarter. Colour peculiar; head black, cross-barred with yellow, body

Long-snouted Whip-Snake with Gecko.

variable, variegated with black and yellow, green or olive; often with conspicuous red markings down the back.

The Flower-Snake lives either on the ground or in trees and bushes; it has remarkable power of springing in a downward-slanting direction. it is oviparous, and feeds chiefly on lizards and frogs.

BULL-DOG-FACED SEA-SNAKE

OTHER NAMES.—Scientific: *Cerberus rhynchops.*

HABITAT.—India east to North Australia.

DESCRIPTION.—Closely resembling a poisonous sea-snake in cross-barred colour and in general shape, but with a tapering and only slightly compressed tail and well-developed belly-shields; lower jaw prominent. It is also a fish-eater and viviparous, and frequents estuaries and the coast: other species of its subfamily have similar characters.

The completely harmless snakes, or *Aglypha,* are often free biters, like some of the last group, and cause much needless alarm. The first genus we need notice is indeed like a grim practical joke on the part of Nature. This is *Lycodon,* the species of which much resemble the deadly Kraits, even to having large fang-like teeth in the front of the mouth.

The best-known is the common

HARMLESS KRAIT

OTHER NAMES.—Scientific: *Lycodon aulicus.*

HABITAT.—India east to Timor; also Ceylon.

DESCRIPTION.—Grows to over 2 ft.; muzzle very flat, with the lips swollen; eye about midway between its tip and corner of mouth. Colour dark brown above, netted or cross-barred with yellow; in the latter case it is extremely like the Krait, but may be distinguished by the different shape of the snout and less forward position of the eye.

Like the true venomous Krait, it often comes into houses, and it also lays eggs.

The Rat-Snakes (*Zamenis*) are good-sized snakes which are liable to be mistaken for cobras, these being not unlike them except when they rear and display their hoods. They are fierce in temper, egg-layers, and feed much on rats, so that they are deserving of encouragement. Their thinner necks and large eyes distinguish them from cobras even in repose.

COMMON RAT-SNAKE

Other Names.—Scientific: *Zamenis mucosus.* Native: *Dhamin*, Hindi.

Habitat.—Central Asia east and south to the Malay Peninsula; also Ceylon.

Description.—Grows to over 7 ft. long, and is said to attain nearly 12 ft.; tail a fourth of total length. Seventeen rows of scales across the back. Colour brown, often cross-barred with black behind, and generally with a light hue in front when young.

The common Rat-Snake often comes into houses; it can be tamed, and possesses a loud voice for a snake, compared to deep growling, which it utters when annoyed, at which time it distends its neck vertically.

EASTERN RAT-SNAKE

Other Names.—Scientific: *Zamenis korros.*

Habitat.—South-Eastern Asia from the Himalayas to the Malay countries and South China.

Description.—Tail longer in proportion than in the last, 2 ft. in a 5-ft. specimen—a large one. Only fifteen rows of scales round the body. Colour brown, often changing to yellow behind, where the scales are edged with black; sometimes olive-tinged. Young narrowly cross-barred with yellow or with bands of white spots.

This Rat-Snake is commoner in the Malay States than the preceding species.

BRONZE TREE-SNAKE

Other Names.—Scientific: *Dendrophis pictus.*

Habitat.—India east to the Malay countries; also the Andamans.

Description.—A snake of ordinary but rather slim form, narrow-necked, large-eyed, and long-tailed, the tail being more than a fourth of the total length, which may reach 4 ft. Colour bronze or olive, with a black eye-stripe and yellow flank-stripe; concealed bases of upper scales bright blue.

This is a very active snake, and feeds on lizards and frogs. It is viviparous. I found it very common in the forest on the Little Andaman; all I got or saw here were black, with green under-parts. They presumably lived on the lizards also very common there, a species (*Gonyocephalus subcristatus*) very like our common garden-lizard in general appearance, but remarkable in that the males had blue and the females yellow eyes.

The Keelbacks (*Tropidonotus*) are close relatives of the familiar Ring-Snake or Grass-Snake at home, and, like it, are egg-layers and frog-eaters. Two are also extremely common in India.

CHEQUERED KEELBACK

OTHER NAMES.—Scientific: *Tropidonotus piscator.*

HABITAT.—India east to the Malay Archipelago.

DESCRIPTION.—Grows to 4 ft., of which the tail is a fourth. Colour yellow or khaki, with a chessboard pattern of black spots, or with four or five black stripes down the back. Two black streaks on cheek. Eye small, nostrils opening upwards.

The Chequered Pond-Snake spends much of its time in the water, taking fish and toads as well as frogs. It was always to be found about our tank at the Calcutta Museum, and I once saw a young one following and striking one of the half-grown young of a pair of dabchicks which bred there.

STRIPED KEELBACK

OTHER NAMES.—Scientific: *Tropidonotus stolatus.*

HABITAT.—Same as the last.

DESCRIPTION.—Grows to over 2 ft.; eye large. Most of upper scales keeled, but not the outer row above the ventrals. Colour olive, with two yellow stripes all down the back, cutting through a ground-pattern of black spots or bars.

This is a land-snake, feeding chiefly on frogs; it ranges up to nearly 6,000 ft. in the Nilgiris.

SMALL-SCALED SEA-SNAKE

OTHER NAMES.—Scientific: *Chersydrus granulatus.*

HABITAT.—Southern India and Burma east to Papua.

DESCRIPTION.—Like a poisonous Sea-Snake in its general form and cross-barred coloration, but, like the Opisthoglyphous Harmless Sea-Snakes above mentioned, with a tapering pointed tail. It may be distinguished from these and all other sea-snakes by the very small scales, which number a hundred round the body, and are granular on the head. Other sea-snakes never have more than seventy round the body, and usually much fewer.

This snake is a fish-eater and viviparous, and found miles from land.

WART-SNAKE

Other Names.—Scientific: *Acrochordus javanicus.*

Habitat.—Siam and Malaysia east to Papua.

Description.—A stout snake, reaching 8 ft. in length, with a short prehensile tail, and very small wart-like scales, more numerous than in any other of our snakes—about 130 round the body, and largest on the spine. Colour brown or olive, with black markings.

This is a water-snake, living in ditches and canals, and viviparous. Fruit has been found in its stomach, an extraordinary food for a snake, but one which has also occurred in the stomach of an Indian python, as has been mentioned above.

AMPHIBIA

THE Amphibians, or Batrachians, used to be classed with the reptiles,* and fossils show a connection between them. They agree with reptiles in having legs and paws when they have limbs at all, as is usually the case, but in youth agree with fish in being aquatic and breathing by gills. They never have any fins, however, but a tail-fringe, and this has no supporting rays as in a fish's tail-fin. In this larval stage they are known as tadpoles. They are easily distinguished from reptiles proper by having, in the case of our species, no claws, or, when limbless, no apparent scales, these being minute and embedded in the skin. The usual species, with legs, have no scales at all, and the skin is often slimy, as in frogs. It is in any case moist, and the creatures breathe through it to some extent, dying if exposed to drought long. They also absorb water through it instead of drinking. They are usually unable to bear salt water, which also kills their eggs; these are balls of jelly generally stuck together in masses or strings. In some cases the fish-stage is gone through before hatching, but generally the creature spends some time as a tadpole.

There are three orders of Amphibians, all represented with us, and readily distinguishable.

The Frogs and Toads (*Ecaudata*) have the limbs strong, especially the hinder, short broad bodies, and no tail.

The Newts (*Urodela*) have a long body, well-developed tail, and weak subequal limbs.

The Cæcilians (*Apoda*) have no limbs and a very short tail, and resemble small soft snakes with transversely wrinkled skins, the scales embedded in these not being noticeable.

ORDER URODELA

We have only one Newt, so its characters may be given under its description.

* Gadow says in the volume on "Reptiles and Amphibia," in the Cambridge Natural History series that, "the great gulf within the vertebrata lies between Fishes and Amphibia." Thus the older arrangement is probably right.

BURMESE NEWT

OTHER NAMES.—Scientific: *Tylototriton verrucosus.*

HABITAT.—Sikkim, Kakhyen Hills, and Yunnan.

DESCRIPTION.—Like a small scaleless, clawless lizard, with large flat head, compressed tail half of the total length, four toes on the fore-feet and five on the hind-feet, not webbed, and a row of large warts along each flank. Colour very dark brown, with the under-side of the tail orange-yellow. Teeth present in both jaws; length 6 in.

Newts generally live in the water during the breeding season, and on land in cool places at other times. They lay their eggs separately, the tadpoles have external gills, and their fore limbs appear before the hind ones. The food of newts is various small animals; their skin exudes a poisonous secretion.

ORDER APODA

Of the Cæcilians we need only mention the two best-known species, both belonging to one genus. They have teeth in both jaws and very small eyes.

PURPLE CÆCILIAN

OTHER NAMES.—Scientific: *Ichthyophis glutinosus.*

HABITAT.—South-Eastern Asia from the Himalayas to Java; also Ceylon.

DESCRIPTION.—Grows to 15 in.; like a small soft snake with circular wrinkles closely set all along the body. Head sub-triangular, the muzzle as long as the distance between the eyes. Tail a mere pointed stump. Colour purple with a yellow stripe all along each side; a short pointed white tentacle between eye and nostril.

This creature is found in hilly country in damp places, or even in mud. According to Major Flower it does not bite, and is usually sluggish, but can crawl quickly if so wishing. In spite of the scientific name it is not sticky or slimy, and its throat constantly throbs like a frog's, while the tentacles are drawn out and in.

The breeding was observed in Ceylon, where it was found that the eggs were large and joined into a string, which was rolled into a ball. This is laid in a burrow near water, where the female coils round it. The young do not leave the eggs till they have lost their gills, when they take to water. Their head is newt-like, and the eyes and tail larger than in the adult, the latter flattened and bordered by a fin.

SHORT-NOSED CÆCILIAN

OTHER NAMES.—Scientific: *Ichthyophis monochrous*.

HABITAT.—Except that it is not known to be found in Ceylon, this Cæcilian has the same range as the last.

DESCRIPTION.—Smaller than the last, but proportionately stouter, with shorter muzzle, not so long as the distance between the eyes. Colour purple-black all over.

ORDER ECAUDATA

The Frogs and Toads are a particularly numerous and familiar tribe, and, unlike reptiles and other amphibians, particularly noisy as well. They usually progress by jumping, and many are good climbers, such being distinguished by sucking-discs on the ends of the toes, which are four on the front and five on the hind-feet. They have no teeth in the lower jaw, and not always any in the upper.

They are usually nocturnal, and feed on small animals, which they will only take if moving; they usually lick them up with the tongue, which is rather long, and attached in front, the point lying back towards the throat when not in use. They do not usually bite, but some have a poisonous secretion which exudes from the skin. In swimming they use the hind-legs only, and together.

They generally spawn in water, and the tadpoles have short round bodies with long compressed tails. The hind-feet appear before the front ones, and when the latter are visible the tail is absorbed and the little creature comes ashore to feed on live food, having previously lived on dead or vegetable matter. Owing to shrinkage, the little frog is often smaller than the mature tadpole, sometimes very much so.

There are several families in the sub-order, but their distinctions are too technical for this work as a rule, so I shall confine myself to describing a few very conspicuous forms among the very numerous species. Their Hindi name is *maindak*. The length given is from muzzle to end of body.

Toads (*Bufonidæ*) have no teeth, and the skin is warty, with a strongly poisonous secretion exuded under pressure, but not slimy. They generally live on land more than frogs.

COMMON INDIAN TOAD

Other Names.—Scientific: *Bafo melanostictus.*

Habitat.—South-Eastern Asia to Malay Islands, ranging up to 10,000 ft. in the Himalayas.

Description.—Grows to more than 6 in.; form stout and head broad and blunt; fore-toes free, hind ones half-webbed, skin with numerous prickly warts, head with ridges on each side and large, long, swollen glands at the back. Colour some shade of brown, the prominent parts black; breeding male with black warts on inner fingers; eyes brassy yellow.

This is one of the commonest land-animals in the East; it is protected by its poison from most enemies, but I have myself seen it taken by the Chequered Keelback Snake, by one of its own species, by a tame Crow-Pheasant allowed to go at large, and by the Roller and Pied Hornbill in captivity. Most likely this cannibalism which I have witnessed is the chief check on its increase, other enemies being insignificant compared with its numerous fellows. In its gait it is a crawler rather than a hopper; it readily comes indoors, and only takes to water when breeding.

The typical Frogs (*Ranidæ*) have teeth in the upper jaw, smooth slimy skins, and long hind-legs.

BULL-FROG

Other Names.—Scientific: *Rana tigrina.*

Habitat.—India east to the Malay Islands; also Ceylon, but not ascending the Himalayas.

Description.—Grows to the same size as the toad, but is slimmer and has a pointed snout; skin not poisonous. Fingers free, toes webbed nearly to tips. Colour, olive green or brown, darker-spotted, and often with a yellow spine-stripe.

This is the largest Indian frog, and very voracious even for its size, attacking even birds and snakes. It spends much time in the water even when not breeding.

WATER-SKIPPING FROG

Other Names.—Scientific: *Rana cyanophlyctis.*

Habitat.—South Arabia east to India and Ceylon, perhaps also to Malaysia.

Description.—Grows to about 2½ in. Toes webbed to the tips, a tubercle like a rudimentary sixth toe on the inside of the foot. Fingers ore slim and pointed than in the Bull-frog. The male can blow out vocal sac on each side of the head. Colour olive or brown, with ırk markings.

This frog spends much time in the water, on which it can skip for : many as a dozen jumps before sinking, according to Major Flower.

SALINE FROG

Other Names.—Scientific: *Rana limnocharis.*

Habitat.—India east to the Malay Islands and north to Japan; so Ceylon; ascends the Himalayas to 7,000 ft.

Description.—Very like the Bull-frog, but not larger than the st species, and with the toes only half-webbed; the hind-legs vary markably in length. Male usually with two black patches on throat.

This is a very common paddy-field frog; it is remarkable among nphibians in readily taking to brackish or even salt water.

CHUNAM FROG

Other Names.—Scientific: *Rhacophorus maculatus.*

Habitat.—India and Ceylon.

Description.—Grows to 3 in.; fingers and toes with sucking scs, the former slightly webbed, the latter for two-thirds of their ngth; skin of back smooth, of belly granular. Colour very variable, tering as in the chamæleon; dark markings present, especially on des of head; thighs spotted behind with yellow.

This is a tree-frog, and also frequents houses. The Malay race of is species (*Rhacophorus leucomystax*) spawns in water-butts, the awn being a frothy mass; in natural haunts it is deposited on leaves ove pools, into which it soon slips.

The Small-mouthed Frogs (*Engystomatidæ*) are remarkable for ıeir small heads and mouths, toothless as in toads; they feed chiefly 1 white ants, and are very plump.

MALAY BULL-FROG

Other Names.—Scientific: *Callula pulchra.*

Habitat.—India east to Malaysia, and Ceylon.

Description.—Grows to 3 in.; toes only slightly webbed. Back nooth, brown, with a broad ragged pink or yellow band on each side; gs grey, with brown and yellow spots; male black-throated.

This frog comes into towns, and makes itself a nuisance by its ud croaking as it floats on the water with swollen throat. The male spawns the eggs in small lumps.

FAT FROG

OTHER NAMES.—Scientific: *Cacopus systoma.*

HABITAT.—Southern India.

DESCRIPTION.—Grows to 2½ in.; particularly plump, small-headed, and short-legged; toes barely webbed; two flattened spurs inside each foot, skin sleek, marbled with dark brown on a pinkish or greenish ground. A vocal sac in the male.

This egg-shaped frog is a common visitor in Madras in the rains.

It may be said, *a propos* of the shape of frogs and toads generally, that this depends to a great extent on circumstances, a specimen which has been having a dry time being very thin-looking, though it will soon absorb plenty of water and become plump when it has access to moisture. These creatures can also puff themselves out under emotion, and, as the colour is likewise generally changeable at short notice, as with so many lizards, considerable allowances must be made in identification of amphibians for temporary alterations in figure and complexion.

INDEX

A.

Agama, Blue-flanked, 296
,, Spotted, 296
Ammon (*Ovis*), 201
Antelope, Four-horned, 231
,, Indian, 227
Argali, 201
Ass, Asiatic Wild, 181
Axis, 252

B.

Badger, Assam, 66
,, Brown Ferret-, 67
,, Grey Ferret-, 67
,, Hog-, 615
,, Honey-, 66
Bamboo Rat, Bay, 161
,, ,, Hoary, 161
,, ,, Large, 162
Bandicoot, 151
,, Smaller, 152
Banteng, 238
Barasingha, 256
Bat, Common European, 40
,, ,, Yellow, 38
,, Dark-brown Leaf-, 34
,, Dobson's Long-tongued Fruit-, 31
,, Fulvous Fruit-, 30
,, Great Eastern Horseshoe-, 33
,, ,, Himalayan Leaf-nosed, 35
,, Hairy-winged, 39
,, Harlequin, 38
,, Hodgson's, 39
,, Indian Pipistrelle, 40
,, Large Leaf-, 33
,, ,, Painted, 39
,, Long-armed Sheath- tailed, 36
,, ,, eared, 37
,, ,, tailed, 35
,, Mouse-tailed, 35
Bat, Noctule, 38
,, Painted, 39
,, Pouched Sheath-tailed, 36
,, Wrinkled-lipped, 37
Batagur, 278
Bear, Brown, 55
,, Cat-, 63
,, Himalayan Black, 57
,, Malay, 58
,, Pied, 64
,, Sloth, 60
,, Sun, 58
Bear-Cat, 108
Bear-Langur, 14
Bharal, 207
Binturong, 108
Biscobra, 289
Bison, 235
Blackbuck, 226
Boa, Sand-, 311
Boar, Indian Wild, 192
Buffalo, 240
Bulau, 2, 250

C.

Cachalot, 124
Cæcilian, Purple, 336
,, Short-nosed, 337
Calotes, Long-tailed Green, 295
,, Malayan Green, 295
,, Moustached, 295
Camel, 197
Capricorns, 217
Caracal, 95
Cattle, 233
Cat, Bay, 91
,, Black-chested, 92
,, Chaus, 93
,, Common Jungle-, 93
,, Desert, 92

Cat, Fishing-, 89
„ Large Tiger-, 89
„ Leopard-, 89
„ Marbled, 88
„ Rusty-spotted, 90
„ Toddy-, 104
„ Waved, 92
Chamæleon, 304
Chaus, 93
Cheetah, 96
Chevrotain, Indian, 198
„ Larger Malay, 200
„ Little Malay, 199
„ Red or Stanleyan, 200
Chinkara, 221
Chiru, 225
Chital, 252
Chittul, 327
Civet, Brown Palm-, 106
„ Burmese, 101
„ Common Palm-, 104
„ Himalayan Palm-, 106
„ Large Indian, 100
„ Malabar, 101
„ Small Indian, 101
Cobego, 41
Cobra, Common, 322
„ King, 323
Colugo, 41
Crocodile, Coast, 267
„ Common, 267
„ Fish-eating, 266

D.

Daboia, 316
„ Western, 317
Deer, Barking, 246
„ Brow-antlered, 257
„ Mouse-, 197
„ Musk-, 244
„ Spotted, 252
„ Swamp-, 256
Dhamin, 322
Dhole, 119
Dhongoka, 279
Dolphin, Common, 129
„ Elliot's, 129
„ Gangetic, 125
„ Speckled, 129
„ Spot-bellied, 129
Dragon, Band-winged, 290
„ Black-spotted, 290
Dragon, Marbled-winged, 290
„ Pale-spotted, 290
Dugong, 133

E.

Earth-Snake, Ocellated, 314
„ „ Red-bellied, 314
„ „ Truncate, 314
Elephant, 1, 174
Eryx, 312
Eyelid-Gecko, Northern, 289
„ „ Southern, 289

F.

Ferret-Badger, Brown, 67
„ „ Grey, 67
Field-Rat, Common, 150
„ „ Short-tailed, 150
Flying-Gecko, 288
Flying-Fox, 27, *tail-piece*
„ Island, 30
„ Malay, 29
„ Nicobar, 30
Flying-Squirrel, Anderson's, 145
„ „ Grey-headed, 146
„ „ Hairy-footed, 146
„ „ Hodgson's, 145
„ „ Horsfield's, 147
„ „ Large Brown, 142
„ „ „ Red, 145
„ „ Orange-bellied, 145
„ „ Particoloured, 147
„ „ Pigmy, 147
„ „ Red-and-White, 145
„ „ Small Kashmir, 147
„ „ „ Travancore, 146
„ „ Woolly, 143
Fox, Common, 122
„ Desert, 122
„ Flying-, 27
„ Hill, 122
„ Hoary, 121
„ Indian, 121
„ Small Tibetan Grey, 122
Frog, Bull-, 338
„ Chunam, 339
„ Fat, 340
„ Malay Bull-, 339
„ Saline, 339
„ Water-skipping, 338
Fruit-bats, 27

Fruit-bat, Dobson's Long-tongued, 31
,, ,, Fulvous, 30
,, ,, Long-tongued, 31
,, ,, Pigmy, 31
,, ,, Short-nosed, 30
,, ,, Small, 31
,, ,, Small Long-tongued, 31

G.

Garial, 266
Gaur, 235
Gayal, 235
Gazelle, Indian, 221
,, Persian, 223
,, Tibetan, 224
Gecko, Asian House-, 286
,, Common House-, 286
,, Flying-, 288
,, Giant, 288
,, Golden, 285
,, Green, 288
,, Narrow-toed House-, 285
,, Twin-spotted, 288
,, Varied House-, 287
Gerbil, Common Indian, 149
,, Desert, 150
Gibbon, Hoolock, 4
,, White-handed, 6
Goa, 224
Goats, 208
Goat, Wild Common, 213
Goat-Antelopes, 217
Goral, 218
Gymnura, Raffles', 50
,, Smaller, 51

H.

Hamadryad, 323
Hamster, Grey, 160
Hangal, 259
Hare, Afghan, 170
,, Black-naped, 169
,, Burmese, 169
,, Common Indian, 168
,, Hispid, 171
,, Sind, 169
,, Upland, 170
,, Woolly, 170
Hedgehog, Afghan, 49
,, Anderson's, 49
,, Collared, 48
,, Hardwicke's, 48
Hedgehog, Large-eared, 49
,, Painted, 50
,, Small-footed or South Indian, 49
Hog, Pigmy, 195
Hoolock, 4
Horse, 183
House-Lizards, 285
Hyæna, 99
Hybrids, Argali-Urial, 206
,, Cat, 90, 91, 93
,, Cattle, 237, 238, 239
,, Markhor-Pasang, 213
,, Spotted and Hog-deer, 255
,, Tahr-Spotted Deer, 216

I.

Ibex, Himalayan, 211
,, Nilgiri, 216
,, Persian, 213
Ichneumons, 109

J.

Jackal, 117
Jarao, 248
Jerboa, Afghan, 163
Jungle-Cat, 93

K.

Kachuga, Blanford's, 279
,, Irrawaddy, 279
,, Red-streaked, 278
,, Smith's, 279
,, Sylhet, 279
Kakar, 246
Kalong, 29
Kanchil, 199
Karawala, 319
Kiang, 182
King Cobra, 323
Krait, Banded, 324
,, Common, 323
,, Harmless, 331

L.

Langur, Barbe's, 11
,, Bear, 14
,, Capped, 11
,, Common, 7
,, Dusky, 12

Langur, Entellus, 7
,, Hanuman, 7
,, Himalayan, 8
,, Madras, 9, 13
,, Malabar, 9, 13
,, Nilgiri, 10
,, Phayre's, 11
,, Purple-faced, 12
,, Red-bellied, 11
,, Rutledge's, 12
,, Silvery, 11
Large-Gland-Snake, Common, 326
,, ,, ,, Red-headed, 326
Leaf-Bat, Dark-brown, 34
,, ,, Great Himalayan, 35
,, ,, Large, 33
Leaf-Monkeys, 6
Lemurs, 22
Leopard, 82
,, Clouded, 87
,, Hunting-, 96
,, Snow-, 86
Leopard-Cat, 89
Linsang, Burmese, 103
,, Indian, 103
Lion, 75
Lizard, Bell's Bordered, 297
,, Blunt-horned Rhinoceros-, 291
,, Common Garden-, 293
,, Fan-throated, 291
,, Indian Sand-, 302
,, Long-tailed, 302
,, Lyre-, 293
,, Naked-horned Rhinoceros-, 291
,, Small Rhinoceros-, 293
,, Snake-eyed, 302
,, Spiny-tailed, 297
Loris, Slender, 22
,, Slow, 22, *opposite Contents*
Luth, 283
Lynx, 94
,, Red, 95

M.

Markhor, 209
Marmot, Long-tailed or Red, 148
,, Smaller Himalayan, 148
,, Tibet, 148
Marten, Beech-, 69
,, White-cheeked, 69
Mastigure, 297
Meminna, 198
Mole, Short-tailed, 43
Mole, White-tailed, 44
Mole-Rats, 150
Mongoose, Ceylon Brown, 112
,, Common Grey, 109
,, Crab-eating, 114
,, Gold-speckled, 112
,, Long-tailed, 111
,, Nilgiri, 112
,, Ruddy, 111
,, Small Burmese, 112
,, ,, Indian, 112
,, Stripe-necked, 112
Monitor, Barred, 299
,, Broad-barred, 320
,, Desert, 299
,, Large Land-, 299
,, Marbled, 300
,, Water-, 300
Monkey, Bonnet, 19
,, Burmese Pig-tailed, 18
,, Crab-eating, 21
,, Himalayan, 17
,, Lion-tailed, 15
,, Pig-tailed, 18
,, Phesus, 16
,, Stump-tailed, 19
,, Toque, 20
Mouse, Brown Spiny, 157
,, Common House-, 155
,, Indian Field-, 157
,, Long-tailed Tree-, 159
,, Malabar Spiny- 149
,, Persian House-, 156
,, ,, Long-tailed Field-, 155
Mouse-deer, 197
Mouse-hares, 171
Muntjac, 246
Musang, Brown, 106
,, Common, 104
,, Ceylonese, 106
,, Golden, 106
,, Hill, 106
,, Small-toothed, 106
,, White-eared, 106
Musk-deer, 244
Musk-rat, 44
,, Shrew, Brown, 46
,, Common, 44

N.

Napu, 200
Newt, Burmese, 336
Nilgao, 229

O

Onager, 182
Otter, Clawless, 74
„ Common, 73
„ Small, 74
„ Smooth, 74
Ounce, 86
Ovis poli, 202

P.

Palm-civet, Brown, 106
„ „ Common, 104
„ „ Himalayan, 106
Panda, 63
„ Giant, 64
Pangolin, Eared, 262
„ Indian, 261
„ Malay, 263
Panther, 82
Paradoxures, 103
Pasang, 213
Phoorsa, 318
Pig, Banded or Island, 195
Pigs, 191
Pika, Himalayan, 171
„ Hodgson's, 172
„ Ladak, 172
„ Large-eared, 172
„ Red, 172
Polecat, Mottled, 72
„ Tibetan, 72
Porcupine, Bengal, 166
„ Brush-tailed, 167
„ Common Indian, 165
„ Crestless Himalayan, 166
Porpoise, Little, 127
„ River, 127
Python, Dwarf, 311
„ Indian, 310
„ Malayan, 310
„ Reticulated, 310

R.

Raccoon, Himalayan, 63
Rasse, 101
Rat, Brown, 152
„ Coffee-, 158
„ Common Field-, 150
„ Common Indian, 154
„ Little Burmese, 154
Rat, Metad, 158
„ Musk-, 44
„ Pepper-, 149
„ Roof-, 154
„ Sewer-, 152
„ Short-tailed Field-, 150
Ratel, 66
Rhinoceros, Burmese, 188
„ Great One-horned, 186
„ Hairy Two-horned, 189
Rhinoceros-Lizards, 291
Rorqual, Great, 232
Rusa, 248

S.

Sambar, 248
Sea-Cow, 133
Sea-Snake, Amphibious, 327
„ „ Common, 327
„ „ False, 327
„ „ Hook-nosed, 327
„ „ Small-scaled, 333
Serow, 217
Sheep, 201
Shou, 260
Shrew, Brown Musk-, 46
„ Common Musk-, 44
„ Himalayan Water-, 47
„ Indian Pigmy, 46
„ Teeth of, 2
Shrews, Tree-, 51
Skink, Blue-tailed, 303
„ Common Hill, 303
„ „ Striped, 303
„ „ Three-toed, 304
Slow-worm, Beaked, 304
„ „ Indian, 292
Snake, Bronze Tree-, 332
„ Chequered Keelback, 333
„ Common Rat-, 332
„ Cross-barred Coral-, 325
„ Eastern Rat-, 332
„ Flower-, 329
„ Hill Night-, 315
„ Rainbow-, 314
„ Red-tailed, 312
„ Rock-, 310
„ Striped Keelback, 333
„ Wart-, 334
„ Common Whip-, 329
„ Long-snouted Whip-, 329
Soft-shell, Brown, 269
„ „ Burmese, 269
„ „ „ Box, 271

Soft-shell, Coast, 270
,, ,, Common Box, 271
,, ,, Ganges, 269
,, ,, Large-headed, 269
,, ,, Malay, 270
,, ,, Phayre's, 270
,, ,, Southern, 271
,, ,, ,, Box, 271
Sperm-Whale, Great, 124
,, ,, Pigmy, 125
Squirrel, Anderson's Flying-, 145
,, ,, Stripe-bellied, 138
,, Bay, 140
,, Berdmore's, 142
,, Black-backed, 139
,, Black Hill, 136
,, Common Striped, 140
,, Dusky Striped, 142
,, Golden-backed, 139
,, Grey-backed, 139
,, Grey-headed Flying-, 146
,, Hairy-footed Flying-, 146
,, Himalayan Striped, 142
,, Hoary-bellied Hill, 139
,, Hodgson's Flying-, 145
,, Horsfield's Flying-, 147
,, Irrawaddy, 139
,, Jungle Striped, 141
,, Large Brown Flying-, 142
,, ,, Grizzled Indian, 137
,, ,, Indian, 136
,, ,, Malay, 136
,, ,, Red Flying-, 145
,, Orange-bellied Flying-, 145
,, ,, ,, Hill, 138
,, Particoloured Flying-, 147
,, Pigmy Flying-, 147
,, Small Kashmir Flying-, 147
,, ,, Travancore Flying-, 146
,, Woolly Flying-, 143
Susu, 125
Swamp-deer, 256

T.

Tahr, Himalayan, 215
,, Nilgiri, 216
Takin, 220
Tapir, 183
Terrapin, Bengal Eyed, 277
,, ,, Three-keeled, 275
,, Bengal Three-keeled Land-, 275
Terrapin, Blunt-beaked Box-, 276
,, Broad Box-, 275
,, Burmese Eyed, 277
,, Casqued, 280
,, Common Three-keeled Land-, 274
,, ,, Roofed, 280
,, Dhor Box-, 276
,, Flat Land-, 274
,, Tree-toed Box-, 276
,, Hamilton's, 277
,, Large Land-, 274
,, Long-tailed, 280
,, Spinous Land-, 274
,, Thick-necked, 276
Thameng, 257
Thurgi, 278
Tic-polonga, 316
Tiger, 77, *frontispiece*
,, Clouded, 87
Toad, Common Indian, 338
Toad-head, Theobald's, 296
Toddy Cat, 104
Tortoise, Brown, 273
,, Burmese Starred, 273
,, Claw-tailed, 272
,, Indian Starred, 272
,, Leith's, 272
Tucktoo, 287
Tupaia, Elliot's, 32
,, Madras, 32
,, Malay, 32
,, Nicobar, 33
Turtle, Green, 281
,, Hawk's-bill, 282
,, Leathery, 283
,, Loggerhead, 282

U.

Urial, 205

V.

Vampire, Indian, 32
,, Malay, 33
Viper, Deceptive, 316
,, Green Pit-, 320
,, Himalayan Pit-, 318
,, Large-spotted Pit- 319
,, Large-scaled Pit-, 320
,, Purple Pit-, 320

Viper, Russell's, 316
„ Saw-scaled, 317
„ Wagler's Pit-, 321
Vole, Sikkim, 160

W.

Wanderoo, Great, 14
„ Nilgiri, 10
„ Purple-faced, 12
Wapiti, 259
Weasel, Himalayan, 70
„ Striped, 71
„ White-nosed, 71
„ Yellow-bellied, 70
Whale, Blue, 132
„ Great Sperm-, 124
Whale, Indian Pilot, 129
„ Pigmy Sperm-, 125
„ Pike, 132
Whip-Snake, Common, 329
„ „ Long-snouted, 329
Wolf, 115
Worm-Snake, Common, 308
„ „ Diard's, 308
„ „ Hook-nosed, 309

Y.

Yak, 239

Z.

Zebu, 233

FLYING-FOXES.

We swarm across the evening sky,
But not in flocks as wildfowl fly,
For each grim vampire singly swings
With smiting sweeps his wide-webbed
 wings
Behind black muzzle keen with greed
On Indian peasants' fruit to feed.
And when again at dawn we come
To the tall trees we call our home,
Each to himself a branch would have ;
And so we snarl and scratch and rave
Till slumber overcomes our spite
And limp we hang where last we light.
Folly in this you mortals see,
Though you would fight for all the
 tree !

F. FINN, *The Masque of Birds and other Poems.*